Today's trade is global. A c
of the world, its production.
Since the first sea-borne con
try has been one of the mai
traces the rise to prominenc
operator – and the internal de
extraordinary expansion betwee
globalisation. With unprecedent
current and former employees,
by The Economist Intelligence U
Register, this is a valuable resour
national business. This first inside
business will also appeal to industry

Visit the fully interactive companion wet

Chris Jephson was, until recently, Direc
graduation in the UK in 1969, he worked
directly in Copenhagen and the UK until i
management team of Maersk Logistics b
Copenhagen in 2004. He has been a long-til
Supply Chain Management Professionals (C:
for Logistics and Supply Chain Management

Henning Morgen is General Manager in Grou
A.P. Moller – Maersk with responsibility for a
documentation and communication. Henning
Maersk in 1998 and is the author of several shorte
based on research in the Maersk archives. Hennil
records management associations in Denmark, Gern
is a member of the Section of Business and Labour
Council of Archives.

Creating Global Opportunities

Maersk Line in Containerisation 1973–2013

Chris Jephson and
Henning Morgen

CAMBRIDGE
UNIVERSITY PRESS

CAMBRIDGE
UNIVERSITY PRESS

University Printing House, Cambridge CB2 8BS, United Kingdom

Cambridge University Press is part of the University of Cambridge.

It furthers the University's mission by disseminating knowledge in the pursuit of education, learning and research at the highest international levels of excellence.

www.cambridge.org
Information on this title: www.cambridge.org/9781107037816

First published 2014

Printed and bound in China by C&C Offset Printing

A catalogue record for this publication is available from the British Library

Library of Congress Cataloguing in Publication data
Jephson, Chris.
Creating global opportunities: Maersk Line in containerisation 1973–2013 /
Chris Jephson and Henning Morgen.
    pages cm
Includes index.
ISBN 978-1-107-03781-6 (Hardback)
1. Maersk Line (Firm) 2. Shipping–Denmark–History. 3. Container ships–
Denmark–History. 4. Containerization–Denmark–History. I. Morgen,
Henning. II. Title.
HE851.J48 2013
387.5′442065489-dc23   2013014545

ISBN 978-1-107-03781-6 Hardback

To Maersk Line's customers, the memory of
Mærsk Mc-Kinney Møller and countless others
who made this whole story possible.

Contents

Figures

Figure 11.2 courtesy of Steven Brandist. All other photographs are from the A.P. Moller – Maersk archives. Image scanning and editing: Jens Nymose, Grafisk Konservering.

Tables

Economist Intelligence Unit data

Boxes

Acknowledgements

This book has been 18 months in the making, but is long overdue – that is one of the many positive and encouraging messages we received when the idea was first put to Maersk Line's management and later to a wider selection of people across the industry.

The book is published in 2014 to celebrate the 100th birthday of Mærsk Mc-Kinney Møller, who as managing owner of the A.P. Moller Group in 1973, was responsible for the decision to containerise the first of Maersk Line's services. This also coincides with the 40th anniversary of that decision and the first steps of a relatively small ship owner in Copenhagen to become the leader of the container shipping industry.

Between the two of us, we have over 50 years of Maersk experience. Once started, the research took many months and involved the A.P. Moller – Maersk archives in Copenhagen, the Sea-Land archives in Charlotte, North Carolina and the P&O and Lloyds Register archives in London. We received prompt and valuable assistance from colleagues everywhere, and in particular from Kasper Nordhoek Johansen in Copenhagen.

Informa, the owner of *Containerisation International* and *Lloyds List* in the UK, was kind enough to provide extensive material from its archives, in particular its yearbooks back to when publication began. Our thanks go particularly to John Fossey and Adam Smallman there.

The Economist Intelligence Unit conducted extensive research for us on global macro developments over the period – political, economic, social, technological, legal and environmental, as well as at the country level. Its material will be found throughout the book. All involved, but particularly Maya Imberg, deserve our sincere thanks for their interest and enthusiasm for the project.

The research was supplemented by an extensive series of interviews. Here we would like to thank all those who gave their time, interest and willingness to provide us with their insights, perspectives and wonderful stories. Some of the printable ones have been included in this book.

Bill Allen in Copenhagen
Finn Bech Andersen in Copenhagen
Poul Bjerregaard in Shanghai
Michael Blach in Copenhagen
Russ Bruner in New Jersey

'Raj' Ambekhar in Copenhagen
Brett Bennett in New Jersey
Henrik Bjørnsen in Copenhagen
Søren K. Brandt in Mumbai
Yim Choong Chow in Penang

Professor Martin Christopher in
    Cranfield
Jessica Lauren Cohen in Copenhagen
Morten Engelstoft in Copenhagen
Kim Fejfer in The Hague
Tim Harris in London
Claus Hemmingsen in Copenhagen
Søren Houman in Copenhagen
Niels Jørgen Iversen in London
Lars Reno Jakobsen in Cape Town
Søren Karas in Copenhagen
Steen Hundevad Knudsen in
    Copenhagen
Ib Kruse in Copenhagen
Peter S. Linnemann in Copenhagen
Duncan McGrath in Minnesota
Captain Michael D. Meisel in
    Copenhagen
Mario O. Moreno in Newark
Lennart Neumann in Copenhagen

Erik Nielsen in Copenhagen
John M. Nielsen in Copenhagen
Marna Nygaard in Copenhagen
Tim O'Connell in New Jersey
Kyu Sun 'Ken' Park in Seoul
Knud Pontoppidan in Copenhagen
Poul Rasmussen in Fåborg
Klaus Schnede in Tennessee
Søren Skou in Copenhagen
Tim Smith in Hong Kong

Rizwan Soomar in Mumbai
Tom Sproat in New Jersey
Professor Martin Stopford in London
Hanne B. Sørensen in Copenhagen

Rune Sørensen in Copenhagen
Robbert Jan van Trooijen in Sao Paulo
Mike White in New Jersey
Dave Zimmermann in New Jersey

John Clancey in New Jersey

Peter Corfitsen in Singapore
Thomas Eskesen in Copenhagen
Jørgen Harling in Tokyo
Jeremy Haycock in New Jersey
Erik Holtegaard in Copenhagen
Bob House in the US
Flemming R. Jacobs in London
Per Jørgensen in Copenhagen
Eivind Kolding in Copenhagen
Thomas Riber Knudsen in
    Singapore
Ole Larsen in Copenhagen
Alan MacPherson in Chicago
Dick McGregor in Charlotte
Carsten Melchiors in Copenhagen

Dick Murphy in Charlotte
Anne Krogh Nielsen in
    Copenhagen
Erling J. Nielsen in Copenhagen
Jeremy Nixon in Singapore
Thorkild Olesen in Copenhagen
Roderic O'Sullivan in London
Torben Petterson in Copenhagen
Henrik Ramskov in Copenhagen
Ted Ruhly in New Jersey
Tony Scioscia in Charlotte
Frans Smit in Laakdal
Captain Henrik Solmer in
    Svendborg
Peter Spiller in Florida
Flemming Steen in Copenhagen
Knud Stubkjær in Seattle
Hans Henrik Sørensen in
    Copenhagen
Nick Taro in New Jersey
Lucas Vos in Copenhagen
Eric B. Williams in Copenhagen
Uffe Østergaard in Copenhagen

We would like to thank our academic reviewer Torben Pedersen, Professor of Strategic Management and Globalisation at Copenhagen Business School, for his input and advice on the drafts. We are also grateful to Birgitte Henrichsen, Lars-Erik Brenøe, Vagn Lehd Møller, Peter K. Miller, Jesper E. Thomsen, Jørgen Theisen Schmidt, Steen Erik Larsen, Poul Bjerre and many others who took the time to provide input and constructive comments on the drafts. We owe particular thanks to Jørgen Harling, Lars Reno Jakobsen and Knud Pontoppidan who, with their collective experience, reviewed the draft manuscripts and provided valuable insights and constructive criticism.

We are very grateful for all the help and guidance provided by our editor, Sally Simmons of the Cambridge Editorial Partnership Ltd, and our commissioning editor, Paula Parish at Cambridge University Press and her team, without whose professionalism, guidance and support this book would never have happened.

Last, but not by any means least, we would like to thank our families, in particular our wives, Elsa and Vibeke, for their patience, support and never-failing interest in the project.

Any errors and failures to draw the right conclusions from all the material, research and input, are ours alone.

Chris Jephson, Henning Morgen
Copenhagen, October 2013

Glossary

Back-haul	The back-haul is the return journey of the container from its destination, usually in the opposite direction to its primary flow. See **head-haul**.
Beneficial cargo owner (BCO)	The legal owner of the goods, an importer of record who takes possession of cargo at the destination.
Berthing programme	This assigns ships to berths in the most efficient manner. It can be used to optimise berth productivity or, alternatively, the ship's productivity.
Cargo-sharing	An arrangement between two or more trading partners to share the goods traffic between them in an agreed proportion.
Cell guides	Vertical guide rails that position and secure containers on board a ship.
Chapter XI	A US bankruptcy protection process that allows companies time to reorganise and restructure their financial obligations without liquidation and while maintaining control over the company.
Chassis	A piece of equipment specifically designed for the movement of containers by road and/or highways to and from container terminals.
Cross-trades	Foreign-to-foreign trade, carried by ships from a nation other than the two trading nations.
Cut-off time	The latest time cargo can be delivered to a terminal for loading onto a scheduled vessel.
Dangerous cargo	Articles or substances capable of posing a significant risk to health, safety or property. Dangerous cargo usually requires special attention when being transported.
Extra-slow steaming	Defined by UNCTAD as 'reducing sailing speed from 24–25 knots to 18 knots'. See **slow steaming** and **super-slow steaming**.
FFE	A container, a 40-foot equivalent unit or 40-foot equivalent
Flag carrier	A vessel of one national registry whose government may give it partial or full rights over international routes.
Freight forwarder	An independent business that dispatches shipments for exporters for a fee. This may happen by land, air or sea and usually includes preparation of documents, booking of cargo space, warehousing, delivery and export clearance.
Geographical rights	When conferences controlled trade routes, geographical and/or tonnage rights were limitations on entitlements of a carrier to serve a route.
Head-haul	The main route on which a ship owner expects to make money. See **back-haul**.
High cube containers	Containers that are 9.5 feet high; normal containers are 8 or 8.5 feet high.

Hub port	A central location to which traffic from many sources is directed and from which traffic is fed to other areas.
Intermodal	Something that is capable of moving between modes of transport, such as a container moving from a ship to a truck or a rail-car.
Intermodal rate-making	The ability of a carrier to set rates across a variety of modes of transport.
Ladings	A traditional word for a loading, hence bills of lading, which cover a shipment that is being moved.
Lien	Retention of property until outstanding debt is paid.
Lighter aboard ship (LASH)	A barge carrier designed to shuttle between ports, taking on and discharging barges.
Liner trades	Operations along definite routes on the basis of fixed schedules. Usually related to general cargo as distinct from bulk cargoes.
Liquid tanks	Tanks on board a ship for the storage of water, oil or, in some cases, cargoes like latex or liquid chemicals.
Liquid tank containers	Special containers designed for the carriage of liquids, such as liquid chemicals, wine or whisky.
Logistics	The efficient and cost-effective management of the physical movement of goods from supply points to final sale.
Loyalty scheme	When conferences controlled trade routes, loyalty schemes, such as discounts payable six months after a shipment, encouraged exporters to be loyal to the conference and not use outsiders or non-conference carriers.
Mini-bridge services	The process of taking inland cargo bound for export to the coast by rail and loading it to the ship.
New-building	A new ship delivered from the shipyard.
Non-Vessel Operating Common Carrier (NVOCC)	A US Federal Maritime Commission licensed cargo consolidator of small shipments in ocean trades, generally soliciting business and arranging for or performing containerisation functions at a port.
Outsider	A non-conference carrier that operates on a route served by a liner conference but is not a member of that conference.
Pallets	A flat structure of wood, metal or plastic that supports goods in a stable fashion while being lifted by, for example, a forklift. The pallet forms the base of a unit load for handling and storage efficiencies. See **unit load**.
Payton	A ton of cargo on which basis the freight is assessed. This can be weight (e.g. 1,000 kg) or cubic (1 m^3).
Positioning	Refers to the movement of empty containers to a site, for example, a factory, where they can be filled. See **Repositioning**.
Reefer cargo	Cargo that requires refrigeration.
Reefer container	A special container designed for the carriage of reefer cargo.
Reefer plug	A plug on a reefer container designed to allow the container to be plugged into an electrical supply.

Repositioning	Refers to the movement of empty containers to a suitable area where they can be re-used; for example, repositioned from Europe to Asia. See **Positioning**.
Rights, tonnage and/or geographical	When conferences controlled trade routes, geographical and/or tonnage rights were limitations on entitlements of a carrier to serve a route.
Route	The movement of a vessel from its first port of call to its final destination.
Slot charter	The chartering of specific container space on board a ship, usually less than the container capacity of the ship.
Slot cost	The cost of providing each container slot to the market as a carrier.
Slow steaming	Defined by UNCTAD as 'reducing sailing speed from 24–25 knots to 21 knots'. See extra-slow steaming and super-slow steaming.
Stabilisation agreement	A discussion forum among carriers where they can meet, exchange market information and conduct research, including discussing ways to manage costs and improve operating efficiency in a trade. As an example, see the Trans Pacific Stabilisation Agreement (www.tsacarriers.org).
String	A series of ships committed to serving a specific route.
Super-slow steaming	Defined by UNCTAD as 'reducing sailing speed from 24–25 knots to 15 knots'. See **slow steaming** and **extra-slow steaming**.
Supply chain	A network involved in the provision of product or service packages to a customer.
TEU	A container, a 20-foot equivalent unit.
Tonnage rights	When conferences controlled trade routes, geographical and/or tonnage rights were limitations on entitlements of a carrier to serve a route.
Tramp trades	A trade in which ships do not operate along a defined route or fixed schedule, but call at any ports where cargo is available.
Trans-load	The transfer of goods from one carrier to another.
Triangular trade	Trade between three ports or regions of the world.
Unit loads	Combines individual items into single units that can be moved easily by forklifts. See **pallet**.
Y2K	The potential inability of computers and software to account for the change from the year 1999 to the year 2000 at the turn of the century.

Prologue

> *Without the container the global village would still be a concept, not a reality, because manufacturing would still be a local process.*[1]
>
> C. C. Tung, CEO of Orient Overseas Container Line (OOCL), 1997

A dynamic but challenging industry

For many, 2008 was a good year – even for some in the shipping industry, with growth in both their businesses and profits. But 2008 was a very tough year for Maersk Line.

Three years earlier, Maersk Line had started the acquisition of a major competitor, P&O NedLloyd. Following approval by the authorities in February 2006, integration proceeded quickly and everything was to be in place within six months. Enormous efforts were made by both organisations to merge the numerous offices around the world – Maersk Line alone had 325 offices in 125 countries.

The newly merged organisation had grown to over 30,000 people from the 22,000 originally in Maersk Line. The fleet had expanded similarly, from about 350 container ships to a fleet of over 600, both owned and chartered. Structuring the fleet network, already a challenging task, now became very complex.

The acquisition, the sixth and largest over the 20-year period from 1987 for Maersk Line, had set out to retain employees but, as importantly, it aimed to retain the customers of both companies. The plan was to grow the customer base with a now unbeatable range of container services, global port coverage, terminals and inland transport capabilities (road, barge, rail or any combination of the three).

The company knew that the biggest challenges would be experienced by the people at the front end of the business whose role was to work with customers on a minute-to-minute, day-by-day basis. These critical roles involved taking bookings, arranging equipment to be in the right place at the right time, responding to queries, issuing essential documentation and collecting freight that was due.

The planning, preparation and action plans were a global effort. The company recognised that, realistically, things were unlikely to go completely smoothly, but expected that they could be managed. As 2006 ended and the new year began, however, it became clear that some serious challenges remained.

With the major integration process underway and a technical platform that was still being enhanced, service delivery issues were causing increasing concern across the global customer base and with management in Copenhagen, notwithstanding the efforts and commitment of thousands of people all around the world. No number of quick fixes would get the process back on track quickly. Some substantial changes were needed.

They began with the management team. In July 2007 the existing dual-CEO role from 2001 was slimmed to a single CEO, and a new management team was put together. New action teams were instituted to get to grips with the underlying causes of the existing challenges, and the development of a new strategy was initiated.

Then, 18 months later, as the year 2008 turned, the global financial crisis hit and world trade began to collapse: global shipping volumes dropped by an unprecedented 20 per cent in one year. Eivind Kolding, then CEO of Maersk Line – the world's largest container operator – described the situation in which he found himself in mid 2009:

At that point in time we were losing at least $3–4 million a day and I had to go to the Board in February or March and say we're not going to make a small profit as budgeted; we're going to lose $1 billion. We felt we had bottomed out because it had never been worse.

But it continued, and in June, when driving home, I knew that over the day, we had probably lost another $9 million.

That month, I had to tell the Board that, well, I told you a $1 billion loss in March. It's going to be $2 billion. And that of course, can keep you up a little bit at night.

But, however desperate it was, I still had the confidence that we would pull through.[2]

The contrast between this account and that of C. C. Tung, with which this prologue opens, could not be more striking. Yet both views are part of this story, one that began for Maersk over a century earlier when the A.P. Moller company was formed. By 2008 Maersk had been in liner shipping for more than 80 of those years.

The main subject of this book is the past 40 years of the company's history, from 1973 to 2013.

Early in 1973, Maersk took the decision to join the container revolution. The investment this entailed was the single largest the company had ever made. By late 1974, Maersk Line was looking ahead to the first year of operation of the new Far East–US–Far East container service that was to be launched in 1975. The projections involved handling just over 30,000 40-foot equivalent containers (FFE or sometimes FEQ). On a like-for-like basis the number handled in 2011 would top eight million.

Projections were in 40-foot equivalent units rather than the industry standard of 20-foot equivalents (TEUs). Although TEU was established as the global industry standard in 1964, in the US trades with Asia the majority of containers moving were either 40-foot or, in Sea-Land's case, 35-foot. As Maersk Line was learning from the carriers in these trades, it was natural to use 40-foot containers as the standard.

That 1973 decision was to take the A.P. Moller company from being a relatively small player in a relatively small Scandinavian country to being a major player in liner shipping and today, the world's largest in containerised liner shipping. It was to help shape the industry over the next 40 years, while the industry would provide a platform on which much of what would be called globalisation could take place.

The quiet revolution

The advent of the container and the innovations within the shipping companies and shippers connected with it has rightly been called a revolution. It began in 1956 when Malcom McLean, who was to found Sea-Land in 1960, organised the first seaborne container transport from Newark to Houston. It was a slow revolution at first, but by the time Maersk Line joined, it had already picked up considerable speed. This quiet revolution was to have a profound and wide-ranging impact on the shipping industry, global commerce and developments in world trade.

As Adolf Adrion, CEO of Hapag Lloyd, commented in 2006, 'the box became both the driving force behind, and the beneficiary of globalisation as an ongoing process. Scarcely has any other industry achieved such high and continuous growth over a period of 40 years.'[3]

Some of the main themes of this book are reflected in the challenges recounted by, and contrasting statements provided by Eivind Kolding, C. C. Tung and Adolf Adrion – and it might be expected to find these corroborated in a wide range of books on globalisation.

However, the opposite is generally the case. With very few exceptions, the limited references to shipping that can be found tend to refer to an earlier revolution – the change from sail to steam in the late 1800s. The role that containerisation has played is poorly researched and documented, and even less well understood. As academics at Copenhagen Business School have stated, 'the theoretical and empirical literature on the role of transport in economic development is surprisingly weak. In general, transport is acknowledged to play an important role as a facilitator of economic development; however the role of transport remains ambiguous and sub-ject to shallow interpretation.'[4]

The aim of this book is to help fill this gap in the market and to appeal to a wide audience, including shipping people, both inside and outside Maersk Line – 'shipping people' in the broadest sense, from Maersk Line's customers globally to those working in the various parts of the supply chain, including the freight forwarders and logistics suppliers, warehous-ing and airfreight companies. The book covers the development of Mercantile into Maersk Logistics and then Damco and the development of APM Terminals – two 'beautiful swans' as one of our interviewees called them, evoking Hans Christian Andersen – outcomes of the development of Maersk Line over the last 40 years.

Apart from research that we have conducted in our own Group arch-ives, we have also reviewed the archives of Sea-Land, now in Charlotte, North Carolina, and material from the P&O archives relevant to this story.

We conducted over 80 interviews with a wide range of people, not only those inside Maersk Line, but also those with Safmarine, Sea-Land, P&O and NedLloyd, and those from the merged P&O NedLloyd. We talked with young and old, those relatively new to the business and those who have retired from it; including people in North America, Africa, Latin America, Europe and Asia, as well as people in Maersk Line's corporate headquarters in Copenhagen. And we talked to a range of customers, some of whom have been moving goods internationally over many years, more often than not with Maersk Line.

While the research generated a wide range of new material, this book is also unique in that it is the first time most of the stories have been told. The A.P. Moller – Maersk archives are private and the Maersk Line records have never been made available to external parties.

While Maersk Line has compiled extensive data about its competitors and the industry in general over the years, we decided not to rely on our own information but to have leading experts in the industry provide their views and their more neutral analyses and input. *Containerisation International* (www.ci-online.co.uk) and Lloyds List (www.lloydslist.com) in particular have been very supportive, providing access to their archives and material covering most of the years of interest.

Similarly, Lloyds Register in London has not only conducted research for us, but has answered all our perplexing questions, providing us with extensive material from its world-renowned archives.

Maersk Line has extensive reports on markets, country developments, commodity movements and general economic development, but rather than rely solely on this material, we commissioned research from the independent Economist Intelligence Unit, and this forms the core of the macro-economic data that is presented throughout the book.

Those interested in further information, for example on trade statistics, commodity movements, changes in trade flows and other details from 1950 to 2010, with projections to 2030, will find it on the website that supports this book. See: www.creatingglobalopportunities.com.

This website is available for the general reader as well as for 'tomorrow's shipping people', those who are studying or contemplating a career in this fascinating industry.

It is therefore our hope that this book will contribute to the general understanding of the role of shipping, and low-cost, reliable container shipping in particular, in supporting and facilitating the development of globalisation, a process that we believe, with all its pitfalls, has contributed to lifting millions of people out of poverty.

Structure

The main text of the book is accompanied by statistics and graphic data and a number of boxes in which readers can find more detailed information. A glossary of terms is provided at the front of the book, while references appear at the end.

The book covers developments at three different levels. The first is the level with which we, as authors, are most familiar – the transition of Maersk Line from being a relatively small liner operator in the early 1970s to becoming the world's largest container operator.

The second level puts this development into a broader context, drawing parallels and considering benchmarks against other carriers and the container shipping industry at large.

The third level puts the industry into the context of globalisation, tracing some of the developments in products and world trade, the rise of the

'Asian Tigers' (Hong Kong, Singapore, South Korea and Taiwan) and, later, the opening up and expansion of China, the factory to the world.

This third level is doubly important because while shipping has acted as a facilitator for globalisation, it is the principles and practices behind free and open trade that have enabled the industry to respond and play this role. Over the years, a number of challenges to free trade have been noted, from conferences working with restrictive shipping practices to legislative activity that imposes trade restrictions and ultimately encourages protectionism.

While developments are traced broadly in chronological order, there are four themes that play throughout the book.

Shipping and globalisation

Some would say that free and open trade has existed since the time of the Phoenicians. We look at the globalisation that has surfaced in relation to liner shipping during the more recent past and trace their implications, such as the role of conferences, UNCTAD and others.

Key developments in world trade are illustrated, and some of the main changes discussed, such as the initial expansion of the east–west, then north–south and more recently south–south trades.

Innovation

The shipping industry is not often characterised as being innovative – at least not when compared with the speed of innovation seen in more technologically advanced industries such as telecommunications and mobile phones. Yet *innovation for the customer* emerges as a significant theme. Overall these have added up to major changes in the way the industry operates, the way it has developed and the way it responds to its customers.

The globalising company

In 1973, Maersk Line had offices in five countries: Denmark and the United States (established in 1919), Japan (1948), Thailand (1951) and Indonesia (1958). By 2007, 35 years later, Maersk Line had offices in 325 cities across 125 countries. Was the company really global by that time? And what were the implications of this development?

Pursuing this theme, the book explores some of the developments in Maersk Line's relationships with exporters, importers, freight forwarders and other suppliers to the industry. The way that companies buy, build and sell their products has changed substantially over this period, whether they are the world's largest retailer or greatest producer of cars. Meeting the demands of the globalising consumer, not just in the more developed economies, but increasingly in Asia, Latin America and Africa is reflected in the rising volumes in the south–south trades and has meant fundamental changes in production, supply chain management and distribution.

Container shipping has needed to adapt and reinvent itself to be able to facilitate these developments. The book touches on the supporting role of communications and technology, crucial enablers of change.

People

It is a cliché that the most important assets a company has are its people, but without the people, this development might not have happened. We look at the role of some key people in driving the development of both Maersk Line's business and the industry, examining selection, training and development processes. How is it that an industry that is often characterised as male-dominated, traditional, family-owned, conservative and far from the most glamorous in the world has been able to attract and retain very special, high-calibre people over the years?

While the industry has been driven by people with vision, energy and commitment to create and build successful companies, it is also sustained by the energy and commitment of people within these companies, from the junior customer service clerk in a front-line office in São Paulo, Brazil, to the operations assistant in Shanghai, China and the HR manager in a service centre in Pune, India.

These people respond to the needs of their customers, sometimes even before the customers are fully able to articulate what those needs are. They continue to facilitate the developments in world trade and globalisation that consumers have come to expect, through the provision of sophisticated yet low-cost, reliable container shipping.

A story to tell

The first 40 years of Maersk Line in containers is a story that flows from a major investment decision, made by a relatively small company, which led that company to become a substantial player in a global industry. It is the story of people who have constantly challenged the status quo, and of an industry that is developing and maturing while undergoing continuous change.

The story needs to be told now, while it is still fresh in the minds of the people involved, including those who were there right at the beginning.

It needs to be told because the role of container shipping in facilitating global trade and globalisation is neither well documented nor well understood.

Finally, it needs to be told because it is an exciting story of a journey undertaken, frequently into the relative unknown, by a cast of thousands on a truly global stage.

1

'Per Aspera Ad Astra'

A Bumpy Journey to the Stars

> *You have not been promised an easy way.*
>   A. P. Møller

The backdrop to our story, and the first point of reference, is Svendborg, one of the main shipping towns in Denmark, at the end of the nineteenth and beginning of the twentieth centuries.

Many Maersk people are familiar with the phrase 'It all began in 1904', which used to precede the presentation of the company's activities in glossy brochures produced in the 1980s and 1990s. Even though the A.P. Moller Group was a much smaller company at the time, within the small country of Denmark it was a large corporation. The 'all' signified the many activities of the group, contrasted with its context within Denmark and within a world of business that was not yet global in the way we understand it today.

However, even in 1904, the perspective of the key players in the company and Maersk's business activities was international. Maersk's people had gained international experience from the relevant markets at the time and used that experience to establish and gradually expand the business.

Shipping in the early twentieth century

At the end of the nineteenth century, the Danish merchant fleet accounted for about 2 per cent of world tonnage, which was dominated by Great Britain, followed by the United States, Norway, Germany and France. Denmark was a largely agrarian country with a substantial foreign trade and, as a coastal country, naturally had a long tradition of crossing the world's oceans.[1]

Led by England and Germany, Europe's manufacturing and agricultural industries underwent significant modernisation and industrialisation during the latter part of the nineteenth century, and shipping prospered from increased international trade. Manufacturing companies imported raw materials and, as the super-national economy emerged, exported finished goods, and so required transport providers.

The technologies that transformed manufacturing evolved into other businesses and led to innovations that would change shipping companies' ability to do business. The emergence of steamships and later motor ships significantly supported the development of increasingly global trade patterns. Fast, reliable transport would become a cornerstone in international trade, as it is today.

Stopford has identified four factors of great importance to these changes:[2]

1. The steam engine, which freed ships from dependence on the wind.
2. Iron hulls, which protected cargo and allowed much larger ships to be built.
3. Screw propellers, which made merchant ships more seaworthy.
4. The deep-sea cable network, which allowed traders and shipping companies to communicate across the world.

Eventually, manufacturing industries required more raw materials from abroad and many of those were obtained in the territories east and south of Suez that had been annexed as colonies in previous centuries. The growing trades presented new opportunities for shipping companies, which took advantage of the technical innovations and set up regular services to the new markets with relatively fast, specially designed ships. These services would change the shipping industry for ship owners as well as their customers. As the trading systems were refined they proved to be 'as revolutionary as containerisation in the twentieth century'.[3]

International transportation of goods has not been the only driver of globalisation, but globalisation would not have developed at speed without the means for fast, reliable international transport. That story is part of this book's story, specifically the developments in the deep-sea liner business, which grew from British shipping companies that had set up regular sailings to the colonies in the nineteenth century, supporting trade and communication between the far-flung countries of the Empire. Steamships allowed the establishment of more reliable services, which were further improved by the introduction of ocean-going motor ships from 1912.[4] As international trade grew, shippers became more dependent on reliable services and shipping companies began to specialise their vessels for the liner business.

The increasingly internationalising market also had an impact on the composition of the merchant fleet in the 1890s. Technical innovations changed the competitive environment, and if they were to stay in business ship owners had to replace their assets. At the turn of the century, 60 per cent of the ships owned in Denmark had been acquired within the previous five years. They came second-hand or new from modern shipyards, primarily in Great Britain.

From sail to steam

When this part of our story begins, at the end of the nineteenth century, Danish manufacturing industries were smaller, developing later than those in the neighbouring European countries, especially Great Britain. Danish shipping companies did not participate greatly in the growth of the international liner shipping system, but focused on the main market for Danish exports, across the North Sea to Great Britain. As in other European countries, many of the new Danish steamship companies were one-ship ventures; only a few ever acquired a second ship, and even fewer had more than two.

The majority of the Danish fleet, all its sailing ships and most of its steamers, were involved in tramp shipping – that is, they did not have a fixed schedule or regular ports of call. If he was not the owner himself, a captain on a tramp voyage would take his ship to any port as directed by the owner or agents, who communicated with him via cables. His first task, having moored in a new port, was to contact the local agent to ask for new instructions, which could include directives to sell the cargo or to obtain new ladings to further ports.

The primary markets for a Danish ship owner were the Baltic Sea, the North Sea and, as time went by, the European Atlantic coast and the Mediterranean, where freight for each voyage was negotiated by the shipping company or the captain. Typical tramp cargoes were commodities in bulk, like grain, coal, timber and iron ore.[5] A ship could be away from its home port for years in its quest for the most profitable cargo.

In Denmark, by 1895 steamships outnumbered sailing ships in tonnage and would remain an important factor in Danish and international shipping for the next 50 years. However, in the Møller family, the transition from sail to steam had been a fact of life since 1884.

New family businesses

After the unfortunate wrecking of the *Valkyrien*, a barque he had commanded since 1874, Captain Peter Mærsk Møller decided to qualify as a steamship master, at the age of 50. He passed his exams in Denmark and also obtained a British master's certificate. After working as a navigator for

Figure 1.1 The steamship *Laura* represented the Mærsk Møller family's entry into the modern age of shipping; steamships were taking over from sailing ships.

ship owners in the United Kingdom for a while, Peter Mærsk Møller returned to Denmark and eventually in 1886 invested his savings in a small steamer, which he renamed *Laura*, after a friend's daughter, thereby thanking him for supporting the purchase of the ship. This was not Peter Mærsk Møller's first investment in shipping – he had owned shares in the sailing ships he had commanded before his move into steamships – but it was his first independent investment. He paid 18,000 kroner and managed the *Laura* through a limited company controlled and maintained by himself until the ship was sold in 1909.

By that time, his four sons had been encouraged to join the company. The oldest, Hans, trained as a navigator and became captain of the *Laura*; his younger brother Oluf was an engineer; and the youngest, Johannes, went into shipbuilding. However, it was Peter's third son, Arnold Peter Møller, known as A. P. Møller, born in 1876, who was to be the initiator and driver of the family businesses.

A. P. Møller had been employed in various trading houses and shipping companies in England, Germany and Russia before he returned to Denmark in 1904 to head the chartering department of the shipping company C. K. Hansen, based in Copenhagen. Before he took up that post,

Figure 1.2 Villa Anna in the town of Svendborg was A. P. Møller's childhood home. It became the first office of the Steamship Company Svendborg, today's A.P. Moller – Maersk.

he and his father had already discussed the possibility of establishing a steamship company.

That became a reality shortly after A. P. Møller took up his new position in Copenhagen. Peter Mærsk Møller's 50 years of shipping experience combined with A. P. Møller's knowledge of the market convinced a group of leading citizens in Svendborg that the young man could lead Dampskibsselskabet Svendborg (the Steamship Company Svendborg). A banker, two merchants, a steam-mill owner and a solicitor were among the investors and they became members of the first Board of Directors, together with Peter Mærsk Møller and A. P. Møller.

The company was founded on 16 April 1904 and in October that year it purchased its first steamer, the *Svendborg*, which was managed from Copenhagen. The *Svendborg*'s initial voyage was a truly international operation, from Cardiff in Wales to Kronstad in Russia. A. P. Møller became the manager of the new company, which got off to a quiet but good start; by 1906 it had acquired its first new building, *Peter Mærsk*, named after A. P. Møller's father.

In spite of good results and a prudent risk-management policy governing the company's financial assets, it became apparent that the day-to-day manager in Copenhagen wanted faster growth than the Board in

Figure 1.3 The first ship to enter the Maersk fleet was the steamer *Svendborg*, which was bought second-hand in England on 6 October 1904.

Svendborg. In order to achieve his ambitions for independent expansion, A. P. Møller established Dampskibsselskabet af 1912 (the Steamship Company of 1912) and terminated his position with C. K. Hansen.[6]

The two shipping companies, Svendborg and 1912, were managed jointly and A. P. Møller rented offices in Copenhagen's old Stock Exchange, where a small staff took care of all the operating tasks in the Maersk fleet, which by 1913 amounted to nine ships.[7] The political developments in Europe that led to the First World War created good commercial conditions for the shipping industry, from which the Maersk companies, like others, benefited.

By 1918 A. P. Møller was able to realise an old ambition by establishing the Odense Steel Shipyard, meaning he could combine shipping with shipbuilding – the basic idea was 'to build ships using our companies' shipping experience and sail them when prices are low'.[8] In 1919 A. P. Møller opened the first overseas office – in New York – under the name of ISMOLCO, short for the Isbrandtsen-Moller Company. The venture was started with A. P. Møller's cousin, Hans J. Isbrandtsen, who had gained some experience from running a company with shipping and pier administration among its activities.

New business ventures

The Svendborg and 1912 companies, managed jointly by A. P. Møller, started with steamships for the tramp trade and called at European, African and American ports during the early years of the twentieth century. In 1921 the first motorised ship was added to the Maersk fleet, which expanded its trading to ports in Asia and Australia during the early 1920s. Within two decades, Maersk trampers had begun sailing all the world's seas.

The global consumption of petroleum products rose dramatically during the same period, and A. P. Møller recognised the opportunity to extend his shipping activities. After successful negotiations with Shell and Standard Oil, he ordered five crude oil tankers for delivery in 1928. This was the beginning of Maersk Tankers, which today is one of the world's largest tanker shipping companies.

In the same year ISMOLCO entered the liner business, primarily on the basis of an agreement with the Ford Motor Company for the transport of car parts from the United States to assembly plants in Asia. Maersk Line's first voyage was from Baltimore on 14 July 1928. The motor vessel *Leise Mærsk* (4,400 tons) sailed through the Panama Canal, called at San Pedro near Los

Figure 1.4 The *Leise Mærsk*, built at the Odense Steel Shipyard in 1921, was the fleet's first motor ship and the first ship to make a Maersk Line voyage in 1928.

The Maersk Line Network 1928

Figure 1.5 From 1928 until 1947 Maersk Line only served the trade from the United States East and West Coasts to Asia and back, initially with monthly sailings and from 1934 with departures every 14 days.

Angeles, and crossed the Pacific to call at Asian ports before returning to North America. We shall come back to this event later in the story.

Expanding the family business

A family business has been described as one where 'a family owns enough of the equity to be able to exert control over strategy and is involved in top management positions'.[9] For an extraordinarily long period of time, nearly 100 years, only two individuals sat at the helm of this particular family business, first one alone, then father and son together until the son took over on his father's death. A. P. Møller's son, Mærsk Mc-Kinney Møller, became a Partner in 1940, at the age of 27, shortly after the outbreak of the

Second World War. He was to remain with the company for another 72 years, until his death in 2012.

Before the Second World War the Maersk shipping companies had 46 ships sailing all the world's oceans. Thirty-six of these ships were outside Danish waters when Denmark was invaded by German forces on 9 April 1940. All were requisitioned and used by the warring countries. The war meant the loss of 150 Maersk crewmen and 25 ships, but due to the delivery of new buildings from the Odense Steel Shipyard immediately after liberation in May 1945, and the relatively fast recovery of the surviving ships, shipping activities were resumed quickly in the period following the Second World War.

The international trade environment underwent significant changes at this time, based primarily on agreements made at the Bretton Woods Conference in 1944. The United States initiated a movement towards universal free access to global markets and raw materials, and the removal of the old colonial trade restrictions, where only select countries had access to specific markets. In the words of Henry Morgenthau, the United States Secretary of the Treasury, the aim was to create 'a dynamic world economy in which the peoples of every nation will be able to realise their potentialities in peace and enjoy increasingly the fruits of material progress of an earth infinitely blessed with natural riches'.[10]

As a result of the Conference, the World Bank, the International Monetary Fund and the General Agreement on Tariffs and Trade (GATT) were created. These initiatives, combined with the later Organisation for Economic Co-operation and Development (OECD), would have a profound effect on world trade and therefore on the shipping world. Over time the former colonies would open their economies and most would become exporting countries.

Maersk Line extended its liner network with routes to Asia, Africa and North America in the 1950s (and to Europe–Asia in 1968). As with developments in other business units in the A.P. Moller Group, Maersk Line's expansion was not the result of a carefully planned strategy to enter first one new trade, then another new geographical market and follow that up with a third initiative as the Maersk fleet grew. Opportunities were taken as they arose, but the overall aim was to expand the liner business.

Maersk Line applied for membership of the Far Eastern Freight Conference (FEFC) in 1950 (see Box 3.1) and correspondence reveals that 'Mr Møller [Mærsk Mc-Kinney Møller representing Maersk Line] is not in any great hurry but he said he was prepared to fight to enter the trade' – in this case the Europe–Asia trade.[11] The father's and son's approach to expanding Maersk Line by taking on the competition in new markets was clearly expressed by A. P. Møller: 'There are, after all, only five continents and I do not believe that anyone can reasonably expect that, just because he arrived first, he has acquired property rights of title to any part of the world.'[12]

The crude oil tanker fleet was restored and expanded throughout the 1950s, when the size of tanker ships increased due to the continued growth in demand for oil products. In response to this, the decision was taken to extend the company's shipbuilding capacity by establishing the modern Lindø ship-yard, which was completed in 1959. In the same decade the A.P. Moller Group expanded, with new industrial companies focused on refined oil products and a relatively new product: plastic. These businesses were attempts to introduce new, rewarding activities in Denmark, but they had a relatively short life. However, another initiative within the oil industry would have far-reaching implications for both the A.P. Moller Group and Denmark.

The motivation for engaging in oil and gas exploration, and later in produc-tion, was typical of A. P. Møller and Mærsk Mc-Kinney Møller. When the opportunity arose, management considerations focused less on potential earnings than how the new ventures of exploration and extraction of hydro-carbon reserves beneath Danish soil might create jobs for the Danish, make Denmark more competitive and increase the group's portfolio of businesses – in this case, potentially closely linked to the transport of crude oil and refining oil products.[13] But a company focused on shipping and industrial manufacturing like A.P. Moller did not have the necessary skills to lead these activities within the organisation when the concession for the exploration of hydrocarbons was assigned by the Danish government in 1962.

A joint venture – Dansk Undergrunds Consortium (the Danish Under-ground Consortium, or DUC) – was established with Shell and Gulf Oil in order to obtain the concession. The first Danish oil was produced ten years later, in the summer of 1972, and over the next few years production was increased, partly due to higher oil prices triggered by the actions of the OPEC countries in 1973–1974.

In 1975 DUC entered into a gas sales agreement with the Danish state, which forced through significant changes in the concession in the early 1980s. In 1984 the production of natural gas was initiated and DUC launched several innovative activities, which led to the development of horizontal well technology.

A diversified business

The expansion of the original Svendborg and 1912 shipping companies into a group of diverse businesses took root in A. P. Møller's time.

Figure 1.6 Maersk's first crude oil carriers of 1928 had a capacity of around 12,000 tons. By 1974 the ships of that particular bulk trade were able to carry more than 330,000 tons and were named ultra-large crude carriers (ULCCs). The *Kristine Mærsk* was one of seven such giants acquired by Maersk Tankers' fleet between 1974 and 1977.

The expansion was not the result of a strategic plan, but rather the result of a talented, opportunistic man's drive to add value to his enterprise and the societies in which he was operating. His decisions to support new business opportunities were carefully planned, calculated and discussed with trusted partners.

The group's shipping activities grew in line with the expanding world economy in the 1960s. The company purchased specialised ships for the transport of goods in bulk, cars and refined oil products. Oil exploration activities in the North Sea led to the establishment of Maersk Supply Service, a shipping operation with anchor handling, support and transport vessels operating around the world.

By the end of the 1960s, Maersk Tankers had a number of very large crude carriers (VLCC) exceeding 200,000 tonnes and in 1974 received its first ultra-large crude carrier (ULCC), which had a capacity of more than 300,000 tons of crude oil. Experience from the hydrocarbon exploration activities in Maersk Oil led to the decision to invest in offshore activities, now consolidated in Maersk Drilling. These initiatives have had enduring

1 Main gate and administration
2 Meeting facilities
   2a: Meeting Centre 1 at the Main Gate
   2b: Meeting Centre 2 at Dock 3
3 Stockyard for steel
4 Plate cutting workshops and profile factory
5 Block assembly workshops
6 Grand block assembly
7 Paint Shops
8 Goods reception and warehouse
9 Dockoffice
10 Apprentice school and senior workshop
11 Outfitting workshop, component and pipe workshops
12 Building docks no. 1 and no. 2: Max. 200.000 dwt
13 Stockyard for blocks from the Baltic Region
14 Building dock no. 3: Max. 450.000 dwt
15 Grand block assembly
16 Outfitting area
17 Stock area
18 Outfitting Quay
19 Gantry Crane (1,000 tonnes)
20 Odense Habour

Figure 1.7 Two of the world's largest container ships under construction at the Odense Steel Shipyard in 2006. New building number 203 is the *Emma Mærsk*, the first of eight sister ships.

value for the A.P. Moller – Maersk Group. Other companies are no longer part of the group's business, but over time contributed to the creation of jobs. Maersk Air passenger activities were divested in 2005, although the short-haul airfreight carrier Star Air continues operations. Maersk Data was sold to IBM in 2004, and industrial companies, including DISA and Rosti, were also sold when the group refocused its activities in the first few years of the twenty-first century. Due to increased competition from Asia, it was decided to stop shipbuilding activities in Denmark in 2012. The last industrial company remaining in the group is Maersk Container Industry, which started production in Denmark in 1991. Now, dry and refrigerated containers are produced at two factories in China, and from 2014, a factory in Chile.

While expansion into some business areas reflects a logical link to the group's core shipping business, the management of A.P. Moller – Maersk has engaged in numerous diverse business ventures over time, many of which have little or nothing to do with ships. For example, A. P. Møller's last major initiative before his death in June 1965 was to take the group into retail. In 1964 he was presented with an ambitious business case by the Danish merchant Herman Salling, who wanted to expand his chain of supermarkets. In consultation with Mærsk Mc-Kinney Møller, A. P. Møller decided to support the venture. Today, the retail arm of the group includes Bilka and Føtex hypermarkets in Denmark and Netto supermarkets in Denmark, Germany, Poland and Sweden.

Some may wonder what motivated other investments, whose link to the group's core business seem tenuous. The Tanganyika Planting Company Ltd in Tanzania was one of these; yet, while the purchase of some rather infertile land in East Africa might seem – literally and metaphorically – off the charts of a shipping company, there was a rationale behind it. A. P. Møller's vision included the possibility of growing enough sisal or sugar to form the base cargo for a liner shipping initiative. In the mid 1970s this venture supported the lives of more than 11,000 people on a sugar planta- tion near Mount Kilimanjaro and became the second-largest sugar produ- cer in Tanzania. However, the government-controlled home market easily consumed the entire yield and Tanganyika Planting Company rarely exported its product. The vision that the shipping arm of the group would expand by transporting sugar from East Africa did not materialise, yet the Tanganyika investment was profitable in its own right, for the owners, the local staff and the society around the plantation, and it is a great example of A. P. Møller's approach to business.[14]

'Constant care'

Mærsk Mc-Kinney Møller had already been with the company for more than 30 years when he took over the leadership following the death of his father in 1965. His own career had started in much the same way as his father's. From his late teens he worked in a series of trainee positions in shipping, trade and financial services, in Denmark and overseas, before returning to Copenhagen in 1938 to work in A. P. Møller's main office, which at the time was located at Kongens Nytorv in central Copenhagen.

When Denmark was occupied by German forces in April 1940, and the bulk of the company's ships were caught in foreign ports with no contact with their owner, Mærsk Mc-Kinney Møller travelled to Maersk's New York office on his father's behalf to manage the employment of the fleet. How- ever, this became increasingly impossible as the war developed and Maersk ships were requisitioned by the United States, United Kingdom, France, South Africa, Holland and Germany for war purposes, many of them still with Maersk crews on board. Remaining in New York, Mærsk Mc-Kinney Møller focused on making preparations for the resumption of the liner trade after the end of hostilities and the quick return of the ships from their war service. After he returned to Denmark in 1947 he rapidly gained experience in day-to-day management as he increasingly deputised for his father, who nevertheless retained his great commitment to Maersk's businesses to the end.

Maersk is a unique company in having been led by only two people over a period of 100 years. A. P. Møller's and Mærsk Mc-Kinney Møller's family values, the continued family ownership of the group and their focus on stability in succession have had a profound influence on the values and culture of the company and its employees. Mærsk Mc-Kinney Møller was fond of repeating his father's words to him when he joined the company in 1938: 'You have not been promised an easy way.'

A. P. Møller's perspective was consistent. When he received the Grand Cross of the Order of Dannebrog, his chosen coat of arms was the well-known seven-pointed white star from the Maersk logo to which he added

Figure 1.8 Mærsk Mc-Kinney Møller (1913–2012) in his office, next to a portrait of his father, A. P. Møller.

the motto 'Per Aspera Ad Astra' – through hardship to the stars. Mærsk Mc-Kinney Møller adopted this motto for himself, when he received his own knighthood, and for the group of businesses he led.

Mærsk Mc-Kinney Møller remained as CEO until 1993 and Chairman of the business and the group's owning foundations until 2003, when he passed the chairmanship of the business Board to Michael Pram Rasmussen, only five months short of the company's 100th anniversary. He remained Chairman of the foundations until his death in 2012, but his formal leadership role in A.P. Moller – Maersk was now effectively over. For that reason he initiated a process that led to the company values being set down in writing and communicated everywhere in the group, which was by now very different from the company he had joined almost 75 years earlier. Before the Second World War there were fewer than 100 employees in the head office in Copenhagen, and even when A. P. Møller died in 1965, having grown and diversified the company to become one of the largest corporations in Denmark, the total administrative staff was still only around 450.

In A. P. Møller's time, the staff was closer to management than is possible today, and everyone learned by doing. A. P. Møller, his son and the company's executives had been highly visible role models. When Mærsk Mc-Kinney Møller succeeded his father as CEO and Chairman, he worked to protect and develop the group, building on his father's basic business principles and the value-based leadership that characterised all the companies within it. Now neither he nor his father would be in the company and their values had to be made accessible to more than 100,000 employees across a large, truly international group of companies.

Mærsk Mc-Kinney Møller's aim was that those values would continue to be guidelines for each individual employee. A statement of company values and business principles was his way of emphasising their importance to all of Maersk's stakeholders, not just employees but also shareholders, customers and business partners. The watchword, guiding principle and one saying that all are familiar with is 'constant care'. The original term is found in a letter from A. P. Møller to Mærsk Mc-Kinney Møller, sent from Copenhagen on 2 December 1946. At the time, Mærsk Mc-Kinney Møller was still in New York, preparing to restart the Maersk Line route from the US East Coast via the Panama Canal and the West Coast to Asia. The letter contains A. P. Møller's guidelines and thoughts in response to Mærsk Mc-Kinney Møller's initiatives. He ended the letter by quoting a maxim of his own: 'No loss should hit us which could be avoided with constant care . . .'

Mærsk Mc-Kinney Møller later commented: 'The letter was not written with a view to how I should run the company when he had passed away;

Box 1.1 A.P. Moller – Maersk Group core values

The A.P. Moller – Maersk core values serve as the anchor for our behaviour and ensure that we make ethically sound decisions that are aligned with our company culture.

The values *constant care* and *humbleness* imply that we must prepare for the future and look for inspiration on how we can continuously improve our practices.

Uprightness requires transparency and accountability in everything we do.

Our employees and *our name* entail striving to make our company an inspiring and challenging place to work, and a valuable and credible business partner.

he wanted to explain how this leadership should be to the benefit of the company.'[15] In rare footage, taken during the filming of a new corporate movie in 2011, Mærsk Mc-Kinney Møller explained further:

> We exercise constant care. And by constant care, I mean care at the time when the action is taken. It's much easier if you do it right the first time, instead of having to correct or add later on. That's difficult. But of course if the care delays decision-making, it can be too much.

Mærsk Mc-Kinney Møller started the Values Process, as the project of formulating and propagating the group's values was known internally, at a meeting at his own home in 2003. The top management of the A.P. Moller – Maersk Group were invited and were presented with five core values based on A.P. Møller's business principles: constant care, humbleness, uprightness, our employees and our name.

All these values were familiar to the managers of Maersk Line, Maersk Oil, Maersk Tankers, Maersk Supply Service and the other Maersk executives – they themselves had been brought up to live the values as they had risen through the ranks of the company. What was new was their formal responsibility to roll out these values in a new fashion; make them known, discuss them in their business units and have their employees accept and live them – rather than passing on the values the way A. P. Møller and Mærsk Mc-Kinney Møller did.

The Values Process started at the top, then cascaded down through the organisation. During 2004–2005 all employees were introduced to the values and discussed ways to implement them in their working lives. Today, all new employees are made familiar with the values as part of their induction to Maersk.[16] In this way, Mærsk Mc-Kinney Møller did all he could to ensure what the Maersk star and the Maersk name would stand for in the future, as he emphasised in his last interview: 'The basic principle is that people can trust us. Authorities can trust us, employees can trust us and business connections can trust us. Your word should be your bond.'

Today, the founding family continues its commitment to the business. The family-controlled foundations are today's majority shareholders in A. P. Møller – Mærsk A/S, the legal name of the operating company. The decisions to establish the Family Foundation in 1946, the A. P. Møller and Chastine Mc-Kinney Møller Foundation in 1953 and the Relief Foundation in 1960 were all based on the constant care value; A. P. Møller took care of today by actively preparing for tomorrow. 'This wise and timely decision has helped the steady development of our company over the years, without the risk of takeover attempts, Danish or international, and without the unrest and uncertainty that would follow. And it will continue to do so', Mærsk Mc-Kinney Møller commented on his father's decision. The ownership structure, with the three Foundations and the basic business principles distilled in the five values, are fundamental to understanding the way A. P. Møller and Mærsk Mc-Kinney Møller operated. A. P. Møller sought independence when he arranged for the A. P. Møller and Chastine Mc-Kinney Møller Foundation to own the majority shareholdings in the Steamship Company Svendborg and the Steamship Company of 1912, which were merged into A.P. Møller – Mærsk A/S in 2003. The Family Foundation and the Relief Foundation own smaller, but significant, shareholdings as well.[17]

The Foundation was created on the basis that it would own the majority of the voting shares in the companies, that its Board would ensure that the A.P. Moller Group activities were managed according to A. P. Møller's business principles and that the group would remain well funded from reserves. Other large Danish and international corporations used the same construction to ensure the continuation of activities after the demise of the first generation of management.[18]

The Board of the Foundation, together with the group management, has the freedom to operate without the risk of a hostile takeover and are in control of the company's destiny. At its core A.P. Moller – Maersk is a privately held company and the management, i.e. A. P. Møller and Mærsk Mc-Kinney Møller, worked to maintain independence in financial as well as operational matters. We will see how this was put into practice when we look at Maersk Line's history in containerisation.

In 2008, Ane Mærsk Mc-Kinney Uggla, the youngest daughter of Mærsk Mc-Kinney Møller and the new chairman of the A. P. Møller and Chastine Mc-Kinney Møller Foundation, said of managing the businesses that 'it is important that each step is handled with a serious and long-term

Figure 1.9 Ane Mærsk Mc-Kinney Uggla succeeded her father, Mærsk Mc-Kinney Møller, as chairman of the A.P. Møller and Chastine Mc-Kinney Møller Foundation in 2012.

perspective that means solutions will last'. This approach has a direct link to the first generations in the company and underlines the strong commitment of the Møller family to the group.[19]

A. P. Møller – Mærsk A/S is listed on the Copenhagen Stock Exchange and more than 65,000 shareholders have interests in the company. There is no longer a family member on the A.P. Moller – Maersk Executive Board, and no family member is part of the top management. Thus, according to our earlier definition, A.P. Moller – Maersk is not strictly speaking a family business. However, as we will show in this book, the Møller family's values and business principles remain the guiding principles for the way Maersk does business.

The Coming Revolution

2

> *When you look at the inventions or innovation of the last 100 years, there are lots of products, most of them in physical form, such as smart phones. But this really low-tech invention of the container has done more for global trade than anything else.*
>
> Søren Skou, CEO, Maersk Line 2012

1966: a critical year

In 1966 Mærsk Mc-Kinney Møller and the Maersk Line management embarked on the journey towards containerisation. Maersk Line had been in the deep-sea liner business for nearly 40 years and was well established in the Pacific, considered one of the larger trades together with the other east–west trades of the Atlantic Ocean and Europe–Asia, as well as several regional trades, primarily in Southeast Asia. However, their competitors had already made the crucial decision to introduce new services, transporting standardised containers. Maersk Line decided in favour of an alternative to the standard container, and it would take nearly a decade for the company to launch its first fully containerised service. On the troublesome way, Mærsk Mc-Kinney Møller and the Maersk organisation would mature and grow into a modern and even more internationally oriented business.

In the mid 1960s, the world was changing rapidly: the global population had increased by one-third in less than two decades and now numbered around 3.3 billion. Trades in Maersk Line's main markets in North America and Asia increased dramatically in the same period. The United States' international trade rose from $19.4 billion to $50.3 billion and Japan's from $1.7 billion to $15.8 billion. Only a limited number of people in and around the shipping industry had the vision to see the opportunities offered by the standard container for facilitating and expanding this trade. The industry would go through significant changes, and indeed itself become a major driver for changing the world as commodities were moved from break-bulk into containers.

Box 2.1 Types of ships

In this book, we mention three types of ships:

- *Bulk carriers* are ships that transport large, homogeneous cargoes, for example grain, iron ore, coal and crude oil. Dry cargoes are moved in bulk carriers and crude oil in very large crude carriers (VLCCs) or ultra-large crude carriers (ULCCs).
- *Specialised ships* transport chemicals, liquefied gases, forest products, wheeled vehicles and refrigerated cargoes. These five types of ships are very different in design.
- *Container ships* are designed with cellular cargo holds to facilitate efficient handling of containers.

Source: M. Stopford, *Maritime Economics*, 3rd edition, Routledge, 2009, p. 36.

Containerisation became a fact of life in 1966, a fact all participants in liner shipping eventually had to confront and make decisions about. The owners of conventional break-bulk cargo ships – and, in the case of Maersk Line, ships designed for handling pallets – were faced not only with potentially overwhelming investments in container ships, but also with expanding their focus from pure ship operations to encompass terminal and inland operations. A race began, where the operators might have seen the short-term potential of containers but were unable to foresee the long-term implications for themselves, their customers and indeed global consumers.

The concept and the consequences

One man, Malcom McLean, who was later to form Sea-Land, had initiated and managed the introduction of seaborne container transport to the domestic American market in 1956 and worked relentlessly to optimise the ships, terminals and inland transport systems and devise a way to supply an attractive product to customers. Other operators followed by introducing container services, and gradually their customers adapted to the opportunities container transport offered. The first containers were either 16, 24 or 35 feet long; standardisation was pivotal to the wider penetration of the container as a means for transport.

Initially, containerisation was a differentiator used by shipping companies in the United States and shortly afterwards in Australia. The story of how containers developed has been told many times. It begins with

Box 2.2 The standard container

In this book we have determined that the container revolution started with the ISO container. However, we do agree that Malcom McLean should be credited with introducing seaborne container transport on the occasion of *Ideal X*'s departure from Newark on 26 April 1956.

Some will argue that containerised transport took place in the seventeenth century, when Portuguese merchants brought home pepper in coconut shells from India; or that the British company Sainsbury's first introduced containers that were easy to transfer from rail to lorry and to ship; or that the Danish shipping company DFDS introduced door-to-door services in the 1950s. We acknowledge all these developments, but it is our contention that it was only when agreement was made on the standard container that international container shipping emerged as an enabler for globalisation.

The US Maritime Administration (MARAD) and the American Standards Association initiated discussions on standardising containers in 1958 and the National Defense Transportation Association joined in 1959. On 14 April 1961 it was decided that a standard container was to be 8 × 8 × 10, 20, 30 or 40 feet, and the US authorities announced that 'only containerships designed for those sizes could receive construction subsidies'.[1]

The International Standards Organisation (ISO) moved to establish international guidelines and the American dimensions were adopted by 1964. Work continued on requirements for the strength and lifting of containers, but the agreement about external sizes meant that ship owners could start designing ships specialised to carry standard containers. In 1967, 107 container ships were under construction and 95 per cent were designed according to the new standards.

converted Second World War tankers and continues with ship owners ordering container ships designed specifically to carry their containers; some favoured 16-foot, others 24-foot and still others 35-foot containers. In 1964, the *Kooringa* of Australia was the world's first fully cellular container ship, a significant innovation in the handling of containers.[2] The new container services were adopted by customers and began to attract the attention of competitors in the global shipping industry. That interest increased sharply when the container revolution took a further step.

Whatever their length, containers provided a safe and efficient means of transporting commodities that were stowed inside their steel or aluminium walls. Trucking and shipping companies offered their customers individually designed containers to encourage them to optimise their operations. However, the differences in length restrained the development of intermodal transport systems, where the container could be moved easily from

Figure 2.1 The start of the container revolution. On 26 April 1956 Malcom McLean and his innovative staff loaded the first containers on board the *Ideal X* in Port Elizabeth in New Jersey, United States. The first voyage was to Houston, Texas.

a trailer to a train to a ship, and vice versa. The first initiative to standardise container dimensions came out of MARAD in 1958 (see Box 2.2). The process of international approval continued until 1964, when the dimensions of containers were agreed, and during the following years the standard was adopted by government bodies, shipping companies and, not least, shippers. This meant that ship owners could start ordering ships that would make transporting goods five times more efficient than the conventional break-bulk cargo ships.

In 1966, containerisation was taken to yet another level when it became truly international. No fewer than three American operators started Trans Atlantic services in the spring of 1966, with U. S. Lines credited for shipping the first ISO-standard 20-foot containers to Europe.

As with many other inventions, the political climate and war created the foundation for faster developments. Liner shipping is dependent on base cargo, that is, agreements with shippers who guarantee a certain quantity of cargo on a regular basis. The dominant shipper in international and intercontinental container shipping in the 1960s was the US Department of Defense. The continuing Cold War and key events like the Soviet invasion of Czechoslovakia in 1968 led to the steady build-up of American military bases in Europe – and those bases needed supplies from North America. A growing proportion of military supplies was shipped in containers. Sea-Land's commercial agreements with the Department of Defense, in Europe and soon afterwards in the Vietnam theatre of war, were of crucial importance for the development of ships, terminals and equipment.[3]

Also, in 1966, another man, an unidentified consultant with McKinsey & Co., grasped the future in a precise manner that is, even with the benefit of hindsight, remarkable. McKinsey was assigned by the British Transport Docks Board to evaluate the longer-term trends in 'land–sea transportation'.[4] The Docks Board was a public sector body created to oversee the adequacy of British port facilities.[5] The McKinsey report concluded that:

- Containerisation is today emerging as the most important and far-reaching single factor in the movement of exports and imports.
- Containerisation represents a fundamental and worldwide process of change. Its economic origins and effects are global.
- Containerisation is a fact right now, not a possible or potential long-term future development. It is already well advanced and proceeding at a pace that has so far been seriously underestimated by virtually all those sectors that will be most affected by it.

Container shipping was emerging in 1966, but it was not nearly significant enough for anyone to produce statistics on container traffic in ports, which of course had neither special cranes nor special trucks for the inter-terminal transport of the containers. In fact, containers were seen as special cargo. But by 1970 credible statistics were in place. And, mirroring the most important trades of the times, the six busiest British ports ranked among the 25 largest in the world in terms of container throughput.

The British Transport Docks Board responded early to the challenge of the container and sought to establish a strategy to meet it. Despite the Board's willingness to confront changes in its business, it must have been difficult for its members to accept the McKinsey predictions in 1966. If you had looked out of the window at the ports in Belfast, Tilbury, Larne, Liverpool, Harwich or Hull, only a few containers would have been in view. Yet just four years later, when the first statistics on container throughput were produced, nearly one million containers passed over the quays of those six ports. Even with the luxury of hindsight, that development is both dramatic and astonishing.

The arrival of American container ships in European ports would have made headlines in the shipping journals of the time and must have been the talk of the day in the industry. The McKinsey predictions, delivered only a few months later, were commissioned by the British Transport Docks Board and were not publicly available. If the McKinsey report had been published it would have emphasised the importance of the development of containerisation and opened the eyes of ship operators much sooner.

McKinsey also predicted widespread consolidation within the shipping industry. Considering the large capacity of container ships compared to ships designed for the conventional break-bulk trade, their report estimated that very few container ships would be needed to carry the entire UK trade with North America, and that only 2 to 4 operators would be left in the container shipping industry, compared to more than 20 operators in the conventional Trans Atlantic break-bulk trade. Capital constraints, combined with limited cargo volumes, would keep the smaller operators from participating in containerisation. Those robust enough to enter the new business would create 'combinations of companies', later known as consortia or alliances. And the combination of forces by these able ship owners would become 'one of the most dynamic forces in the rapid diffusion of container shipping'.[6]

The unit: the new mode of transport

The development of pallets to unitise cargoes was recognised as a major factor in increasing the efficiency and productivity of the transportation function. McKinsey viewed containerisation as one further step in this evolutionary process, which it foresaw taking place in a relatively short period of time. There were three crucial factors: the timing of container ships coming into service; the fact that most operators viewed containerisation as a race; and lessons learned from sea and inland transport experiences in the United States that would allow more rapid development in other parts of the world.

The 1966 McKinsey report that urged the British Transport Docks Board to recognise containerisation as a fact of life also recommended that it should prepare for partnerships with operators to obtain user agreements to optimise the use of port facilities. A threat was posted: worldwide container transportation companies may become large enough to undertake terminal operations themselves. McKinsey effectively predicted the containerised door-to-door, intermodal transport concept, and that it would be the foundation for global trade.

This is where developments in the liner shipping industry stood in the pivotal year of 1966. The shipping industry might have been global in its individual trades, but it still did not serve a global economy. And despite the combined experience of many great shipping executives in the world's most prominent shipping companies, only a few had the vision and courage to take significant steps into containerisation at this time.

Early Maersk Line developments

Like many other shipping companies, Maersk ships have never traded primarily in their native country but have served international shippers since the first inter-European voyage by the steamship *Svendborg* in 1904. Maersk ships called at African ports for the first time in 1910, the Americas in 1913, India in 1921 and Australia and China in 1923. Maersk ships were deployed in the tramp trade and although it was increasingly prominent in Denmark, the fleet still played only a small role in the global economy.

Maersk opened its first international office in New York in 1919. The US-based company was to be a general shipping business, including chartering, with the view to 'settling down into permanent trades'.[7] A. P. Møller was convinced that over time the liner trade would take over a considerable share of the tramp trade, but acknowledged that the liner and tramp trades were two entirely different disciplines. The new American company had a quiet start and despite a number of initiatives it did not find the right customer base to secure sufficient cargo intake for a regular service.

Very few manufacturing companies had established production facilities away from their home country. In 1928, however, a contract was signed with the Ford Motor Company to transport car parts to the Ford assembly factories in the Far East, and on 14 July 1928 the motor ship *Leise Mærsk* made its historic first journey from Baltimore to Japanese and Philippine ports. By 1934, Maersk Line was making fortnightly sailings but did not expand into other trades until after the Second World War, while the fleet's tramping activities continued to decline.

Profiting from the post-war increase in exports from the United States to Asia, liner activities on the Panama Line were resumed in 1946. Maersk seized business opportunities in the inter-Asia trades and soon established a range of services from Japan in the East to Persia in the West, and even a round-the-world service via the Suez Canal. In the late 1950s, North Atlantic and West African ports were included in the network, and in 1968 the Europe-Asia route was established in cooperation with Kawasaki Kisen Kaisha's Kawasaki Line of Japan.

Figure 2.2 The original Maersk Line logo.

It is obvious from the literature on developments in the container liner trade in the late 1960s and the early 1970s that in 1966, when Maersk Line's containerisation story starts, the company was an insignificant player in the container liner market. Simply put, Maersk Line was not mentioned among the operators who were active with container services on selected routes. Commenting on the situation in the increasingly global container line business in 1980, Broeze describes Maersk Line as 'a well-established shipowner but until now only a modest participant in the liner business'.[8] He was describing a business unit in the A.P. Moller Group that had been active in the conventional liner trades for more than 50 years, but had not yet containerised the greater part of its network.

Back in 1966, when the first American 20-foot containers arrived in Europe and McKinsey predicted a radical change in the transport of goods, the Maersk Line fleet consisted of 44 break-bulk cargo vessels, a few of them nearly 20 years old, most of them bought in the 1950s and some less than five years old. Two years previously, in 1964, Maersk Line had made a strategic decision about unitised cargo – but not containers. It would develop systems and processes around the pallet.

The unit load

To optimise the product – the unit load – Maersk decided to order ships specifically designed to handle palletised cargo efficiently. These seven fast

Box 2.3 The change from break-bulk liner shipping to container liner shipping and the mechanisation of cargo handling

Liner ships operate on regular schedules, whether carrying break-bulk cargoes or containers. Typically, they call at many ports on their route to load and discharge. Liner ships are equipped to carry specialist cargoes such as refrigerated products, machinery, liquid cargoes, whether those cargoes come in break-bulk or containers.

The conventional break-bulk liner services 'were complicated by the need for multi-port loading and discharging as well as the need for the operator to offer transhipment to other ports not served directly'. The handling of many different commodities in many different types of packaging made operations in port more expensive, more time consuming, more dangerous and, as trade grew, inefficient.

Companies developed various solutions: pallets of different sizes for boxes of manufactured goods, ready to be moved directly from the factory floor to storage or consumption. But it was the container that won in the market place.

One container, one unit. Easy to move, easy to stow and easy to prevent damage and pilferage. The container was readily moved from truck chassis to train to ship's cargo hold, with a minimum of delay, setting the scene for low cost, efficient shipping that 'opened the floodgates for global commerce'.

New technologies were used to standardise and automate cargo handling and sea transport developed to be a part of an integrated through-transport system. Ship design was changed dramatically to adapt to the new technologies and systems of efficient cargo handling and stowage.

The practical stowage of boxes of shoes, bales of cotton, frozen fish and the many other commodities that are shipped was now moved from the cargo holds of the liner ship into the container. When the container was filled with its cargo and the container doors sealed, the container was moved and the cargo left untouched.

As much as the introduction of scheduled liner services was a revolution in its day, the shift in paradigm represented by moving the cargo hold of the ship into that of a container changed the economics of transporting commodities around the world.

Source: M. Stopford, *Maritime Economics*, 3rd edition, Routledge, 2009, pp. 28–41.

break-bulk carriers, which became known as C-ships after the first letter in their names, were contracted in Bergen, Norway, and Malmö, Sweden. The decision to market the unit load concept was supported by a report commissioned from the Stanford Research Institute in the United States in 1966.

In 'A Study of Alternative Unit Load Systems for the Maersk Line', Stanford examined the market, the anticipated quantities and types of

Figure 2.3 *Christian Mærsk* was one of the seven C-ships, fast conventional break-bulk ships designed for the unit load/pallet trade and introduced on the Maersk Line network in 1967–1969. *Christian* Mærsk is carrying a diverse load of cargo on deck, including a few containers.

cargo, freight costs at all stages of transportation in the United States and Canada, and Maersk Line's primary markets in Southeast Asia. The aim was to compare the profitability of the conventional cargo-load, represented by the unit load concept, and container transport.

The Stanford Research Institute emphasised the developments within container transport among Maersk Line's competitors and the need for Maersk to respond to them. The report stated that Maersk Line would not be sure of success simply by following the initiative of others, and that the company was already behind its competitors. It predicted that the competition would gain market shares simply because they were the first in the market with dedicated container ships.

The report concluded that:

- Traffic would switch direction; exports from the United States would fall and imports increase.
- Japan's exports would increase significantly.
- Exports of manufactured goods from developing countries would increase.
- A very large proportion of cargoes would be compatible between unit load and containers.

- 90 per cent of all cargo would fit on pallets or larger units.
- Approximately 75 per cent of all cargo would be shipped in quantities that fitted into a 20-foot container.
- Approximately two-thirds of the cargo could be shipped using the unit load concept.

Based on the report's conclusions, Maersk Line chose to continue the development of the unit load concept. The systems and processes were incorporated not only in the C-ships, which were being built in Norway and Sweden, but also in the other ships deployed on the Maersk Line network.

The choice of unit load was a strategic one, reflecting Maersk Line's market opportunities at the time of the decision. Lacking efficient infrastructure, Maersk Line's main markets in Asia were not ready for large-scale containerisation. Even four years later in 1970, by which time containerisation was firmly established and credible statistics began to emerge, only three Asian ports counted among the world's top 25 ports in terms of container traffic, and those were Japanese. Maersk Line had a strong market position in Southeast Asia and the results of trading were satisfactory; it had the right product for its markets at the time.

Marketing efforts at this time included a 19-minute film entitled 'Focus on Unit Loads – Focus on Maersk Line'. The storyline featured pallets with boxes of candles from a factory in Kobe, Japan, and showed all the links in the transport chain until the candles arrived – efficiently and safely, of course – at a warehouse in Philadelphia in the United States. As a ship owner, Maersk Line focused on its modern ships with side ports for easy handling of the pallets, but the fork-lift pallet truck is really the hero of the film. Pallets are moved directly from the factory floor to the lorry, from the lorry to the ship, internally in the ship's cargo holds and vice versa until the pallet reaches the designated storage site in the Philadelphia warehouse.[9] The combination of well-packed cartons on pallets and the fork-lift truck provided shipping companies with safer and more efficient cargo handling, resulting in significant savings for the shippers. The unit load concept was promoted by the Oslo-based Unit Load Council. Working with road hauliers, Maersk Line and others developed systems to optimise pallet-handling procedures. Maersk Line staff attended courses with the aim to better understand the opportunities and advantages unit loads offered and to be able to provide professional advice to their customers.[10]

The indications for change, however, were becoming clearer. Competing ship owners were preparing to containerise services between the four most developed regions of the world: North America–Japan, North America–Europe, Europe–Australia, North America–Australia and

Japan–Australia.[11] The British company Overseas Containers Limited (OCL) ordered ships for the Europe–Australia trade. Sea-Land did not enter the Pacific commercial trade until late 1968, but was active with outbound containerised cargoes for the US military. The first new ocean-going cellular container ships designed for the standard ISO container were launched in 1968 and all competitors – including the Germans, Japanese and British – raced to be the first to deploy them. But the Americans won. U. S. Lines introduced a service with a cellular container ship in the summer of 1968.[12]

Maersk Line was established in the Pacific trade and monitored the developments closely. In 1966 Japan was less important for Maersk Line than Indonesia, Thailand and the Philippines, but those markets soon changed and the decision to focus on the unit load concept, which had seemed far-reaching and indeed strategic at the time, had to be reconsidered.

The international deep-sea liner business was about to change dramatically, but obviously it was impossible for anyone to predict the future – not the American ship owner who had just decided to order dedicated container ships with ISO-specifications; nor the British Transport Docks Board,

Figure 2.4 Mechanised movement of unitised cargo significantly improved efficiency on piers as well as on board ships and the fork-lift pallet truck played a leading role.

who had to digest McKinsey's recommendations to change its business plans radically; nor a relatively small ship operator, based in Copenhagen.

Time for change

The year 1966 was not the time for big decisions in the Maersk headquarters on Copenhagen's central square, Kongens Nytorv. A. P. Møller had died in 1965 and Mærsk Mc-Kinney Møller, feeling the loss of both a father and his mentor in the business, was still finding his way as the head of the group. Remembering her father in the A.P. Moller – Maersk Annual Report for 2012, Mærsk Mc-Kinney Møller's daughter, Ane Mærsk Mc-Kinney Uggla, stated that Mærsk Mc-Kinney Møller paid 'profound respect' to A. P. Møller and 'the values that he had created and instilled. However, his attention was also directed towards new opportunities of an increasingly globalised world.'[13] It was crucial for Mærsk Mc-Kinney Møller to have a strong foundation in place, to ensure the long-term stability of the group's activities before new initiatives were launched – but as we will see shortly, it did not take him long.

Mærsk Mc-Kinney Møller had worked in his father's company since 1938 and had been responsible for day-to-day operations in Maersk Line since 1947. In the 1950s and 1960s Maersk was still organised as it had been in the 1930s. The company was focused on ship ownership and operations; the commercial activities – trampers, liners, tankers and later bulk ships – were run separately, while technical operations and developments, the sale and purchase of ships and staffing were joint operations covering all commercial arms of the shipping business. Although all the individual commercial activities had their own separate management, central leadership was strong and all far-reaching decisions, and indeed lesser ones, had to be confirmed by A. P. Møller and now by Mærsk Mc-Kinney Møller. The company culture and business principles derived from the founding family, who were the controlling owners of all activities, and even personally owned some of the ships.

An international perspective

Very few Danish business people had such a large and significant international network as Mærsk Mc-Kinney Møller. He had formed his first international contacts during his apprenticeships in Germany, England and France in the 1930s, but he learned the importance of meeting in the right forum to exchange ideas and experiences during his time in the United States between 1940 and 1947.[14] After Mærsk Mc-Kinney Møller

Figure 2.5 The Lindø shipyard at the time of its inauguration in November 1959, with the production facilities at the front and the housing project for employees in the background.

took over the leadership of the A.P. Moller Group in 1965, he continued to develop his knowledge of international affairs to support the expansion of the group. Eventually, Mærsk Mc-Kinney Møller became a board member in the Morgan Guaranty Trust Company and IBM Corporation, and stayed with these prominent organisations until he stepped down from the CEO post in A.P. Moller in 1993.

Mærsk Mc-Kinney Møller made regular business trips to the group's offices all round the world and local staff introduced him to important political and business partners. His insight into the potential developments of the liner business was established through an increasing interest in the customers, competitors and opportunities presented by the container.

Shipping remained the core activity of the A.P. Moller Group businesses, but the group also owned the Odense Steel Shipyard, which A. P. Møller had started in 1918 to build cheap and efficient ships, taking advantage of the experience and knowledge the company had gained in shipping. The original shipyard had become obsolete during the 1950s, as tankers increased in size, and a new, modern shipyard was inaugurated at Lindø, near Odense, in 1959. At the old shipyard, ships were constructed on building berths, then released into the sea and completed at an outfitting quay. At the new shipyard, ships were to be constructed using modern assembly-line methods, in docks rather than on building berths. The layout of the new shipyard was like that of a factory, with the raw materials (steel) entering the facility at one end of the construction process and the product (ships) sailing out at the other.

Implementing these new methods proved to be challenging, and the shipyard decided to call in American consultants with expertise in production methodology and shipbuilding. A. P. Møller was the chairman of the Odense Steel Shipyard, Mærsk Mc-Kinney Møller was a member of the Board and both were deeply involved in its management, and Maersk Line and the other shipping divisions of the group were important customers of the yard. Both A. P. Møller and Mærsk Mc-Kinney Møller had consulted external experts on many occasions before, recognising the need to look outside the organisation at certain decisive moments. The year 1966 had been one of those moments, when Maersk Line had commissioned the report from the Stanford Research Institute. This time, Mærsk Mc-Kinney Møller turned to the McKinsey consultancy, which had produced that impressive set of predictions for the British Transport Docks Board. It is probably safe to assume that McKinsey did not keep their findings to themselves. Two years later the report and its recommendations were to have significant importance for Maersk Line.

Mærsk Mc-Kinney Møller first met the McKinsey consultancy in 1968 and formal cooperation was initiated in 1969. The task assigned to McKinsey was to conduct a survey of the A.P. Moller Group's potential and to develop a plan for improvements. All the business units were evaluated and the general assessment for Maersk Line was that the operation worked better than its competitors. The main problem was identified in a question: 'What must [Maersk Line] do to protect the Panama Line in the light of the container threat?' In its conclusions, McKinsey referred to the 1966 British report – clearly, the matter of containerisation was considered very urgent.

Solving the problem posed by McKinsey would require the attention, energy and commitment of Mærsk Mc-Kinney Møller and not least his staff of dedicated liner people over the next five years – and continues to require that attention today.

A selection of important developments: 1950–1954

Political

- 1950 UN membership stands at 60 nations. By 2012 there will be 193 member nations.[15]
- 1950 The Korean war begins. An armistice is signed in 1953, establishing the boundary between North and South Korea at the 38th parallel.[16]
- 1950 Nationalist China's leader, Chiang Kai-shek, forms an anti-communist government on the island of Taiwan (Formosa).[17] China takes control of Tibet.[18]
- 1950 India's constitution is promulgated, establishing the country as a secular, democratic republic.[19]
- 1951 Australia, New Zealand and the US sign the Pacific Security Treaty (ANZUS Treaty), creating a mutual defence pact.[20]
- 1952 Japan and the US sign a bilateral security treaty.[21]
- 1954 The Southeast Asia Treaty Organization (SEATO) is created, mainly to formulate a regional defence treaty to oppose communism in Asia. The body will be disbanded in 1977.[22]

Economic

- Early 1950s The reconstruction of Europe follows the end of the second world war in 1945.[23]
- Early 1950s Through the Marshall Plan, the US provides grants over the period 1948–1952 worth around US$12.5bn, equivalent to around 1% of that nation's GDP for each of the four years. This will promote growth in participating states and introduce pro-market reforms.[24]
- Early 1950s The US dollar becomes the world's major reserve currency. US corporations assume leading positions in many industries. Europe and Japan spend the immediate post-war decade undergoing extensive reconstruction, heavily dependent on official aid from the US.[25]
- Early 1950s The Soviet Union Council for Mutual Economic Assistance (CMEA; 1949–1991) is created with the purpose of fostering economic collaboration between communist countries.[26]
- 1950–1973 World merchandise exports rise by more than 8% per annum in real terms over the period.[27]
- 1950 Under the Saudi-Aramco "50/50" Agreement, Arabian American Oil Company (Aramco) agrees with Saudi Arabia to share oil revenue equally, setting a precedent for distributing royalties between foreign firms and governments in the Middle East.[28]
- 1950 Agricultural products make up 40% of world merchandise trade.[29]
- 1951 The European Coal and Steel Community (ECSC) treaty is signed in Paris. It will form a community consisting of France, Germany, Italy and the Benelux countries, with the aim of organising free movement of coal and steel.[30]

Social

- 1950 The world's urban population stands at 29%. By 2008 it will reach 50%.[31]
- 1950 The women's participation rate in the workforce in the US is 35%. By 2010 it will reach 58%.[32]
- 1950 The number of TV sets in US homes reaches 6m. By 1960 this will increase tenfold, to 60m.[33]
- 1952 The International Planned Parenthood Federation, the Population Council and a national population policy in India raise concern over the rising global population.[34]
- 1952 The first commercial jet flight leaves London for Johannesburg.[35] In 2010 the annual number of commercial flights will exceed 30m.[36]
- 1953 New Zealander, Edmund Hillary, and Nepalese Sherpa, Tenzing Norgay, are the first men to reach the summit of Mount Everest.[37]

Technological

- 1950 The Diner's Club card is introduced and becomes the first credit card accepted at multiple retail establishments.[38]
- 1951 The first vessels designed to carry containers begin operation in Denmark.[39]
- 1951 The first commercial computer, the UNIVAC, is introduced by Remington Rand, a typewriter manufacturer.[40]
- 1952 Tetra Pak introduces aseptic packaging for milk in Sweden.[41]
- 1952 Herbicides treat 11% of corn and 5% of cotton acreage. By 1982, these percentages will rise to 95% and 93%, respectively. Despite increasing crop yield, intensification of pesticide use raises concerns about its impact on the food chain.[42]
- 1953 James Watson and Francis Crick discover the DNA double-helix structure.[43]
- 1954 The Rose Parade, a carnival held in California, features in the first programme ever broadcast in the NTSC colour television format.[44]

Legal

- 1950 The UN adopts the Principles of the Nuremberg Tribunal, creating new international laws on crimes against humanity, crimes against peace and war crimes.[45]
- 1952 The World Customs Organization is established.[46]
- 1954 The UN Convention on the Political Rights of Women, designed to promote the equality of rights between men and women, enters into force.[47]
- 1954 The International Institute of Refrigeration is established as an intergovernmental organisation.[48]

Environmental

- 1950 The World Meteorological Organization is established.[49]
- 1950 Dr Arie Haagen-Smit identifies the causes of smog in Los Angeles as the interaction of hydrocarbons and oxides of nitrogen from auto exhaust. By 1959 the California Motor Vehicle Pollution Control Board will be established to test vehicle emissions.[50]

A selection of important developments: 1955–1959

Political

- Late 1950s Decolonisation gains momentum in both Africa and Asia. Sudan, Morocco, Tunisia (1956), Ghana, the Federation of Malaya (1957), Burkina Faso, Guinea and Singapore (1958) gain independence.[51]
- 1955 Newly independent West Germany joins the North Atlantic Treaty Organization (NATO).[52]
- 1955 The USSR establishes the Warsaw Pact, a counter alliance to NATO.[53]
- 1955 The Bandung Conference of developing nations takes place. The conference leads to the formation of the Non-Aligned Movement.[54]
- 1956 Egypt nationalises the Suez Canal. A UK and French military response fails.[55]
- 1956 Juscelino Kubitschek is elected president of Brazil and launches a Plan of National Development for energy, transport, food and education, as well as the construction of a new capital, Brasilia.[56]
- 1957 The European Community (EC) is established by the Treaty of Rome, favouring Western European integration.[57]
- 1958 Nikita Khrushchev demands the withdrawal of UK, US, and French troops from Berlin in part to prevent East German citizens from crossing into West Berlin.[58]
- 1959 Fidel Castro overthrows Cuba's president, Fulgencio Batista, turning Cuba into a socialist state.[59]

Economic

- Late 1950s Decolonisation leads to newly independent countries seeking partial or total self-sufficiency in food production owing to a lack of trust in imports following wartime and post-war shortages. Food self-sufficiency becomes a standard feature of most national development plans.[60]
- Late 1950s With the US and Canada as the major producers of industrial and agricultural goods, the US dollar comes under pressure. Many countries with financing difficulties, particularly Latin American nations, respond by restricting their imports.[61]
- Late 1950s The Port Authority of New York and New Jersey plans and builds the Port Newark-Elizabeth Marine Terminal, which will open in 1962. This is the first port in the world designed for containerisation.[62]
- 1953–1957 China's first Five-Year Plan is implemented. Government investment in agriculture and industrial planning reportedly increases GDP by 12% in real terms.[63]
- 1956 Japan becomes the world's leading shipbuilding nation.[64]
- 1958 Mao Zedong launches the Great Leap Forward campaign to facilitate Chinese industrialisation.[65]
- 1958 The Bretton Woods system of freely convertible currencies at fixed exchange rates becomes fully operational. All major European currencies become convertible for current-account transactions.[66]
- 1959 The European Free Trade Association is established.[67]

Social

- Late 1950s Decolonisation and labour demands for reconstruction increase migration flows to Europe from former colonies.[68]
- 1957 The peak birth year of the "baby boom" era (1948–1964) in the US:[69] 123 of every 1,000 women aged 15 to 44 years give birth.[70]
- 1958 The first transatlantic passenger jetliner service begins, connecting London to New York.[71]
- 1959 The US Department of Defence MIL-Q-9858 standard is issued, encouraging the notion of *quality assurance*. This is a precursor to the International Standard for Management Quality Assurance ISO 9000.[72]

Technological

- Late 1950s "Just-in-time", a production strategy which minimises inventory in order to reduce costs, is implemented by Toyota.[73]
- 1955 The first transatlantic telephone TAT 1 cable is laid, allowing up to 48 calls to be made simultaneously.[74]
- 1956 Thermo King Corporation produces the first *reefer container*,[75] a ship equipped with refrigeration technology to transport perishable commodities.
- 1957 Sputnik, the first artificial satellite, is launched into space by the Soviet Union.[76]
- 1957 Gateway City, the world's first purpose-built container ship, enters service.[77]
- 1958 Jack Kilby, a Texas Instruments employee, invents the *integrated circuit* – or *microchip* – to make smaller electronic circuits.[78] Microchips will subsequently be used in all electronic equipment, including computers, mobile phones and other digital home appliances.
- 1959 Xerox 914 is launched, the first automatic plain-paper office photocopier, which becomes among the top-selling industrial products of all time.[79]

Legal

- 1958 The Inter-Governmental Maritime Consultative Organization (later renamed the International Maritime Organization) is established.[80]
- 1958 The International Convention for the Prevention of Pollution of the Sea by Oil comes into force.[81]
- 1958 US president, Dwight Eisenhower, signs the National Aeronautics and Space Act, creating the National Aeronautics and Space Administration (NASA).[82]

Environmental

- 1958 The Food and Agriculture Organization (FAO) expresses concern over the growth of forest industries and their impact on the world's forests.[83]
- 1958 The UN Conference on the Law of the Sea is convened. A major issue is outer-continental-shelf resource exploitation and fishing.[84]
- 1958 A scientist, Charles David Keeling, starts regular measurements of levels of carbon dioxide in the atmosphere.[85]
- 1959 The 2,300-mile St Lawrence Seaway opens, linking the Atlantic with the Great Lakes in North America.[86]

A selection of important developments: 1960–1964

Political

- 1961 The Berlin border is closed and the construction of the Berlin Wall begins.[87]
- 1962 The Cuban Missile Crisis begins with a USSR–US stand-off over secret USSR plans to install a missile base in Cuba.[88]
- 1963 The Nuclear Test Ban Treaty is signed in Moscow by the US, the Soviet Union and the UK. The treaty bans all tests of nuclear weapons, except those conducted underground.[89]
- 1963 The Organisation of African Unity (OAU) is formed in Addis Ababa with 32 members. Its goal is to decolonise Africa and remove European rule in Southern Rhodesia, South Africa, Mozambique and Angola. In 2001 the African Union (AU), loosely modelled on the European Union (EU), will replace the OAU.[90]
- 1964 China detonates its first atomic bomb. It becomes the fifth country to develop nuclear weapons, after the US, the Soviet Union, the UK and France.[91]

Economic

- Early 1960s High-performing Asian countries access the world economy through labour-intensive manufactured exports. These nations promote exports through a mix of policies: relatively free trade, convertible currencies, macroeconomic stability and a set of innovative institutions (including export-processing zones, duty exemption schemes, and incentive packages for foreign direct investment, FDI).[92]
- Early 1960s Rapid growth in automobiles and highways in industrialised countries accelerates demand and a shift in fuel consumption from coal to oil.[93]
- Early 1960s Development of the Eurodollar market in London contributes to the expansion of international liquidity.[94]
- 1960 The Organization of the Petroleum Exporting Countries (OPEC) is founded with the objective of co-ordinating members' petroleum policies.[95]
- 1960 The Organisation for Economic Co-operation and Development (OECD) replaces the Organisation for European Economic Co-operation (OEEC).[96]
- 1964 The first United Nations Conference on Trade and Development (UNCTAD) is held in Geneva, in light of growing concerns about the place of developing countries in international trade. Given the complexity of the issues, the conference will be institutionalised to meet every four years.[97]
- 1964 The G77 is formed in order to represent developing countries at the UN and promote South-South co-operation.[98]

Social

- 1960 The contraceptive pill is launched in the US.[99] By 2011 over 100m women worldwide will be using it.[100]
- 1961 The UN names the 1960s as the "Decade of Development", with rapid decolonisation marking a new level of engagement with the third world.[101]

- 1964 Anti-apartheid leader, Nelson Mandela, is sentenced to life imprisonment for high treason in South Africa. He will be released in 1990, eventually winning the Nobel peace prize and serving as the country's first post-apartheid president.[102]
- 1964 The Civil Rights Act is passed to reduce discrimination in the US. Lyndon Johnson's Great Society agenda gains momentum.[103]

Technological

- Early 1960s The advent of the floating rig allows the development of offshore oil and gas production.[104]
- 1960 Theodore Maiman demonstrates the first optical laser.[105] Lasers will be at the core of a variety of inventions over the following decades, including compact disc (CD) and digital versatile disc (DVD) players, printers, laser-surgery equipment and industrial welding applications.
- 1961 The International Organization for Standardization (ISO) sets standard sizes for shipping containers: 20-foot and 40-foot lengths.[106]
- 1963 Cancer-screening mammography is shown to be a valuable tool for detecting the presence of breast tumours.[107]
- 1964 Murray Gell-Mann and George Zweig independently propose the existence of *quarks* – fractionally charged particles within protons and neutrons.[108]
- 1964 The first line of Japan's high-speed train system (Shinkansen) opens.[109]
- 1965 The Mont Blanc Road Tunnel in the Alps mountain range opens.[110]

Legal

- 1960 Charles D. Prater and James Wei of Mobil Oil Corp file the first software patent application.[111]
- 1960 Canada's indigenous peoples, the First Nations, gain the right to vote in federal elections.[112]
- 1963 The Codex Alimentarius Commission, established by the Food and Agriculture Organization (FAO) and the World Health Organisation (WHO), develops harmonised international food standards, guidelines and codes of practice to protect the health of consumers and ensure fair trade practices in the food sector.[113]

Environmental

- 1960 Jacques Cousteau and Prince Rainier III of Monaco publicly oppose the French plan to dump radioactive waste into the Mediterranean Sea. The French government decides not to go ahead.[114]
- 1961 The World Wildlife Fund (WWF) is founded.[115]
- 1962 Rachel Carson publishes *Silent Spring*, exposing the hazards of the pesticide dichlorodiphenyltrichloroethane (DDT), and providing impetus for the environmental movement. DDT will be banned in the US from 1972.[116]

Merchandise trade by country

Global population: 2.5bn

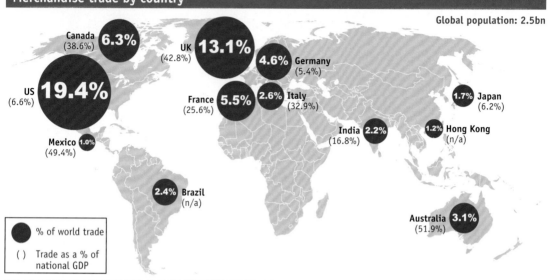

Canada (38.6%) 6.3%

UK (42.8%) 13.1%

4.6% Germany (5.4%)

US (6.6%) 19.4%

France (25.6%) 5.5%

2.6% Italy (32.9%)

1.7% Japan (6.2%)

Mexico 1.0% (49.4%)

India 2.2% (16.8%)

1.2% Hong Kong (n/a)

2.4% Brazil (n/a)

Australia 3.1% (51.9%)

● % of world trade

( ) Trade as a % of national GDP

1955

Global population: 2.8bn

Canada (39.8%) 5.8%

UK (40.0%) 10.6%

6.9% Germany (9.2%)

US (6.6%) 16.0%

France (24.0%) 5.1%

2.6% Italy (39.9%)

South Korea, 0.2% (n/a)

2.5% Japan (11.4%)

Mexico, 0.9% (32.9%)

India 1.5% (18.2%)

Hong Kong, 0.6% (n/a)

1.6% Brazil (n/a)

1.2% Argentina (n/a)

Australia 2.2% (32.9%)

Note. The maps are based on January 2013 boundaries. Trade is based on merchandise exports and imports.
Sources: The Economist Intelligence Unit (EIU) calculations using trade data from IMF, *Direction of Trade Statistics* and GDP data from EIU; IMF, *International Financial Statistics*; and World Bank, *World Development Indicators* (via Haver Analytics). Population data from UN (via Haver Analytics).

World merchandise exports

US$ trn (at 2005 prices)

0.4   0.6
1950 1955 1960 1965 1970 1975 1980 1985 1990 1995 2000 2005 2010

Note. World exports have been rebased to 2005 constant prices using world export volumes from the World Trade Organization (WTO).
Source: EIU calculations using WTO data.

The Economist — Intelligence Unit

1960

Merchandise trade by country

Global population: 3.0bn

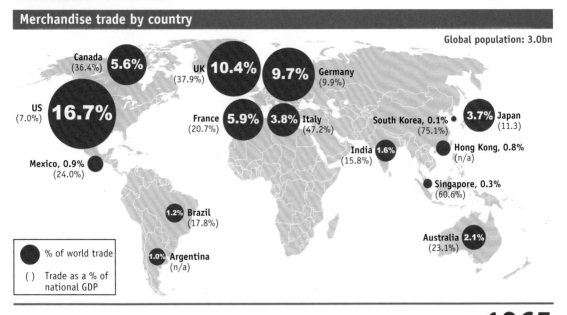

Canada (36.4%) **5.6%**

US (7.0%) **16.7%**

UK (37.9%) **10.4%**

9.7% Germany (9.9%)

France (20.7%) **5.9%**

3.8% Italy (47.2%)

South Korea, 0.1% (75.1%)

3.7% Japan (11.3)

Hong Kong, 0.8% (n/a)

India (15.8%) **1.6%**

Singapore, 0.3% (60.6%)

Mexico, 0.9% (24.0%)

1.2% Brazil (17.8%)

1.0% Argentina (n/a)

Australia **2.1%** (23.1%)

- ● % of world trade
- ( ) Trade as a % of national GDP

1965

Global population: 3.3bn

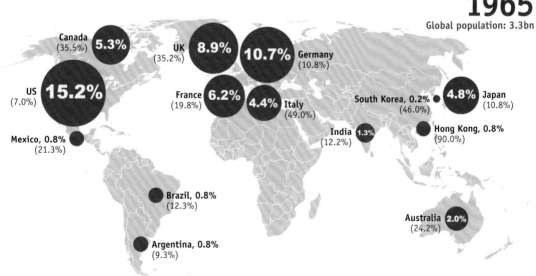

Canada (35.5%) **5.3%**

US (7.0%) **15.2%**

UK (35.2%) **8.9%**

10.7% Germany (10.8%)

France (19.8%) **6.2%**

4.4% Italy (49.0%)

South Korea, 0.2% (46.0%)

4.8% Japan (10.8%)

Hong Kong, 0.8% (90.0%)

India (12.2%) **1.3%**

Mexico, 0.8% (21.3%)

Brazil, 0.8% (12.3%)

Argentina, 0.8% (9.3%)

Australia **2.0%** (24.2%)

Note. The maps are based on January 2013 boundaries. Trade is based on merchandise exports and imports.
Sources: The Economist Intelligence Unit (EIU) calculations using trade data from IMF, *Direction of Trade Statistics* and GDP data from EIU; IMF, *International Financial Statistics*; and World Bank, *World Development Indicators* (via Haver Analytics). Population data from UN (via Haver Analytics).

World merchandise exports

US$ trn (at 2005 prices)

0.4	0.6	0.8	1.2									
1950	1955	1960	1965	1970	1975	1980	1985	1990	1995	2000	2005	2010

Note. World exports have been rebased to 2005 constant prices using world export volumes from the World Trade Organization (WTO).
Source: EIU calculations using WTO data.

The Decision

3

Taking Maersk Line into Containers

> *It was a question of one big step or none at all.*
>
> Mærsk Mc-Kinney Møller, at the inauguration of Pier 51 in Newark, New Jersey, 1975

Facing the facts

Maersk Line started sailings on the Panama Line from ports on the US East Coast via the Panama Canal and Los Angeles to the Far East in 1928. However, it did not establish itself as a major player in the Pacific until after the Second World War. In its 1966 report, the Stanford Research Institute stated that regional trades were expected to change over the coming years and that Maersk Line was well positioned to meet this development. The numerous inter-Asia routes that had been in operation since the 1950s would prosper from the growing economies in the region, notably Taiwan, South Korea, Hong Kong and Singapore. In its 1969 report on the potential of the A.P. Moller Group, McKinsey outlined the position of the competing liner operators in the Pacific trade – Sea-Land, APL, NYK and Mitsui, among others. They were either considering containerisation or already preparing for the delivery of fully cellular container ships. Maersk Line lagged significantly behind in that specific trade.

In fact, in the autumn of 1968 Mærsk Mc-Kinney Møller and Maersk Line had already initiated internal evaluations and discussions with Kawasaki Kisen Kaisha, Maersk Line's partner on the newly established Europe–Asia trade, to determine how to address the container challenge. The two partners were very much influenced by messages coming out of the Far Eastern Freight Conference (FEFC), where other members – those building container ships at shipyards in Europe and Asia – discussed rates and conditions for the transport of containers. The predictions made in 1966 by McKinsey were now being talked about across the table and were very much a fact of life. Maersk Line knew it had to respond.

Mærsk Mc-Kinney Møller had discussed the container question with representatives from McKinsey in their first meetings in the autumn of 1968 and more specifically as their report was developed during 1969.[1]

However, the management focus on container transport was first formally registered in the minutes of a joint meeting on 31 October 1969, where the Boards of Directors of the Steamship Company Svendborg and the Steamship Company of 1912 participated.

Possibly the company was a little late, but developments had come so quickly that already today even contracts made a year ago would be out of date on several points.

This extract suggests that Mærsk Mc-Kinney Møller accepted McKinsey's question – 'What must APM [i.e. Maersk Line] do to protect the Panama Line in the light of the container threat?' – as relevant for the business. The first step to answering it was to establish a team to investigate the pros and cons of containerisation for Maersk. This was not a formal project group with a declared purpose and set deadline, but rather an investigative team working to prepare a base for a future decision. The participating Maersk Line offices, all located in the division's main market places in the United States, Japan, Thailand and Indonesia, were asked to submit detailed information on current and potential markets relevant for the evaluation of Maersk Line's opportunities in container line shipping.

On 26 August 1970, the Line Department delivered a presentation to Mærsk Mc-Kinney Møller in which the feedback from the local offices formed the basis of its recommendation against containerisation of the Panama Line, for four main reasons:

1. Conversion to container ships would require large investments in ships and equipment.
2. The Panama Line route was long and had many ports. Implicit in this statement was the fact that the ports were not equipped to support pure container operations.
3. There was a great imbalance in the cargo distribution – larger quantities were foreseen inbound to the United States, fewer outbound to Asia.
4. There would be a great need for transport of empty containers.

The presentation was followed by a discussion of issues such as whether sailings should be on fixed weekdays or dates; the fact that container ships were becoming increasingly expensive; the distribution of 20-foot and 40-foot containers; the risk of protectionism (which would be an advantage for Japanese and American competitors); and the possibility that Maersk Line might become a member of a conference as a container carrier. The conclusion was that Maersk Line 'alone should not invest in container ships, nor transform the existing tonnage to container ships, but continue to operate the semi-conventional ships in this trade'.

Box 3.1 The background to the conference system

It is believed that the opening of the Suez Canal in 1869 led to the classic problems of excess shipping capacity between Europe and Asia, as the available ships that had previously sailed around Southern Africa could now make the journey more quickly via the canal.

The consequence, exacerbated by seasonal fluctuations, in particular in the tea trade with China, led to cut-throat competition and rate wars, undermining the concept of regular and reliable liner services.

The Ocean Steam Ship Company (OSS), owned by Alfred Holt, as well as a number of other British (Peninsular & Orient, Glen Line, Shire Line and Ben Line) and continental carriers (e.g. Messageries Maritime of France) were all operating on this route and had been since the 1840s.

In 1866, Alfred Holt offered the China agency for OSS to John Swire and, in partnership with a UK exporter of woollen goods, Richard Butterfield, they created the trading house Butterfield & Swire in Shanghai, operating as agents for Holt.

Swire started trading in his own name on the China coast and found that competition was already being mitigated by understandings between some of the operators. These understandings covered sets of sailings, uniform rates and even revenue pools. John Swire believed such agreements could be extended to longer-haul services.

The Calcutta-to-Europe trade saw the first conference, established in 1875, and in 1879 an 'Agreement for the Working of the China and Japan Trade' was established.

Sources: National Maritime Museum, *The Early History of Freight Conferences*, Trustees of the National Maritime Museum, 1981; V. Rolls, *The Far Eastern Freight Conference 1879–2004*, CAS, 2005.

This was a reference to the break-bulk and pallet ships that more often than not carried containers on deck. Customers were moving into containers and Maersk Line was meeting their requirements on a limited scale, but container handling on conventional break-bulk ships was obviously not optimal. Nevertheless, it was possible and it represented significant business for Maersk Line in the early days of containerisation, even though the main product was still the unit load concept.

With hindsight it is easy to judge negatively the Line Department's reluctance to take advantage of the new opportunities presented by containers, but we have to remember the context, which was highly positive. The investigative team had carried out its research on potential cargoes, equipment, terminals and not least profitability, and had been faced with a dilemma. Even though the investigations were based in the Line Department, the innovation of containerisation represented a potential threat to the Line Department's existing and indeed profitable trades.

Maersk Line had very fast and efficient ships and operations that won in the market place. Both McKinsey and the Stanford Research Institute had placed Maersk Line at the top of the market in the conventional break-bulk and pallet services, and the self-confidence of the Maersk Line management and staff was largely justified. The potential innovation of focusing on containers was not necessarily welcomed by all.

A new organisation

The growth of the Maersk Group of activities and companies in A. P. Møller's time cannot be attributed to strategic planning; the nature of the expansion was more a reflection of a knowledgeable and creative man seizing opportunities as they arose.[2] Traditionally, Maersk's shipping activities had been divided into trampers, tankers and liners. When Mærsk Mc-Kinney Møller returned to Copenhagen from the United States in 1947, he and his father divided their management tasks between them, so that A. P. Møller retained responsibility for trampers and tankers, while Mærsk Mc-Kinney Møller took control of liners, supported by his cousin Georg Andersen, who became a Partner in A.P. Moller in 1959. Because of this, A. P. Møller's death in 1965 did not affect the management of Maersk Line significantly. However, it did mark the point at which changes in the

Figure 3.1 Kongens Nytorv 8 was the main office of the A.P. Moller Group from 1915 to 1979, when the headquarters moved to its present location at Esplanaden on the Copenhagen waterfront.

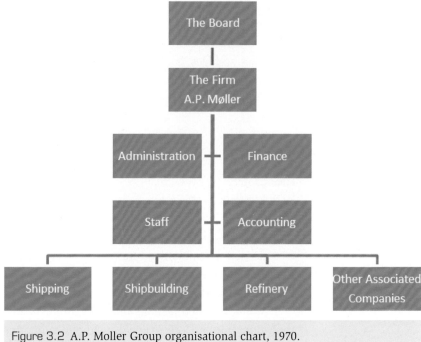

Figure 3.2 A.P. Moller Group organisational chart, 1970.

A.P. Moller Group became less evolutionary and more the result of strategic planning.

Mærsk Mc-Kinney Møller and the McKinsey team worked to translate the 1969 report findings into relevant consequences for the A.P. Moller Group. The result was a new organisation plan that covered the corporate head-quarters and the individual groups within the shipping business. Mærsk Mc-Kinney Møller decided to adjust the company's organisation according to the recommendations of the report and implemented a new organisational structure from July 1970.

There were four principal activities in the shipping division.

1. Tankers. The fleet consisted of 25 21,000–210,000-ton crude oil carriers and two small product tankers, a relatively new addition to the business.
2. Maersk Line.
3. Bulk and special vessels. The six bulk vessels were designed to carry large homogeneous cargoes, like grain or iron ore. Two specially designed bulk carriers were added to the fleet in 1969, fitted out to transport cars from Europe to North America and bulk cargoes on return voyages.
4. Maersk Supply Service. This business unit was started in 1967 as part of growing off-shore activities in the Danish part of the North Sea. Maersk

Supply Service had only two ships at the time and was not considered a separate profit centre.

Generally, McKinsey concluded that operations in the company's shipping departments were 'efficient and well managed' but that the group's leadership (Mærsk Mc-Kinney Møller and Georg Andersen) should delegate responsibility for the day-to-day management to others, senior as well as junior staff, and focus on strategic rather than operational issues.[3] It stressed that, if the A.P. Moller Group was to exploit its potential, individual managers should have full responsibility for their departments and the freedom to act within the general guidelines drawn up by the Partners. In 1969 Georg Andersen was 65 and had been the day-to-day head of the Line Department since 1945, continuing in that position after Mærsk Mc-Kinney Møller returned from the United States. In 1970 he was replaced as day-to-day manager by Christian Lund; however, Andersen retained overall responsibility for the Line Department until his retirement in 1978.

Profit centres

McKinsey proposed the establishment of decentralised profit centres, where management reported to the Partner responsible; for the Line Department this was Georg Andersen. The aim was to ease the burden of management for the Partners and to let the department managers, now profit centre managers, focus on creating the required results. In addition to the three profit centres, which were referred to as the Line Department, the Tanker Department and the Bulk and Special Vessels Department, two staff functions were established. The Technical Organisation was to organise new buildings and the operation of the fleet, including machinery and inspection and ship personnel services, while the Planning Section encompassed the Sale and Purchase Department, which would arrange the buying and selling of ships as well as the development of new ships.

The new organisation plan was the first major result of the generational succession in the A.P. Moller Group. Its overall objective was to ensure continued growth and to maintain the group's stature and reputation by attracting, developing and promoting top-quality managers. Mærsk Mc-Kinney Møller made the decision to professionalise the structure of the group and move away from the evolutionary model by which the group had previously expanded its activities.

The prominent Danish financier and industrialist Carl Frederik Tietgen (1829–1901), many of whose companies are still operating today, once stated that his management philosophy was to delegate and have a professional organisation do all the work.[4] However, there is no evidence that Mærsk Mc-Kinney Møller was moved to delegate more of the day-to-day running of the group.[5] As senior Partner he continued to be tirelessly involved in the operational implementation of the significant investments made in shipping, oil exploration, offshore and industrial businesses during this period.

A strategy for Maersk Line

After the introduction of the new group organisational structure in 1970, the immediate task for Maersk Line's management was to ensure that any strategic gaps would be closed, and to alter the course of the business to meet the corporate objectives. For that purpose a strategy was developed for the liner business. The objectives were to provide competitive liner services in each trade, to maintain (at least) existing share positions in major trades and to average 12 per cent return on assets at market value before tax, depreciation and administration.

Specific strategic approaches were outlined for management:

1. Build up an effective head office marketing programme and develop a practical sales management system for guiding agent sales activities.
2. Evaluate older-ship services to determine whether to renew or phase out these trades, making return-on-investment calculations for continued sailing.
3. Complete evaluation of the container ship issue on the Panama and Europe Lines and decide how to meet or respond to container competition.
4. Seek out new trades suitable for break-bulk or containers.

The Copenhagen office represented the legal entities, the ship owner, the managing partner and indeed the daily management of the Steamship Company Svendborg and the Steamship Company of 1912. In its report and its recommendations, McKinsey targeted the group leadership, and in less than two years – from the first encounter with McKinsey in Paris in late 1968 to the establishment of a modern headquarters organisation during 1970 – Mærsk Mc-Kinney Møller had set the scene for Maersk Line: increase the contribution to the group's bottom line and do so by deploying the right services on trades that provided a sufficient return on investment. Also, the Maersk Line management had to take into consideration the roles and responsibilities of the organisation outside Denmark, the very import-ant offices in the United States, Japan, Thailand and Indonesia, together with the agents. That organisation also had to deliver.

Figure 3.3 *Clara Mærsk*, deployed on the Panama Line with break-bulk cargo in the holds and the increasingly important containers on deck.

Despite the decision that Maersk Line management had taken to continue with the unit load concept, containers were already a fact of life. Every day, all round the world, an increasing number of containers arrived for shipment in ports. Maersk Line sales staff had to accept that some customers considered a unit load to be a container, not a pallet – the shipper would choose 'the system that best fits his needs from a cost and effectiveness standpoint'.[6] This meant that containers were being increasingly carried on ships designed to take a very different type of load.

Maersk Line was faced with precisely the challenges that McKinsey had predicted would confront independent ship operators: capital restraints, cargo mix and the potential need for partnerships or even consolidation. And the Maersk Line organisation was not yet ready for the container challenge.

Maersk Line, the FEFC and containerisation of European trade

Since the 1950s, A.P. Moller had been communicating with the FEFC about the possibility of acquiring rights to serve the Far East–Europe and Mediterranean–Far East trades. Remembering A. P. Møller's assertion – that 'there are ... only five continents and I do not believe that anyone can expect that, just because he arrived first, he has acquired property rights of title to any part of the world' – the Maersk Line management was frustrated that its competitors were successful in keeping Maersk Line out of the European market. Application letters had been put forward in 1950, 1952 and 1956, and in 1957 Maersk Line obtained rights to serve Genoa in Italy with its around-the-world service, which was considered a small gain in the continuing battle for market shares.[7]

Independence was preferred, but in order to enter the Asia–Europe trade without risking too much, Maersk Line found a partner equally eager to join. In May 1967, the new service Maersk was developing in association with Kawasaki Kisen Kaisha applied to the FEFC for rights to Northern Europe. The application was rejected in the following month. Consultation took place with Maersk Line's European agents (Detjen in Hamburg, Hudig and Veder in Amsterdam and De Keyser Thornton in Antwerp). As a consequence, in November 1967 it was announced that the service would operate as 'outsiders', that is, not adhering to the rules and regulations of the FEFC.[8] On 9 March 1968, the semi-container and pallet ship, *Charlotte Mærsk*, commenced loading in Antwerp. The first voyage of the new service was noted by the Boards of the Maersk shipping companies as having lost $49,000.[9]

As Kawasaki Kisen Kaisha had not received approval from the Japanese authorities for the new service, Maersk Line initially operated alone as 'Maersk Line – forerunner for Maersk-Kawasaki Line'.[10] Discussions with the FEFC continued but a draft agreement between Maersk-Kawasaki and the FEFC at the end of March 1968 still did not meet the needs of the two carriers. Neither the major lines nor the authorities in Japan appreciated outsiders, particularly where two potentially significant carriers were involved, and the new line came under substantial pressure to join the conference. And so, in June 1968, after nearly four months operating as an outsider, an agreement was signed with the FEFC allowing the new Maersk-Kawasaki Line to serve North European ports, excluding ports in the United Kingdom, among others. This agreement superseded the original 1957 Maersk agreement. On 20 June, Kawasaki's *France Maru* loaded in Kobe, Japan, initiating the joint monthly sailing, with each party providing two conventional break-bulk ships with pallet and container capacity.

These changes took place against the background of rapid developments in the organisation of bulk shipping and shipping lines elsewhere. In September 1965, Overseas Containers Ltd (OCL) had been formed from the amalgamation of Ocean Steamship of Liverpool, P&O, Furness Withy and British & Commonwealth steamship companies. In response, in January 1966, Associated Container Transportation (ACT) was created, consisting of Ellerman, Blue Star, Ben Line, Harrison Line and Port Line.[11] These consortia were set up 'to coordinate the investigation, planning and implementation of a substantial United Kingdom flag container shipping strategy, investment and service'.[12]

In the spring of 1966, Malcolm McLean's Sea-Land had started its Trans Atlantic container services to Rotterdam, Bremerhaven and Grangemouth in competition with other American lines. 'The voyage astonished the shipping world: cargo sent to Europe arrived at its destination fully four weeks faster than its equivalent had before.'[13] The Board of the Steamship Company Svendborg was informed in April 1969 that the Maersk-Kawasaki service was by now generating 'good results', but that discussions were taking place between the English, German and Japanese conference members to implement container services in the Europe–Far East–Europe trades from 1971. Two months later, the June Board meeting heard that OCL had now ordered four container ships and it was believed that Maersk Line and Kawasaki would soon have to take a similar decision. The October meeting was told that Scan-Service (a combination of the Danish and Swedish East Asiatic Companies and Wilhelmsen of Norway) had also ordered four container ships, for delivery in 1972.[14]

Maersk and Kawasaki Kisen Kaisha had started discussions about the potential containerisation of the Europe–Asia line in the summer of 1970 and agreed to establish Project ITINONE, a service from Japan via the United States to Europe and vice versa – with container ships. But the venture was not implemented. Meanwhile, other members of the FEFC, who had formed consortia to finance and operate container ships, moved more quickly and had ordered container ships for delivery during 1971 and 1972. Maersk Line and Kawasaki Kisen Kaisha negotiators recognised that if Maersk-Kawasaki Line 'had aspirations to stay competitive',[15] pure container ships had to be contracted.

This reality was made clear at a meeting of the FEFC in the winter of 1970, where it was determined that from 1972 at least 27 container ships would be deployed in the Europe–Asia services. After that meeting the Partners took the decision to build a container ship. During the spring of 1971, specifications were agreed and Maersk Line and Kawasaki Kisen Kaisha contracted one container ship each. In June 1971 a contract was signed with the Ishikawajima shipyard in Japan. The *Svendborg Mærsk*, of about 1,800 TEU, would eventually be delivered in January 1974. On delivery, she would be the first ship to be painted with the brand name 'MAERSK LINE' on her hull.

At the time that Maersk-Kawasaki placed the order for their two container ships they were in fierce competition with other operators. British, German and Japanese shipping companies had formed the TRIO alliance, which within two years would boast a total of 17 container ships. The

Figure 3.4 The Maersk Fleet's first cellular container ship *Svendborg Mærsk* was chartered out to OCL in 1974–1975 until it joined the A-ships on Maersk Line's Panama Line from September 1975.

ScanDutch, formerly Scan-Service, alliance brought six container ships into the market in the same period. In Western Europe alone, more than 30 ports were being transformed into efficient container-handling terminals. Containerisation was here to stay. In 1972, Maersk Line asked the Stanford Research Institute to compile a report on 'intermodal containerisation' and deliver its view of the liner shipping world. To put its report in context, the Stanford Research Institute outlined recent developments in the major deep-sea container trades. Table 3.1 omits the details of which vessels were deployed on the individual trades, their container capacity, whether they carried standard ISO containers, the number of sailings, consortia members, and so on; nevertheless, it gives a clear idea of the strength of the competition at this time.

Yet despite these imminent threats, the decision to order the ships was not followed by close cooperation on how to develop an integrated container service on the Europe–Asia line – on the contrary.

Throughout 1972, discussions continued between the partners as to how to operate the ships and how to market the capabilities that would become available with the new container ships. At Maersk Line, internal work groups were established to look into how to operate the containerised service, including the question of whether to continue the partnership with Kawasaki and, if so, how. And then, in the days between Christmas and New Year, a telegram was received in Copenhagen to say that Kawasaki

Table 3.1 Cellular container ships 1970*

In 1967, 68 cellular container ships were under construction at shipyards around the world. In 1968 the number was 47.

By November 1970, shipping companies had taken delivery of 167 fully cellular container ships.

* Lloyd's Register of Shipping Annual Reports, 1967, 1968; Lloyd's Register of Shipping Statistical Tables, 1970

Kisen Kaisha had decided that due to 'circumstances', they would cancel the existing agreement, with effect from 9 January 1973.

While the decision was received in Copenhagen with considerable dismay, Maersk Line was committed to the trade and decided to carry on alone. It would continue to serve the trade with its seven conventional break-bulk ships – known internally as the Seven Cs – where there was capacity to carry a limited number of containers on deck. The newly commissioned *Svendborg Mærsk* container ship, the new flagship of the Maersk fleet, was chartered out to another carrier. It would not return to Maersk until 1975, when the containerised service on the Panama Line began.[16] But we are running ahead of the story.

Maersk Line's conventional services

The full picture of the situation in Maersk Line at this time is incomplete without considering the other liner services. Containerisation was growing rapidly in the early 1970s, but had not reached all corners of the world – indeed, it continues to grow today. As part of a regular evaluation of the services, the Persian Gulf Line (Japan/Middle East) was reviewed in the summer of 1972. The process of the evaluation and the considerations clearly show the state of the liner shipping business. The main issue was the option for changes in the schedules in order to obtain more cargo. However, the potential deployment of pure container vessels was not included in the analysis because the ports on the service were not equipped to receive container ships as we know them today. Instead, they accommodated ships with their own cranes that would handle a variety of cargo types, such as general cargo in unit loads, goods in bulk (like grain) and (not least) standard containers.

Along with the evaluation of the Line Department, work was continuing in the Technical Organisation's new building department. Here, experienced naval architects and technicians worked to create solutions that would meet the commercially based requirements for new ships specified

Figure 3.5 *Mc-Kinney Mærsk* (1974) approaching Pier 11 in Brooklyn, New York, which was Maersk Line's main port in the United States between 1958 and 1975. The four M-ships acquired in 1974–1975 had a capacity of 628 TEU on deck and in the top cargo holds.

by the Line Department. The solution to the evaluations made during the Persian Gulf Line review was to recommend the construction of four semi-container ships for the liner trade in the Middle East. These four ships – *Marchen*, *Margrethe*, *Mathilde* and *Mc-Kinney*, all with the second name *Mærsk*, and known internally as the M-ships – were a new design, because each ship could accommodate 628 20-foot containers in the top cargo holds and on deck. Containers could be stacked three high on the hatch covers. However, the design had essentially the same functionality as the conventional break-bulk cargo and pallet ships that had entered the Maersk fleet in recent decades. The four ships were ordered in November and December 1972 at the Danish Nakskov shipyard and delivered in 1974–1975. The division of responsibilities in Maersk Line was emphasised when the M-ships were listed as liner vessels and not as container vessels in the A.P. Moller Annual Report in 1975.

The course of events in 1972–1975 clearly illustrates the division of responsibilities in the Maersk Line organisation. The 'old' Line Department, which had been made into a profit centre in its own right when the A.P. Moller Group was reorganised in 1970, operated the conventional services and was not directly involved in the preparations for containerisation.

Table 3.2 Trade routes and dates of inception of container services

Canadian East Coast and Europe	1965
United States East Coast and Europe	1967
United States and Canadian West Coast and Asia	1967
United States East Coast and the Mediterranean	1968
United States and Canadian West Coast and Europe	1968
United States and Canadian East Coast and Australia	1969
Europe and the Mediterranean and Australia	1969
Japan and Australia	1969
United States and Canadian East Coast and Asia	1970
Europe and Asia	1971

Containerisation of the Panama Line: a business case

The stalemate in the talks with Kawasaki Kisen Kaisha did not halt the progress of Maersk Line's container investigations; 1972 was a busy year. Work on the container challenge was carried out despite the fact that the organisation chart for the Line Department did not show a separate unit charged with the task of preparing a business case for containerisation of the Panama Line. In August, a Crash Committee was formed to undertake a six-month study preparatory to making a business case for containerisation of the Panama Line. The committee was formed in response to the competitive situation (most competitors had made moves to containerise their services) and the market situation: Maersk Line's main markets had matured and provided enough business to sustain a containerised service. Maersk management was persuaded by a number of reports (internal and external, formal and informal) on the market. The committee collected data in the main markets and sent them to Copenhagen for evaluation; ports used by Maersk Line's conventional break-bulk cargo ships and potential new ports were visited by committee members; and the results of the studies were included in the preparatory work leading to a container presentation in October 1972.

The final round of meetings on the container project was launched on 26 October 1972. The information gathered over the previous 2–3 years was updated by Niels Iversen, who was the main driver in Copenhagen, assisted by the country managers in the United States (Poul Rasmussen), Japan (Wagn Jacobsen), Thailand (Hans Georg Andersen) and Indonesia

(Per Jørgensen). Iversen also managed the preparation of the business case, writing a lot of it himself, and presented it to the management group. Mærsk Mc-Kinney Møller had requested a unanimous recommendation from the Crash Committee.

This was not forthcoming in October, nor when the business case was first presented on 18 December. The decisive moment came at an adjusted presentation on 31 January and 1 February 1973. The event was attended by Mærsk Mc-Kinney Møller and Georg Andersen, the two Partners representing the A.P. Moller Group; Christian Lund, the head of the Line Department; the four country managers (Rasmussen, Jacobsen, Andersen and Jørgensen); the Copenhagen-based working group led by Niels Iversen, assisted by Bengt Henriksen and Ove Jensen; and Dr Rodney Leach of McKinsey, who had helped the Crash Committee compile and organise the relevant data. The Crash Committee was assisted by colleagues from the Line Department and Technical Organisation's new building department, led by Ib Kruse, who would shortly be assigned a critical role in the project. The six-month study concluded that

"the US/Far East liner trade is dominated by continuing growth and the rapid adoption of containerisation, which will increase demand for an integrated, intermodal, door-to-door service. This is an entirely new concept in methods of transportation in which ocean shipping is only a part. Maersk Line has responded to these trends by adapting existing vessels to carry containers – a development that has

- been well received by our customers;
- improved our profitability.

However, these adaptations are largely a 'stop-gap', or interim, step."

On 1 February 1973 everyone round the table gave the nod to the Crash Committee's recommendation that

"Maersk Line should develop a large-scale, door-to-door full container service that will replace the present services operating between the United States/Canada and the Far East."

In May 1973, the Boards of the Steamship Company Svendborg and the Steamship Company of 1912 approved the implementation of the container project. In the following month it was announced that a total of nine container vessels had been contracted for delivery between February 1975 and June 1976, from two German shipyards. In fact, the A-vessels, as they became known, were somewhat delayed and *Adrian Mærsk* was the first to be delivered, on 22 August 1975. On 5 September the ship left Newark, New Jersey, on the Panama Line and Maersk Line began its first fully containerised service.

Meanwhile a new department called Maersk Container Line was established within the group. The name was used internally only; externally, the brand name remained Maersk Line. It was indeed a very new department. On the organisation chart dated 31 December 1973 names were attached to only a few positions. By the end of 1974 Maersk Container Line had expanded significantly and all the important posts were occupied. The Crash Committee had recommended that the overall management responsibility should be given to Ib Kruse, based on his proven abilities to get things going and solve problems.[17] Other functions in the new department were traffic & operations, finance & systems, marketing & sales and service planning. Ib Kruse came from a position as head of the Technical Organisation and had no significant liner experience; however, others in his new organisation had experience of the conventional break-bulk and pallet trades.

The end of one journey and the start of another

'Per Aspera Ad Astra' – the road to containerisation had certainly been long and bumpy. Mærsk Mc-Kinney Møller was right in 1969 when he told the Boards of the A.P. Moller shipping companies that Maersk Line was a little late. Even after that statement it had taken more than three years to decide to containerise the Panama service. It had not been easy, but in February 1973 Mærsk Mc-Kinney Møller had achieved what he had been aiming for over the last five years – a leadership group that was in unanimous agreement to move Maersk Line into containerisation, to take on the competition and to do so with unprecedented tools. And they were – the ships themselves were costly as no other ships had been in the history of A.P. Moller. But the capacity of the nine ships, which was 50 per cent larger than the seven C-class ships deployed on the United States–Asia–United States route until 1975, represented a real step up in the service, which also went from sailings every ten days to a weekly service. The decision to reach for the stars had been taken.

There had been many factors to consider, not the least of which was the allocation of funds for investment in the group. The take-off of the domestic airline Maersk Air was in 1969; Maersk Data, which evolved out of the A.P. Moller Group's internal Electronic Data Processing (EDP) Department to become an independent service provider, was established in 1970; oil and gas exploration continued in the Danish North Sea – the investigations about the possible containerisation of Maersk Line's Panama service was only one of many initiatives that Mærsk Mc-Kinney Møller introduced in a very short space of time. Maersk Line's plans were very significant to the A.P. Moller Group, but the competition for funding was fierce.

Flemming Jacobs, who was the personal assistant to Mærsk Mc-Kinney Møller at the time of the first meetings with McKinsey, summed up the situation:

Knowing Mr Møller a little bit, I think he would be very careful not to put a ton of money into a new activity like that. You know, you buy one tanker, and then you are in business. You buy one container ship, and you are not in business.[18]

The independent ship owner

With hindsight, it could be said that Maersk Line should have acted earlier on the recommendations from the Stanford Research Institute and McKinsey. If it had containerised its main trade earlier it would probably have won market share sooner. But Maersk Line waited, for two main reasons. It waited to contradict one of the predictions made by McKinsey in 1966, that ship owners who wanted to participate in containerisation would have to do so (primarily) through alliances. And it waited to see the business case that supported an independent entry into the container trade.

Mærsk Mc-Kinney Møller was actively transforming the company he had taken over from his father, but a vital part of the foundation of that company was independence. He supported partnerships where they were needed to advance A.P. Moller Group activities, but generally independence was preferred. Maersk Line had experienced some of the difficulties associated with partnerships when the talks with Kawasaki Kisen Kaisha did not produce the anticipated results. Although the two partners had agreed to build ships for joint operations, they were unable to agree on how those operations should be conducted. The experience did not encourage the A.P. Moller Group to look for new partners. On the contrary, management stressed that Maersk was focused on independent operations wherever possible.

By 1973 the containerisation question had become critical: it was a case of either being in or not participating at all. Had Maersk Line decided at that point that it would not replace the conventional break-bulk service with a fully containerised service, it would rapidly have been forced out of the liner business. Constant care – A. P. Møller's watchword – had been shown in the preparation leading to the decision to containerise the Panama Line. But the work put into calculating the risks and challenging the status quo was worth the wait: little time was needed to contemplate the recommendations and implement the strategy. Once it had decided to act, Maersk Line did so swiftly.

Preparations for container transport

When the Crash Committee put forward the recommendation for containerisation of the Panama Line in February 1973, the very last paragraph in the paper set the scene for the following years' work in Maersk Container Line:

The Committee cannot too strongly emphasise *that a door-to-door container service is a very different business for the traditional liner service*, and no time must be lost in developing the new skills we shall need if we are to be successful.[19]

Comprehensive preparations for operations on the Panama Line began in the summer of 1973, when the decision to contract the A-vessels was taken and continued after the delivery of the first vessel in August 1975.[20] The Line Department still had a business to run during the decision-making process for the new containerised service; a very important part of the group's shipping activities needed to get the results in and it was not feasible simply to move people from the ranks of the Line Department to the new Maersk Container Line organisation. Moreover, operating a container service was completely different from the conventional break-bulk and pallet services.

The Container Line Department was put together during 1974 and new offices established in the group's headquarters at Kongens Nytorv in Copenhagen. Flemming Jacobs vividly remembers the outpost at the back of the office complex: 'The office was above Arvidsen's butchers shop and the smell ...! The indoor temperature was almost indistinguishable from outside weather conditions.'[21] The team members felt like entrepreneurs and their physical surroundings only emphasised that feeling. While working on the transition from one type of service to another on the Panama Line, cooperation between Maersk Line and the new Container Line developed. Market conditions on the break-bulk and pallet services were closely monitored and Maersk Container Line representatives attended the Line Department's daily morning meetings. In its 1972 report to Maersk Line, the Stanford Research Institute had stated that a container liner company would have to consider 'extensive organisational and operational changes (e.g. larger and more sophisticated marketing staff, computer systems for equipment control and management information) which will impose considerable additional costs'.[22] Adding to the continuous stream of information from Maersk Line's offices abroad, Maersk Container Line began work on solving the many tasks related to marketing and sales, infrastructure and equipment, systems, training and traffic and operations.

Marketing and sales

'We had as a philosophy that we were not going to copy.'[23] Ib Kruse was clear that the new Maersk Container Line organisation was to copy neither the rules of operation used in the traditional break-bulk liner services, nor the manner in which other container lines operated. The new operational mode was based on the door-to-door concept, giving the customer the option to allow the operator to arrange the entire journey from supplier to recipient. The aim was to plan for Maersk Container Line to have control of the deliveries from A to Z.

The sales project members confirmed ports of call and designed a 'schedule for container ships'. It is clear from the wording of the project plan that many terms and concepts were novel and exciting – new ground was being broken. Two tasks from the marketing plan give an idea of the amount of work involved:

1. Describe the commercial requirements for a competitive door-to-door service and determine the type of service to be offered by Maersk Container Line.

Figure 3.6 Maersk Line had a good track record in obtaining orders for the transport of heavy-duty machinery on conventional cargo ships. To retain that business the container-sized artificial tween-deck was introduced and it became a significant differentiator for Maersk Line in the early years of containerised services.

2. Emphasise where Maersk Container Line should operate differently to achieve superior service.

The challenge was immense, but ambitions were high and new standards were to be established. At the start, the ports of call were not entirely clear. The conventional Panama service was being containerised, but many of the ports served by the conventional break-bulk Maersk Line service were not ready for container ships. Maersk Line had been successful in offering transport of special cargoes, such as large and heavy construction machinery, to those ports. The Maersk Container Line project plan specified the need for 'identifying ... opportunities for capturing specialised traffic, e.g. liquids, motor-cars, large items of machinery'. Alternative ports of call, including Jamaica, the Persian Gulf, India and Australia, were also on the list for investigation.

Then there was branding to consider. Since 1928, when Maersk Line started operations, nearly all A.P. Moller ships had had a first name that was Møller-family related and 'MÆRSK' as a second name. Until 1955, when the Maersk Blue that characterises today's ships was introduced, the ships were painted either black or grey. They carried the house flag, light blue with a white, seven-pointed star; the ship's funnel was decorated similarly. The new service needed its own logo and a version of a ship's funnel was chosen to represent the service. With only minor changes, the 1928 design remained until 1972, when the Danish designer and architect Acton Bjørn was commissioned to develop a new logo and a special font for Maersk lettering. When *Svendborg Mærsk*, the first container ship in the Maersk fleet, was taken over in 1974, 'MAERSK LINE' was painted on its hull sides.

Based on Acton Bjørn's new design, Maersk's Communication Department issued a manual that detailed the styles to be used to produce everything associated with the new Container Line, from how to paint containers and chassis, to route schedules and office stationery. Visual identity had always had the attention of management, but the communication manual was a further step to professionalise the organisation and a serious step up the branding ladder.

Infrastructure and equipment

Niels Iversen had visited a number of terminals in the spring and summer of 1973 to gather information for the planning of the container service. It was an interesting task, breaking new ground on both sides of the table; Maersk Line had just decided to enter containerisation and was in the midst of negotiating orders for the ships that Iversen was to introduce to the port

Figure 3.7 The original Maersk Line logo compared to 3.8 below.

Figure 3.8 The current Maersk logo and MAERSK letter fonts were developed for Maersk Line but were eventually introduced in most business units in the A.P. Moller – Maersk Group.

authorities in the presumed ports of call. Even today, with the communication tools available, such a situation would be delicate to navigate properly. In 1973, it was difficult. In typical A.P. Moller fashion it was decided to go quietly and not reveal details of the plans for containerisation of the Panama Line; in fact, the hope was to keep the project a secret for as long as possible. As a consequence, Iversen had to investigate without being able to answer many of the very relevant questions a port authority would be interested in asking.

The main factors in deciding which ports to choose were:

- location as a local consumer/transit and exporting area;
- location for import/export cargo to hinterland destinations (considering rates and service levels for rail and trucking);

Box 3.2 Container usage

Containers are packed in four ways:

1. CFS/CFS: packed at a carrier's container freight station (CFS) or warehouse at origin, it is stripped by the carrier at a similar facility at the destination. Shipments moved this way are generally small lots, where an exporter or importer does not expect other shipments from an origin with which the shipment in question could be combined. This is generally the most expensive way to move goods in containers as the goods are handled manually at both ends of the process and is also known as LCL/LCL.
2. CFS/CY: packed at a carrier's CFS at the origin, where the CFS operator receives multiple small lots, often from a range of suppliers, but where the goods are all destined for one consignee. The container can therefore be delivered from the carrier's container yard (CY) and unpacked at the importer's premises without any intermediate handling of the contents. This is also known as LCL/FCL.
3. CY/CFS: this type of usage is unusual but possible. It implies that the container is packed at an exporter's premises and then delivered to the carrier's CY at origin as a full unit; however, at destination the importer would take delivery of the goods from the carrier's freight station.This would be known as FCL/LCL.
4. CY/CY: this is normally the most economical mode of container use and implies that the exporter packs the container at origin and delivers it to the carrier's CY, while the importer takes delivery from the carrier's CY and strips the container at its own facility. This is also known as FCL/FCL.

Source: Maersk Line resource.

- terminal facilities;
- legal aspects, especially if agreements between ports about cargo allocation/throughput would hamper operations.[24]

The results of Iversen's observations were included in the work that preceded the contractual negotiations with the authorities in the ports Maersk Line had chosen for the new liner network. In close cooperation with Maersk Line's local offices, agreements were concluded with inland depots, local trucking companies that would transport containers between terminals and customers, and railway operators that would transport containers cross-country. Containers and chassis were purchased from the United States, Japan, Hong Kong, Thailand and Taiwan.

The nine A-vessels were scheduled for the service from the US East Coast via the Panama Canal to Asia, and were to call at New York, Philadelphia, Baltimore and Charleston before passing through the canal to call at Long

Beach and Oakland on the US West Coast. In Asia the ports, in order of call, were: Hong Kong, Singapore and then back to Hong Kong before calling at Keelung, Nagoya, Kobe and Tokyo in Japan on the return voyage to Long Beach and via the Panama Canal to New York.

In order to deliver the best possible service to existing customers, and to achieve the best possible use of capacity in these large vessels, a series of feeder vessels were chartered and deployed to call at smaller ports. The 45 acres at Pier 51 in Port Newark near New York became the first container terminal for the exclusive use of Maersk Line.

Systems

When the decision was made to initiate the first full container service, it was clear that it would need the support of advanced information and communications technology. One of the first steps the new Maersk Container Line team took was to approach Maersk Data in Copenhagen and Moller Steamship Co. in New York with a question: how will we track these containers once they leave a port, so that we know where they are?

The remit was to have a draft recommendation agreed by all the parties involved by mid 1973 and subsequently developed by Maersk Data to be ready for operation by 1 January 1975. Birger Riisager, head of Finance and Systems, and Vagn Lehd Møller visited Japan to investigate what was needed there and to understand, in terms of documentation, how the manifest information could be transferred from Japan to the US West Coast prior to the vessels' arrival, minimising the risk of delays with US Customs on the short eight-day transit of the Pacific Ocean. A complicating factor for the documentation system was that a number of international organisations were in the process of reviewing the standard documents used in international trade in efforts to bring them to the required levels of standardisation and risk management that container transport was beginning to require.

The container control system was a top priority, and following further discussion with the offices involved, including visits to existing container terminals and some competitors, an initial paper was ready by April 1973, only two short months after the management approval of the plan to containerise the Panama Line. Maersk Data would develop the software, but an even more significant (and more expensive) step was the decision to establish Maersk's own proprietary satellite communications network, with dedicated leased lines and software development assistance from Cable and Wireless in London. This network evolved rapidly to become the central nervous system of the growing global organisation.

The US National Committee of International Trade Documentation (NCITD), the International Chamber of Shipping, the Banking Committee of the International Chambers of Commerce and the UK's Simpler Trade Procedures Board (SITPRO) were all working under the UNCTAD umbrella (see Box 4.3) to enhance and simplify transport documentation and to iron out the legal issues related to documents such as the combined transport bill of lading; way bills; received for shipment bills as well as others, such as shipped bills of lading and shipper-provided bills of lading.

While many, primarily US-based, exporters, such as DuPont, Union Carbide, General Motors, Ford and Standard Brands were very much involved, the shipping community was represented by Dart Lines, Prudential-Grace Lines, Sea-Land and Maersk Line. While these discussions continued, Maersk Container Line created its own combined transport bill of lading that attempted to take the best market-centric approach for the launch of the new service in 1975 and beyond.

One consequence of the new containerised service was therefore the decision to invest in technology. But technology in 1975 was very different from the technology we are familiar with today. To illustrate, in April that year Olivetti presented the world's first personal computer: it weighed 40 kilograms, had 48 kilobytes of random access memory (RAM) and a 32 alphanumeric character plasma display. It was only in 1981 that IBM was able to bring the personal computer into the mainstream when they introduced a model that sold for under $1,600.

Box 3.3 Transport documents

The bill of lading is a document issued by a carrier to a shipper, signed by the captain, owner or agent of a ship. The bill provides written evidence confirming the receipt of the goods, the conditions on which transport is arranged (known as the contract of carriage) and the commitment to deliver the goods to the lawful holder of the bill at the destination. It is therefore both a receipt for goods and a contract to deliver the goods at a destination for a fee (the freight).

There are a variety of different types of bill of lading, including air way bills. For containerised transport, the most commonly used bills are combined transport (or multi-modal) bills of lading. These bills cover two or more modes of transport, such as ship, canal, rail and/or road, and are most frequently used when the shipment has to be moved from point-to-point rather than purely port-to-port.

The other documents mentioned in the text are variants on these two documents.

Source: Internal Maersk Line material and E. G. Hinkelman and S. Putzi, *Dictionary of International Trade*, World Trade Press, 2002, p. 423.

Marna Nygaard, a senior communications specialist who had joined Maersk Line in 1970, recalled the office in which she worked in 1979: 'We were eight ladies sitting in a two-windowed room, each with a huge, very noisy electronic typewriter, the modern kind with magnetic cards where you could save your document – you could retype and correct as much as you needed.'[25] These noisy FACIT 1620 typewriters were supplemented by a manual process for collecting and distributing messages for each department. Printed on yellow (inbound) and blue (outbound) paper, these were transmitted between the head office and the ships and offices globally, initially using the Maersk Telex System (MTS), which in due course was superseded by the Maersk Communications System (MCS).

Unlikely as it may seem, these developments created the technical and communications platform that was to be a hidden differentiator for Maersk Line right until the rise of the internet. Jørgen Harling, now Managing Director of Maersk Japan, identified Maersk's communications system as the thing that stood out most during this period: 'Our ability to communicate globally... was unheard of in those days.'[26] Although this system was not without its challenges, it inspired a significant part of the development of Maersk Data, while encouraging Maersk Line to keep abreast of what else was going on in the technology market place, for competitive reasons. Mærsk Mc-Kinney Møller (a personal friend of Thomas Watson Junior) was the first non-American to be invited to join the IBM Board of Directors in 1970, and his active involvement with IBM provided a natural entry point into that organisation. Warren Hume, a retired senior IBM executive, was frequently used as a sounding board when Maersk Container Line and Maersk Data considered service standards, new developments and cost initiatives. It also meant that when an internal Maersk company called Mercantile expanded substantially in the early 1990s, the business had an internal supplier in Maersk Data that could respond positively and with proven capability to get development off the ground.

Training

Because container transport differed fundamentally from conventional liner trade, and the vessels were bigger and carried more cargo, sales efforts had to change and be strengthened. The sales teams, operations people and administrative staff participated in training courses, arranged both locally and at the headquarters in Copenhagen.

Traffic and operations

Although the liner trade is characterised by scheduled departures and arrivals, the reality is less rigid than such timetables suggest. If a customer was delayed in delivering containers, the ship's departure could be postponed; this naturally had consequences for the ship's arrival in the next ports of call. Everything was to be different from September 1975: the fixed voyage plans were to be kept and that meant arrival and departure on time, to the hour. This played a dominant role in the marketing of the new service from Maersk Line and was a new situation for staff as well as customers: in some instances, ships would depart without the cargo ordered for the voyage. Ib Kruse remembers:

We had negotiated terminal contracts to guarantee that our vessels would be handled immediately when they arrived at the agreed time of day. So, the instruction to the vessels was to adjust speed to arrive at the scheduled date and time.[27]

As it turned out, the punctuality of the Maersk ships would be one of the most significant differentiators for Maersk Line's sales staff. It represented reliability for the customer. Flemming Jacobs remembers checking his wristwatch while lunching with customers in San Francisco, and telling them, 'Oh, in five minutes, Maersk will be arriving' – and five minutes later drawing their attention to a Maersk ship entering the harbour, bang on time. Radio spots were produced to promote Maersk Line's special on-time feature, and the saying 'You can set your watch by Maersk' became common parlance not only in San Francisco, but also in the other ports served by the new Maersk Line container ships around the world.

The first voyage

In early September 1975 Maersk Line invited dignitaries and business partners to Pier 51 in Port Elizabeth, close to Newark International Airport in New Jersey, where Mærsk Mc-Kinney Møller hosted the reception to inaugurate Pier 51 as Maersk Line's exclusive terminal facility in the New York area. The Manhattan skyline was visible from the quay.

In his speech Mærsk Mc-Kinney Møller talked about his father's initiative to start the Maersk Line service in 1928 and how 'new and improved vessels were constantly added' over time: 'With this dynamic society goes a constant demand for improvement and change, and so here we are to inaugurate yet another pier – geared primarily to containers – that relatively new American mode of transport.'[28] But he also made it clear that it had not been easy to make the decision to containerise the Panama Line and hinted that Maersk Line had not chosen the timing themselves: 'You

Figure 3.9 The Maersk gantry crane was not ready for operation when *Adrian Mærsk* arrived at Pier 51 in Port Elizabeth, New Jersey, on 3 September 1975. But the brand new and shining containers were all clear for shipment on Maersk Line's new flagship, by using neighbouring cranes.

may feel that we are courageous and indeed we are. But it was a question of one big step or none at all.'

Ib Kruse felt the same: 'I would say that the decision took itself . . . There was no other way than going into the container business.'[29]

It had never previously been thought necessary to detail the voyage of one of its ships, but in the November 1975 issue of the internal A.P. Moller Group magazine, *Mærsk Post*, a four-page article was dedicated to the first voyage of the *Adrian Mærsk* and containerisation of the Panama Line was celebrated throughout the organisation. The ship was taken over from a shipyard in Hamburg, Germany, on 22 August 1975 and made its maiden voyage across the Atlantic towards New York. As the new ship passed under the Verrazano Narrows Bridge en route to Pier 51 on 3 September, the entire management group of the Moller Steamship Company was waiting to greet it.

In the newly built terminal area nearly 1,000 silver 40-foot containers were waiting to be distributed to the ports of call on Maersk Line's new service. Every container was clearly marked with the white seven-pointed Maersk star and MAERSK LINE, written in the new Maersk font. Not all were empty; the sales organisation had been successful in obtaining some cargo from customers. On 5 September the *Adrian Mærsk* left Pier 51 carrying 385 containers, mostly 40-foot units – on time. It was a historic day for Maersk Line; the Panama Line was containerised and the company was now truly part of the new world of transport. Another 50 containers were loaded in Philadelphia and yet more in Baltimore, before calling at Charleston, the last port on the US East Coast. After passing through the Panama Canal, the *Adrian Mærsk* reached its next destination, the Pacific Container Terminal at Long Beach, California. A welcome party had been arranged and about 400 shippers and other business contacts visited the new ship. At Oakland a large contingent of customers visited Maersk Line's new flagship before it left for Asian ports on 23 September.

Two years later, Mærsk Mc-Kinney Møller took stock of the situation, writing in the *Mærsk Post*:

Two years have now passed since the *Adrian Mærsk* was delivered, and entered the service between the USA and the Far East as the first fully containerised vessel.

This ship has since been joined by eight sister ships.

Today we are happy to say that all nine ships are serving well and steadily on this line, which is operating according to plan.

The many correlated initiatives, brought about by the decision in favour of this great investment, have also been carried through:

- Thus, nine new Maersk Line offices have been opened in the USA, and in the East another seven offices have been added to the A.P. Moller organisations.
- A number of container terminals have been established – partly for the exclusive use of Maersk Line, partly in co-operation with others.
- A comprehensive building programme regarding containers and other equipment has been carried through, feeder services have been established for ports not directly called at by the big containerships, new EDP [IT] systems have been developed, etc.
- And considerable efforts have been made to secure the necessary cargo flow.

Taken as a whole, a great installation phase has been successfully terminated. This is gratifying, and many staff members at home, in the offices abroad, and on board the ships of the MAERSK fleet deserve to be complimented for this.

Our task will now be to pursue what has begun so well, to ensure that the great investment really meets with success.

Maersk Line's entry into containerisation was based on a conservative, careful business plan that would turn out to be downright pessimistic. But in 1973, neither the Maersk Line management, nor the rest of the shipping industry – including the few people who had seen the potential consequences of the standard container back in the 1960s – could envisage the dramatic annual growth rates (around 20 per cent) that would become the reality in container shipping during the next decade.[30]

A selection of important developments: 1965–1969

Political

- Late 1960s Decolonisation continues. Former European colonies in Africa, the Caribbean, and the Pacific gain independence, including: Gambia, Rhodesia (1965); Barbados, Botswana, Lesotho (1966); Nauru, Equatorial Guinea, Mauritius and Swaziland (1968).[31]
- 1966 Mao Zedong launches the Cultural Revolution in China to reassert control over the Communist Party, following criticism of his rapid-industrialisation policy.[32]
- 1967 The Bangkok Declaration establishes the Association of Southeast Asian Nations (ASEAN).[33] ASEAN was founded as a force against the spread of communism through Asia.[34]
- 1967 Singapore, previously expelled from the Malaysian Federation owing to ideological differences, uses ASEAN as a vehicle to develop its vision of becoming the Asian hub for multinational corporations.[35]
- 1967 Arab-Israeli conflicts in the Middle East culminate in the six day war, resulting in Israel taking control of the Sinai Peninsula, Golan Heights, Gaza Strip and West Bank.[36]
- 1968 The Soviet invasion of Czechoslovakia following the Prague Spring heightens cold war tensions.[37]
- 1968 The US and the Soviet Union propose a nuclear non-proliferation treaty limiting nuclear weapons to the five existing nuclear powers. The treaty will come into force in 1970.[38]

Economic

- Late 1960s A backlash against multinational corporations in Latin America and foreign control of national resources sees foreign direct investment (FDI) contract in the region, as well as in newly independent nations in other parts of the world.[39]
- 1965 Asia's economic rise begins. Hong Kong, Singapore, Taiwan, Korea, China, Malaysia, Thailand and Indonesia will grow at an average of over 5.5% per year in real GDP per capita terms between 1965 and 1990.[40]
- 1967 The Kennedy Round, the sixth round of trade negotiations since the establishment of the General Agreement on Tariffs and Trade (GATT) in 1946, ends with tariff concessions worth US$40bn.[41]
- 1967–69 OPEC strengthens its cartel with the admission of the United Arab Emirates and Algeria.[42]
- 1968 The slogan, "Trade not Aid", gains international recognition when it is adopted by UNCTAD to emphasise the establishment of fair trade relations with the developing world.[43]
- 1968 Japan overtakes West Germany to become the world's second-largest market economy after the US.[44]
- 1969 Bolivia, Chile, Colombia, Ecuador and Peru form the Andean Pact (from 1996 known as the Andean Community of Nations, CAN) to encourage greater regional development and self-sufficiency.[45]

Social

- 1965 Ralph Nader's *Unsafe at Any Speed* is published. Highly critical of the American automotive industry, it helps to launch the consumer rights movement.[46]
- 1967 The Radarange – the first affordable counter-top microwave model – is introduced.[47]
- 1968 Student protests ignite across the globe, surrounding issues such as education reform, war, imperialism, civil rights and gender equality. Music, literature and lifestyles reflect a protest-driven Western counterculture.[48]
- 1969 The Stonewall Riots in New York prompt a US campaign for gay rights.[49]

Technological

- Late 1960s Third Generation Computing using integrated circuits is developed, resulting in greater reliability and reduced size. The concepts of the operating system, multi-programming and parallel processing are also introduced, and used in weather forecasting, airline reservations and banking services.[50]
- 1965 Arno Penzias and Robert Wilson's discovery of *cosmic background radiation* confirms the Big Bang theory.[51]
- 1965 Moore's Law – postulating that the number of transistors on a single integrated circuit would double every two years – is formulated.[52] In 2011, the Law will still hold true.[53]
- 1966 Computer-scanned binary signal codes (*bar codes*) are used commercially for the first time.[54]
- 1967 Dr Christiaan N. Barnard and a team of South African surgeons perform the first human-heart transplant.[55]
- 1969 The Advanced Research Projects Agency (ARPA) goes online, connecting four major US universities. Designed for research, education and government organisations, it will become a founding platform for the Internet.[56]

Legal

- 1965 The SOLAS Convention (Safety of Life at Sea) comes into force. It will modernise regulations in line with technical developments in the shipping industry.[57]
- 1966 The UN General Assembly adopts the International Covenant on Civil and Political Rights and the International Covenant on Economic, Social and Cultural Rights.[58]
- 1967 The UN World Intellectual Property Organization (WIPO) is established.[59]

Environmental

- 1967 The Don't Make A Wave Committee, a Quaker peace group, is founded. It will become Greenpeace in 1971.[60]
- 1968 Scientists at Antarctica's Byrd Research Station drill the first ice core through 7,000 feet of ice in order to study historical temperature and atmospheric changes.[61]
- 1968 The UN Biosphere Conference recommends setting up an international research programme on man and the biosphere.[62]

A selection of important developments: 1970–1974

Political

- Early 1970s Decolonisation continues. Fiji and Tonga become independent in 1970, the United Arab Emirates in 1971, the Bahamas in 1973, Guinea-Bissau and Grenada in 1974.[63]
- 1970 Biafran forces surrender after a 32-month fight for independence from Nigeria. Unsuccessful attempts to deal with the famine arising from the conflict will lead to the creation of Médecins Sans Frontières a year later.[64]
- 1971 The People's Republic of China joins the United Nations,[65] taking over Taiwan's seat in the General Assembly and the Security Council.[66]
- 1971 Indo-Pakistani tensions over East Pakistan increase, leading to the Bangladesh liberation war. A ceasefire leads to Bangladeshi independence.[67]
- 1972 US president, Richard Nixon, visits mainland China and meets with Chinese Communist Party (CCP) chairman, Mao Zedong. This follows an easing of relations between the US and China, known as "ping pong diplomacy", involving a series of exchange visits by table tennis players between the two countries.[68]
- 1973 The last US troops leave Vietnam as a peace deal is signed.[69]

Economic

- Early 1970s Following a coup which brought Augusto Pinochet to power, free market economic policies begin to be pursued, supported by the "Chicago Boys", a group of Chilean economists trained at the University of Chicago.[70]
- 1971 The US severs the US dollar's convertibility to gold, effectively ending the Bretton Woods monetary system and eventually leading to a system of floating exchange rates.[71]
- 1971 The National Association of Securities Dealers Automated Quotations (NASDAQ) stock exchange begins trading. The NASDAQ is the world's first electronic stock market and will become one of the largest stock markets in the world.[72]
- 1973 The UK, Ireland and Denmark join the European Economic Community (EEC) in its first enlargement.[73]
- 1973 The Tokyo Trade Round of the General Agreement on Trades and Tariffs (GATT) begins, with 102 countries participating. Continued efforts by the GATT progressively to reduce tariffs will lead to substantial cuts in customs duties. However, the round will not resolve fundamental issues affecting agricultural trade.[74]
- 1973 Following the Arab-Israeli war, OPEC countries impose an embargo on supplies to the US and the oil price increases. This will lead to a recession in 1975, the first of a number of economic downturns caused in part by oil price increases.[75]
- 1973 Closed regional trading blocs modelled on the EEC are established in Africa (the Economic Community of West Africa) and the Caribbean (CARICOM).[76]
- 1974 Shipbuilding collapses owing to excess capacity, arising from overproduction in the 1960s and early 1970s. The industry will not recover for many years.[77]

Social

- 1971 Southwest Airlines launches in Dallas. It will become the first significant low-fare, high frequency, point-to-point carrier.[78]
- 1972 The Bangladesh Rural Advancement Committee (BRAC) is founded to assist refugees after the country's secession from Pakistan. BRAC will become the world's largest non-governmental organisation (NGO) with 110,000 staff.[79]
- 1972–74 Two disastrous world harvests bring about a global food shortage.[80]
- 1972 World Bank president, Robert McNamara, states that developing countries should redesign their policies to meet the needs of the poorest 40% of their populations.[81]

Technological

- 1970 IBM introduces the floppy disk.[82]
- 1971 The first single-chip microprocessor (Intel 4004) is introduced.[83]
- 1971 Ray Tomlinson invents software to send emails with the application of the "@" key.[84] In 2011 the number of email accounts worldwide will reach 3.1bn.[85]
- 1971 An American probe, Mariner 9, orbits Mars, becoming the first spacecraft to orbit another planet.[86]
- 1972 Hewlett-Packard produces the world's first scientific pocket calculator (the HP-35).[87]
- 1973 Godfrey Hounsfield uses *computed tomography* (CT) scanning to create cross-sectional X-ray images of body tissues.[88]
- 1973 The recyclable polyethylene terephthalate (PET) bottle is created.[89]
- 1975 Sony introduces the Betamax-format video recorder, capable of recording an hour of video footage.[90]

Legal

- 1973 The Conference on Security and Co-operation in Europe (CSCE) opens. This will lead to the signing of the Helsinki Accords in 1975 by 35 European states, defining ten security principles for relations between signatories.[91]
- 1974 In response to concerns regarding infringement upon individuals' privacy rights by computerised databases, the US government passes the Privacy Act.[92]

Environmental

- 1972 The United Nations Environment Programme (UNEP) is founded.[93]
- 1973 The European Economic Community issues its first action plan for applying protective measures to the environment.[94]
- 1974 Researchers report evidence that freon and other chlorofluorocarbons (CFCs) destroy stratospheric ozone.[95]

Merchandise trade by country

Global population: 3.7bn

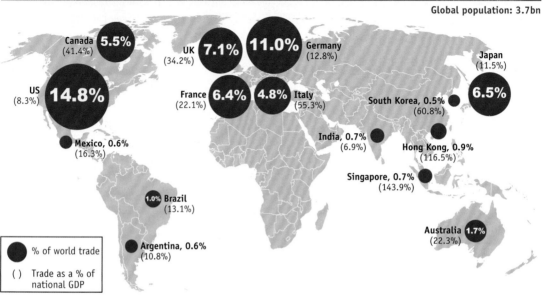

Canada (41.4%) **5.5%**

UK (34.2%) **7.1%**

11.0% Germany (12.8%)

Japan (11.5%)

US (8.3%) **14.8%**

France (22.1%) **6.4%**

4.8% Italy (55.3%)

South Korea, 0.5% (60.8%)

6.5%

Mexico, 0.6% (16.3%)

India, 0.7% (6.9%)

Hong Kong, 0.9% (116.5%)

Singapore, 0.7% (143.9%)

1.0% Brazil (13.1%)

Australia **1.7%** (22.3%)

Argentina, 0.6% (10.8%)

- % of world trade
- ( ) Trade as a % of national GDP

Note. The map is based on January 2013 boundaries. Trade is based on merchandise exports and imports.
Sources: The Economist Intelligence Unit (EIU) calculations using trade data from IMF, *Direction of Trade Statistics* and GDP data from EIU; IMF, *International Financial Statistics*; and World Bank, *World Development Indicators* (via Haver Analytics). Population data from UN (via Haver Analytics).

World merchandise exports

US$ trn (at 2005 prices)

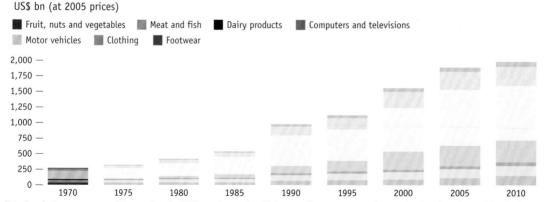

0.4	0.6	0.8	1.2	1.8								
1950	1955	1960	1965	1970	1975	1980	1985	1990	1995	2000	2005	2010

Note. World exports have been rebased to 2005 constant prices using world export volumes from the World Trade Organization (WTO).
Source: EIU calculations using WTO data.

World exports of selected commodities

US$ bn (at 2005 prices)

- ■ Fruit, nuts and vegetables
- ▨ Meat and fish
- ■ Dairy products
- ▨ Computers and televisions
- ▨ Motor vehicles
- ▨ Clothing
- ■ Footwear

2,000 —
1,750 —
1,500 —
1,250 —
1,000 —
750 —
500 —
250 —
0 —

| 1970 | 1975 | 1980 | 1985 | 1990 | 1995 | 2000 | 2005 | 2010 |

Note. In order to compare commodities over time, the EIU has made a number of judgment calls on category groupings, as there have been three revisions in the way that UN commodity data are classified. The data have also been rebased to 2005 constant prices using world export prices from the WTO. The motor vehicles category refers to road motor vehicles, including cycles, trailers, and parts and accessories; clothing includes headgear, excludes travel goods and handbags.
Source: EIU estimates using UN Comtrade, *DESA/UNSD* and WTO data.

Merchandise trade by country

Global population: 4.1bn

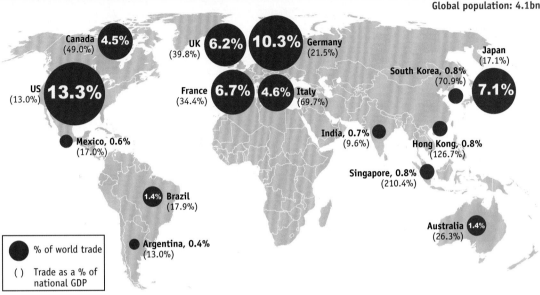

Canada 4.5% (49.0%)

UK 6.2% (39.8%)

Germany 10.3% (21.5%)

Japan 7.1% (17.1%)

South Korea, 0.8% (70.9%)

US 13.3% (13.0%)

France 6.7% (34.4%)

Italy 4.6% (69.7%)

India, 0.7% (9.6%)

Hong Kong, 0.8% (126.7%)

Mexico, 0.6% (17.0%)

Singapore, 0.8% (210.4%)

Brazil 1.4% (17.9%)

Australia 1.4% (26.3%)

Argentina, 0.4% (13.0%)

% of world trade

( ) Trade as a % of national GDP

Note. The map is based on January 2013 boundaries. Trade is based on merchandise exports and imports.
Sources: The Economist Intelligence Unit (EIU) calculations using trade data from IMF, *Direction of Trade Statistics* and GDP data from EIU; IMF, *International Financial Statistics*; and World Bank, *World Development Indicators* (via Haver Analytics). Population data from UN (via Haver Analytics).

World merchandise exports

US$ trn (at 2005 prices)

0.4	0.6	0.8	1.2	1.8	2.3						
1950	1955	1960	1965	1970	1975	1980	1985	1990	1995	2000	2005	2010

Note. World exports have been rebased to 2005 constant prices using world export volumes from the World Trade Organization (WTO).
Source: EIU calculations using WTO data.

World exports of selected commodities

US$ bn (at 2005 prices)

■ Fruit, nuts and vegetables   ■ Meat and fish   ■ Dairy products   ■ Computers and televisions
■ Motor vehicles   ■ Clothing   ■ Footwear

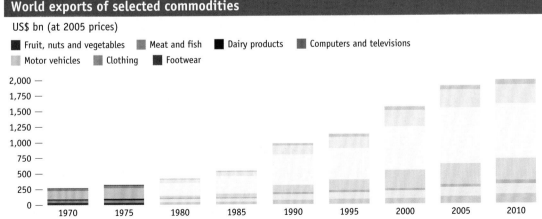

Note. In order to compare commodities over time, the EIU has made a number of judgment calls on category groupings, as there have been three revisions in the way that UN commodity data are classified. The data have also been rebased to 2005 constant prices using world export prices from the WTO. The motor vehicles category refers to road motor vehicles, including cycles, trailers, and parts and accessories; clothing includes headgear, excludes travel goods and handbags.
Source: EIU estimates using UN Comtrade, *DESA/UNSD* and WTO data.

Building the Base (1978–1984)

4

'Do you know what freight is?' McLean would ask a visitor. 'You can look it up in the dictionary, but I'll tell you. It's something added to the cost of the product.'

All his life he worked to make that 'something added' as low as possible.

O. E. Allen, *The Box, An Anthology Celebrating 50 Years of Containerisation*[1]

The world container ship capacity in 1970, according to *Containerisation International*, was 195,362 TEU (20-foot-equivalent container units). By 1985, this number had passed two million. When Maersk Line entered containerisation in 1975, it had two ships built specifically for transporting containers – the *Adrian Mærsk*, the first A-class ship, and the *Svendborg Mærsk*. Six years later, it had 25 cellular container ships in its network and was operating just under 5 per cent of the world's container fleet.[2] Only Sea-Land and Hapag Lloyd were larger. How these developments took place is the next part of this story.

The agents' meeting, 1976

Very early in 1976 Maersk Line's management was greatly concerned about the results of the new container service. To that end, a meeting was called in Copenhagen attended by representatives of agents from the United States, Indonesia, Thailand, Singapore, Hong Kong, Taiwan and Japan. They met to discuss ways and means to turn the results around. In preparation for the meeting, Birger Riisager, responsible for Finance and Systems, sent the offices details of the original 1969 Stanford Research Institute study. The forecasts for 1976 received from the agents departed widely from the Crash Committee projections for 1976 and 1977, and the discrepancies needed to be addressed. The outbound numbers from the United States to the Far East were a particular concern. Volumes were about 10 per cent below the original projections, while freight rates were 'substantially lower'. It was clear that 'the very slow outward market had made all carriers look for lower-paying commodities'.[3]

Two proposals were put forward. The first was to operate only seven vessels and provide a nine-day service; the second to serve only Asia to the US West Coast, using mini-bridge services to the East Coast – that is, moving goods by rail from the West Coast to the New York area. Looking for extra volume and revenue, Flemming Jacobs, responsible for Maersk Container Line's sales and marketing, initiated analyses of other possible markets, including calling at Boston, Jamaica and/or Mexico.

The homebound market was doing well, but in what was a typical Maersk approach to the business, agents were asked to consider what they could do to be even better. Bearing in mind that the service had been operating for only a few months at that stage, some of the suggestions were quite innovative. They included reducing the percentage of container-freight station (CFS) cargoes carried. The high cost of handling these goods and the added time needed were not felt to be fully compensated by the rates obtained. Other efforts included reducing the number of 20-foot containers, as handling costs for these were nearly the same as for the larger units, while the revenue obtained per move was significantly lower.

Erik Holtegaard, head of Maersk Container Line's Conference and Pricing team, put forward questions related to intermodalism as well as on membership of conferences and the relevant talking agreements. Niels Iversen, head of Traffic and Operations, had numerous suggestions about what could be done to cut costs, and a further letter from Riisager on 12 January added another item to the agenda: 'Review of operation of various management systems including the container control system, documentation, repair and maintenance, sales management, allocations and performance control systems'.[4]

No one realised it then, but this meeting took place at a time that probably marked a turning point in the flow of goods. According to Flemming Jacobs, up to this point the head-haul – the major trade and therefore the trade on which a ship owner would expect to make most revenue and margin – had been from the United States to the Far East:

This was when it shifted and if we've ever done anything right in life, it was establishing our own organisations around the world because that enabled us to capture what was happening and we could react to it very quickly.[5]

Machinery, chemicals and other goods, including raw materials, had been moving in volume to the Far East as Korea, Japan, Taiwan, Hong Kong and Singapore built up their own industrial capabilities. While these products continued to flow, the flow of goods from Asia into the United States began to take off significantly as retail buyers, in particular, identified opportunities to obtain good-quality but relatively low-cost items such as footwear, textiles, clothing, toys and sports goods. These movements supplemented the growing volumes of Japanese cars that were beginning to penetrate the American market.

Chaired by Ib Kruse, the meeting was held over three days at the end of January 1976 with the objective to take pro-active steps to address management's concerns. The discussions resulted in a range of decisions that were implemented over the coming year, of which the principle was not to tamper with the service or schedules that had by now become established and accepted in the trade. Essentially, it was agreed to keep going, focusing on cutting costs and maximising revenues. When the meeting was over, everyone, whether from Asia, the United States or Denmark, went away with an action plan.

Containerisation was still a new discipline and a less pressing but nevertheless important issue arising from the meeting was the desire among offices for clearer guidelines on acceptance of goods. New manuals on the Accommodation of Dangerous Cargo in Containers and the Accommodation of Special Commodities were quickly developed and implemented. The latter was the result of a study that was already under way under the aegis of the *Beratungs und Forschungsstelle for Seemässige Verpackung* (Centre for Research and Consulting in Seaworthy Packaging) in Hamburg, Germany. It furnished descriptions, photographs and the pros and cons of stowing containers for some three dozen commodities, including cassia, seedlac, cow hides, coffee, spices, rubber, tobacco, vegetable fats, cocoa butter, ground nuts, citronella oil, tapioca, cloves and dried jelly fish. These commodities are a good indicator of the level of industrial sophistication in some of Maersk Line's key markets, many of which had not yet experienced the container revolution that had started elsewhere in the late 1960s, but now found themselves in the middle of it.

To put these developments into a broader context, world merchandise exports doubled between 1975 and 1980, when they reached $3,753 billion. Japan, Korea, Hong Kong and Singapore significantly increased their share of world trade. And by 1980, China was also starting to appear in trade data for the first time, representing 1 per cent of global trade, following the normalisation of relations with the United States in 1978, as did Taiwan, at 1.1 per cent of world trade. Although there was some further growth in world trade in 1981, the early 1980s were poor growth years, particularly across Western Europe, and it was only in 1985 that world trade once again surpassed the 1980s overall value.[6]

Mercantile Consolidators: into logistics

Most of the new, rapidly developing export commodities moving particularly from Korea, Hong Kong, Taiwan and Singapore, were being sold on free on board (FOB) terms (see Box 5.12).

Under FOB terms, while the exporter could influence the carrier to be used, the final control lay with the importer. By now, the major importers in the United States were beginning to understand how to make the best use of containers as they started to buy more goods from suppliers in Asia. However, orders placed with such suppliers were driven by anticipated customer demand at destination, and while these often generated enough volume to be shipped as full container loads from origin right through to destination (FCL/FCL), some orders could fill neither a 40-foot nor a 20-foot container efficiently. Existing shipping legislation in the United States prevented carriers from helping their customers with the shortfall in these loads.

Sea-Land had addressed this business opportunity by creating Buyers Consolidators Inc., and a small number of other carriers did likewise. Lines, when asked for such extra services by an importer, would bring in their associated consolidator, so that the requirements and modus operandi could be discussed, defined and agreed, and the customer relationship maintained.

And so, in 1977 a new Maersk venture was formalised. Mercantile Consolidators Ltd was established in Taiwan, Hong Kong and Singapore, with a small corresponding office in New York. Activities had been conducted under that brand name since 1975, but had now developed to the point where a formal and independent company structure was needed. As the name implies, consolidation was the new company's key activity. The services provided by Mercantile were primarily to complement the carrier's role, to work with the various exporters and assemble their small lots and overflows from larger shipments, frequently from a variety of different suppliers.

As all were destined to the same consignee, these loads moved as LCL/FCL, less than container loads, packed for full load delivery at destination, against a handling fee usually levied per cubic metre of cargo.

The main market at this stage was major US importers, such as S. S. Kresge, Sears Roebuck and Montgomery Ward, and their requirements were basic. But as they became more sophisticated, rapid communication (by cable and telex) developed between the parties to determine the best shipping process.

Figure 4.1 The distinctive Mercantile logo. The business unit was renamed Maersk Logistics in 2000 and introduced its current identity, Damco, in 2007.

The consolidator would book the shipments with the carrier, pack the container and provide the carrier with all the shipment details. The job also entailed issuing a consolidator's receipt to the exporter, allowing for payment by the appropriate bank against the importer's letter of credit. Finally, the service included collecting the relevant bills of lading from the carrier and providing all the paperwork to the importer by mail and later by courier, so that US customs clearances and distribution planning could take place at the destination.

Mercantile continued to develop slowly, and by 1990 employed approximately 85 people worldwide. Meanwhile, it took retailers, manufacturers and their suppliers some time to grasp the significance of 'supply chain management', a concept first iterated by Keith Oliver, a consultant at Booz Allen and Hamilton, in an interview with the UK *Financial Times* in 1982.

Box 4.1 What is a letter of credit?

A documentary credit is a written promise by a bank, on behalf of a buyer, to pay a seller the amount specified in the credit, provided the seller complies with terms and conditions outlined in the credit.

The terms and conditions of a documentary credit revolve around the presentation of documents that evidence title to goods shipped by the seller and payment. Banks act as intermediaries to collect payment from the buyer in exchange for the transfer of documents that enable the holder to take possession of the goods.

Documentary credits provide a high level of protection and security to both buyers and sellers engaged in international trade.

Source: Internal Maersk Line resource, based on the *Dictionary of International Trade*, 5th edition, World Trade Press, 2002, p. 360.

Maersk Line and Maersk Container Line

Internally in Copenhagen two liner departments – Maersk Container Line, with its one fully containerised service and Maersk Line, with its range of conventional services – were learning how to work together.

Containers were inter-changed between the services, container control information needed to be kept up to date and container repair costs needed to be allocated to the right account. To save time and energy, agreements were put in place to govern the working relationship between the two departments covering, among other things, trans-shipment cargoes and container management.

US East Coast strike, 1977

While Maersk Line continued to work on the opportunities to improve the results of the new container service, the US East Coast was hit by a strike by the International Longshoremen's Association (ILA), which lasted some two months. Thomas Gleason, then president of the ILA, maintained that 'the container is digging our graves and we cannot live off containers'. Levinson illustrated the impact of containerisation on dock workers by summarising the changes in employment in Manhattan over little more than a decade. In the period 1963–1964 employers used 1.4 million days of longshore labour, and by 1975–1976 this was down to 127,041 days.[7] The impact of containerisation was no less significant in other ports along the US coasts.

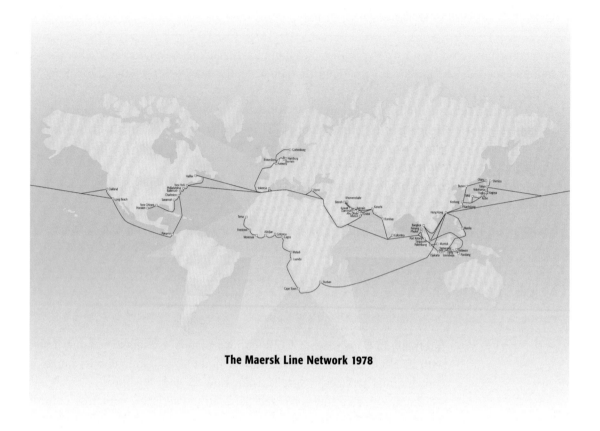

The Maersk Line Network 1978

Figure 4.2 Maersk Line was present in all of the three main markets of the world in 1978 – North America, Europe and Asia – plus the Middle East and Africa. Specialised container ships served North America, Asia and the Middle East.

Nor was the United States the only area where such changes were noted. In the UK, the Transport and General Workers Union imposed a ban on handling containers at the Port of Tilbury from January 1968, and in doing so opened the door to the development of the Port of Felixstowe, which in 1974 handled over 137,000 containers and never looked back.

Coverage of Southeast Asia

One of the strengths of the new Maersk Line container service was its ability to build on the previous Panama Line and its robust market shares from the United States to ports in Southeast Asia. To enhance the services

Figure 4.3 The container revolution arrived slowly but surely in ports around the world. Even though the tools may seem simple, the container itself and the yard hustler represent a significant improvement in cargo handling. *Maersk Mango* is waiting for more cargo in the port of Singapore.

to these markets, a number of chartered feeder ships had initially been taken on. While the large, main-line ships served the main ports, these smaller container ships served other ports, feeding containers to and from the main-line ships. As the services developed, Maersk Line built its own feeder ships to provide coverage of these markets, and so in 1978 the *Maersk Tempo* and *Maersk Mango*, both built in Japan (Taihei 329 and 331), entered service. With their own cranes and a capacity of about 400 TEU,[8] these ships provided ideal coverage of their markets.

Maersk Tempo mainly acted as a feeder between Hong Kong, Manila in the Philippines and Kaohsiung in the south of Taiwan. *Maersk Mango* went straight into the Singapore–Bangkok trade and continued to serve Bangkok until 1986. These ships were later to change their names to *Maersk Clementine* and *Maersk Claudine*, respectively, when they were transferred to the West Africa service in 1986, operating as feeder vessels between West African ports and Algeciras in Spain.

A number of chartered container ships continued to be taken on to supplement the coverage. Chartered ships normally retain their owner's colours; however, to reinforce the Maersk brand, even the chartered ships in the new service were repainted in Maersk Line colours and given Maersk names, with the personal approval of Mærsk Mc-Kinney Møller. *Maersk Rando*, *Maersk Mondo* and *Maersk Pinto* joined the fleet, serving Jakarta,

Surabaya and Belawan Deli in Indonesia and Port Kelang and Penang in Malaysia. They operated on a 'butterfly' service – so called because on a map the ports represent the wings of a butterfly, with Singapore as the body.

Then, on 19 September 1977, Maersk Line suffered a major setback. That day, as the *Adrian Mærsk* was leaving Hong Kong bound for Taiwan at about 18 knots, the ship ran aground on Lamma Island, the consequence of a navigation error. Major damage was incurred to the underside of the ship's hull and the engine room was flooded. Nearly 600 containers had to be discharged and forwarded separately. Eventually the ship was lightened and pulled off by four powerful tugs and taken for repair to the Innoshima yard in Japan.[9]

Svendborg Mærsk and A-class lengthening

In the meantime, Maersk's competitors continued to expand their network. For example, in 1979, Sea-Land took delivery of the *Sea-Land Patriot*, the first of 12 new buildings of about 2,500 TEU capacity.

Back in 1977 Maersk Line had made the decision to extend its nine existing container vessels by adding one container hold section into the hull. This extension operation was conducted by the Hitachi shipyard in Japan and was timed to the minute, with the lengthening of all nine ships to be completed by the end of 1978.

The first ship to undergo this technically advanced operation was the *Anders Mærsk*, with the *Svendborg Mærsk* taking over its loading position. *Svendborg Mærsk* had been chartered out for most of 1974 to serve in the Australia–Europe container service, a joint service of Overseas Container Limited (OCL), Hapag-Lloyd, Messageries Maritimes, NedLloyd and Lloyd Triestino. It had been positioned to Japan to become part of the phasing in of the Far East–United States–Far East service in September 1975. The *Svendborg Mærsk* was now to prove its worth: its availability meant an uninterrupted service could be maintained during the lengthening process with a ship of similar size and speed to the existing ships – an important customer consideration in the decision.

The lengthening operation itself was complex and involved a very tight schedule.[10] The cutting and re-welding operations each took less than a day.[11] The return on the investment was calculated at 43.3 per cent. As one ship was completed, it took over the loading position of the next ship, without any break in the service schedule. The net effect was to increase the capacity of each of the nine ships by approximately 100 TEU, to about 1,800 TEU, based on carrying containers stacked four-high on deck. This

Figure 4.4 The nine A-ships were lengthened in 1978 and, as shown here, four were rebuilt in 1983–1984, when the original turbine engine was replaced with a much more economical diesel engine and yet another container section was added. It took the Hitachi yard at Innoshima, Japan, only two months to complete the operation.

Box 4.2 A half-century

1978 marked the 50th anniversary of Maersk Line's services between the United States and the Far East. To commemorate the event the advertising agency Young and Rubicam was commissioned to develop a set of advertisements that could be run in the relevant areas, to promote the line and thank its loyal customers. Two weeks before the campaign was to roll out, it was presented to Mærsk Mc-Kinney Møller.

He studied the material, complimented the team that had developed it, and then, after a long pause, said, 'Thank you for an excellent approach – but I don't think it is what my father would have wanted. Instead, I will write a personal letter of thanks to our top customers.' Which is what happened.

A. P. Møller had always ensured he was away from home on personal anniversaries. He declined to celebrate them and he preferred not to be part of public functions. Mærsk Mc-Kinney Møller decided to continue the tradition his father had established.

Source: A.P. Moller – Maersk archives.

procedure was repeated in 1983–1984 when some of the ships were lengthened again by the same amount and the engines changed from steam turbine to diesel.

Relations with the FEFC

The year 1979 saw a significant development in the ongoing saga with the FEFC. At the start of its discussions with the FEFC, Maersk Line had felt, despite its history in the trade, that it was being treated as a newcomer, some of its competitors having been in existence for well over a century. The FEFC itself had celebrated its 100th anniversary in 1977. But these meetings had also provided the opportunity to build relations with both the FEFC management and the management of many of the lines that made up the core of the conference. Although it was still a small player by the standards of the main consortia, by working constructively, being thoroughly well prepared and slowly building relations, over time Maersk Line had established itself as a committed and respected operator within the conference. However, those hard-won relationships were soon to be shaken.

The Newton ships

With so many of the trades either containerised, or in the process of being containerised, the writing was on the wall for the continuation of conventional, semi-container services, unless these were to serve specific niche markets. Broeze summarised the development of containerisation in the major North–South routes as:

1972	Europe–East Asia
1973	United States–Latin America
1974	United States–Middle East and India
1976	Europe–Caribbean
1977	Europe–South Africa
1977	Europe–Middle East
1978	Japan–Middle East
1978	Europe–India and Pakistan
1978	Europe–West Africa
1979	Europe–China
1980	Europe–Latin America.[12]

Understanding the implications of this from a competitive service perspective, early in 1978, Maersk Line in Copenhagen decided to purchase a number of state-of-the-art vessels of 2,124 TEU capacity at four layers on

Figure 4.5 Odense Steel Shipyard new building number 88, which joined the Maersk Line fleet as *Luna Mærsk* in 1982. It had two extra rows of holds for 40-foot containers compared to the first five of the Newton (new tonnage) ships; its capacity was 2,536 TEU plus four 360 m^3 tanks for liquid cargoes.

deck, known internally as the Newton ships, to containerise its existing Europe–Far East–Europe service.

The first four ships, Lindø new-building numbers 83 to 86, were ordered immediately, and shortly afterwards a further two ships were added, Lindø 87 and 88. A tug boat strike in New York from early April to the end of June 1979 provided some operators with a sharp lesson: these ships were all to be equipped with both bow and stern thrusters to enable them to enter and leave port unassisted.

Other innovations, such as an adaptive autopilot and changes to fuel additives, were all designed to improve the vessels' performance and reduce fuel consumption. And another – internally developed – innovation, a new cell guide system known as 'slim guides', provided flexibility in combining 20-foot and 40-foot capacity while saving about one metre in the length of each hatch. At the time, the world's largest diesel engine of 47,000 shaft horse-power (SHP) provided the most fuel-efficient power unit available.

Another innovation for the Far East–Europe–Far East trade was the inclusion in all six ships of four semi-permanent tanks. Each tank was the size of six 40-foot containers, three high by two wide, and had a capacity of 360 cubic metres, totalling 1,440 cubic metres per ship. The objective, which was successfully met, was to continue to serve the latex and liquid chemicals markets that would otherwise have had to be covered by parcel tankers or trampers.

The service plan

Starting in late 1980 with the arrival of the new container ships, the service would replace the existing Maersk Line semi-container service covering the Europe–Far East–Europe trade. Sailings would integrate in the Far East with the existing Far East–United States–Far East service and its feeder operations, adding extra throughput to the existing terminals and feeder vessels. This allowed for the negotiation of sliding-scale terminal rates. The service rotated from Singapore to Hong Kong, Keelung, Busan, Kobe and Tokyo, returning to Europe via Keelung, Hong Kong and Singapore. Malaysia was fed from Singapore, Manila and Kaohsiung in the south of Taiwan via Hong Kong. In Europe, Rotterdam, Antwerp, Bremerhaven and Hamburg were covered direct.

Although the new ships could reach in excess of 26 knots, the service was planned to operate at an average of about 23 knots, with buffers in the schedule ranging from two hours (a short leg) to 24 (e.g. Singapore to Suez). The result was a schedule in both directions and for each port-to-port combination that was at worst comparable with the competition and at best significantly better than the best competing services (TRIO, ScanDutch or ACE Group) for most ports.

At this time in Maersk Line's development, both inflation and interest rates were relatively high by today's (2013) standards. By providing customers with a fast and reliable service, the schedule was building on the proven success criteria already available to customers of the US service and providing cargo owners with the opportunity to minimise inventory-holding costs.

Busan, in Korea, was a new operation, but otherwise the Asian terminals were known, as was Maersk Line's reputation for punctuality. The container terminals in Europe were new to Maersk Line and so took more time to put in place. As Ib Kruse was quoted as saying in Chapter 3, the instruction to the ships was to arrive at the scheduled date and time. China was to be served, as it was in the Trans Pacific, via Hong Kong.

Several thousand 20-foot units and 40-foot units were acquired to build up the equipment fleet for the service. Extra refrigerated containers were purchased at a cost 3.2–3.7 times the price of standard dry equipment. The plan included a significant step-up in refrigerated container capacity compared to the A-class ships, as they had only initially been equipped for ten refrigerated containers and prospects had been minimal. We will come back to this development later in this chapter.

Opening European offices

Maersk Line had made agency agreements with its first third-party agents in the early 1930s, when the United States–Far East service had been established. As Flemming Jacobs had pointed out, own representation in key markets had shown its value in enabling the Maersk Line organisation to monitor and quickly respond to changes in the market. Building on this experience led to the opening of a range of new Maersk Line offices for the Far East–Europe trade.

Notice had to be given to Detjen Schiffahrtsagentur GMBH in Hamburg, Kompass in Hanover, Cargo Reederei in Düsseldorf, Axel von Wietersheim in Frankfurt, De Kayser Thornton in Antwerp and Hudig & Veder B. V. and Vinke & Co. in Holland. Most of the notices were hand-carried by senior Maersk executives so that the decision could be explained personally. All were completed during December 1979, with one year's notice.

While notice was being given, searches were conducted for suitable office space in the key cities, companies were registered, organisation charts developed and advertisements created to attract senior personnel. The plan was to have all these in place by 1 September 1980.

In Germany, a head office was opened in Hamburg with supporting offices in Bremen, Düsseldorf, Nuremberg, Stuttgart, Frankfurt and Munich. In Holland, Rotterdam was established as the head office, with Amsterdam as a sales office, while Antwerp handled both head office and all other functions for Belgium. As cargoes in Europe move into and out of the hinterland via all these ports, the offices were to be responsible not only for local activities but also for managing their cross-border flows. The main offices were brought online immediately and also handled the documentation for the hinterland offices. Once the service had been launched, all the hinterland offices would quickly be linked to the network, including Maersk Line's unique e-mail system, MCS.

The systems would also cover documentation production and management, container control, marketing statistics, freight accounting and local accounting for the agents' office. Maersk Data, a separate company within the A.P. Moller Group, was contracted to make the necessary adjustments so that the existing systems could also be used effectively in Europe. A key challenge was the need to be able to manage shipments in both US dollars and any one or more of the multiple European currencies.[13]

To put these technical developments into an appropriate context, it is worth noting that in 1980, the term 'personal computer' was about three years old, as was Apple Computers' Apple 1 personal computer. Only three years previously, in 1977, Wang Laboratories had introduced the first computerised word processor; and the first cellular telephone network, in Tokyo and operated by NTT, was just one year old.

The United Kingdom

While there was no agreement with the FEFC for Maersk Line to cover the United Kingdom with the planned container service, the management there and in Copenhagen decided to investigate the UK market to build understanding of what would be required if Maersk were to serve that market at some later stage. In November 1979, an unattributed confidential analysis was commissioned from a consulting company – Maersk Line was not to be identified as the client company.

The consultants' report was delivered in March 1980 and described the key components of the market, trade forecasts, freight rates and modus operandi including Freight Liner rail operations, inland container depots (ICDs) and ports. The report included a summary of a survey of the likes and dislikes of importing, exporting and freight forwarding customers, their attitudes to the FEFC and to the individual carriers operating in the market – at that stage heavily dominated by the British lines, with only minor penetration by other FEFC members.[14]

Customers had close financial ties to the conference through the FEFC's deferred rebate scheme. This encouraged loyalty to the FEFC by rewarding such customers with a deferred freight discount on shipments, subject to their not using non-conference carriers. On the other hand, there was a significant level of frustration in the market place, which could provide an opportunity for a strong, quality outsider.

Mærsk Mc-Kinney Møller and the senior management of Maersk Line reviewed the Europe–Far East project in June 1980, noting that of the 32 members of the FEFC, 18 were now working in three consortia (Trio, ScanDutch and ACE Group), providing weekly services and commanding a market share of about 90 per cent of the overall market. Other than Maersk Line, only Evergreen played any significant role outside the consortia.

The rights discussion

The major discussion point within the FEFC was the state of the market. Although there was strong competition and generally full vessels from the

Far East to Europe, there was evidence of unofficial discounting. Maersk Line's internal project review made it clear that the original decision base for the four-ship, fortnightly service loading Maersk Line's full rights in each direction, had therefore been eroded and the projected profit now looked like a loss. Nevertheless, Maersk Line needed to go ahead and put forward a number of options to resolve the issues.

At that time, each of the member lines in the FEFC had rights to lift specific shares of the market. Maersk Line's rights allowed the loading of about 6 per cent of the market in each direction. Maersk Line had no rights to or from the UK and Eire, from Le Havre in northern France, or from Europe into Thailand, and no rights to load from the Far East into the Gulf of Aden or the Red Sea.

At the same time, FEFC analyses showed that the Trans-Siberian railway was lifting about 15 per cent of the total Asia to Europe trade, with 75 per cent of its volume from Japan, by far the largest Far East market.[15] Volumes also originated from Korea, Hong Kong and Taiwan. Rates were 'considerably below those of the FEFC, and in most cases commercially unviable on the all water routes'.[16] Evergreen, as a non-conference outsider, had about 11 per cent of the total westbound market.

The challenge was clear – Maersk Line had not started its container service and an approach to the FEFC was not considered viable. Several other carriers, including Maritime Company of the Philippines (MCP), Korean Shipping Company (KSC) and Malaysian International Shipping Corporation (MISC), all had outstanding tonnage and geographical rights issues with the FEFC and under the UNCTAD code could argue their national flag status, entitling them to a 40 per cent share of their national trades.

A special Owners' Committee of the FEFC was in the process of reviewing the overall situation, so Maersk Line's plan was to await the outcome of these deliberations, which was due in 1981. In the meantime, steps were initiated to strengthen its bargaining position.

One option that was considered, but rejected, was to leave the FEFC and operate as an outsider. The main reason for this decision was the politics of the growing global trade. National flag lines could play the UNCTAD Code card and keep Maersk Line from significant cargoes. However, the implications of government intervention – for example, Korea's implementation of a waiver scheme to limit outsider loadings – would be difficult to address. Operational risks in Japan were considered too problematic. Maersk Line might have acted with a certain degree of self-confidence in the FEFC, but it was realistic about its position should it leave the conference. So, working with, rather than against, the conference requirements and goals, Maersk Line focused on regaining profitable cargo volumes that had been lost to

Box 4.3 The United Nations Conference on Trade and Development (UNCTAD)

From a maritime perspective, UNCTAD developed out of discussions in the early 1960s between the OECD countries, which sought to resist introduction of government control over an industry that was essentially in private hands, and the Group of 77 (developing countries) who were in favour of state control of maritime transport.

A consensus was achieved in 1964, which recommended that while liner conferences were needed to provide stability and regular services, a process was also needed to deal with shippers' complaints. This led to the creation of Shippers' Councils and other organisations to represent trade interests.

Debates continued until 1974, when the United Nations Convention on a Code of Conduct for Liner Conferences was put forward. Once ratified, this was a legally binding agreement. The Code defined liner conferences as:

A group of two or more vessel-operating carriers which provides international liner services for the carriage of cargo on a particular route or routes within specified geographical limits and which has an agreement or arrangement, whatever its nature, within the framework of which they operate under uniform or common freight rates and any other agreed conditions with respect to the provision of liner services.

The Code covers other aspects of conferences, including participation, sharing of services and cargoes, and is best known for the 40/40/20 rule, which was a compromise giving the developing countries' national shipping lines the opportunity to carry a generally greater share of their maritime trade (i.e. up to 40 per cent).

At the time, independent carriers were not as significant as they later proved to be.

Source: L. O. Blanco, *Shipping Conferences under EC Anti-Trust Law*, Hart Publishing, 2007.

outsiders. With local market input from the Maersk Line offices, a range of proposals to compete more effectively with outsiders was advanced to the FEFC and influential member lines for their consideration.

The announcement and staff training

In early 1980 a trade press release was issued announcing that Maersk Line planned to containerise its Europe–Far East–Europe service and would be establishing its own offices across mainland Europe. In March advertisements for senior positions hit the main shipping press across Europe.

In April, after studying a number of options, an internal work group recommended that the container service should continue to be built on the same on-time principles that applied to the Far East–United States–Far East service. This would mean moving to 26 sailings per year from 1981. A comparison of the resulting reliable, fortnightly scheduled transit times with the top three consortia clearly demonstrated the advantages of this approach.

Meanwhile, in Korea Maersk Line was negotiating with E. Sun Lee's Worldwide Maritime Company, to acquire 50 per cent of the company. With the service including a direct call at Busan, in Korea, the importance of managing it directly in Korea had increased.

At 7:30 a.m. on Saturday 28 June 1980, the new senior external recruits from Germany, Holland and Belgium met for the first time in Copenhagen for a full induction and briefing day with Maersk Line's management and the project team. While the head of each country would be a Dane, with a few exceptions, the new organisations were to be staffed with local talent recruited from across the shipping and forwarding industries. Their main

---

Box 4.4 The European Union maritime approach

Influenced by Hugo Grotius' work 'Mare Liberum' of 1609, enshrined in the UN Convention on the Law of the Sea (1982), competition rules in Europe had not applied to international trade.

Prompted by the UNCTAD Code, in 1979 the European Commission proposed a common maritime position, ultimately called the Brussels Package, which was seen as a political gesture of good will to the developing countries while maintaining self-regulating liner conferences and free access to cargoes.

During the 1980s the EU's Consultative Shipping Group (European member states) and US authorities moved to ensure open and free access to trade. This led ultimately to the US Shipping Act of 1984.

The European Commission put forward proposals concerning inland transport in 1983, air transport in 1984 and maritime transport in 1985.

In 1986 these proposals became Regulation 4056/86, which legitimised liner conferences under a block exemption from competition rules, while giving the European Commission powers to investigate and impose fines for abuses.

In 1987 the Transport Division of the Directorate General for Competition of the European Commission (DGIV) was formed.

In 2001–2002, an OECD report proposed that if liner conferences were not eliminated, then they should be subject to economic regulation by an independent regulator. This led the Commission to review Regulation 4056/86 in 2003 and to propose the abolition of the block exemption in 2005. Regulation 4056/86 was repealed in September 2006, taking effect from October 2008.

Source: L. O. Blanco, *Shipping Conferences under EC Anti-Trust Law*, Hart Publishing, 2007.

task was to understand how far the project had developed and, working in teams, define what still needed to be done, by when and by whom to ensure a successful start-up of the new organisation. The day concluded with a semi-formal dinner where the new managers were encouraged to get to know one another.[17]

Later in the year, country management and their new employees were brought together for training sessions in sales (ensuring a consistent approach to customers across the markets throughout the new European offices), operations and electronic data processing (EDP) systems, so that the new offices would be properly equipped to take and handle bookings from day one.

Resignation from the FEFC

Meanwhile, negotiations with the FEFC continued. In January 1981, Jane Boyes, the highly respected editor of *Containerisation International*, paid a visit to Copenhagen and met a number of Maersk Line executives, writing a five-page summary of Maersk Line in containers from 1975 to that year. In the section covering the new Europe–Far East service, she concluded: 'That Maersk is prepared, if need be, to depart from its traditional policy of conference membership is evidenced by not only its recent resignation from the PNAC (Philippines North America Conference), but also by the fact that its new Mediterranean/US service is non-conference.'[18] This new service was managed by Maersk Line's conventional service team, who were also in the process of upgrading it to a full container service.

And, continuing the trend of having its own offices wherever possible, towards the middle of the year, Tabacalera, Maersk Line's agents in the Philippines, celebrated its centenary, having operated as Maersk Line's agents for almost half a century. Now the agency became a 50/50 joint venture with Maersk.

Despite regular meetings between the FEFC and Maersk Line's management, little progress was being made in resolving the rights issues and on 4 June 1981, a letter to the FEFC indicated that 'it is unlikely that Maersk Line will be able to continue to operate very much longer within the constraints of the current agreement'.[19] The reasons cited were:

the strong and increased competition from non-conference operators both East-bound and Westbound [which] has reduced the FEFC share of the market in which we all participate. This combined with rate actions has drastically affected the economic results ... It is of course essential that membership be based on agreements which make it feasible to operate an economically viable service and with ability to meet the increasing threat of non-conference competition which operates on an unrestricted basis.[20]

The FEFC's reaction was one of concern, and representatives of both parties met in Copenhagen on 18 June. There was considerable tension among FEFC lines at the time for exactly the reasons cited by Maersk Line, namely the declining FEFC share caused by the increased market penetration of the TSR, Evergreen and Korean outsiders.[21] *Containerisation International* estimated that, at this stage, 'non-conference lines controlled nearly 20 per cent of the TEU capacity on the North Europe/UK to Far East all water route and over 40 per cent in the Mediterranean/Far East all water market'. And outsiders were not only a threat there: 'In the North Atlantic outsiders probably offer at least one third of the slots deployed. In the Trans Pacific arena their presence grew steadily from about 23 per cent in 1978 to an estimated 35 per cent by the end of 1981.'[22]

As Vernon Rolls, FEFC Conference Manager, pointed out, although Maersk were relative late-comers to operating fully containerised vessels in the FEFC trade, their position had altered beyond recognition since the Owners' Meeting in June 1966 which had concluded that there was presently 'no room in any part of the FEFC trade for Maersk.'[23] Maersk Line was now acting as a catalyst for some of the most significant changes in the FEFC's modus operandi. The effect, as we will see, would be to help bring the conference thoroughly into the 20th century.

But getting agreement across such a disparate group of competing carriers was not going to be easy. In September, an FEFC Policy Committee meeting provided an opportunity for the FEFC to tell Maersk Line's representative that there were as yet 'no concrete proposals from the conference and that the only way to deal with our request for increased rights would be for Maersk Line to join one of the existing consortia'. Maersk Line did not see this option as being feasible.

During October, meetings took place between the FEFC's negotiating committee and Maersk Line in which a number of alternative solutions were discussed. Solutions included other lines slot chartering on the new Maersk service and allowing a gradual increase in Maersk Line's tonnage rights through to 1984. The difference between the parties was 150,000 tons but proved to be too much, notwithstanding that both sides recognised that Evergreen was lifting in excess of 1.4 million tons at the time. A final meeting took place on 5 November where, despite the news that Yang Ming of Taiwan would also be starting a service between Asia and Northern Europe in mid 1982 as an outsider, and despite significant attempts by both sides to bridge the gap, differences remained.

On 17 November 1981 Maersk Line wrote to the FEFC giving six months' notice to terminate its agreements with the conference from 30 November. It would leave the FEFC on 31 May 1982.

The letter also noted that during the course of negotiations two items had come to light of which Maersk Line had previously been unaware – namely that members of the ACE Group had been granted some 30 per cent more than their formal rights and that other lines were exceeding their rights by considerable margins. Brian Allen, Director General of the FEFC, formally acknowledged receipt of the termination in a letter dated 20 November 1981.

Parallel developments

While turbulence might characterise the Asia–Europe trade, things were settling down on the existing Trans Pacific service. In 1978, Moller Steamship had opened a number of new offices in the United States as well as in Canada, while Maersk Line had opened an office in France.

In 1979, Ib Kruse, responsible for the container service, was promoted to Partner in A.P. Moller.

An internal analysis of the Trans Pacific services reliability in 1979 showed that inbound from Asia the ships had arrived 100 per cent on schedule into Long Beach and 95 per cent into New York, and outbound from the United States 98.1 per cent into Hong Kong. Similarly, departures from Tokyo were at 96.1 per cent, while departures from New York were 100 per cent on schedule. The market outbound from the United States was subject to space pressure for much of the year, with the US dollar relatively weak. This provided the United States with opportunities to grow exports to its more traditional markets in South and Southeast Asia, and also into the new growth area of the People's Republic of China.

Homebound to the United States, the market was weaker and the cargo waiver system implemented by Korea was of such concern that, with the active involvement of the Danish Ship Owners' Association, a shipping agreement at governmental level was eventually implemented between Denmark and Korea. Freight rates were generally under pressure.

Ib Kruse's book-closing summary for 1979 recorded the initiation of a number of IT-related projects, including investigations into replacing the existing documentation system; the implementation of enhancements to existing EDP systems so that their use could be extended to other services as they became containerised; and a review of the entire structure of the EDP set-up to ensure it was optimal to serve the business on a global basis, including the overseas offices.

Overall, the biggest risk to the business globally and to all the services was two rapid rises in the price of oil in quick succession in the spring of 1979. This had put a damper on the optimism prevalent at the end of 1978, when the general view had been that the world economy had recovered from the longer-term impacts of the oil crisis in 1973.

Early in 1980, management in New York was asked to consider the possibility of operating some of the container ships under the US flag in order to protect the line against the risks developing under the UNCTAD Code, flag discrimination generally and further bilateral trade agreements. In addition, as a further attempt to control its own destiny, Maersk opened up discussions about the possibility of buying a shareholding in Modern Terminals Limited (MTL) of Hong Kong, a discussion that eventually resulted in Maersk acquiring an 8 per cent shareholding. MTL was a critical Maersk Line hub and the ability to influence its development was seen as an important long-term step, as well as a sound investment.

It was also opportune as MTL was undergoing substantial redevelopment, including installation of additional cranes, and the work was causing delays with ripple effects on other ports in the Maersk Line network. That autumn, Ib Kruse wrote to Admiral Yuan, then Director of Keelung Harbour Bureau in Taiwan, to thank him and his staff for their efforts in helping to manage the irregularities in Maersk Line's otherwise airline-type schedules.

Two other developments are worthy of note. One was the decision to set up a small unit to be responsible for the control and development of A.P. Moller's communications facilities. The result was the development and expansion of a communications capability that, until the advent of the internet, gave Maersk Line a differentiating edge over its competitors.

Figure 4.6 The Telex Department at the A.P. Moller Group headquarters, where in 1982, 4,500 telex messages were handled on a daily basis – 3,000 incoming and 1,500 outgoing messages.

The second was the growing relationship between the managements of Maersk Line and Sea-Land. Ib Kruse and Charles Hilzheimer, then Chairman of Sea-Land, agreed to review operations jointly and to meet at the end of 1981 or early in 1982. Maersk was particularly impressed with Sea-Land's container control systems.

The Maersk Line fleet was developing rapidly. From a TEU capacity of 6,740 in 1975, by the end of 1981 this had grown to 32,174. *Containerisation International* calculated that the May 1982 capacity, with new buildings and conversions, would probably achieve 44,874 TEU, a 39 per cent increase from the previous year.[24]

The first two Newton ships, *Laura Mærsk* and *Leise Mærsk*, were launched towards the end of 1980, inaugurating the containerised Europe–Far East service. Two more ships followed, *Lexa Mærsk* in March 1981 and *Lica Mærsk* in May. They replaced the C-class semi-container ships that were already being converted to full container ships. *Charlotte*

Box 4.5 Cumulative world containership capacity 1970–1984

Year	TEU capacity	Annual increase (%)
1970	195,372	
1971	258,186	32.2
1972	382,428	48.1
1973	478,492	25.1
1974	518,944	8.5
1975	568,363	9.5
1976	639,971	12.6
1977	788,115	23.1
1978	982,681	24.7
1979	1,189,317	21.0
1980	1,354,012	13.8
1981	1,456,592	7.6
1982	1,550,808	6.5
1983	1,719,229	10.9
1984	1,849,277	7.6

Source: Containerisation International Yearbook 1983 © 1983, reproduced with the permission of Lloyds List Group.

Figure 4.7 Loaded with an unusually homogeneous cargo of near-identical containers, *Laura Mærsk* is seen leaving Singapore. *Maersk Mango* is entering the port on its Butterfly Service.

Mærsk and its sister ship *Chastine Mærsk* were the first to be converted, this time to 1,200 TEU container vessels. Conversion was both cheaper and faster than building new ships and in October 1980 these ships became operative on an existing service covering the Middle East, upgrading it to a new container service.

While the internal Maersk Container Line department ran the Trans Pacific and the newly containerised Europe–Far East service, this new Middle East service was managed by the conventional Line Department (see Chapter 3). The service had been operated with semi-container vessels since the mid 1970s. Linking the United States with the Middle East, the independently priced homebound call into the Mediterranean was the new element in the return journey to the States. The service was well received and allowed improved economies of scale to be achieved in the growing Maersk Line organisation in North America.

Another service in the conventional Line Department was also being containerised. The Japan–Far East–Middle East service had provided a semi-container and roll-on–roll-off (RO-RO) service with new ships since 1979.[25] These were E-class ships, built at the Lindø shipyard and now providing RO-RO capability in the trade at a time when heavy equipment and materials for the construction industry were beginning to flow in volume.

From March 1981, one of the trades in which Maersk Line had operated the longest, the Japan–Indonesia service, was also containerised. Since the service began in 1952 it had gone from a break-bulk to a pallet to a semi-container service, and now it would be served by two converted C-class ships, *Cecilie Mærsk* and *Cornelia Mærsk*, of 1,200 TEU each. As some of the ports (e.g. Surabaya in Indonesia) were not yet equipped with container cranes, the two ships were provided with their own.

As the M-class semi-container ships built in 1974–1975, such as *Marchen Mærsk*, were replaced on the Trans Pacific service by the new A-class container ships, the M-class ships were transferred to the Japan–Far East–West Africa service, where they continued to provide a monthly service focused on pallets, but with a container capacity in excess of 600 TEU per vessel available for suitable cargoes and customers.

In another development, in 1980–1981 Maersk Container Line conducted a detailed study into serving the Australia and New Zealand markets based on a containerised relay operation over either Hong Kong or Singapore. The proposed service showed that it could be profitable, but was not deemed very attractive and was put on hold for the time being.

At the end of her visit to Copenhagen in early 1981, Jane Boyes concluded:

As to its future intentions, whatever they may be, Maersk remains as tight-lipped as ever ... It is of interest, though, that the worldwide network of container links it now maintains gives it endless routing possibilities ... [I]t has a worldwide network of facilities, largely under its own control, a strongly service-oriented philosophy and a multiple service pattern which enables it to balance out fluctuations in the fortunes of one market against those of another ... Maersk is now as well placed as any of the major container carriers to operate profitably in the 1980s.

The only risk Jane Boyes noted was its:

vulnerability as a cross-trader in a liner shipping environment that is increasingly shifting towards bilateral agreements and ratification of the UNCTAD Code of Conduct for Liner Conferences with its 40/40/20 cargo sharing provisions. However, this is not a new predicament for Maersk, whose whole service oriented philosophy has been built on the premise that if you are a cross-trader, you have to try just that bit harder.[26]

In an interview with Mitsuo Ikeda of Japan's *Shipping and Trade News* towards the end of 1980, Ib Kruse was asked for Maersk Line's view on the UNCTAD Code. He summarised it by saying:

Box 4.6 More on UNCTAD

The implications of the UNCTAD Code were summarised in an internal Maersk Line paper in 1981. The main points were:

- The Code is a guideline for conference standards, relations between conference members, between the conference and applicants for membership and between the conference and shippers' organisations.
- The Code contains a good amount of flexibility, providing a chance for the convention to become universally acceptable.
- Its success depends on the good will of governments to make use of the harmonising elements of the Code to build a bridge between conflicting national shipping legislation.
- The Code is basically for the conduct of liner conferences. The ball is in the liner conferences' court, while it remains the responsibility of governments to provide the environment permitting the Code to operate.

However:

- Conferences are open for national lines. Entrance for cross-traders or third flags depends on certain conditions.
- National lines at both ends of the trade have the right to participate in the freight and volume of the trade carried by the conference on an equal basis.
- Cargo-sharing guidelines refer to the trade carried by the conference. They do not refer to the part of the trade carried by independent lines.
- The Code provides for control of conference practices by consultation between liner conferences and the organisations of the shippers.
- A resolution annexed to the Code confirms the right of shippers to choose between conference lines and independent lines.

Source: Internal Maersk Line paper, 19 May 1981, A.P. Moller – Maersk archives.

basically we are opposed to the concept of the Code as we consider it detrimental to the free flow of world trade, since the Code's intended 40/40/20 principle imposes restrictions on the practice of exporters and importers making their own independent choice of who is to carry their cargoes ... a principle of expedience, whereby ships of all nations compete with each other offering merchants the best means of having their goods transported and thus helping to develop world trade at the lowest and most competitive cost.

Ib Kruse was representing the views of both Maersk Line and the A.P. Moller Group shipping divisions. In the very early years of his career, A. P. Møller had been an active spokesman for liberal economic policies. He maintained that in Denmark, as in the foreign markets relevant for Maersk, 'a free market economy would, in the final analysis, lead to the greatest overall prosperity whereas state subsidies, flag discrimination and other protectionist measures had a distorting effect on competition and, from a socio-economic viewpoint, were also irrational.'[27] This viewpoint still held in 1980.

Ib Kruse went on to say,

> however, in order to assist in solving the problem, we subscribed, together with other Danish liner operators, to Denmark's adherence to the E.E.C. compromise ... the so called Brussels package ... which, very simply, is that we support the request of the developing nations to participate with up to 40 per cent of their own liner trade, with the remaining 60 per cent to be handled on a commercial basis.[28]

Of course, the world was changing. The Vietnam War ended in 1975, Vietnam was reunified the following year, and in 1978 the United States formally recognised the People's Republic of China. That same year, Deng Xiaoping launched the economic reforms known as 'socialism with Chinese characteristics', including opening trade with the outside world. Also in 1978, the US Senate supported a treaty to transfer control of the Panama Canal to Panama in 1999; and in 1979, the European Council agreed to create the European Monetary System based on the concept of fixed but adjustable exchange rates and the European currency unit (ECU), was created.

At the end of 1980, Ronald Reagan was elected as President of the United States and in early 1981, British Prime Minister Margaret Thatcher, the first

---

Box 4.7 A summary of the Brussels Package

The Brussels Package, adopted by the EEC Council of Ministers on 15 May 1979, enabled member states of the European Union to ratify the UNCTAD Liner Code under certain conditions, namely:

- The term 'national shipping line' includes any vessel-operating shipping line established on the territory of such member states in accordance with the EEC Treaty.
- The cargo-sharing guidelines shall not be applied in EEC trades, respectively trades between EEC countries and like-minded OECD countries on a reciprocal basis.
- The two groups of national shipping lines will coordinate their positions before voting on matters concerning the trade between their two countries.
- If no agreement is reached on the distribution of cargoes between EEC member lines, the matter can on request of one of the parties be referred to conciliation.

Source: Internal Maersk Line paper, 19 May 1981, A.P. Moller – Maersk archives.

Box 4.8 The Organisation for Economic Co-operation and Development (OECD)

The OEEC (Organisation for European Economic Co-operation) was established in 1947 to run the US financed Marshall Plan for the reconstruction of a continent ravaged by war, by making governments recognise the interdependence of their economies.

Based on its success, Canada and the US joined OEEC members in creating a new OECD convention that came into force on September 30th 1961. Since then about 40 other countries have joined so that the OECD covers approximately 80 per cent of world trade and investment.

The OECD promotes 'progressive liberalisation of current and capital account operations ... its approach to open markets finds expression in the Code of Liberalisation of Capital Movements and the Code of Liberalisation of Invisible Operations which covers cross/border services'.

Completeness and resolve in carrying out economic reforms is of crucial importance to establish and maintain credibility during the liberalisation process.

Source: OECD website, 2013

foreign leader to be invited to visit the new president, declared on her arrival in the country, 'We are both determined to sweep away the restrictions that hold back enterprise.'[29] Over the coming years, President Reagan and Mrs Thatcher would implement policies based on laissez-faire philosophies that would seek to stimulate their respective economies through tax cuts and de-regulation.

A diversion: into cool cargoes

When the A-class ships were designed in 1974, ten reefer plugs were installed on each of the ships. Prospects indicated that on average, these plugs would only be used about 20 per cent of the time. Yet the 1979 global trade in perishable refrigerated products was estimated at 30.3 million tons, and the volumes moving internationally by sea were estimated to be about 24 million tons.[30] North America and Northern Europe were the main importing regions, with exports from Latin America and the eastern Mediterranean growing the fastest. Fruit, vegetables and bananas were the most important cool commodities, and meat and fish the main frozen items.

There were probably two main reasons for the conservative evaluation. First, at the time most of these products were moving in refrigerated ships dedicated to carrying them. With about 630 specially designed refrigerated ships available globally, these ships had made solid inroads into what refrigerated liner traffic there had been since the 1960s.[31]

Second, the average size of these specialised reefer ships increased significantly, absorbing most of the growth in demand. However, from a customer's perspective, reefer ships had one significant weakness; when a specialised reefer ship arrived in Hong Kong or Singapore with 3,000–5,000 tons of oranges from the US West Coast, the market price of an orange would drop significantly as the market would be temporarily flooded.

Refrigerated container traffic, although beginning to make inroads into the frozen and chilled meat trades by the early 1970s, was really limited to moving non-traditional commodities, mainly photographic films and enzymes, in smaller lots.

In the 1970s, two main cooling methods were used in reefer containers. The port-hole reefer was an insulated container with two holes for the supply and return of cold air. This required the ship to operate centralised refrigerating machinery with corresponding ventilation plant and duct systems for cooling the containers on board. Port-hole containers were generally loaded below deck and were less flexible as commodities in the same stack needed to be kept at identical temperatures. Ship installation was therefore complicated and expensive, as were terminal operations. This system was mainly in use in the Australia trade, where ships were designed to accommodate 800–1,000 reefer units.

The second type of cooling method was the self-contained reefer container, which could be driven electrically or by a combination of electricity and a diesel motor. The electrically driven units could also be provided with generator sets (gen-sets) during road or rail transport. These units were more flexible when it came to handling various temperatures, accommodating more flexible stowage positions on board ship and conveying various commodities and environments. Ship installation was relatively simple, as were terminal operations. However, the capacity of these reefers was about 1 cubic metre less than the port-hole unit and, because the refrigeration unit was in-built, could accommodate some 400–600 kilogram less payload. They were also significantly more expensive to buy.

In 1986, a major internal investigation examined the opportunities to penetrate the global reefer market. The investigative team reported:

- This is a technically complicated operation calling for reliability, competence and flexibility in the carrier.
- Overall cost comparisons between self-contained and port-hole reefers clearly indicated that up to 300 units per ship, self-contained units were

more cost-effective and flexible in terms of temperature, commodity stowage, refrigerating techniques and terminal handling.

- Containerised solutions can be offered at freight rates competitive with traditional reefer tramp vessels and still be an attractive business.

By May 1986, Maersk Line's own reefer capacity had already grown and the 28 container ships in the fleet now averaged about 160 plug connections per ship or an estimated 5 per cent of world reefer capacity. A new development of more than 1,300 high cube reefers (40 × 8 × 9.5 feet) were now in operation in the Maersk Line fleet, all capable of operating globally.[32]

Maersk Line was beginning to offer significant reefer capacity on each of its services. Contribution margins were generally considered good, at between $3,900 and $6,000 per container in the major trades. A significant part of the investigation went into identifying and proposing ways and means to bring more balance into the equipment flows, as there was high usage in the trades from Europe and the United States to Asia, but low usage outbound from the Far Eastern markets.

The other main part of the report analysed a series of markets and advanced a number of proposals for new or expanded services:

- covering Australia and New Zealand with an extension of the Europe–Far East service via Singapore;
- extending existing coverage of the Philippines to transport bananas to Japan;
- covering the Central and South American markets via feeder services to the US East Coast or via Kingston, Jamaica, or via the US West Coast for on-carriage to the Far East.

For each market, the report analysed the size of the markets, the main commodities, the customers and their requirements, as well as who controlled the cargo, competition and transit times to main importing ports. It also summarised the risks. The report ended with a summary of the team's recommendations. This report was to guide and stimulate a series of developments over the next few years.

The impatience in the organisation for growth and development is not limited to this analysis, as it is clear that Maersk Line was actively looking for development opportunities. Several other investigations were conducted, including the feasibility of creating a separate US Pacific–Far East service, with coverage of the US Pacific North West and the US interior by mini-bridge, and coverage of the Trans Atlantic. Maersk Line's Japan-based organisation also challenged the status quo by putting forward proposals to improve the coverage of Japan, Asia's largest market and one that Maersk Line in the American trades really only served homebound to the United States, rather than in both directions.

Competition

Among all its competitors, from the earliest days of Maersk Line's venture into containerisation, it was Sea-Land that management in Copenhagen monitored most closely. In 1975, Sea-Land opened a container terminal in Algeciras, southern Spain, which was to become its major link between the Mediterranean, the Middle East and European ports. Other initiatives followed: its 1976 service to the Middle East with its first port in Dammam; its opening of offices in Montreal and Toronto, Canada; its 1978 development in Jebel Ali, Dubai, which led to the creation of the largest port complex in the Middle East.

None of these developments escaped the notice of Maersk Line because with them Sea-Land's ability to move containers around the world increased. In 1979, Sea-Land added a container service to India and provided bi-weekly sailings between Dubai, the United Arab Emirates and Bombay and Cochin in India. The sailing that same year of the *Sea-Land Patriot*, the first of 12 new diesel-powered container vessels, marked the largest private ship modernisation of any carrier.

After the resignation

With Maersk Line's resignation from the FEFC coming into effect, life was busy for both parties.

From Maersk Line's perspective, the real implications of operating as an outsider had been defined. Work programmes were set up to ensure that everything was done to make the new service a success. The decision meant that a Maersk Line freight tariff for both the outbound and the homebound trades needed to be put in place.

The UK market was now a possibility and the analysis that had been developed earlier in 1980 received substantial management attention, with a view to being ready to launch at the beginning of June 1982. Offices had to be found and opened and people selected. Meetings had to be held with ports, contracts negotiated and road and rail operations defined.

By 1981 Maersk Line was the world's third largest operator of container ships, so the news of its resignation from the FEFC created interest in the shipping and trade press in many parts of the world. Over the weeks and months that followed, Maersk Line developed a steady stream of press releases to keep the market (and the FEFC) aware of its plans for the new service.

From the FEFC's perspective, action was being taken. Three key areas were addressed, the first of which was a review of the informal Inter-Group Agreement (IGA). The IGA existed outside the formal structure of the FEFC as an agreement between the member lines of the TRIO, ScanDutch and ACE Group consortia. Within the FEFC, tonnage and geographical rights continued to govern the individual lines serving the trade. The concepts in the IGA were now made conference-wide and the old structure with rights and tonnage limitations was eliminated. This firm agreement was intended to be the platform for important stabilisation.[33] A second initiative was the creation of the first real FEFC container freight tariff. Formal tariff rates had begun to move away from the real levels in the market place, so when this tariff was introduced, the rates were presented as 'temporarily reduced rates'. However, as Vernon Rolls observed, 'like so many temporary arrangements, it was eventually to become permanent'.[34] As part of this development, the FEFC was also in discussion with the European Shippers Council (ESC) on the wording of the FEFC's binding loyalty contract. This discussion had been going on since before the era of containerisation, but resurfaced when the ESC

Box 4.9 The FEFC five-part tariff

The original objectives of the FEFC container tariff from the early 1970s were to reassure early container users that they would not be paying more under the new system than they would have paid under the old and to produce common rules for the complete process of door-to-door transport.

As its name suggests, there were five steps in the tariff process:

1. From a point of loading, e.g. factory or warehouse.
2. Through the terminal for export.
3. On board ship, rated in the traditional per ton structure until 1982 when container rate tariffs were fully implemented;
4. Through the importing terminal.
5. Out to its destination, e.g. warehouse, distribution centre or factory.

Developed by work groups of experts from within the industry in consultation with shippers, the tariff was ready when the first full FEFC container service began from Japan in December 1971.

Source: V. Rolls, *The Far Eastern Freight Conference 1879–2004*, CAS, 2005.

raised concerns that containerisation made the validity and practicality of such contracts doubtful.

The third FEFC action area was to find out if an accommodation could be reached with Evergreen Marine. Evergreen was not prepared to join the conference but it would eventually agree to an understanding with the FEFC as a 'tolerated outsider'. As might be expected, the agreement was very difficult to maintain and after operating for about two years it was dropped in September 1984. But for a period, it provided the stability needed in the trade.

In principle, once Maersk Line's resignation was announced, contact between the FEFC and Maersk Line's management also ceased. However, life is rarely that straightforward and some contact was maintained. The resignation was due to become effective from 31 May 1982, but the FEFC management had been busy with these major initiatives, and early in May renewed contacts led to a new agreement being put in place on 24 May. The FEFC opened up Maersk Line's rights to allow full coverage of Europe as well as Asia and the loading of up to 8 per cent of the market under the new, open-to-all IGA. A limit on a sliding scale was maintained on liftings to and from the UK, a scale that increased substantially over the period 1982–1985. That largely dealt with Maersk Line's issues.

The new open IGA was to run until the end of 1985. New eastbound and westbound tariffs were implemented and an independent neutral body, similar to that already operating in trades to and from the United States, was put in place. A senior Rating Committee was established to target commodities where the outsiders had achieved 30 per cent or more penetration, with the objective of bringing these movements back to the FEFC carriers.

To rephrase Rolls slightly, 'the conference's operating methods had been radically updated'. As *Containerisation International* noted in the 1983 yearbook,

Put quite simply, containerisation and its intermodal implications have rendered obsolete some of the cherished, and until recently, unquestioned, tenets on which the conference system was founded.[35]

The Far East–United States–Far East service was unaffected by these issues because conferences related to the US trades were open – that is, they were obliged to grant access to new members and to allow existing members to leave subject to very minimal conditions. This does not mean, however, that conferences covering trades to and from the United States were benign or lacked activity, as we will see in Chapter 5.

Jumbo-ising again

While there was heavy activity on the Europe services, the Far East–United States–Far East service was also continuing to develop, and in 1982 Maersk Line signed a new contract to jumbo-ise the A-class ships for the second time. At the same time, the ships were re-engined, converting them from turbines to diesels. This lengthening increased their capacity to 2,050 TEU and took most of 1983 to complete.

The next competitive threats came from two different angles. While a number of other operators were ordering ships in relatively small numbers, Evergreen had a total of 24 container ships on order, of which 20 were rated at 2,728 TEU and four at 2,928 TEU. However, the real threat was else-where. Having sold Sea-Land to the tobacco conglomerate R. J. Reynolds in the late 1960s, Malcom McLean finally sold his shares and left his seat on the Board in 1977.

But he was not the type of man to stay still for long, and in October of the same year, McLean bought United States Lines (USL). In 1982 USL placed orders worth $770 million for 14 new container ships to be built, without any subsidy from the US government, from Korea's Daewoo shipyard. These ships were called 'jumbos': they were to provide a major leap in capacity at 4,148 TEU apiece, by far the largest container ships ever built. The ships were scheduled to serve in an extensive new round-the-world service.

In its 1984 yearbook, *Containerisation International* observed:

It is difficult to accurately calculate the current degree of over capacity in the container liner market, and even harder to predict how it will develop in the future. Nevertheless, the common wisdom of many carriers seems to suggest that it has risen to around 30 per cent from about 20 per cent in 1980/81 and can be expected to climb further in the future ... Thus, as a result of over-capacity and low rates, the liner industry is in an extremely depressed state.[36]

A selection of important developments: 1975–1979

- 1975 The Khmer Rouge take control of Phnom Penh. Khmer Rouge leader, Pol Pot, will rule Cambodia from 1975 to 1979, during which 1.7m people will be killed or die as a result of torture, disease, overwork or starvation.[37]
- 1975 The fall of Saigon to the North Vietnamese ends the Vietnam war and Vietnam is reunified in 1976.[38]
- 1975 Following the military coup in Portugal (1974), General António Ribeiro de Spinola becomes president and implements a policy of decolonisation, ending wars in Angola and Mozambique. Other Portuguese colonies to gain independence are Guinea-Bissau, Cape Verde, Sao Tomé and Principe.[39]
- 1978 The US recognises the People's Republic of China and relations are normalised.[40]
- 1979 US president, Jimmy Carter, and Soviet general secretary, Leonid Brezhnev, sign the SALT II treaty in Vienna, banning new missile programmes. The treaty represents a further step towards disarmament in US-Soviet bilateral relations.[41]
- 1979 The North Atlantic Treaty Organization (NATO) agrees to deploy intermediate-range cruise and pershing missiles in Europe. NATO will adopt a "dual-track" strategy: a simultaneous push for arms-control negotiations and the deployment of intermediate-range, nuclear-armed US missiles.[42]
- 1979 The Soviet Union invades Afghanistan. It will occupy the territory for nearly a decade.[43]

Economic

- 1975 Paul Volcker heads the US Federal Reserve during a period of *stagflation* (a period of rising prices, slow economic growth and high unemployment). He will implement monetary policies espoused by economist, Milton Friedman, as a counter-inflationary strategy.[44]
- 1975 A G6 economic summit at Rambouillet (France) endorses floating currencies.[45]
- 1978 China's Deng Xiaoping launches the economic reform known as "socialism with Chinese characteristics". The first reforms will consist of opening trade with the outside world. Farmers to be allowed to sell surplus crops on the open market.[46]
- 1978 The US Senate backs a treaty to transfer control of the Panama Canal to Panama in 1999.[47]
- 1979 The fall of the Shah in Iran causes a second oil-price shock. Oil prices will rise further owing to the Iran-Iraq war in 1980. In the period 1978–81 the real price of oil doubles.[48]
- 1979 The European Council agrees to create the European Monetary System (EMS), based on the concept of fixed, but adjustable, exchange rates; the European Currency Unit (ECU) is created.[49]

Social

- 1975 The first global UN Women's Conference is held in Mexico City, with the goals of establishing full gender equality and the elimination of gender discrimination.[50]
- 1975 Donald Carl Johanson and his team find the partial skeleton of a human ancestor more than 3.2m years old and nickname it "Lucy".[51]
- 1976 Concorde operates its first commercial flight. British Airways (BA) flies from London to Bahrain and Air France from Paris to Rio de Janeiro.[52]
- 1978 The world's first *in vitro* ("test tube") baby is born in the UK.[53]

Technological

- 1976 Apple Computer (founded by Steve Jobs, Ronald Wayne and Steve Wozniak) introduces the Apple I personal computer.[54] Apple's market value will exceed US$600bn in 2012, becoming the world's largest company by value.[55]
- 1977 Wang Laboratories introduce the first computerised word processor.[56]
- 1977 The artificial heart is patented by Robert Jarvik.[57]
- 1979 The first cellular telephone network is built in Tokyo by NTT.[58]
- 1979 The Walkman TPS-L2, the world's first portable stereo, goes on sale in Japan.[59]

Legal

- 1977 The UN adopts the Geneva Protocols – additional protocols to the 1949 Geneva Conventions, which are designed to protect victims of international armed conflicts (Protocol I) and victims of non-international armed conflicts (Protocol II). This builds on the original Geneva Convention by covering civilians.[60]
- 1979 The Convention on the Elimination of All Forms of Discrimination against Women – the bill of rights for women – is adopted by the UN General Assembly.[61]

Environmental

- 1976 The US National Academy of Science warns of damage to the ozone layer by chlorofluorocarbon (CFC) gases.[62]
- 1978 During the period of the Arab oil embargo, the US government asks a US firm, ADM, to convert a new beverage-alcohol plant into a synthetic-fuel plant. An ethanol production plant is established.[63] By 2012 the number of ethanol plants in the US will reach 209.[64]
- 1979 As the Three Mile Island nuclear power plant in Pennsylvania loses coolant, a nuclear meltdown ensues. This accident will hit the development of the nuclear power industry in the US.[65]

A selection of important developments: 1980–1984

Political

- 1980 Lech Walesa launches Solidarity, a trade union, aimed at improving workers' rights in Poland. In 1990 he will be elected president of Poland.[66]
- 1981 UK prime minister, Margaret Thatcher, is the first foreign leader invited to the US by the Reagan administration.[67] She declares on arrival: "We are both determined to sweep away the restrictions that hold back enterprise".[68]
- 1981 Egyptian president, Anwar Sadat, is assassinated and replaced by vice-president, Hosni Mubarak.[69] Mr Mubarak will rule Egypt for almost 30 years, before being overthrown in a wave of mass protests in 2011.[70]
- 1982 US President Reagan launches the Strategic Arms Reduction Talks (START) to reduce nuclear arsenals.[71]
- 1983 Mr Reagan launches the Strategic Defence Initiative (SDI) for space-based anti-nuclear defence systems.[72]
- 1984 An agreement is made between both countries for the UK to hand over Hong Kong to China in 1997.[73]
- 1984 Indian prime minister, Indira Gandhi, is assassinated by Sikh bodyguards in retaliation for the storming of the Golden Temple in Amritsar, which was intended to remove Sikh separatists from the shrine.[74]

Economic

- Early 1980s The economic policies of US president Reagan become known as "Reaganomics". These espouse reducing government spending, marginal taxes on labour and income, curtailing government regulation of the economy, and using monetary policy to help keep inflation rates low.[75]
- Early 1980s Increased leveraged-buyout activity sees a proliferation of private-equity firms, such as Bain Capital, the Blackstone Group and the Carlyle Group.[76]
- 1982 Mexico's difficulty in servicing its debt sparks a Latin American debt crisis. Brazil, Argentina and Venezuela follow. Between 1983 and 1989 much of this debt will be restructured.[77]
- 1983 Australia abandons its management of the exchange rate, opting for a floating currency.[78]

Social

- 1980s The United Nations (UN) declares the 1980s to be The Decade of Clean Drinking Water, to highlight limited access to safe drinking water. At this time, only one person in five has access to safe water worldwide.[79]
- 1980 The Cable News Network (CNN) is launched, creating the 24-hour news cycle.[80]
- 1980 The US recycles only 9.6% of its municipal rubbish. By 2007 the rate will increase to 32%. Austria and the Netherlands by 2007 will recycle 60% of municipal waste.[81]

- 1981 A rare outbreak of Kaposi's sarcoma and pneumocystis pneumonia mark the discovery of Acquired Immune Deficiency Syndrome (AIDS).[82]

Technological

- 1980 Minoru Abe patents a wind turbine to produce energy.[83]
- 1981 The International Standards Organisation (ISO) introduces ISO 6346:1981, the standard for freight containers coding, identification and marking.[84]
- 1981 IBM brings the personal computer into the mainstream by introducing its first model for under US$1,600. Two decades earlier, an IBM personal computer cost as much as US$9m.[85]
- 1983 Fred Cohen develops the first Trojan computer virus.[86] With *cybercrime* becoming a growing risk for individuals and businesses, global spending on *cyber security* will reach US$60bn in 2011.[87]
- 1983 Motorola commercialises DynaTAC 8000X, the world's first truly portable mobile phone. The handheld is priced at US$3,995.[88]
- 1984 Dr Alec Jeffreys, a British geneticist, invents DNA fingerprinting, which is later used in forensics.[89]

Legal

- 1982 The Paris Memorandum of Understanding (MoU) on Port State Control comes into force, authorising the inspection of vessels in order to reduce substandard shipping and ship pollution, and to improve living conditions on ships.[90]
- 1983 Marpol 73/78 – the International Convention for the Prevention of Pollution from Ships – comes into force. It is designed to minimise pollution of the seas, including dumping and oil and exhaust pollution.[91]
- 1983 The UN Convention on the Law of the Sea (UNCLOS) on territorial waters is signed by 117 nations, but not the US.[92]
- 1984 The UN adopts the Convention against Torture and Other Cruel, Inhuman or Degrading Treatment or Punishment.[93]

Environmental

- 1980 ECOLO, the Green party of French-speaking Belgium, is founded. It will win seats in parliament in 1981, becoming the first green party to enter parliament at a national level.[94]
- 1981 The National Aeronautics and Space Administration (NASA) reports satellite evidence that the stratospheric ozone layer is being depleted globally.[95]
- 1982 The UN General Assembly approves the World Charter for Nature.[96]
- 1984 Over 3,000 people die in Bhopal, India, when toxic gas escapes from a Union Carbide pesticide plant. Compensation is eventually paid to 570,000 victims.[97]

1980

Merchandise trade by country

Global population: 4.5bn

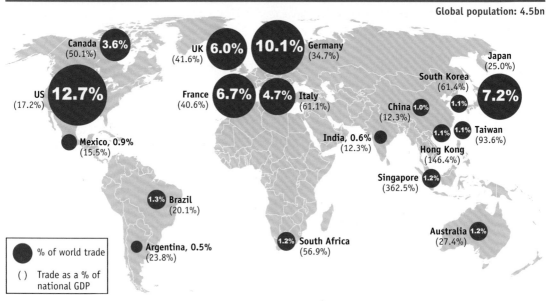

Canada **3.6%** (50.1%)

UK **6.0%** (41.6%)

Germany **10.1%** (34.7%)

Japan (25.0%)

South Korea (61.4%) **1.1%**

7.2%

US **12.7%** (17.2%)

France **6.7%** (40.6%)

Italy **4.7%** (61.1%)

China **1.0%** (12.3%)

Taiwan **1.1%** (93.6%)

Mexico, 0.9% (15.5%)

India, 0.6% (12.3%)

Hong Kong (146.4%) **1.1%**

1.3% Brazil (20.1%)

Singapore (362.5%) **1.2%**

Argentina, 0.5% (23.8%)

1.2% South Africa (56.9%)

Australia (27.4%) **1.2%**

% of world trade

( ) Trade as a % of national GDP

Note. The map is based on January 2013 boundaries. Trade is based on merchandise exports and imports.
Sources: The Economist Intelligence Unit (EIU) calculations using trade data from IMF, *Direction of Trade Statistics* (via Haver Analytics) and GDP data from EIU. Population data from UN (via Haver Analytics).

World merchandise exports

US$ trn (at 2005 prices)

0.4	0.6	0.8	1.2	1.8	2.3	3.0						
1950	1955	1960	1965	1970	1975	1980	1985	1990	1995	2000	2005	2010

Note. World exports have been rebased to 2005 constant prices using world export volumes from the World Trade Organization (WTO).
Source: EIU calculations using WTO data.

World exports of selected commodities

US$ bn (at 2005 prices)

■ Fruit, nuts and vegetables ▨ Meat and fish ■ Dairy products ▨ Computers and televisions
▨ Motor vehicles ▨ Clothing ■ Footwear

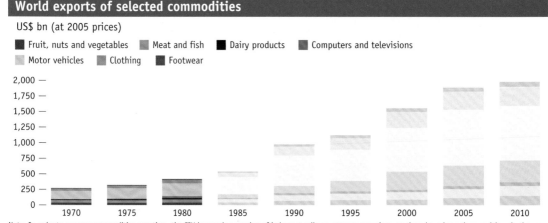

Note. In order to compare commodities over time, the EIU has made a number of judgment calls on category groupings, as there have been three revisions in the way that UN commodity data are classified. The data have also been rebased to 2005 constant prices using world export prices from the WTO. The motor vehicles category refers to road motor vehicles, including cycles, trailers, and parts and accessories; clothing includes headgear, excludes travel goods and handbags.
Source: EIU estimates using UN Comtrade, *DESA/UNSD* and WTO data.

Merchandise trade by country

Global population: 4.9bn

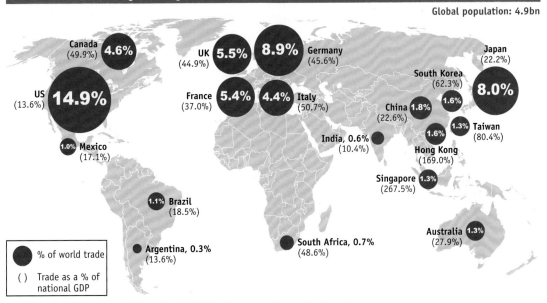

Canada (49.9%) 4.6%

UK 5.5% (44.9%)

8.9% Germany (45.6%)

Japan (22.2%)

US (13.6%) **14.9%**

France 5.4% (37.0%)

4.4% Italy (50.7%)

South Korea (62.3%)

8.0%

China 1.8% (22.6%)

1.6%

1.3% Taiwan (80.4%)

1.0% Mexico (17.1%)

India, 0.6% (10.4%)

1.6%

Hong Kong (169.0%)

Singapore 1.3% (267.5%)

Brazil 1.1% (18.5%)

Argentina, 0.3% (13.6%)

South Africa, 0.7% (48.6%)

Australia 1.3% (27.9%)

● % of world trade

( ) Trade as a % of national GDP

Note. The map is based on January 2013 boundaries. Trade is based on merchandise exports and imports.
Sources: The Economist Intelligence Unit (EIU) calculations using trade data from IMF, *Direction of Trade Statistics* (via Haver Analytics) and GDP data from EIU.
Population data from UN (via Haver Analytics).

World merchandise exports

US$ trn (at 2005 prices)

0.4	0.6	0.8	1.2	1.8	2.3	3.0	3.3					
1950	1955	1960	1965	1970	1975	1980	1985	1990	1995	2000	2005	2010

Note. World exports have been rebased to 2005 constant prices using world export volumes from the World Trade Organization (WTO).
Source: EIU calculations using WTO data.

World exports of selected commodities

US$ bn (at 2005 prices)

■ Fruit, nuts and vegetables   ▨ Meat and fish   ■ Dairy products   ▨ Computers and televisions

▨ Motor vehicles   ▨ Clothing   ■ Footwear

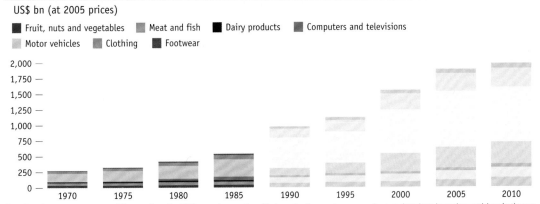

Note. In order to compare commodities over time, the EIU has made a number of judgment calls on category groupings, as there have been three revisions in the way that UN commodity data are classified. The data have also been rebased to 2005 constant prices using world export prices from the WTO. The motor vehicles category refers to road motor vehicles, including cycles, trailers, and parts and accessories; clothing includes headgear, excludes travel goods and handbags.
Source: EIU estimates using UN Comtrade, *DESA/UNSD* and WTO data.

5

Planning the Next Steps (1984–1987)

> *Containerisation has certainly been the clear catalyst or boost to globalisation. There is no question – to put it bluntly – that it has been a major contributing factor to the rapid growth of world trade ... producing the same impact on transportation that fibre optics has had on the telecommunications industry, for example.*
>
> Nariman Behravesh, Chief Economist, *Global Insight*[1]

The Global Steering Committee

The mid 1980s saw a number of significant developments and innovations within Maersk, particularly in the use of information technology, but also in respect of the FEFC and its rights structure, as well as in Maersk Line's approach to other trades. Although these did not necessarily materialise in a long series of record-breaking ships, they did result in a developmental blueprint for the business for much of the next ten years. A key driver was the challenge Ib Kruse set the global management team – to double the size of the business over a five-year period.

In November 1983, after a general business review, a new Global Steering Committee was established. Comprising Per Jørgensen (Asia), Ted Ruhly (United States), Karsten Borch (London) and chaired by Ib Kruse, the objective being to tap into the expertise and ideas that the new, stronger, locally based organisations in the 19 country offices were able to provide. These offices, which were close to the customers, were at a point where their knowledge and expertise meant more involvement would be sought from them.

By mid 1984 the Committee was able to recommend that 'Maersk Line's strategy should be to engage in and efficiently handle any worthwhile transportation requirement.'[2] Ib Kruse, when interviewed,[3] stressed that there was 'no strategy' as such and Jørgen Harling, recollecting a contemporary interview with Kruse in *Containerisation International*, remembered Kruse's reaction when asked: 'Strategy? I just need to make some money!'[4] On the other hand, it is also evident that Tom Peters' works on

Figure 5.1 Ib Kruse (third from left) inspecting the inland container terminal facility outside Keelung, Taiwan, with representatives from Maersk Line's agent Tait and Co. and the terminal operator, around 1975.

organisational effectiveness and excellence were being widely studied in the management group. It is clear that starting in early 1984 and continuing for some time to come, the initiatives launched by the Steering Committee had wide developmental implications. With an emphasis on profitability, service second to none, innovation and industry leadership, whenever economically justified, Maersk Line was to control all aspects of its service.

The On-Line Committee

To deliver effectively on the technical side of these initiatives, the Committee delegated key activities to other, more specialised teams. One of these was the On-Line Committee, which was to put forward recommendations for systems developments. With nearly all of Maersk Line's offices working online, the Steering Committee briefed the team that 'Maersk Line should strive to become a leader in this area by developing its own first-class and innovative systems for the exchange of information with customers, authorities, etc.'[5]

Early in 1985, the team proposed the Maersk Advanced Global Information Concept (MAGIC), a wide range of system developments, including online tariffs, a new booking system, a sailing schedule system, a cargo-

Figure 5.2 Customer service with the most modern facilities of the day – head set and all relevant information available on the computer screen.

tracking system, automated customs documentation and a measurable performance standards system.[6] MAGIC was to include PC dial-up-based information services and support for new technologies, such as satellite-based voice synthesising and recognition, optical character recognition, electronic data interchange (EDI) and imaging.

As part of the system definition process, for the first time ever a wide range of customers were interviewed to understand their needs and requirements. The decision was for this development to be given top priority.[7] Sea-Land was understood to be moving in a similar direction.

Finding the right balance between front-line needs for fast, responsive pricing to meet market requirements and the management responsibility of ensuring a positive bottom line for a service has always been a challenge and remains so. Markets are constantly in flux and even decentralised decision-making can rarely keep up with the dynamics of the market place. To move the process forward, it was agreed that minimum revenue requirements would be developed for each type of equipment in the major corridors. This was seen as a stop-gap solution while the On-Line team investigated how to make the freight tariffs directly accessible through the planned MAGIC system.

Other items discussed by the Global Steering Committee included upgrading the sales processes and the development and implementation of a Global Sales Training programme, headed initially by Erik Nielsen and later by Carsten Melchiors. The initial plan was to run the programme globally in mid 1985, with further sessions planned for 1986. In addition to the skills training, emphasis was put on reducing the administrative burden on sales managers to allow them to better manage their team's sales efforts.

The organisation globally had been expanding very quickly, with new recruits coming up through the ranks but also from outside Maersk, from other shipping companies as well as the freight forwarding industry. There was therefore a need 'to capture a common language across a very fast expanding organisation ... to create a common understanding of what it is that Maersk Line (whether conventional or container service) actually sells' and changing 'what was a product-oriented company to a customer-oriented company'.[8] Ultimately, the objective was to profession-alise the role of sales in Maersk Line, setting new standards.

There was also a need to ensure that the organisation globally was aligned on the importance of quality in the services provided to custom-ers. To support this, a global effort was made, with help from the American consultants Philip Crosby Associates, to create a common language and approach to quality and an understanding, among other things, of the price of non-conformance (PONC), as waste and mistakes were labelled.

The global market place

In October 1983 the UNCTAD Code of Conduct for Liner Conferences came into effect. Trade protection schemes were developing in Nigeria, Taiwan, Chile, the Philippines and elsewhere. Discussions at the Box Club indicated that although Western governments had generally been quite successful at defending their principles of free trade, fair competition and an open market, in the liner trades, it appeared that the majority of UNCTAD members preferred closed trades. National cargo reservation schemes were leading to aggressive fleet expansion and real concern was growing that this would result in over-tonnaging, not only in the container industry but also in the tanker and bulk trades.

Already in 1981, the Box Club had noted that the Chinese fleet had quadru-pled over six years and now exceeded seven million gross register tons (GRT). The only consolation for the container operators was that this expansion was directed at the bulk shipping market. Fears about shipping capacity were worsened by what was perceived as aggressive Soviet fleet expansion. In July 1983, the OECD published a paper headed 'The Long-Term Soviet Shipping

Box 5.1 The Box Club

The International Council of Containership Operators, known as the Box Club, comprises the CEOs of the major container ship operators. The membership has varied over the years as consolidation has reduced the number of major players, companies headquartered globally and serving all the world's major trade lanes.

Founded in the 1970s by Hans-Jakob Kruse, then Chief Executive of Hapag Lloyd, the purpose of the Council is to provide a forum for the open discussion of all areas of concern to the carrier members in providing scheduled container ship common carrier services in international commerce by those persons with primary responsibility for the policies and actions of the respective carrier members.

The Box Club's authority, granted by the Federal Maritime Commission,[9] covers 'the exchange of information to facilitate long-range maritime industry planning with respect to a broad range of factors, such as environmental controls, intermodal regulations, technological developments, fuel and energy requirements, monetary and fiscal policies, port development, government-controlled fleets and government programmes that affect maritime activities'.

'Members shall not engage in conduct prohibited by the Shipping Act of 1984, as amended.'[10] This specifically prohibits discussion on the pricing of services.

Policies Strategy'. This stated: 'Soviet intrusion in some trades is serious and the share they have secured in a short time by means of under-quotations is disquietingly high.'[11] At the same time, legislative developments in both the United States and Europe were advancing. In the United States, Senators Biaggi and Gorton were drafting what was to become known as the Gorton Bill, while in Europe the European Economic Community (EEC) was drafting competition rules for sea transport.

With these events as the backdrop, 1983 was a year in which world trade was stagnating and few, if any, signs of recovery were evident. The Line Department's book-closing file for 1983 did not make pleasant reading. The Far East–West Africa trade was down by 35 per cent compared to 1982. The Far East–Middle East trade was suffering because of the Iran–Iraq war and OPEC's decision in March to cut the price of oil, leading to cuts in the Middle East's development budgets. Hellenic Lines had gone bankrupt and Waterman Steamship Company was in serious financial difficulties. Box 5.2 charts world imports and exports between 1980 and 1990. The decline in world merchandise trade from 1980, the lack of growth in 1982–1983 and the return of some growth from 1984 are plain to see.

Box 5.2 World imports/exports 1980–1990

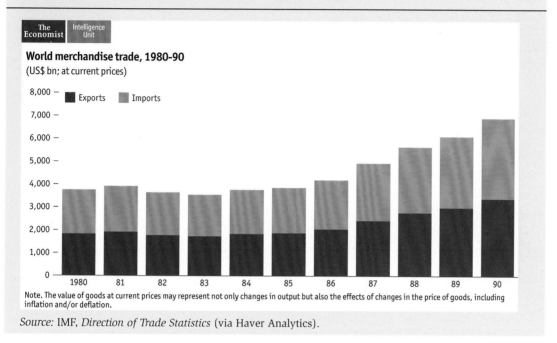

World merchandise trade, 1980-90
(US$ bn; at current prices)

■ Exports   ▨ Imports

Note. The value of goods at current prices may represent not only changes in output but also the effects of changes in the price of goods, including inflation and/or deflation.

Source: IMF, *Direction of Trade Statistics* (via Haver Analytics).

Under the circumstances, there were relatively few reasons to be optimistic about the future. But the management of Maersk Line decided to take the long view. Looking at the numbers in Box 12.1 that trace some of the main financial data related to the business between 1975 and 2012, one can surmise that the management's view of the first ten years of Maersk Line in containers had been acceptable, with maybe only 1983 providing significantly below-par results since the start-up year of 1975. The platform was solid and while global trade had just over doubled, Maesk Line was on a trajectory of growth with revenues that had grown seven-fold over the period.

In February 1984, a new study into serving the Trans Atlantic concluded that it would still not be profitable enough to recommend management to move forward. The key to that trade had not yet been found. At about the same time, an investigation was initiated into serving Vietnam. Maersk Inc. in New York was asked to investigate and sound out sources in Washington. On the basis of the advice received, it was decided to wait.

As well as these exploratory efforts, a major initiative was launched: the reorganisation of the Panama service.

Reorganising the Panama service

Box 5.3 The Panama Canal

Historically, the Panama Canal concept goes back to 1534, but in reality to 1904 when work started. Completed in 1914, it was first used on 15 August 1914.

The current Panama Canal is the first to directly link the Pacific Ocean and the Atlantic Ocean, cutting across the Isthmus of Panama. There are locks at each end to lift ships to the level of the Gatun Lake, 26.5 metres above sea level. This reduced the amount of work needed to create the canal.

- Overall length: 77.1 kilometres
- Locks: 33.5 metres wide, 320 metres long
- Transit time: 10–11 hours
- Two lock systems:
  - Atlantic end, Gatun locks, three chambers;
  - Pacific end, Pedro Miguel lock, one chamber, and Miraflores locks, two chambers
- Maximum draft: 12.6 metres
- Daily transits: approximately 40 per day.

The Panama Canal involved the excavation of over 150 million cubic metres of earth, the creation of the then largest dam in the world and man-made lake (Gatun), the pouring of more than 1.5 million cubic metres of concrete and three sets of double ships locks. Widening and other improvements are currently under development, as well as new locks, which will be 40 per cent longer and 60 per cent larger than the present locks. Completion is expected by 2015.

Maersk Line had over 500 transits of the canal in 2012, with an average canal fee charge of $270,000 per transit. Maersk Line accounted for 3.6 per cent of the total transits and 15.9 per cent of all container vessel transits, generating 7.7 per cent of the annual revenue of the Panama Canal Authority due to the large size of the average Maersk Line ship transiting the canal.

Maersk Line Panama was formed in 1992 and maintains offices in Panama and Colon. Damco Panama was formed in 2002 and APM Terminals opened an office in Panama in 2007.

Source: Maersk Line Panama

Early in 1983 a plan was put forward to split the existing Panama service and reorganise it as two separate services. The first, using nine ships, would continue to serve the US East Coast weekly, as previously, but would add calls at Kobe and Tokyo outbound from the United States, and

Miami on the journey back to the US East Coast. The Japan calls had been strongly recommended by the management of Maersk Japan for many years.

The second service would be a weekly service covering Hong Kong, Taiwan, Korea and Japan to the US West Coast, calling at Seattle, Oakland, Long Beach and Oakland again on the way back to Asia. The objective was to obtain market share at least equivalent to Maersk Line's share of sailings, while also supporting the upgrade of vessels on the Panama service, from the A-class to the new and larger L-class.

This plan reflected Maersk Line's continual monitoring of the competition on its lines and its push for differentiation. The new services were implemented in 1985. The decision to call at Japanese ports as first ports of discharge outbound from the United States allowed Maersk Line to penetrate this major new market, including the major reefer trade from the US West Coast to Japan.

The Policy Coordination Group

The Global Steering Committee remained in place. Towards the end of 1985, the Committee's composition began to change and in June 1986 it was renamed the Policy Co-ordination Group (PCG), known familiarly as 'the Quartet'. However, the objectives that the original Steering Committee had defined for Maersk Line did not change:

To be the most profitable international container transportation company in the world through:

- First-class and superior services in all respects.
- Global coverage to satisfy all customer requirements and to level out changes in trade balances and seasonalities.
- Door-to-door services to ensure maximum routing control and enhanced profits.
- Well-educated and highly motivated staff worldwide.
- Tailor-made and superior customer service.
- Maximum cost efficiency.

To achieve the objectives, it was necessary to be, and be perceived externally as, a 'leader' and not as a 'follower'. [12]

In essence, this is not fundamentally different from the simple and direct recommendation made by the original Crash Committee in 1973, that Maersk Line should go into a 'large-scale, door-to-door full container service'. However, it is certainly a more segmented and perhaps more sophisticated definition, reflecting the lessons learned during the first ten years of operations.

This relatively simple set of statements was to guide much of Maersk Line and Mercantile's development over the coming years.[13]

Opening up for lateral local expansion

A further outcome of the global leadership team was a list of possible new investment opportunities. Ib Kruse recalled: 'Figures showed that the ocean freight was far from sufficient to make a reasonable return on investment and stressed the need for side earnings from related or unrelated activities.'[14] A number of teams were put together to progress the key items and in September 1984, a letter signed jointly by Flemming Jacobs and Poul Rasmussen (then head of Maersk Line's conventional services) was sent to all Maersk Line offices. It included the guidance:

> In order to expand the range of services to Maersk Line customers, we ask that you note that Maersk Line Copenhagen encourages agencies, subject to their own independent decisions, to engage in customer related activities such as warehousing, consolidation/deconsolidation, forwarding, customs broker activities, trucking …[15]

This letter was to stimulate a development where the local country manager (a 'Maersk Top' in Maersk Line parlance) would go out and develop his local business. 'His' is deliberate: at this time, Maersk Tops were typically young, energetic, Danish men, inspired by the persona of A. P. Møller and Mærsk Mc-Kinney Møller and keen to demonstrate that they could be successful as local entrepreneurs.

The PCG also recommended investigating the feasibility of offering airfreight services from 'areas such as Hong Kong, Taiwan, Korea, and Singapore', and early in 1985, Maersk Line Hong Kong Ltd acquired 50 per cent equity in Concord Express Ltd, a prominent local air cargo consolidation company. Similar investigations continued in Frankfurt for West Germany and in Amsterdam for Holland.

Another initiative involved the provision of professional cargo insurance for customers who requested it and it was agreed to 'pursue an underwriting agency contract with the Royal Insurance Company Ltd., with the intention to make the Europe–Far East–Europe trade a pilot project'.

The PCG had a further important recommendation: that all services provided to the market 'must be of a first-class quality and fully competitive with other services in the market place and satisfy the expectation and requirements of the customers'. Finally, the PCG recommended that 'all affiliated activities directly related to the customer, such as terminals,

Figure 5.3 In the developing Maersk Line hub and spoke network, the Algeciras container terminal was one of a series of hubs.

should whenever feasible carry the Maersk name, and the name of Mercantile should be promoted for auxiliary cargo services'.

Connecting Point Spain (CPS)

A notable development at this time was the implementation of the Algeciras terminal for Maersk Line. In July 1984, the *Anna Mærsk* became the first vessel inbound from Asia to call at Algeciras with cargoes to West Africa. This development enhanced the coverage of the Spanish market, but it did more than that by opening up a wave of other opportunities. The vessels serving West African ports from Algeciras (the geared container ships *Maersk Claudine* and *Maersk Clementine*) were now able to load containers not just to and from Asia, but also Northern Europe, the Mediterranean and North America. The opportunities were even more extensive as Spanish exports to West Africa, North America and Northern Europe could also be catered for. Despite the costs involved, the overall effect was positive within the first year of service.

The implementation of the Algeciras hub provided shippers and consignees in many parts of the world with new options to buy, sell and trade goods to new markets. The flexibility and access to markets provided by hub ports at that time substantially outweighed any disadvantages:

Box 5.4 The role of the hub port in creating opportunities for trade

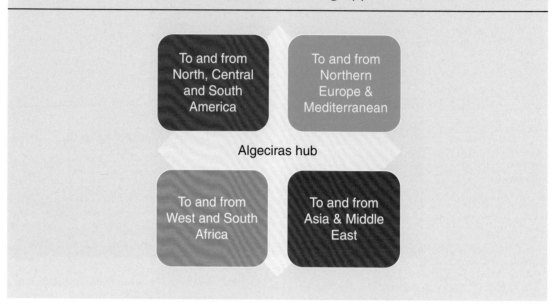

To and from North, Central and South America

To and from Northern Europe & Mediterranean

Algeciras hub

To and from West and South Africa

To and from Asia & Middle East

Shippers can benefit from the unit cost advantage of inter-connecting routes and having a single entry-point for the purchase of global shipping services.[16]

From another perspective, Jørgen Harling commented: 'The Algeciras hub port put us in a unique position to grow a lot faster and to roll out our concept globally much, much faster than any of our competitors could do.'[17]

A review of the CPS concept late in 1986 by a team led by Maersk Line's head of Finance and Systems, Ole Larsen, concluded that developments were on track. Expansion of the terminal area was recommended to ensure space was available to accommodate the expected volume growth. It was also recommended that Maersk in Spain evaluate the possibility of 'selling' berthing programmes to acceptable third parties – that is, carriers whose need for the berth did not conflict with Maersk Line's needs – in order to also reduce the fixed costs of the terminal.

At that time, Maersk Line's use of the facility was highly concentrated at weekends.[18] In contrast, today's usage spans most of the week, with between two and five ships calling every day, including feeder ships. To cater to the growth, a third crane was added in 1989 and today the terminal operates a total of 19 cranes, normally deploying seven or occasionally eight cranes on an Emma-class ship, with productivity of up to 220 moves per berth-hour.[19]

The overall success of CPS stimulated investigations in 1986 into further possibilities: developing a Connecting Point Caribbean and expanding on the existing Connecting Point Singapore.

Competition and the market

All these initiatives were important steps in at least keeping pace with competition. By the end of 1985, Evergreen was the largest container operator in the world, with a 95,000 TEU capacity and was in the process of receiving 16 new ships, the G-class vessels that would give them the capability of running two round-the-world services, westbound and eastbound. The second largest carrier was another outsider, US Lines (USL), which had now received six of its 'jumbo' ships and would shortly be operating 66,000 TEU. Maersk Line was running third with 63,000 TEU and Sea-Land fourth with 51,000 slots.

Market volumes to the United States were at last beginning to increase and rates were also improving. Those monitoring the trade began to see the effect of competition from outsiders. While the total Far East to United States volumes had risen by over 25 per cent, the conference market had grown by less than 15 per cent, indicating further penetration by outsiders. Outbound from the United States, rates had fallen to the level of a decade earlier, and although Maersk Line's volumes were about the same as the previous year (1984), the outbound freight list was only $2.85 million per sailing, compared to $3.81 million in 1981.[20]

Figure 5.4 *Karen Mærsk* and *Sine Mærsk* at APM Terminals' Pier 400 facility near Los Angeles. Its 484 acres are nearly ten times larger than the Long Beach terminal of 1985.

Box 5.5 Competitors and changes over time

Top ten carriers	1983*	Capacity (TEU)	1996	Capacity (TEU)	2001	Capacity (TEU)	2006	Capacity (TEU)	2012	Capacity (TEU)
1	US Lines	88,028	Evergreen	204,061	Maersk-Sealand	692,574	Maersk Line	1,523,347	Maersk Line	2,200,491
2	Evergreen	69,728	Sea-Land	196,483	P&O NedLloyd	381,481	MSC	736,301	MSC	1,983,174
3	Sea-Land	61,002	Maersk Line	194,071	Evergreen	355,100	Evergreen	470,234	CMA CGM	1,326,575
4	Hapag Lloyd	53,636	COSCO	163,650	Hanjin/ Senator	301,378	CMA CGM	424,494	COSCON	623,221
5	Maersk Line	51,250	NYK	127,400	MSC	300,543	APL	326,291	Hapag Lloyd	620,060
6	NedLloyd	51,186	Mitsui-OSK	121,085	APL	244,934	China Shipping	317,541	Evergreen	597,623
7	OCL	43,986	Hanjin	111,900	COSCO	239,958	COSCO	308,223	APL	583,949
8	Mitsui-OSK	33,349	NedLloyd	106,889	CMA CGM	187,497	NYK	292,304	Chine Shipping	534,450
9	OOCL	32,717	Hyundai	101,992	NYK	167,588	Hanjin	291,207	CSAV	528,026
10	NYK	30,595	MSC	99,306	CP Ships	160,206	Mitsui-OSK	240,391	Hanjin	513,070
Totals		515,477		2,001,816		4,269,032		6,880,568		12,892,595

Source: Containerisation International Yearbooks © reproduced with the permission of Lloyds List Group. *1983 includes ships on order

Box 5.6 The US shipping approach

The US Shipping Act of 1916 was the first statute in the world to cover liner conferences, laying down rules for the public control of conferences and cartels. It also created the Federal Maritime Board, now Commission (FMC).

Discriminatory practices were prohibited but otherwise conferences were exempt from anti-trust laws. Conferences were to be open to new members and allow members to leave. Loyalty agreements with shippers were permitted. The Act was reformed in 1961 through the Bonner Act, which required all carriers to file tariffs with the FMC.

In the 1980s proposals for new legislation put before Congress resulted in the 1984 US Shipping Act, which reinforced most of the provisions of the 1916 Act and added the right of independent action on freight rates, with the exception of service contracts unless a conference specifically allowed that possibility. Loyalty contracts were made illegal. Consequently, unless a conference gave permission, members could not enter into individual service contracts or leave a contract between a conference and a shipper.

In 1998, this latter provision was changed under the Ocean Shipping Reform Act, which also abolished the requirement to file tariffs with the FMC and allowed conference members to enter into individual service contracts. Overall, this Act 'moved the centre of gravity of the organisation of US trade away from open conferences and towards discussion agreements and voluntary guidelines concerning individual service contracts'.

Source: L. O. Blanco, *Shipping Conferences under EC Anti-Trust Law*, Hart Publishing, 2007.

Container-handling manpower was short in Long Beach, causing delays to the ships, and requiring increased bunker consumption in order to maintain schedules. Another consequence of space pressure, which had a ripple effect throughout the process chain, was an increase in turn-around time on equipment.

The Maersk Line terminal in Long Beach also suffered from space pressure and to alleviate this an agreement with the Port of Long Beach was concluded with Maersk Line moving to a new terminal facility with a total of 54 acres of land in mid 1985.[21]

The 1984 US Shipping Act

Following on from the significant deregulation of the US trucking and rail industries in 1980, a number of proposals to update US legislation on shipping had been under way. Initiated originally by Senator Inouye in 1980, then by Congressman Murphy, the new approach by Senators Slade Gorton and Mario Biaggi had seen passage of a bill that was, as the Box

Box 5.7 The General Agreement on Tariffs and Trade (GATT)

In 1947, more than 150 countries entered into an arrangement known as the General Agreement on Tariffs and Trade (GATT). Its purpose was 'the substantial reduction of tariffs and other trade barriers and the elimination of preferences, on a reciprocal and mutually advantageous basis'.[23]

This agreement initiated the Kennedy and subsequently the Tokyo Rounds of multi-lateral trade negotiations, which ended with the Uruguay Round in 1995. When launched, the GATT did not apply to trade in services.

The Uruguay Round was the most ambitious of the series and led to new agreements covering services, capital movements, intellectual property rights, textiles and agriculture. It also created the World Trade Organization (WTO), which came into being on 1 January 1995.

The WTO implements tariff and trade agreements, provides a forum for negotiating other reductions in trade barriers and also settles policy disputes while enforcing trade rules.

The ninth round of these discussions, the Doha Development Agenda, was launched in 2001. Pending completion of the Doha Round, a large number of regional and bi-lateral trade agreements have been put in place, while others are under development.

Club minutes from their meeting in Paris in February 1982 indicated, 'a truly historic document recommending the revision of 65 years of US shipping regulatory policy'.[22]

The environment was one where the UNCTAD code of practice had come into effect at the end of 1983 and trade discrimination practices were being taken seriously. Waivers were required for cargoes moving between the Philippines and the United States and Indonesia and the United States, in direct contradiction to the US position on free trade. Unless a waiver was obtained, carriage was limited to ships flying either the flag of the originating country or of the United States. In addition, the GATT was active in encouraging the development of guidelines on 'trade in services', which also included shipping services.

The Bill, which became the 1984 US Shipping Act, was to fundamentally change the rules for international shipping as they related to the United States, while domestic shipping continued largely to be covered by the 1916 Act, restricted to US flag operators. The Act freed intermodal rate-making from anti-trust constraints; this, combined with the deregulation of rail transport in the United States, led to a new competitive element being established. American President Lines (APL) quickly led the way by establishing a comprehensive 'double-stack' rail network to distribute

Figure 5.5 The impressive sight of a double-stack container train crossing the vast openness of the northern United States between the container terminal in Tacoma, Washington, and the city of Chicago.

containers across the United States. *Containerisation International* noted that 'as of late 1985 seven ocean carriers and two railroads were operating dedicated stack-trains for their own account, generating 44 departures of up to 560 TEU each per week'.[24]

The Sea-Land organisation had been a major influence in defining the new rules, which were designed 'to be non-discriminatory and to reduce regulation, to provide an economic system for liner shipping in harmony with and responsive to international maritime practice and to encourage the development of a US flag liner fleet capable to meeting national security needs'.[25] John Clancey, President of Sea-Land, maintained that Sea-Land had had 'a message that we needed to get out regarding containerisation' on a continuous basis since the 1960s. Initially, 'all the laws and all the rules were built and predicated on break-bulk operations ... [E]very customer wanted individual contracts and I had met enough shippers and spent enough time with members of Congress to know that, unless we addressed their concerns, Congress was going to address their concerns.'[26] This was confirmed from a wider industry perspective by Ib Kruse, who commented that 'Sea-Land was very instrumental in liaising with influential people behind US shipping policy and also with shipper organisations in the United States. Whether authorised or not, they were really speaking for the industry.'[27]

The Act also created the right of independent action and automatically gave those rights to all carriers on registration of the action with the FMC and on public notice of the rate change. Some of the details, such as the essential terms, volume commitments and corridors, were to be publicly available through the FMC, although the rates themselves were not. From a customer perspective, these changes provided an opportunity for more flexibility and added competition.

Other clauses meant that the FMC became the sole arbiter in maritime affairs. The Act was to remain in force from 1984 until the Ocean Shipping Reform Act (OSRA) came into effect in 1999.

The independent action clause was a major driver of the creation of the Trans Pacific Westbound Rate Agreement (TPWRA), established in an attempt to minimise the risk of a rate war. However, it failed to prevent such activity, as over 1984 and into 1985, for example, reefer rates from the US West Coast to Hong Kong for oranges fell from $5,044 per 40-foot container to $2,424.[28]

Interest in European short sea services

While Ib Kruse indicated that there had been no specific strategy for Maersk Line, a number of business opportunities did present themselves and some were pursued.

One was building an integrated network that would serve the inter-European market, complementing Maersk Line's deep-sea capabilities. Actively promoted by Karsten Borch, at that time Managing Director of The Maersk Company Limited in the UK, the idea was to develop and/or acquire services that could be built into an integrated capability.

In August 1983, a pilot proposal was put forward by Maersk UK to launch a service covering Hull in the UK, Bremerhaven in Germany, Gothenburg in Sweden and Aarhus in Denmark, but this was ultimately not pursued. Other avenues were explored on a regular basis. In 1984, an effort was launched to acquire a company called PortLink, but at the last minute the company was sold by its owners to Stena Line of Sweden.

Not to be put off, Karsten Borch noted one day in the *Times* of London that Unilever was in the process of selling a wide range of subsidiary companies, and made enquiries to determine whether the sale included Norfolk Line, a major ferry and cargo trailer operation. After several months of negotiation, Norfolk Line became part of the Maersk organisation. Norfolk Line was to go through a series of changes and developments, including expansion with Kent Line and Brit Line, investment in a series of new, larger ships, a move from its original UK base in Great Yarmouth to

Figure 5.6 Norfolk Line ferries passing while crossing the Channel en route between Holland and the United Kingdom.

Felixstowe, and the development of a short sea container operation that specialised in services to and from Ireland. However, it never developed into the integrated service network that was originally conceived, and some 25 years later, in 2009, Norfolk Line was sold to the Danish ferry operator DFDS.

Over this period a number of other European distribution companies were also acquired. These included Skandi, a road/rail swap-body operator that moved goods mainly between Scandinavia and Northern Europe, and Mahé Transport, a similar company. In 1994, in parallel with the beginning of deregulation of the European rail operations, European Rail Shuttle (ERS) was formed, initially with P&O and Sea-Land, to manage the rail distribution of containers between the main European ports and interior hubs.

On the Europe–Far East–Europe service

The year 1984 saw the last of the A-class ships lengthened and re-fitted with diesel engines. A review of the use of the rather unusual liquid tanks on the L-Class ships noted that it was ahead of budget, being mainly used for latex from Southeast Asia to Europe and liquid chemicals in the opposite direction. Reefer capacity was also growing. Maersk Line's reefer market shares in the main trades were doing well, despite rates being under pressure in several areas of the world.

U.S. Lines (USL) started its round-the-world service and many were watching to see how it developed. Barber Blue Sea of Norway introduced large roll-on–roll-off (RO-RO) vessels into the Middle East trades, while Waterman Steamship of the US withdrew due to economic difficulties. USL continued to develop but it was clear that it faced challenges. In August 1986, it was reported to have lost more than $150 million in the first six months of the year; by December it was reporting the loss of a further $90 million in the third quarter and was expected to file for Chapter XI protection. That month, its Econ ships began to be arrested for failure to pay outstanding bills – one ship in Singapore, two in Hong Kong and a smaller ship in Bremen. 'The company's problems dented the McLean mystique as nothing else could have done.'[29]

At this point, the story of USL becomes messy: it slowly came to light that the Export-Import Bank of Korea held first priority lien on the Econ ships, while seven other banks, including CitiBank and Bank of America, held the remaining debt. Second priority liens were held by Daewoo Corporation, the builders of the ships. USL was now in Chapter XI bankruptcy protection, with all their services stopped, but for some time to come there was real concern that Daewoo might take the ships over and operate them.

But as one competitor receded, another appeared, this time in the shape of Senator Lines, another outsider headed up by Karl-Heinz Sager, a former Hapag-Lloyd executive, and based at the old Hanseatic port of Bremen in Germany.[30]

Competition and the FEFC

There were other competitor developments in 1984, with implications for the FEFC. In Europe, continuing issues over the capacity of Evergreen and Yang Ming lines were discussed regularly at FEFC meetings. When Yang Ming announced that it would put four new buildings of 3,000 TEU capacity into the trade, it was estimated that the outsider share of the total trade would climb from 28 per cent in 1982 to 44 per cent by 1986.

The Trans-Siberian Railway (TSR) had moved some 14,000 TEU to Iran and 20,000 TEU to Western Europe in the first six months of 1984, while the new Baikal-Amur line under construction at the time would allow commercial capacity to double. The inexorable growth in outsider shares also led to the breakdown in the working agreement between the FEFC

Box 5.8 Comparison of the United States and China in world trade development 1980–2010 (at current prices)

	1980	1985	1990	1995	2000	2005	2010
United States							
Merchandise trade (billion dollars)	478.3	575.3	910.1	1,354.9	2,010.6	2,637.0	3,245.8
Percentage of world trade	12.7	14.9	13.2	13.2	15.5	12.4	10.7
Percentage of gross domestic product	17.2	13.6	15.7	18.3	20.2	20.9	22.4
China							
Merchandise trade (billion dollars)	37.6	69.8	116.6	281.1	474.4	1,422.9	2,974.3
Percentage of world trade	1.0	1.8	1.7	2.7	3.7	6.7	9.8
Percentage of gross domestic product	12.3	22.6	28.8	37.1	39.8	62.2	50.0

Source: Economist Intelligence Unit

and Evergreen, which was cancelled with effect from July 1984. The good news, however, was that trade with China was beginning to grow rapidly, albeit from a very low level. That growth would continue, and really take off in the first few years of the 21st century.

In the FEFC, within the Inter-Group Agreement (see Chapter 4), Maersk Line was doing well with a share of just over 8 per cent. TRIO continued to be by far the largest carriers with about 50 per cent, while ScanDutch and the ACE Group had about 20 per cent each. Irrespective of this, the FEFC faced a number of risks, and pressures were building. Among other items, Maersk Line's agreement with the FEFC was due to expire at the end of 1985. In February that year, the chairman, Kerry St Johnston of P&O, initiated a discussion with member lines on ways and means of finding a more flexible compromise on tonnage rights within the conference. C. H. Tung of OOCL proposed that they should be made fully flexible, and while Maersk Line supported this position, it was not considered realistic at this stage. At the end of the year, the *Far Eastern Economic Review* reported OOCL's half-year results as a loss of $228 million.

In February 1986 the FEFC noted that Deutsche SeeRederei (DSR) of Rostock, East Germany, was likely to exceed its rights by substantial margins. DSR, which was operating inside the FEFC but was not a

---

Box 5.9 Maersk Line in China

China: some key economic facts
- Foreign direct investment in China exceeds $1.2 trillion.
- China's capital outflow was estimated at $60 billion in 2012, making it the fifth largest overseas investor country.
- China has about $3.5 trillion in capital reserves.
- China's manufacturers do not need to look beyond their own borders for sustainable consumer demand.[31]

China has evolved into an independent engine of regional growth and a larger source of final demand for a number of emerging developing economies, including the Philippines, The Republic of Korea and Taiwan, Province of China.[32]

Maersk Line had been serving China via Hong Kong with a representative office in Guangzhou since 1984, but in late 1994, following political pressure from the EU Commissioner Sir Leon Brittan, licences were obtained that allowed Maersk to open its first offices there. Lars Reno Jakobsen was asked to move to Beijing to start the process, before handing the fledgling organisation over to Tom Behrens-Sørensen in 1994.

Today, Maersk's liner, logistics, terminal and other related activities involve some 125 offices and over 21,000 employees. Activities in China are managed from Maersk's Hong Kong office, which also has regional responsibility for Japan, Korea and Taiwan. These activities involve:

- Maersk Line: operating in China since 1994. Some 41 offices, a staff of over 1,900 people and a freight turnover in 2012 estimated at over $7.5 billion.
- Damco: operating in China since 1998. Now has offices in 21 cities, seven warehouse facilities, a staff of over 3,000 and a turnover in excess of $900 million.
- APM Terminals: with investments of over $450 million in facilities in Shanghai, Qingdao, Dalian, Xiamen, Tianjin and Guangzhou, as well as 13 offices and over 7,000 staff.

Other activities include MCC Transport; Maersk Container Industries, with two factories and over 6,000 staff; salvage experts Svitzer; and a global service centre in Chengdu with over 1,200 staff. Since late 1996, Maersk has purchased over 110 ships from yards in China with an accumulated value of over $3.5 billion.

Source: Maersk China, 2013

signatory to the Neutral Body agreement, asked for substantially improved rights, a request Maersk Line supported with the proviso that DSR then join the Neutral Body agreement. The Box Club meeting in Mexico that month also recorded that 'the total two-way trade between the EEC and Taiwan amounts to approximately 190,000 TEU in 1985, whereas the Taiwanese companies Evergreen and Yang Ming are able to offer 500,000 TEU slots annually on the Europe/Far East route'. In September 1986, Maersk Line wrote to the FEFC also requesting additional rights 'to allow a fair return on investment and customer satisfaction'.

While the request was rejected, Kerry St Johnston of P&O used corridor discussions at another meeting to sound out a number of other owners and on his return to Europe, through a number of telephone conversations, he indicated that Maersk Line's aspirations could be resolved by buying someone else's tonnage rights. Although Ib Kruse was sceptical, Kerry had a proposal.

CMB and CR 'rights'

His idea was for Maersk Line to buy the rights from Companie Maritime Belge (CMB) and Chargeurs Réunis (CR), both members of the ACE Group consortium. Contact between the various parties was established, and a letter from Copenhagen to Marc Saverys of CMB in mid-November 1986 summarised what Maersk Line was interested in acquiring, but CMB/CR's reply suggested that no commonality was being achieved.

Kerry St Johnston, as FEFC Chairman, hosted a meeting with Maersk at the beginning of December to understand the issues, and in mid-December a meeting was arranged in Antwerp where all the interested parties met. Discussions progressed but a number of internal ACE Group issues needed to be resolved before CMB/CR rights could be sold.

While these discussions were continuing, a message was received from OCL that they would be changing their name with effect from 1 January 1987 to P&O Containers Ltd (POCL) to coincide with P&O's 150th anniversary.

Meanwhile, the FEFC was also working to improve the effectiveness of the Neutral Body through the implementation of a new manifesto, committing the senior management of the lines to the straight and narrow. Flemming Jacobs, now head of Maersk Line and reporting to Ib Kruse, commented at an FEFC meeting that 'the level of malpractice [authors' note: discounting] had increased tremendously even since the last meeting in September'.[33]

The telephone lines between London, Copenhagen, Paris and Brussels carried a lot of extra traffic in January 1987 as a series of proposals was debated. A number of meetings between Maersk Line, CMB and CR ended with one in Antwerp on 19 February which broke through the impasse and concluded the deal. Maersk Line's first acquisition was in place. With it,

Maersk Line bought rights in the FEFC to and from Northern Europe and the Mediterranean, being 'the entire volumes of such liftings by Chargeurs Réunis, Companie Maritime Belge and Franco-Belgian Services ... and which is presently estimated to correspond to 5.63 per cent eastbound and 5.09 per cent westbound of the total IGA volumes as presently calculated with the IGA and that these entitlements are granted without any sub-limitations whatsoever'.[34]

Despite this agreement, the other lines serving the Mediterranean were not comfortable with Maersk Line serving that part of the world. Maersk Line mobilised its lawyers – Holman, Fenwick & Willan in London – prompting Kerry St Johnston to complain about the sending of 'exceedingly legalistic messages, which took a barrage of lawyers to interpret', but the gesture had the desired effect. On 4 March, the FEFC issued a press release advising the trade that the IGA had been committed to by all the FEFC carriers for another four years. The Chairman noted that 'this should be a valuable contribution towards stability in a major trade'.[35]

The same day as the FEFC press release, Maersk Line issued one of its own, announcing that with effect from April 1987, the existing fortnightly service via the Suez Canal would be upgraded to three monthly sailings and that from the end of 1988 the service would be upgraded further to weekly sailings, all as the result of having purchased the CMB/CR rights. Maersk Line was now a significant player in the overall Europe–Far East–Europe trade, achieving an aspiration that went all the way back to the 1950s.

The Middle East, Africa – and some casualties

The overall FEFC solution was certainly a key development in the mid 1980s; however, it was not the only one. Several other developments had been moving forward in parallel.

In 1984, Sea-Land had emerged from the R. J. Reynolds Corporation as an independent, publicly traded company with stock trading on the New York Stock Exchange. That year, the company achieved the highest revenues and earnings in its 28-year history. However, in 1986, Sea-Land would be acquired by CSX Corporation for some $800 million; CSX's strategy was to integrate its rail, sea and overland cargo movements into an holistic service capability with annual transportation revenues of some $7 billion.

1984 saw Waterman Steamship being relieved of its two lighter aboard ship (LASH) ships by the US Maritime Administration (MARAD) and ending its Far East services. A casualty of the late 1970s had been another

Box 5.10 The Suez Canal

Historically, the Suez Canal dates back to Pharaoh Senausret III (1878–1839 BCE), who was the first to link the Mediterranean with the Red Sea via the River Nile.

The current Suez Canal is the first to link the Mediterranean and the Red Sea directly and was opened for navigation on 17 November 1869.

- Overall length: 193.3 km
- Transit time: 12–16 hours
- Southbound: two convoys per day
- Northbound: one convoy per day
- Two passing areas: Port Said by-pass: 36.5 km; Great Bitter Lakes: 27.5 km
- Maximum draft: 26.4 m
- Maximum deadweight: 240,000 tons
- Permissible speed: 11–14 kmh
- Daily transits: approximately 50 per day, both ways.

The Suez Canal is the longest canal in the world with no locks. Navigation takes place day and night and is managed through a Vessel Traffic Management System radar network.

Maersk Line made 1,569 transits of the canal in 2012, with an average canal fee charge of $455,000 per transit. Maersk Line accounted for 9 per cent of the total transits, but 14 per cent of the annual revenue of the Suez Canal Authority due to the large size of the average Maersk Line ship transiting the canal.

Maersk Line Egypt SAE was formed in 1998 and maintains four offices: Cairo, Alexandria, Port Said and Suez.

Damco Egypt was formed in 1999 and operates from offices in Cairo, Alexandria and Port Said.

APM Terminals has been operating the Suez Canal Container Terminal since 2004. The facility includes 18 quay cranes and handled 3.2 million TEU in 2011.

Source: Maersk Line Egypt

LASH operator, Pacific Far East Lines, while in 1981, Seatrain Container Lines filed for bankruptcy, owing some $515 million. In Japan, too, there were casualties, with the container operator Yamashita Shinnihon Line merging initially into Japan Line, both of which were eventually taken over by Mitsui-OSK Line in 1989.

The national freight bureaus, mainly set up by the African countries, were very active in Europe and were not only allocating volumes to carriers, but were also setting transport rates and charging commissions.

A number of countries had established such operations; meanwhile Germany, Holland, Belgium and Italy had protested and were working with other EEC countries in an attempt to bring these developments under control and create a common EEC approach.

The continuing Iran–Iraq war was heavily impacting trade in the Middle East, with many development projects either stalled or stopped. Meanwhile in West Africa, Maersk Line's services to and from the area initially provided a monthly and later a fortnightly service via Algeciras in southern Spain – competing with the conference that covered this area, which was still largely based on conventional or semi-container services operating direct.

Maersk Line was also working on other developments. To support the new Pacific Northwest service, Ted Ruhly's North American organisation was opening offices in Vancouver and Seattle, while in China a unique (for its time) terminal operation through the port of Zhang Jia Gang was being investigated.

Meanwhile, Mercantile had nominally opened a representative office in Shanghai in 1985 and was now offering consolidation services to Europe, the first service provider to do so.

And, at the end of 1985, Ib Kruse formed a team to analyse the worldwide reefer trades, as Maersk Lines' reefer volumes were growing rapidly.

From a legislative perspective, a lot was also happening. The US Shipping Act had now been in place for about a year and the FMC was complimented on its operation by the Box Club at its meeting in Singapore: areas of ambiguity were being addressed quickly. The only area of significant concern to ship owners was the independent action clause, which was already seen as weakening the rate-making authority inherent in the conference system.

Holland and Germany had ratified the UNCTAD Code of Conduct, while the UK and Scandinavia were about to accede. At the same time, the EEC was working on a common maritime policy that would include competition rules for liner conferences.

Korea, meanwhile, was implementing rules that would directly support the Korean lines while India announced that it would use the UNCTAD code to reserve 40 per cent of its cargoes for Indian ships. Other Asian countries were also implementing discriminatory trade practices, while the Soviet, Polish and Chinese fleets were expected to increase by some 60–70 per cent by the end of 1985.

Maersk Line's position on these developments was made known not only via the Box Club, but also in active participation in the Danish Shipowners Association, where Knud Pontoppidan and his small team worked assiduously, particularly with the European Commission, both to raise the issues and minimise the worst effects of these discriminatory moves.

In its 1986 yearbook, *Containerisation International* summarised these developments:

There is no doubt that the container shipping industry is currently experiencing a period of profound structural change . . . which in many ways [is] as fundamental as the original switch from conventional break-bulk to container liner services proved to be.[36]

Of course, it was not just shipping that was experiencing profound change. US President Ronald Reagan was pursuing what became known as 'Reaganomics', by reducing government spending, marginal taxation on labour and income and curtailing government regulation of the economy, while using monetary policy to keep inflation low. Meanwhile, countries like Mexico were struggling to service their debts, leading to default in 1982, followed by Brazil, Argentina and Venezuela.

One Maersk Line

During the containerisation process it had been practical to maintain two departments responsible for liner activities, one managing the conventional liner services and the other focusing on container activities, 'with a view to achieving optimal integration and future expansion of services as well as to avoid duplication in administration'. By 1985, most of the previously significant conventional services had been containerised or were planning to become so. At the end of 1985, Maersk's PCG recommended merging the two profit centres into one. And so, in January 1986, it was announced that from 1 May the conventional Line Department would be merged with Maersk Container Line, taking the consolidated name of Maersk Line.

By this time, the management of the A.P. Moller Group had also been strengthened and now consisted of a total of five Partners: Ib Kruse, Leif Arnesen, Karsten Borch, Jess Søderberg and the senior Partner, Mærsk McKinney Møller. Ib Kruse retained overall responsibility for the new Maersk Line, but his time was taken up more and more with his other major responsibility, Maersk Oil and Gas. The day-to-day management of Maersk Line passed to Flemming Jacobs, closely supported by the quiet-spoken but deeply knowledgeable Knud Erik Møller-Nielsen, known to all as Erik.

Maersk Line now had to find the optimal way of structuring the organisation in Copenhagen. The individual services were established as largely self-contained business units, with responsibility for day-to-day commercial and operational issues. This structure also ensured fast decision-making and clear bottom-line responsibility and would 'assist to develop all-round shipping people dedicated to maximising net profitability for the individual investments'. In effect, all these steps were a direct follow-up on the original 1970 McKinsey approach and the subsequent HR strategy of the A.P. Moller Group.

The reorganisation revealed a shortage of experienced staff in Maersk Line and the PCG consequently emphasised 'the necessity of a planned, coordinated, cohesive and consistent staff management and training, thereby creating an *international* pool of staff' and also advanced suggestions as to how this could be achieved in conjunction with the Staff Department.

The need for qualified staff was reinforced by a review of agency representation, which concluded that Maersk Line needed to strengthen its representation in a number of areas. Offices were opened in Italy, Switzerland and Austria, as well as in the Ivory Coast, Togo and Senegal in West Africa. In the Middle East, work was conducted to develop exclusive 'Maersk units' within the local agents' organisations, while in China it was decided to strengthen and expand the organisation further, in view of the potential of the market.[37] Maersk Line's relative lack of experience in India and Pakistan meant that decisions about offices there were postponed.

Conference affairs had been discussed regularly, and in November 1985, the PCG concluded that the future liner environment would be fairly deregulated and that carriers would need greater responsiveness, flexibility and innovative pricing in addition to other service qualities. Consequently a certain degree of 'freedom to act' in Maersk Line's best interests would be needed. The recommendation was that Maersk Line must not hold on to a general policy of being a conference member, but take a more flexible approach to individual trades.

Service pricing was to have the flexibility to be handled on a customer basis when a global customer with multiple trade lanes was involved; a growing development in the business. The key service parameters were 'the necessity to react quickly to customer enquiries and the importance of immediate reaction to changes in the market place',[38] to enable the front-line offices to work effectively.

Another notable shift in mindset was the understanding that transit-time and reliability – critical criteria for port-to-port services – should be extended to door-to-door services. In the days of conventional shipping, services were port-to-port and the importer had to pick up goods at the port of entry; little cargo now moved on that basis as containers generally moved point-to-point, that is, from factory to distribution centre or store. As part of this approach, owned and/or managed terminals in key areas were seen to increase control and enhance scheduling security.[39] Similar to Sea-Land and P&O's approach, control of such facilities could also be developed into profitable businesses.

The day-to-day business

The financial results at the end of 1985 and beginning of 1986 were not at the levels management wanted to see. The conflict between Iran and Iraq that had been running since September 1980, and would not come to an end before August 1988, continued to have an impact. Overall, general market conditions were not very favourable throughout much of the early 1980s: 'The decade began with a rapidly escalating crisis which reached its deepest point by 1983 as the impact of a structural tonnage glut was exacerbated by a severe global trade recession.'[40] In response, major cost-trimming exercises were implemented, followed by further annual cost reduction efforts.

In April 1986, the major analysis of the global reefer trades was concluded. The report looked not only at the container trades, but also at the strengths and weaknesses of the reefer ships and put forward a number of suggestions for Maersk Line to expand into new reefer trades. The team noted that by mid 1986, Maersk Line was already providing the market with reefer container capacity equivalent to 33 average-sized reefer ships. A relatively small investment could increase the reefer capacity on the container ships by another 50 per cent.

A second report that month, from Erik Møller-Nielsen, summarised opportunities in the Caribbean and Central and South America. At that time the Caribbean and Central America area was seen as offering only limited volumes. However, it was believed that the United States' Caribbean Basin Initiative, which aimed to offer financial assistance, lower import tariffs and preferential quotas, would lead to growth, while competition came mainly from Sea-Land and Evergreen. It was recommended to enter this area with transfers via Miami if or when a Trans Atlantic service was implemented.

Erik Møller-Nielsen and Maersk's North American management saw South America as a definite opportunity, despite its economic challenges and rigid cargo reservation schemes. Local criticism of these schemes was seen as a sign that relaxation was likely to follow at some stage. Brazil had substantial trade with North America and Europe and the main commodities moving were coffee, footwear, textiles, automobiles and spare parts – all capable of moving in containers. Maersk Line's levels of service were expected to 'undoubtedly have a great impact on the trade ... The US government, US shippers, US consignees and Brazilian exporters all want to change the present cargo reservation schemes.'[41]

While these reports were being developed, one of the first actions of the newly merged Maersk Line was to conduct a review of its current liner services and consider new opportunities 'with the aim of rationalising and expanding Maersk Line's liner services' in direct continuation of the McKinsey recommendation of 1969.[42]

A Crash Committee delivered an initial report in June 1986, but work continued throughout the rest of the year. The report recommended expansion for the period 1986–1990 and reviewed the availability of ships, including the transfer of ships from one service to another. The report looked at each service in turn, and it was clear that the main challenges were the Far East–Middle East and United States–Middle East trades. The continuing Iran–Iraq war was distorting and reducing trade flows and volumes and making predicting these nearly impossible.

The Far East–Middle East service was to be continued with the Optima ships (built 1978–1979). As the name implies, these ships were designed to cater for the wide range of commodity types moving in this trade. They combined a very flexible under-deck capability to accommodate pallets as well as containers, with a stern loading ramp giving access to 900 metres of trailer deck for wheeled vehicles. The ships were also equipped with their own cranes and, working in tandem, could accommodate heavy lifts of up to 120 tons.

The recommendation for the United States–Middle East service was to continue with chartered ships until the converted C-class ships were

Figure 5.7 The diversity of the Optima – containers and own cranes on deck, wheeled cargo and a variety of break-bulk cargoes in the cargo holds.

available. The conversion would provide a fleet of seven 'new' container ships in a short space of time and at a much lower price than new buildings.

Based on the success of the new operation via Algeciras, which was to be expanded, new offices were opened in Abidjan, Dakar and Lome in 1986. They got off to a good start, and investigations continued into opening an office in Nigeria. In Europe, Switzerland and Austria received their own representation and Maersk Line acquired its agent in Denmark, Thor Jørgensen, together with its subsidiaries in trucking, warehousing and distribution.

The L-class ships, built in the early 1980s, now went through a lengthening process and had their bridges lifted to allow additional containers to be carried on deck while maintaining the required line of sight from the bridge.

Supporting the plan

The next few years were to see rapid growth, geographically and at sea; the investment in ships and container equipment would exceed $1 billion for the first time. On 10 December the Crash Committee's recommendation was put forward to order three 4,023-TEU ships for delivery in early 1988. Unusually, because orders for ships built at the A.P. Moller Group's yard at Lindø in Denmark were not normally communicated to the press, the *Kaiji Press* in Japan noted the order for the three new ships on 23 December.

Finally, right at the end of the year, a plan to serve Australia with three vessels connecting via Singapore was put forward, with the proviso that this should be done as soon as capacity was available. This followed a thorough analysis of the Australian and New Zealand markets by small teams from Copenhagen, who met some of the main exporters and importers.

Globalisation

This book is mainly about the story of Maersk Line, and that is where our focus lies. However, this chapter covers a key period when Maersk Line and its competitors were confronting an economic and geopolitical phenomenon: globalisation. The literature on globalisation provides many varied definitions of the term and as many widely varying suggestions as to when globalisation actually began – ranging from the early Phoenician traders to the Reagan and Thatcher years. However, the crucial drivers of modern globalisation for this story were the introduction of seaborne container transport and the sophistication of the services connected with the transport of containers from A to B.

As Marc Levinson puts it, 'it is hard to fathom just how much the container has changed the world'[43] in the period since Malcom McLean shipped the first containers in April 1956. Since that time, innovations have enabled unimaginable technologies to be installed in space, ships, offices and people's pockets; it was the time of 'the coming of the nuclear age, the emancipation of colonies, the renewed expansion of trade and investment and the economic rise of Northeast Asia'.[44]

In the third quarter of the twentieth century, Maersk Line was able to grow in a world of expanding international trade. Super-national bodies like the United Nations and the World Bank started collecting data about countries, their development and economic activities. In our story, we have reached the mid 1980s. It is a good point to take stock of the developments: approximately 40 years since the end of the Second World War, 20 years after the start of containerisation and some ten years or so into the history of Maersk Line's venture into this business.

Before we take that step, it may be helpful to see how we have defined globalisation. Of the many definitions available, a combination of two fits the Maersk perspective: 'a process fuelled by, and resulting in, increasing cross-border flows of goods, services, money, people, information',[45] 'where production is coordinated on a global scale'.[46] The economist Joseph Stiglitz provides a similar definition and one that lies very close to the thesis of this book, namely that globalisation is 'the closer integration of the countries and peoples of the world which has been brought about by the enormous reduction of costs of transportation and communication, and the breaking down of artificial barriers to the flows of goods, services, capital, knowledge and (to a lesser extent) people across borders'.[47] These definitions contain the seeds of a significant and continuing challenge to the industry, that of increasing visibility and availability to customers globally of 'information' and 'communication'. The challenge is the potential for commoditisation of services.

By 1985, the world's population had nearly doubled from about 2.5 billion in 1950 to just under five billion. Unemployment, which had been relatively low in the Western world in the 1960s and 1970s, had increased by 1980 following the oil crisis in 1979 and the ensuing economic slowdown.[48] Meanwhile, some 157 countries were now identified as nation-state members of the United Nations and 92 books had been published featuring the words 'global' or 'globalisation' in the title.[49]

From a political perspective, it would be difficult to argue that the world was significantly concerned about globalisation in the 1960s. Rather, it was a world divided, with the erection of the Berlin Wall in 1961, the Cuban missile crisis in 1962, and the growing US engagement in the war in Vietnam. Throughout the decade, the Cold War was the main focus of attention. In the 1960s and well into the 1970s one ex-colony after another achieved independence, some quietly, some bloodily. In the meantime, China remained introverted, despite the detonation of its first atomic bomb in 1964 and the launch of the Cultural Revolution. Also in 1964, Nikita Krushchev was replaced as Head of the Communist Party and Prime Minister of the USSR by Leonid Brezhnev and Alexei Kosygin. The Cold War was brought even further into focus in Europe in 1968 when the Soviet Union invaded Czechoslovakia following the 'Prague Spring' of that year.

Change was coming, however. The assassination of President John F. Kennedy in 1963 led to President Lyndon B. Johnson's efforts to develop 'the Great Society' in the US. A year later, Martin Luther King was awarded the Nobel Peace Prize for his role in the non-violent civil rights movement for racial equality in the United States. In 1971, the People's Republic of China took its seat in the United Nations. This was followed by a period of 'ping-pong diplomacy' with slowly easing relations between China and the United States, which culminated in President Richard Nixon's visit to China in 1972. Even with this breakthrough, the United States would not recognise China nor put relations on a 'normal' footing until 1978, after which China's leader, Deng Xiaoping, visited the United States in 1979.

The early 1980s saw continuing change at an increasing pace. *Solidarity* emerged as a political force in Poland, while two of the most significant political developments of the period saw Margaret Thatcher elected Prime Minister of the UK in 1979 and Ronald Reagan elected President of the United States in 1980. While their approaches were often controversial, both leaders implemented similar *laissez-faire* policies in their countries. These involved initiating tax cuts and driving deregulation, reducing government spending, privatisation and using monetary policy to keep inflation low while raising productivity. Both leaders were in power for a significant period – President Reagan for eight years until 1989 and Mrs Thatcher as Prime Minister until 1990 – during which time they promoted these policies globally, having major political and economic impact not just in the 1980s but also beyond.

'Asian Tigers'

Things were also changing in Asia. Although Japan continued to dominate the region's manufacturing and export, a major economic shift had started to take place. A combination of economic policy tools, such as export processing zones, duty exemption schemes, and incentive packages to generate foreign direct investment, were frequently noted. These, combined with the mix of relatively low-cost, labour-intensive manufacturing, led countries such as Hong Kong, Singapore, Taiwan and South Korea to see the beginning of the growth that in the 1970s would earn them the name 'Asian Tigers'. See Box 10.11 to put this development into its longer term perspective.

As C. Y. Tung, founder and former Chairman of OOCL said:

Most people you talk to will tell you the world is round, but in Hong Kong and the Far East, the world is not round. It is a box. The box is a container. Without that container, none of what went on in Asia could have happened.[50]

Kyu Sun 'Ken' Park, until recently President of Maersk Line in Korea, had grown up with the business there, having started in sales in Seoul, South Korea in 1974.[51] He summarised the development of the region by tracing the growth of Korean companies from the early 1970s to the late 1980s, when they began manufacturing goods on an original equipment manufacturer (OEM) basis for US and European importers. They acted as both manufacturer and exporter and the larger companies also acted as traders on behalf of other, smaller companies. Daewoo and Samsung were trading houses that sold light industrial goods to importers in the United States and Europe. The major commodities were textiles, garments, luggage, handbags and toys. Electronic goods were a key commodity from LG, Samsung and Daewoo – sold to companies such as J. C. Penny, Sears Roebuck, Macy's, K-Mart and others.

From the mid 1970s, footwear was an important commodity and Korea was the largest footwear manufacturing country until the late 1980s, when it lost the position to China and the Southeast Asian countries. Nike, Reebok, LA Gear, Meldisco, Adidas and many others all imported footwear from a variety of supplier-owned factories in Korea.

At the time, almost 90 per cent of South Korean exports to the US and Europe were on a free on board (FOB) basis, with the buyer controlling the shipping. In many cases these were large department stores that sometimes established buying offices in Korea. Manufacturers and exporters had little say but they still had influence in the choice of shipping line.

The Hyundai Group was into shipbuilding, automobiles and also had a general trading house, but they were more active in the heavy industrial commodities such as petro-chemicals and steel products, and so did not have much business for shipment by containers.

From the late 1980s into the early 1990s, the larger Korean conglomerates started to work to establish their own brand names instead of selling

Box 5.11 Li & Fung

One of the best examples of companies that developed in the 1970s, 1980s and beyond to support the growth in manufacturing in Asia is Li & Fung. Founded in 1906 in Guangzhou, China as an export trading company, it relocated to Hong Kong after the Second World War.

In the early 1970s, William and Victor Fung returned from the United States and rejoined the business, William with an MBA from Harvard Business School and Victor with a PhD from Harvard University and two years' teaching at Harvard Business School.

The 1980s saw Li & Fung expand its network of offices throughout Asia as more sources of supply developed in the rapidly industrialising Asian economies. In 1995, Li & Fung bought Inchcape Buying Services (formerly Dodwell), which enabled the company to expand into Europe, the Indian sub-continent and the Mediterranean.

By 2000, Li & Fung was turning over $2 billion, sourcing and managing global supply chains for high-volume, time-sensitive consumer goods for clients such as The Limited, Warner Brothers, Abercrombie & Fitch, Tesco, Avon Products, Levi-Strauss and Reebok, among many others.

To illustrate Li & Fung's supply chain management role: the filling for a down jacket may come from China, the outer fabric from Korea, the zippers from Japan, the inner lining from Taiwan and the elastic, labels, Velcro and other trim from Hong Kong. The garment might be dyed in Southeast Asia, stitched in China, sent back to Hong Kong for quality control and finally packed for delivery in the United States or elsewhere.

As Victor Fung summarised, 'Effectively we are customising the value chain to best meet the customer's needs.'[52]

Customers benefit through:

- Access to an unrivalled global sourcing network;
- Shorter order fulfilment processes;
- Reduced credit risks when dealing with small, distant suppliers;
- Access to on-the-spot quality inspection services.

As Victor Fung said in an HBS Alumni Bulletin in December 2011, 'We were there at the beginning of globalisation of labour-intensive manufactured goods. We were in the middle of it, but we didn't know what to call it until the academics told us it was globalisation!'[53]

on an OEM basis. At the same time, to maintain competitiveness they started establishing production facilities in China, Southeast Asia, North America and Europe – especially in East-Central Europe. We will return to this story to see how it developed in subsequent chapters.

In describing the development of Korea's exports, the term 'free on board' was used. This is one of a range of buying and selling terms used

Box 5.12 International commercial terms of the International Chamber of Commerce, Paris 2000

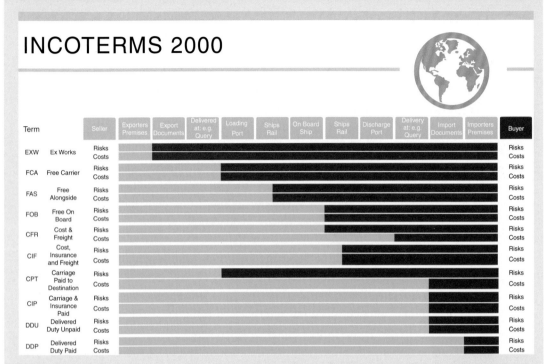

Other terms exist, such as Delivered at Frontier (DAF), Delivered ex Ship (DES), Delivered ex Quay (DEQ). Detailed definitions and applicability of each can be obtained from the International Chamber of Commerce in Paris and from many international Banks.

Source: Dictionary of International Trade, 5th edition, World Trade Press, 2002, pp. 331–59.

globally. The various terms reflect in some cases the relative power balance between the buyer and the seller, while in other cases it can be a question of who has the greater competence in managing the flow of product. Box 5.12 summarises some of the main buying and selling terms.

Turbulence

Despite this economic development, the 1970s had seen significant turbulence when the Bretton Woods monetary system was replaced by floating exchange rates in 1971, and when two disastrous world harvests in the period 1972–1974 led to a global food crisis. In 1974 OPEC increased oil prices significantly, leading to a substantial downturn in global economic activity.

Other influences had more positive impacts on economic developments including the 1967 Kennedy Round of trade negotiations, which saw significant tariff concessions, and its successor, the 1973 Tokyo Round, which led to further reductions in tariffs and cuts in customs duties. Then, in 1978, Deng Xioaping launched the economic reform known as 'socialism with Chinese characteristics', of which one of the key elements was the opening up of trade with the outside world. As an indicator of things to come, in 1984 the former Norwegian Prime Minister, Gro Harlem Brundtland, was appointed Chairman of the World Commission on Environment and Development and its report, known as the Brundtland Commission, put forward influential proposals on how countries could pursue sustainable development.

The 1980s was also a decade of economic turmoil. A major topic for discussion at the Box Club meeting in Miami in February 1983 was 'world trade is stagnating without signs of a quick recovery' – a second economic slow-down impacted trade in 1985–1986. Caused, among other events, by the collapse of the Middle East trades as a consequence of the continuing Iran–Iraq war, the price of oil dropped back to about $10 per barrel. The situation was made more challenging by the Plaza Accord of 1985, which allowed the US dollar to devalue against the German mark and the Japanese yen in an attempt to rebalance the world economy. The Black Monday stock market crash of October 1987 was a very visible sign of the prevailing economic uncertainty.

Summing up a theme that will recur in the chapters that follow, three Scandinavian professors wrote:

the shipping industry was by far the most important carrier of the expanding global trade in goods and raw materials, which made possible the wave of out-sourcing and trans-nationally integrated value chains ... The industry was more global in its growth strategies and political and institutional structures than most other industries ... Finally, the cyclical movements of modern shipping could be regarded almost as an economic 'Richter Scale' measuring the varying amounts of energy released by globalisation. The fate of shipping is thus closely linked to the ebb and flow of economic activity and world trade.[54]

6

Laying the Foundations for Expansion (1987–1990)

> *What is attractive with the business is really that it is so international. Just in Copenhagen, we have 70 to 80 different nationalities in the 1,000 or so people we have here. For young people who want to travel and see the world, this is actually a pretty good industry to be in.*
>
> Søren Skou, CEO, Maersk Line[1]

During the final years of the 1980s, Maersk Line concentrated on establishing a solid platform from which it could develop and expand. As in previous years, there was plenty of action but the main acquisitions were to come later, in the second half of the 1990s. A great deal of work, including cooperative efforts with other carriers, had to be put in place to build the platform before those later acquisitions could take place.

In Chapter 5 we looked at the success of an early hub port, Connecting Point Spain in Algeciras. Now, Maersk Line began to look at expanding Connecting Point Singapore. But connecting to where? Singapore was already a feeder hub with services to and from Indonesia, some Indonesian out-ports and to the main ports in Malaysia and Thailand. The main additional area not covered yet was Australia and New Zealand.

Maersk had established a representative office in Australia in 1966, but the main focus had been on shipping ventures other than the liner trades. The market for Maersk Line had been investigated on a fact-finding trip by two liner representatives back in October 1981. They had concluded that the service might be viable if the space could be made available, but at the time, the ships were full. In May 1986, their study was updated, and showed a potentially positive result after start-up costs. In the same month, Maersk Line's major reefer study was presented. Putting these two reports together highlighted the size of the reefer markets out of this area and the value of using available surplus reefer equipment in the Far East to serve this trade.[2]

To verify this, among other opportunities, a new team travelled to the area to meet customers and possible agents. Their report was delivered on 4 December 1986. The estimated results for the proposal were not

Box 6.1 A comparison of Oceania with four other developed countries

	Australia	New Zealand	West Germany	Japan	UK	United States
Area ('000 km²)	7.682	269	249	378	243	9.166
Population (millions)	15.4	3.2	61.4	119.3	55.6	233.7
GDP per capita ($)	10,988	7,671	10,689	8,973	9,351	13,152
External trade						
Exports (FOB; $million)	23.986	5.358	169.784	170.132	94.538	217.888
Imports (CIF; $million)	23.424	6.01	151.246	136.492	105.616	341.177
Balance of trade ($million)	562	−652	18.538	33.640	−11.077	−123.289
Inflation rate 1986 (%)	7.7	12.6	0.2	0.7	3.6	1.6
Projected inflation 1987 (%)	5.5	9.0	1.0	1.0	3.0	3.0
Exchange rate to dollar (budget 1987)	1.43	1.84	2.00	150.00	0.65	1.00

Source: Maersk Line Report, 4 December 1986.

intrinsically exciting, but recommended that the opportunities in Oceania be included as a consideration in the plan to increase the frequency of the Europe–Far East service. On that basis a number of new possibilities presented themselves, including the ability to spread the risk of Maersk Line becoming too dependent on the main economies of the United States, Far East and Europe. Further, seasonality in the Australia–New Zealand fruit trades could complement seasonalities in other trades (e.g. apples from Oregon, United States), improving reefer equipment balances. Overall, it would enhance Maersk Line's global coverage and the existing organisation's sales portfolios around the world, with few extra resources needed beyond representation in the area.

The level of cargo controlled by the Producer Boards was noted. These boards dominated key exporting industries and, to varying degrees, managed the global distribution of produce on behalf of their members. While some boards focused on dairy produce, others handled meat or fruit. But with the right services, a strong local organisation and a structured approach, generating the needed support was considered feasible.

The report concluded: 'It is recommended that as soon as the necessary extra capacity can be made available on the Europe-Far East service, Maersk Line should also extend its service to cover Australia and New Zealand.'

Internal developments

On 24 June 1986, the price of oil reached $11.50 per barrel and the indications were that it would continue to rise. A letter from Sheikh Abdullah Kanoo, Maersk Line's agent in Saudi Arabia, indicated that oil prices might stabilise at about $18–20 per barrel, so investigations began into the pros and cons of forward buying to minimise the risks. Sure enough, by December of that year, the price had risen to $18 per barrel. Forward buying was to become a feature of the business.

In May that year an article appeared in *Fortune* magazine analysing the *Challenger* space shuttle disaster of 28 January 1986. A number of learning opportunities for NASA were clearly stated and included the need for managers to be willing to listen; to cooperate internally, particularly with those with expertise in specific areas; to outline realistic goals; and the critical role of communication, whether conveying good or bad news. With a growing and geographically widely dispersed organisation, effective communication and cross-border cooperation were pre-requisites for Maersk Line's continuing success. Management was always open to opportunities to learn from mistakes, external as well as internal. The *Fortune* article was circulated to all senior managers for internal discussion and consideration of how the lessons learned could be internalised in Maersk Line.

The budget process

Maersk Container Line's budget process had begun in the mid 1970s as a relatively simple procedure, with one service and relatively few offices involved. Following the merger of the two liner departments to create one Maersk Line in 1986, the range of services and offices involved meant this had developed into a substantial annual task. Budgeting was not just a question of reviewing the services. Each office around the world contributed input to the process, and also carried out its own local reviews and budgets. When these had been reviewed, and discussed with management in October, Maersk Line had a detailed plan for the coming year and projections for the next four years. Management had a clear view on ships, equipment and other investments, as well as market and market share developments, forecast gross and net results, and an agreed base line against which developments could be evaluated as the year progressed. It also provided the forecasts that, when aggregated at the A.P. Moller Group level, allowed for cash flow and investment planning considerations.

Supported by a monthly accounting system which received global input and the annual divisional book-closing process that ran from January to March each year, there was little that could fall through the cracks in terms of management or managers, at any level in the organisation, not knowing their numbers.

Profit improvement plans (PIP)

Containerisation International's yearbook for 1987 reported that profitability for 1986 throughout the industry was down on 1985: 'Over-ambitious expansion plans and general over-capacity in all sectors of the container market obliged many companies to master "the three Rs" of rationalisation, restructuring and regeneration.'[3]

The preliminary budget numbers for 1987 were better than 1986 was expected to be, but both revenue enhancement and cost reduction efforts were needed. Specific market segments were identified, and service by service, specific PIP plans were established and actions initiated. This included focus on schedule reliability to ensure that Maersk Line was in 'number one position in terms of adherence to schedule'. A separate management report showed that Mercantile Consolidators had the opportunity to double its level of business and got the go-ahead to do so.[4]

In October Flemming Jacobs proposed to senior management that a task force be established to prepare for the new, expanded services based on the upgraded Europe–Far East service (going to weekly from fortnightly). The team would report to Ib Kruse, Ted Ruhly (President of Moller Steamship Co. in the United States) and Jacobs himself. Erik Møller-Nielsen was asked to consider options for strengthening the Line Department in Copenhagen, as there was concern about the level of experience and availability of the right people – so many were now out in the field, running Maersk Line's local or country-based organisations. Language skills were also a focus, particularly for French speakers for the growing organisations in France and West Africa. The head of HR, Svend Vilborg, noted that overall, staff had grown by some 60 per cent over the previous eight years. He and his team were actively working on career planning, particularly for the 30–40 age group.

It was understood that there might be a need to increase the pioneer spirit, as many of the planned developments would be in new developing areas, such as Africa, Pakistan, India and China. Maersk Line now had an office in Shanghai and the Beijing office was under development. Although running a Japan–North China feeder at the time was of marginal profitability, it was considered important to have a presence.

Ted Ruhly was proud of the US developments, where Maersk Line now had 34 offices. Bridge Terminal Transport (BTT), a Moller Steamship-owned trucking company responsible for Maersk Line's extensive chassis fleet and road-based container distribution, had 48 state licences allowing it to operate across nearly all of the United States. Moller Steamship was also working on developing its own stevedoring companies and Ted Ruhly also reported that Columbus Line, part-owner of the Global terminal adjacent to Maersk Line's own in New Jersey, might be interested in selling the facility to Maersk, an opportunity that would give the extra space needed to accommodate a Trans Atlantic service.

The Maersk International Shipping Education (MISE) programme

Rather than enrol young people in further education, both A. P. Møller and Mærsk Mc-Kinney Møller relied on practical learning provided by trainee-like positions in shipping-related companies, combined with relevant courses taken in evening classes. This on-the-job approach was the typical way of training potential leaders in the first half of the twentieth century.[5] In the 1950s some Danish companies set up their own internal training programmes, inspired by American management courses introduced via the European Recovery Programme – more familiarly known as the Marshall Plan – put in place by the American government following the Second World War.[6]

For Maersk, as well as others, the aim of the training was the interaction between theory and practical work in the day job. When it was launched in 1993, the Maersk International Shipping Education programme built on an earlier programme called The A.P. Møller Shipping School.[7] This had covered subjects as diverse as charter parties, communications, shipping law, accounting, book keeping and other useful background that all 16–17-year-old trainees at Maersk were required to take and pass. Run in Danish, it called on both internal experts and external trainers to supplement the programme with specialised knowledge. By the early 1980s the Shipping School was providing training for between 30 and 40 young, intelligent, energetic and ambitious Danes each year, mainly men, but with a smattering of women. As they graduated and developed further, they were placed

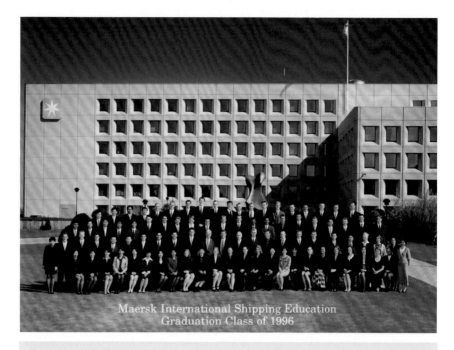

Figure 6.1 The Maersk International Shipping Education graduates of 1996 around A.P. Moller Group CEO Jess Søderberg and his fellow Partners Ib Kruse and Flemming Jacobs.

in key roles across the new organisation. However, by the end of the decade, this was no longer enough.

In 1993, Oscar Rosendal, at that time responsible for management development in the Staff Department, proposed fundamentally restructuring the programme. The changes were accepted and were implemented by the Staff Department.

The main changes involved a global recruitment process to generate the candidates, gradually moving the MISE from an international programme for Danes to being truly international. The numbers also grew, from the original 40 or so trainees per year in the 1970s to 55 by 1987, and over 450 at its peak. While some elements of the programme remained the same, such as the training by a mix of internal and external experts, more academic content began to be included. Initially Copenhagen Business School, later supplemented by the Indian School of Management, actively supported and delivered the content.

The programme content was increasingly delivered using automated learning tools. Trainees had to work with others from their cohort in teams across the world, doing research, writing papers and submitting them for review and marking by the course providers. Additionally, the cohort for each year would meet at a training facility outside Copenhagen for a number of weeks of intensive training, culminating in an exam that had to be passed. Failure to pass could lead to dismissal, and certainly meant that the candidate was unlikely to qualify for the third-year overseas assignment. While this programme was run for the A.P. Moller Group as a whole, Maersk Line was the largest business unit with the most overseas offices, so the largest numbers tended to go to Maersk Line.

Targeted largely at young people between the ages of 18 and 22, most trainees initially did not have a university degree. At its peak in the late 1990s and early 2000s, Maersk received some 70,000 applications from around the world. From this number of applicants, some 450 trainees a year from about 45 countries would be selected. Eric Williams, later head of Sales Excellence, said, 'the MISE programme was very attractive, particularly as it was in a business that was multinational'.[8]

For more than 40 years, Maersk has used the same type of assessment tools. Focused on cognitive and learning ability as well as personality, these provide valuable supplementary information when trying to predict the future success of an individual. As Jessica Lauren Cohen, a young American graduate, said of her interview, 'when the HR consultant read back the profile to me, I was amazed at how well she knew me'.[9] Today, the main tools are administered over the internet. As the balance of trainees shifted away from Denmark, towards the developing economies in particular, the level of qualifications required also shifted towards first and Master's degrees. Intelligence, energy, enthusiasm and commitment remain the key decision points.

When it was initiated, MISE was probably the best training programme in shipping available anywhere in the world and provided Maersk with a significant source of competitive advantage. The MISE programme was a strategic approach to solving a specific issue. The programme continued to develop until 2009–2010, when it underwent another major restructuring to better fit the needs of twenty-first-century business through the smaller, more focused but equally intense Maersk Line Graduate Program. Today, ex-MISE trainees can be found all over Maersk Line and the other divisions, but also in most shipping and logistics companies of any size, anywhere, and often at a senior level.

The beginnings of a terminals business

In the late 1980s, Maersk Line was also moving towards creating yet another separate activity, namely a terminals business.

By 1987, Maersk Line, with its share holding in Modern Terminals (MTL) in Hong Kong, represented something like 30 per cent of all of MTL's business. The terminal was negotiating for land in order to undertake further expansion. For Kwai Chung, the area in which most of the terminals were situated, this was difficult because of the lack of available space; nevertheless, it was needed to meet the rapidly growing demand for capacity as exports from South China and Hong Kong ballooned. Extra land would only become available in 1989, as would space in the adjacent terminal operated by Sea-Land, whose new container freight station (CFS) was the world's largest industrial building when it opened there.

Leif Arnesen, a Partner in A.P. Moller, was due to visit MTL and was briefed to ensure his meeting with David Gledhill, Chairman of MTL and John Swire & Sons, made the point that MTL's poor performance was impacting Maersk Line's 'second to none' service. Shortly afterwards, an Extraordinary Board Meeting of MTL was called to approve the provision of berthing preferences to Maersk Line to ensure that 'if we arrived on time, we would be handled and would depart on time'.[10]

Meanwhile, in May 1987 the PCG noted that Maersk Line now either owned or was in the process of acquiring 19 terminals around the world. A working group was established to consider the future terminal needs for

Figure 6.2 A busy day in Hong Kong with two ocean-going A-class ships and one feeder ship at the MTL terminal facilities.

technology and operational layouts, based on what had been learned operationally to date.

The Rokko Island terminal at Kobe was opened formally by Ib Kruse in March 1987 and in 1988 the terminal at Aarhus, Denmark would also receive substantial Maersk Line investment. Both would be operated internally. In August 1989, Ib Kruse took the step of taking Maersk Line more formally into the terminals business by creating the Terminal Planning and Implementation Team, 'to achieve more cost-effective arrangements on a profitable basis'.[11] This was followed at the end of the year by the creation of another team, the Future Terminal Concept Group, to define the types of terminals, layouts and operational technology that would be needed to meet the future production aspirations of the business.

Developments in information technology

With the growth in the business, it was becoming clearer that global systems managed centrally from Copenhagen would not provide the flexibility needed to meet either internal or customer needs. The technology itself was also changing, as 1985 had seen the launch of the Microsoft Windows application. To ensure that operational rules were established, Ole Larsen, head of Finance and Systems, together with the North American organisation, developed a set of rules that were to guide these developments. The principle was that Copenhagen would not interfere with local systems, but would retain the responsibility for ensuring that local systems did not conflict with any central system.

Supporting this, Steen Hundevad Knudsen, Managing Director of Maersk Data, and Poul Bjerre, from Maersk Line's IT organisation, reviewed developments, plans for the future and the direction information technology was taking. The price of computing power was continuing to decline rapidly. As an illustration, in 1985, $1 would buy about 13,600 bits of memory, while by 2004, at constant 2000 prices, the same dollar would buy nearly 94 million bits. Then, in 1989, Tim Berners-Lee invented the World Wide Web protocols, a development that by the end of 2011 would have over 2.3 billion users.[12]

To address these developments, a Strategic Systems team was created, led by Aksel Nielsen and Maersk Line's systems development group was expanded, while a major new equipment management system was commissioned for delivery in 1990.

Duncan McGrath, now Container Freight Manager at Cargill Incorporated in Minnesota, but in the early 1990s a freight forwarder in Portland, Oregon, recalls:

We did have some business going from Portland over to Africa, Nigeria and a few other places. Maersk was really the only game in town and while the span of the service was impressive, what was even more impressive was that whenever we had shipment troubles, it was very easy for Maersk to figure out exactly where the boxes were. That was a capability that nobody really had at the time.[13]

As Maersk Line needed that information for its own operational management, it was only one step further to supply it to its customers, although the company was probably still underestimating the value that the information contained.

Another development, and one where Maersk Line was in competition with Sea-Land and APL, was the use of technology to hook-up with customers and thereby share information, cutting both errors and costs. Now a customer could send the carrier a shipping instruction through electronic data interchanges (EDIs), and in due course receive some of the shipping documents needed and an invoice.[14] Ted Ruhly's organisation in New York had five customers ready to pilot the process, while one of the Japanese car companies was moving in the same direction. Once the standards were established, the process developed rapidly.

The rise of Shipper Associations and Councils

As the 1980s came to an end, many container ship operators had begun the transition from being maritime entrepreneurs into total transport service providers. The focus was not limited to seaborne container transport, but was expanding to include management of the total supply chain. This need in the market was developing as globalisation took off, and many industries became less tied to local manufacturers, moving their purchasing or selling into the new, fast-developing areas of the increasingly integrated world.

The language was also changing, as Martin Christopher, Emeritus Professor at Cranfield University, recollected:

Before the 1970s, it was really called distribution. In 1972, I became the first professor in the UK to have the word 'logistics' in my title. And today, certainly in larger companies, you now often have a Vice President or Director of Logistics and it has become much more common to find such people in the Board Room.[15]

As the implications of extended global trade grew, so did the need for wider and deeper transport-related knowledge, and many companies opted to bring a new breed of transport professionals into their organisations. Klaus Schnede, now Manager of Marine, Air and Facilities Procurement for Eastman Chemical Company in the United States, had started with Maersk Line in 1988. He moved to a freight forwarder in 1995 and joined Eastman

Chemical in 2005. Duncan McGrath spent a number of years as a freight forwarder – 'a great way to learn the nuts and bolts of the business because you get exposed to all the problems that happen along the way'[16] – before joining Cargill Incorporated in 1997.

Professionals like these, in producing, importing and exporting organisations, concerned about supporting and facilitating the growth and development of their businesses, also served to move Shipper Associations and Shipper Councils into a much more powerful and influential role.

One area where this influence became highly visible was the debate over the Hague-Visby Rules and their proposed replacement by the Hamburg Rules. These rules had so far governed the application of insurance to movements by sea and were the basis for the management of risk for ocean carriers, importers and exporters alike. Changing these rules was perceived by some as breaking the trust on which the whole basis of modern shipping rested. The Hamburg Rules, if enacted, would transfer liability from the shipper to the ocean carrier. A number of Shipper Associations were driving this development and lobbying to have the Hamburg Rules implemented in Europe as well as the United States. Significant discussions took place with special industry-wide sessions to determine the best way forward.

All the major shipping nations were opposed to the changes; however, the timing had been well chosen. The UNCTAD Code was to be reviewed at the end of 1988 at a meeting in Geneva. In the United States, the 1984 Shipping Act was to undergo a five-year review and a Presidential Advisory Commission was set for 1990, with Congressional hearings for 1991 and action by Congress in 1992. Discussion of the Hamburg Rules was incorporated into all this activity.

In the meantime, in Europe, the EUROCORDE investigation involving the Trans Atlantic trade by the EEC was moving forward, driven by a complaint from the British Shippers' Council. In its purview were items such as rules relating to consortia, cargo reservation schemes and maritime policies.

In October 1989, 22 large US shippers announced that they favoured repeal of all US-related conferences' anti-trust immunities. Carrier representatives at senior levels were growing significantly concerned and considering whether to put together serious lobbying efforts to counter the trends.[17] During the year, Sir Leon Brittan of the UK became EEC Commissioner for Competition and Karel van Miert became Commissioner for Transport.

In July 1991, the European Shippers' Council lodged a complaint with the EEC's Competition Directorate over the application of a Middle East Emergency Surcharge during the Gulf War; in December 1992 the British and French Shippers' Councils filed complaints over rate increases in the Trans Atlantic trades. The same month, the Competition Directorate

Box 6.2 The Hague-Visby, Hamburg and Rotterdam Rules

The Hague-Visby Rules were originally drafted in Brussels in 1924, covering the international carriage of goods by sea (as the Hague Rules), and subsequently have been amended several times, most recently in 1979. The rules imposed duties on both the carrier and the shipper and became the Hague-Visby rules in 1968.

The carrier's duties require a reasonable standard of professionalism and care, including not deviating from the usual route except in emergencies. However, the rules also include a wide range of exemptions from liability, including neglect or default of the ship's master.

The shipper also has obligations, being required to pack the goods appropriately for the journey, describe them correctly, have them ready for shipment as agreed, not to ship dangerous cargo without prior agreement and ultimately to pay the freight.

All the major trading nations and many others have ratified the rules, which over decades of commercial use, including litigation, became established in international commerce.

The Hamburg Rules were a product of the United Nations International Convention of the Carriage of Goods by Sea and were adopted in Hamburg in 1978. The driving force behind that convention was the developing countries. This was picked up by Shipper Associations, seeing an opportunity to reduce costs by shifting risk from shippers to carriers.

The main effect of these rules was to increase the carrier's liability for cargo damage and loss and reduce the carrier's exemptions from liability. Ratified by the required 20 countries, they came into force in May 2011 as another international convention. No major trading country has yet ratified these rules.

The Rotterdam Rules cover the latest conventions, and are an attempt to create a comprehensive and uniform legal structure for the rights and obligations of those involved in international sea transport. They were adopted in December 2008, and 20 countries were needed to ratify the convention. To date, over 20 countries have become signatories, including the United States, Denmark, France, Greece and the Netherlands.

Source: Maersk Line material and United Nations International Convention of the Carriage of Goods by Sea, 1978.

responded to a complaint from the German Shippers' Council about the FEFC's inland transport rates, and deemed some practices illegal, a decision that was to have significant consequences in that market place.

UNCTAD and national cargo reservation schemes

Erik Møller-Nielsen continued his investigations into how to respond to the developments with UNCTAD and remained concerned that the only long-term solution might be to move at least some of Maersk Line's ships under the US flag.

Meanwhile, trade discriminatory issues had not gone away. In fact, the UNCTAD 40/40/20 principles were very much to the fore in certain parts of the world. For example, the Togolese Shippers' Council decided on the strict enforcement of cargo sharing in 1991. Danish governmental intervention was needed before this practice was changed, while a similar approach in Nigeria was countered by a delegation of ambassadors from EEC countries who persuaded the Nigerian Ministry of Transport to review the regulations positively.

In the meantime, there was serious concern about over-tonnaging. By 1987 the developing countries' fleets accounted for about 18 per cent of the world's merchant fleet, while the EEC fleet stood at 19 per cent, down from over 30 per cent in 1975. 1989 saw the EEC taking these developments increasingly seriously and involved in negotiations with a total of 25 West and Central African countries, addressing their unilateral shipping policies and use of freight bureaus, while at the same time working to avoid any political confrontations.

Soviet fleet activities remained a shipping policy issue, but change was coming. By early 1988, the Cold War was clearly drawing to a close, relations between the US and the USSR were thawing and it was predicted that Soviet shipping would again be allowed into US ports.

The Trans Atlantic trade: the missing link

In 1986 Maersk Line was not serving the Trans Atlantic trade. But it had done so immediately after the Second World War, and the memories of that difficult time remained, particularly with Mærsk Mc-Kinney Møller.

In the spring of 1947 the Trans Atlantic Line had been set up and operated within the North Atlantic Conference. Managed by Copenhagen's Tramp Department, it had provided sailings between the US East Coast, French Atlantic coast ports, Antwerp, Rotterdam and, later, German ports.

After a few years, competition became extremely intense ... The governments of the USA and several European countries reacted to the difficulties facing their national liner companies by introducing a series of protectionist measures that made it difficult for shipping companies of third party countries to compete. Since the Maersk ships had been sailing at a loss for a considerable time and there was no improvement in sight, it was decided in 1954 to discontinue the Trans Atlantic Line.[18]

A number of reviews of the Trans Atlantic trade had been conducted but none had proved interesting nor particularly profitable. The key had not been found. But Flemming Jacobs' attitude was 'just never give up'.

This was the oldest container trade and we had to be there in order to serve our customers. And Mærsk Mc-Kinney Møller was reminding us of what happened and he was of course right, we needed to think about this very carefully. So, proposal 1, thrown out. Proposal 2, thrown out. And, proposal number three was a lot better than the other two, so it was good that he had forced us to think.

Mærsk Mc-Kinney Møller wanted to ensure that Maersk Line would not be yet another victim of a failed attempt to conquer the trade. The Atlantic was littered with the flotsam of earlier casualties, as Box 6.3 illustrates.

The third proposal was to extend the Panama service across the Atlantic. The secret of its success was its ability to provide full coverage of both the US and European markets but by adding only three ships. This proved to be the key: the profitability and return on investment projections looked solid, as the lower level of investment (three ships instead of four) for the same amount of income provided the needed margins while also allowing flexibility of operations.[19]

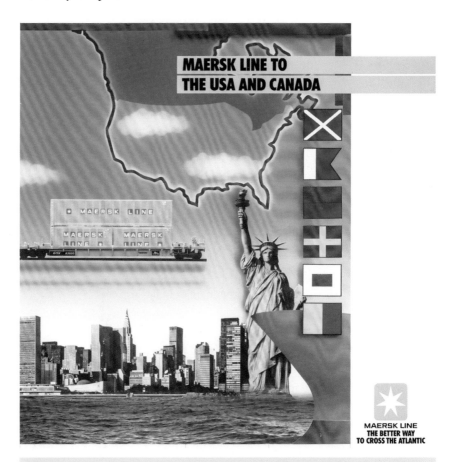

Figure 6.3 A ship owner's riddle for shipping people: six signal flags with a special meaning. MAERSK was spelled out with signal flags to attract attention when the Trans Atlantic service was introduced.

It is a measure of Maersk Line top management's concern about the introduction of this service that, early in 1987, shortly before its launch, they decided to make one further, final, independent senior-level review to ensure that the plan would achieve its objectives and that the financial results were realistic.[20]

A positive report was returned in August 1987, and identified a number of opportunities for further improvement over the Crash Committee's plan.[21] The analysis also indicated that rates were very sensitive and concluded that the service should operate as an independent in the trades from Europe to the United States, focusing on service contracts. Other rates would be at the same level or close to that of the conference.

From the US Gulf and US East Coast to Europe, the service would operate within the conference. Jørgen Harling, who was one of Maersk Line's representatives at the conference meetings at that time, believes that Maersk Line effectively broke up a comfortable club and, as such, was not at all welcome. Tim Harris of P&O saw it from a different angle, describing Maersk Line's approach as long-term, accepting that weaker lines would succumb in what he characterised as a 'blood-bath'.[22]

Box 6.3 Carriers that left the Trans Atlantic 1982–1992

Transatlantic westbound trades (excluding Canada, Mexico)

Carrier	Nationality
Dart Lines*	Asian
Shipping Corporation of India	Asian
Atlantic Express Line	European
Baltic Shipping Company	European
Barge Container Ro/Ro Lines	European
Breakbulk & Container Line GMBH	European
CGM	European
CGM/IncoTrans Euro/Pacific	European
CMB	European
Convoy Lines	European

Box 6.3 (cont.)

EAC	European
Gearbulk Container Services	European
Gulf Container Line	European
Gulf Europe Express	European
Inco Trans	European
Johnson Scanstar	European
Ocean Star Container Line	European
Pacific Europe Express	European
PVC Lines	European
Scan Pacific	European
Star Shipping	European
Trans Freight Lines	European
Troll Carriers	European
Uiterwijk Shipping Lines	European
Amco	American
Amtrans	American
CMC	American
Euro-Gulf	American
Fednav Lakes	American
Ibero	American
Milwaukee Lines	American
Sylvan Shipping Co	American
Topgallant	American
United Fruit Company	American
US Lines	American
Waterman	American
Westwood Shipping Lines	American
Total	37 carriers

* Now part of OOCL

Source: Containerisation International Yearbooks © 1997, reproduced with the permission of Lloyds List Group.

Carsten Melchiors recalls the tremendous significance of the new service:

> By introducing the Trans Atlantic service ... Maersk Line was global. It was psychologically hugely important. The beauty of the service was that it was possible to introduce by far the best product, we had the best features in the marketplace at the time, by only using three ships ... The build-up was absolutely fantastic and this was a typical strength of the way [Flemming] Jacobs operated at the time. He would pick a few people, stroke their backs, and then throw an enormous task at them.[23]

The campaign to launch the Trans Atlantic service in 1988 was the largest public relations exercise Maersk Line had ever implemented. It covered a relatively short period of a few weeks, but was intense and built on the strong US- and Europe-based organisations that Maersk Line already had in place. It involved teaser adverts in the leading media, with no captions but using the signal flags for MAERSK. A still attractive publication, *Maersk Line Sales and Service Guide for the Trans Atlantic*, was distributed internally and to customers, providing clear and well-illustrated information on every imaginable aspect of the service. Teams of people from across the Maersk Line organisations were given the opportunity to participate in one launch event after another, not just in the major cities and ports involved, but also in places less well connected to the sea, such as Vienna in Austria and Lyon in France. As an example, in London the US Ambassador hosted a cocktail party for about 150 guests in the foyer of the American Embassy, something that would be unthinkable with today's security.

Inaugurated by the *Marchen Mærsk* at the end of April 1988, the initial outbound sailings from Europe to the United States were below budget. The key commodities needed for success in the trade were wines and spirits. The Wine and Spirits Association had taken the opportunity to negotiate a new conference agreement and it took some time to penetrate this major product flow.

Marchen Mærsk had ultimately left Europe with below-planned revenues, but *Louis Mærsk*, arriving in Europe as the first inbound sailing, did exceptionally well, with major support from customers moving refrigerated products. While this was something of a 'maiden voyage' special, reefer loadings continued to remain well above plan. As an aside, the June 1988 issue of *Containerisation International* contained an interesting note. Having attended the inauguration of the service in Felixstowe when *Marchen Mærsk* called there, Troels Dilling, then Managing Director of Odense Steel Shipyard, was quoted as saying that although it was rated at 3,900 TEU, the *Marchen Mærsk* was actually 'a Panama-ximum masterpiece' of 5,000 TEU capacity.

Figure 6.4 Odense Steel Shipyard new building number 123 under construction. It would become the largest container ship to pass through the Panama Canal and be named *Marchen Mærsk* when it entered the Maersk Line fleet in April 1988.

The competitive market place

A PCG meeting in 1987 had noted that both APL and Evergreen's turnover were of a similar size to Maersk Line's and efforts were being made to benchmark and learn from their activities. At a further PCG meeting early in 1988, Ted Ruhly, President of the newly renamed Maersk Inc. (formerly the Moller Steamship Company), reported that while Black Monday (the global stock market crash in October 1987) had not yet impacted volumes, markets were beginning to experience turbulence and it was agreed that 'a tremendous effort was necessary to bring results up to standard'. To strengthen the management team and to allow enough time for full focus on cost management, Vagn Lehd Møller returned to Copenhagen from his role as Managing Director of Norfolk Line, with effect from 1 February 1988.

A number of service reviews were conducted to improve profitability and a significant change was made in the services covering the Middle East. Erik Møller-Nielsen's review concluded that by integrating the Middle East Container Line (MECL) service with the Far East–Middle East services, the MECL service would return to a 'good' bottom line.

Box 6.4 Ships and the Panama Canal

When the M-class ships were being designed, the required TEU capacity given to the naval architects proved impossible to develop. After several attempts, they had to come back and say that a ship with the required capacity, which must also be able to transit the Panama Canal, was not possible to design due to the length limitations the canal authorities applied.

After considerable discussion, Mærsk Mc-Kinney Møller asked if anyone had actually visited the canal authorities to discuss the issue with them. No one had.

Shortly afterwards, a proud Bent Hansen, head of Maersk's Technical Department, was able to report that the canal authorities had agreed that Maersk ships could be up to one metre longer than the rules allowed.

Jørgen Harling recollected: 'Sailing through the Panama Canal, the pilot would be standing on the bridge wing and looking down on the surface of the quay at a sign in Maersk blue, "Maersk ships stop here". The M-Class ships were literally shoe-horned into the locks.'

The concern had been about the lock length, but the actual issue was the ships' turning capability on a corner in the canal on the way to Gatun Lake, not an issue with ships equipped with bow and stern thrusters.

That solution allowed the designers to add an extra 20-foot bay on the ships, achieving the required capacity.

This was duly done. The investment was also changed to three Optima ships (see Figure 5.7) and the addition of two C-type container vessels.[24] The Trans Pacific services were expected to be roughly on budget for the period, but, for the first time, the Europe service was the overall bread winner.

Teams reporting to Michael Fiorini, head of the A.P. Moller Group's Finance Department, were brought together to improve the results of the other services. On the Trans Pacific, over-capacity was expected for 1988 and vessel usage was expected to decrease. In October the first meeting of the new Trans Pacific Discussion Agreement was held in San Francisco. Erik Møller-Nielsen was not very optimistic about the outcome, but was convinced that if Maersk Line did not attend – the invitation had arrived in August – the meeting was likely to be cancelled because a recession was expected in the United States in 1989.

Meanwhile, Per Jørgensen reported on the demise of Japan Lines' liner business and the probability that the Japanese lines would reorganise; NYK was considered likely to swallow Showa Line and Yamashita Shinnihon (YS) Line.[25]

Aggressive PIP plans were implemented to find the needed savings to ensure a reasonable result, and as Maersk Line's turnover that year would be about $1.6 billion, 'it was expected to be possible'.[26] Container turn-around times and inland transport arrangements were key focus areas with a transnational team set up under Jens Raun. Their primary objective was to reduce these costs; however, the team was also able to support Maersk's continuing operational independence and desire for control by establishing and/or acquiring relevant land based transport activities, thus at least 'keeping the money Maersk blue'. Many of these operations were later to form the core of another business activity, 'Inland Container Services' (ICS), which is today managed as a separate business area within APM Terminals.

As always, staff costs were also reviewed and in the middle of 1988 it was acknowledged that staff numbers in Maersk Line Copenhagen were above budget at 214 people, covering Finance, Operations, the Europe desk, the Trans Atlantic desks, the established Trans Pacific as well as Sales and Marketing. By excluding trainees and those on short-term assignments, the number was brought down to plan, over time.

Non-vessel operating common carriers and Mercantile Consolidators

Up to this point, Maersk Line had not focused significantly on the non-vessel operating common carriers (NVOCCs) market, the freight forwarder part of the individual markets, generally working direct with beneficial cargo owners (BCOs), whether shippers or consignees. Now, particularly with the entry into the Trans Atlantic, a more nuanced approach was needed and a number of parallel initiatives were set in motion.

In the United States, a legal issue needed to be considered, namely whether Mercantile Consolidators was sufficiently distanced from Maersk Inc. After taking legal advice, it was decided to set up Mercantile as a legally separate entity in the United States, as Maersk had already done in Asia and was in the process of doing in Europe. Irrespective, Mercantile would not be developed as an NVOCC at that time, as it would be in direct competition with a growing number of Maersk Line customers.

In Europe, the PCG agreed that Mercantile should be encouraged to expand, as 'it would be particularly important for a weekly Far East/Europe service'.[27] Meanwhile, a team was put together, headed by Hans Henrik Sørensen, to investigate how Maersk Line could serve the strong Trans Atlantic NVOCC market as effectively as possible.

Maersk Line was not alone in thinking of containerisation in a broader context as the concept of supply chain management began to mature.

As *Containerisation International* reported in 1988, that previous year, Bruce Seaton, Chairman of American President Lines, had delivered an address to the US-based Containerisation and Intermodal Institute in which he quoted 'the example of a garment importer/retailer on the US East Coast to show how the diverse cost elements which go to make up a firm's distribution process are broken down'.[28] Seaton also argued that the time-value of money invested in the retailer's inventory had to be taken into account.

Early in 1988, Steen Hundevad Knudsen returned from a meeting with the Index Group keen to share some business insights. He met Flemming Jacobs for a brain-storming session and found that they shared a similar view on many development opportunities. To turn some of these into practical steps, Knudsen commissioned the Maersk Electronic Transport Information Solution, later known as the METIS Report, and towards the end of 1988, Flemming Jacobs initiated the Maersk Materials Management (3M) Committee, which discussed the ideas behind the business concept of supply chain management during 1989. The PCG gave solid backing, although Ted Ruhly in the US was concerned about the possible level of investment that might be required.

New relationships, new ventures, old conflicts

Reviewing developments at the end of the 1980s, one interesting change is visible in the number of visitors that pass through the Maersk Line offices at Esplanaden in Copenhagen. These included a senior delegation from Sinotrans of China in mid 1987 and again in 1989. By mid 1989, Maersk Line Hong Kong had five representative offices in China, in Beijing, Guangzhou, Shanghai, Nanjing and Tianjin, a joint venture with Sinotrans to operate a 450-TEU chartered vessel as a feeder serving Tianjin, Kobe and Nagoya, while another service was also under negotiation with Sinotrans.

Jackson Baker, Chief Operating Officer of Sea-Land and Bengt Kock, Chairman of Atlantic Container Line, visited, as did a management team from both CGM and CMB. Another visitor in 1988 included C. H. Tung of OOCL, while a growing number of senior customer delegations from companies like BASF in Germany, Marubeni in Japan and Dupont in the US also spent time there.

The PCG continued to monitor competitor developments. Per Jørgensen (Japan) took NYK and MOSK while Wagn Jacobsen (head of Management Secretariat) took on OOCL and Evergreen, Ted Ruhly in the US took on Sea-Land and APL and Flemming Jacobs in Copenhagen took P&OCL. The idea continued to be to learn from their operations, costs, agency set-ups, and so on – a benchmarking process that was to provide solid input for developments later in the Maersk Line story.

As a consequence of the continuing Iran–Iraq war and attacks on international commercial shipping, evaluations had been made to ascertain if ships could obtain assistance from friendly warships in the area. The conclusion for Danish flag ships was negative, as Denmark had no warships of its own in the area at the time. However, on 22 April 1988, President Ronald Reagan expanded his Persian Gulf policies to allow US warships to come to the aid of neutral merchant ships that were under attack. Shortly after this, a meeting between Maersk Line and senior US officials clarified what US Navy ships would or would not do. The conditions for Maersk ships were that they should register with the US Navy before entering the Straits of Hormuz and confirm that they were not carrying arms, ammunition or implements of war. This would ensure rapid assistance in case of need. In the event of attack, a mayday message was to be sent immediately and contact established with the nearest US warship. At the time, the US had 17 warships in the area and a further 10 in nearby waters. A note dated 10 May indicated that, to date, three A.P. Moller ships had been attacked. Two Maersk seamen had been killed and four wounded.

New ships, new offices, new markets and an old problem

A press release in December 1988 announced an order for 12 container vessels, 9 from the A.P. Moller Group's own shipyard at Lindø and 3 from the Tsuneishi shipyard in Japan. The order included 3 Panamax M-class ships for delivery in 1991, and a new series of 9×950 TEU C-class feeder ships with their own cranes to be delivered during 1991–1994 from Lindø and Japan. Of the 19 feeder ships operated at that time by Maersk Line, only 2 were owned. Analyses showed that charter rates were expected to continue to increase, so this was the right time to buy.

In addition, orders were placed in November for a wide range of additional containers covering 20-foot dry units, 20-foot open tops, flatracks and reefers, 40-foot reefers and a substantial number of 40-foot dry units. A separate order was placed in Taiwan for 950 45-foot high-cube containers (9.5 feet high – a new standard height that had been approved in early 1988) and in an innovative approach, Erik Møller-Nielsen recommended the purchase of 200 45-foot reefers, saying in his memo that 'there is presently no direct demand for this type of equipment, but, if forty-five-foot reefers were available we may be able to create a demand'. It was approved.

Figure 6.5 *Charlotte Mærsk*, one of nine feeder ships with a capacity of around 950 TEU, passing the Sugar Loaf Mountain near Rio de Janeiro in Brazil.

New offices were opened in Nigeria, Benin, Togo, Ghana, Monrovia, Senegal and Finland and a visit to Vietnam planned. With the fall of the Berlin Wall in 1989, Wagn Jacobsen was ready with a plan to cover the opening up of the Eastern European countries, with Maersk Line Germany initially taking responsibility for exploring new opportunities in Poland, Czechoslovakia and East Germany. Copenhagen did the same with Hungary, Bulgaria, Romania and Yugoslavia.

The growing organisation required support and guidance, and to that end, global sales training continued to be a focus with over 5,000 training days implemented worldwide. As Flemming Jacobs described it, it was 'to have sales managers trained in how to manage a sales force including how to coach and council people'.[29]

Outside, the wider world continued to change at a remarkable pace. Mikhail Gorbachov had become leader of the Soviet Union in 1985 and was moving that vast nation towards *glasnost* (openness) and *perestroika* (restructuring). In 1987 the Louvre Accord, following on from the Plaza Accord, looked to stabilise the US dollar once it had reached a sustainable level, and that same year Alan Greenspan was appointed Chairman of the US Federal Reserve.

Box 6.5 Maersk Line service and market shares 1988

Service	1988 Market share (%)	Service	1988 Market share (%)
Trans Pacific		**Europe to Far East**	
United States to Far East Total	8.9	Europe to Far East (reefer)	32
United States to Japan	5.6	Europe to Far East (IGA)	9.2
United States to Taiwan	3.7	Scandinavia to Far East	20.9
United States to Hong Kong	12.3	UK and Eire to Far East	5.7
United States to Singapore/Malaysia	40.1	North Continent to Far East	7.8
Far East to United States Total	8.3	**Far East to Europe (IGA)**	11.7
Japan to United States	5.8	Japan to Europe	11.4
Taiwan to United States	7.8	Taiwan to Europe	21.1
Hong Kong to United States	10.1	Hong Kong and PRC to Europe	12.8
Singapore/Malaysia to USA	16.9	Korea to Europe	6.5
Middle East Container Line (MECL)		**Mediterranean**	
United States to Middle East	17.8	Mediterranean to Far East	11.6
United States to India, Pakistan	12.5	Far East to Mediterranean	13.7
United States to Spain	3.8		
United States to West Africa	12.8	West Africa	
Spain to Middle East	8.5	Far East to West Africa total	37.9
Italy to United States	13.5	West Africa to Far East total	49.6
France to United States	24	Europe to West Africa	3.8
Spain to United States	7.5	West Africa to Europe	3.9
Far East to Middle East		**Europe to Middle East**	
Far East to Middle East	13	Europe to Middle East (dry)	1.7
		Europe to Middle East (reefer)	8.8
Indonesia Service	23.4	Europe to India/Pakistan	2.6
Far East to Indonesia			
Indonesia to Far East			

Source: Maersk Line monthly report, June 1988.

In 1989, Soviet troops left Afghanistan, and began to pull out of Hungary. Mikhail Gorbachov and Deng Xiaoping met in the first Sino-Soviet summit meeting in 30 years, and in the same year the Berlin Wall fell, paving the way for German reunification. In Asia, the Asia Pacific Economic Cooperation (APEC) forum was founded to facilitate economic growth, cooperation, trade and investment across the Asia Pacific region.

Continued FEFC issues

Meanwhile, in the FEFC, despite all the hard work, things were not going smoothly. In 1988, Kerry St Johnston, Chairman of the FEFC, was still working hard to bring the westbound trades, from Asia to Europe in particular, under control. With the Korean lines expected to leave the FEFC at the end of 1988, Ib Kruse corresponded with Jiro Nemoto, President of NYK, in mid 1988 on issues in the trade. His letter illustrated the problem clearly: when Maersk Line had operated a fortnightly service between Asia and Europe its share had been about 8 per cent of the trade with Japan. Since then, Maersk Line had bought rights from CMB and CR, and had upgraded the service to a weekly operation. Yet Maersk Line's share of the Japan-to-Europe trade had now fallen below that level. On this basis Kerry St Johnston's efforts were fully supported by Maersk Line, and Maersk Line's position was fully supported by the role of the Neutral Body.

An article in Lloyds List of May 1989 summarised the TRIO Group's expansion plans to provide three separate services with 27 ships and increase its capacity to 450,000 TEU (up from 385,000 TEU). With their traditionally strong market positions in Japan, Germany and the UK, this would create further risk of turbulence in the trade. Maersk Line's plan for 1990, however, was not fundamentally dissimilar; with the arrival of the new L-class ships into the Europe trade, capacity would increase from 145,000 TEU to 180,000 TEU.[30]

Substantial efforts continued in the FEFC through 1989 to create an agreement with the ACE Group within the Inter-Group Agreement (IGA) framework, including the creation of a new, more competitive tariff structure in both the eastbound and westbound trades and a 'stabilisation agreement' with the outsiders. The process continued throughout 1990, after Kerry St Johnston handed over the job of FEFC Chairman to William R. E. Thomson of Ben Line in mid 1989. A new tariff, known as NT90, was introduced and attempts made to bring rates back to more compensatory levels by a series of increases over that year.

In the Trans Pacific, rates were also under pressure as more capacity was added. Flemming Jacobs decided to attend the Asia North America

Eastbound Rate Agreement (ANERA) owners meeting. The management team responsible for Maersk Line's Trans Pacific services was seriously considering leaving the conference.

A valuable lesson for Maersk, which was beginning to consider itself a global organisation, was learned around this time. A senior American manager from Maersk Line in the United States, interviewed by the US *Journal of Commerce,* heavily criticised the conference system. A few days later, the article came to the Board's attention in Copenhagen and Mærsk Mc-Kinney Møller asked what guidelines existed for managers around the world when dealing with the press. Wagn Jacobsen investigated and reported back that there were indeed clear guidelines for all the external office managers. They dated back to January 1978 and were all in Danish. Not all the internal procedures in the growing Maersk organisation had yet adjusted to the globalised world!

A selection of important developments: 1985–1989

Political

- 1986 A coup and popular demonstrations topple the Philippines' president, Ferdinand Marcos.[31]
- 1989 The last Soviet troops leave Afghanistan[32] and the Soviet Union begins to pull troops out of Hungary.[33]
- 1989 A summit is held in Beijing between Soviet and China leaders, Mikhail Gorbachev and Deng Xiaoping. This is the first Sino–Soviet summit for 30 years.[34]
- 1989 China's army forcibly ends student demonstrations in Tiananmen Square, Beijing, leaving around 800 people dead.[35]
- 1989 The Berlin Wall falls, paving the way for the reunification of Germany.[36]
- 1989 The European Bank for Reconstruction and Development (EBRD) is created to facilitate development in post-communist countries in Eastern Europe.[37]
- 1989 Former pro-democracy dissident, Václav Havel, becomes Czechoslovakia's new president.[38]

Economic

- 1985 The Plaza Accord is signed between France, West Germany, Japan, the US and the UK. The agreement aims to devalue the US dollar against the German deutsche mark and Japanese yen in order to reduce the US current-account deficit and rebalance the world economy.[39]
- 1986 Mexico starts market reforms and joins the General Agreement on Tariffs and Trade (GATT). In 1980 trade accounted for only 17.5% of Mexico's GDP. By early 2012 it will increase to around 60%.[40]
- 1986 The Cairns Group, a coalition of 19 agricultural exporting countries, is created to reform international trade in agrarian goods.[41]
- 1987 The Dow Jones Index plunges 508 points, or 22.6% in value, its largest single-day percentage drop in what will be labelled the Black Monday stock market crash.[42]
- 1988 The G10 agrees on the Basel (I) Accords. Basel I is an attempt to standardise and set a minimum capital requirement for the world's banks, in order to minimise risk in the financial system. It will come into force in 1992. Basel I will later be replaced by subsequent accords.[43]
- 1989 The Japanese Nikkei Share index reaches its peak of 38,957.[44] It does not recover to this level in subsequent years, standing at 10,395 on December 28th 2012.[45]
- 1989 The Asia-Pacific Economic Cooperation (APEC) forum is founded to facilitate economic growth, co-operation, trade and investment in the Asia Pacific region.[46]

Social

- 1985 *Liberation theology*, the notion that the Church should be an agent of change within the working classes, sweeps Latin America.[47]

- 1985 The Free Software Foundation is established to promote the freedom to use, study, copy, modify and redistribute computer programmes without restriction.[48]
- 1986 Desmond Tutu becomes the first black African archbishop of Cape Town.[49] He will later play a major role in South Africa's reconciliation process.[50]
- 1988 Max Havelaar, the first Fairtrade label, is launched under the initiative of a Dutch development agency, Solidaridad. Ethical labels have since become major players in the food industry.[51]

Technological

- 1985 Microsoft Windows is released.[52] By 2012 over 80% of personal computers will use a Microsoft Windows operating system.[53]
- 1985 The price of computing memory continues to fall. US$1 (at constant 2000 prices) buys 13,646 RAM Bits, by 2004 it will buy 93,945,000 RAM Bits.[54]
- 1985 US federal agencies approve the first two experimental releases of genetically modified organisms: anti-frost bacteria for strawberries and tumour-resistant tobacco plants.[55]
- 1987 China launches its policy to encourage technology transfer from the West by pursuing *import substitution* – a policy of reducing dependency on imports by favouring domestic production – in the auto industry.[56]
- 1989 Tim Berners-Lee invents the World Wide Web protocols.[57] By end-2011 the global number of Internet users will reach almost 2.3bn.[58]

Legal

- 1986 The Computer Fraud and Abuse Act comes into force in the US, making it a crime to break into computer systems.[59]
- 1987 The Montreal Protocol to phase out stratospheric ozone-destroying chlorofluorocarbons (CFCs) is signed.[60]
- 1989 The UN adopts the Convention on the Rights of the Child, allowing for "children to develop their full potential, free from hunger and want, neglect and abuse".[61]

Environmental

- 1986 A Soviet nuclear power station explodes at Chernobyl, scattering radioactive material worldwide; 350,000 people are subsequently resettled.[62]
- 1986 The International Whaling Commission (IWC) bans commercial whaling to allow stocks to recover.[63]
- 1987 The Intergovernmental Panel on Climate Change (IPCC) is established.[64]
- 1988 The Brazilian government begins using satellites to monitor deforestation of the Amazon.[65]
- 1989 An oil tanker, Exxon Valdez, spills over 11m gallons of crude oil in Prince William Sound in Alaska.[66]

7

The 1990s

> *Globalisation accelerated in the 1980s and really started to take off in the 1990s following the fall of the Iron Curtain, which opened up the markets of Russia and East Europe, and, most dramatically, as China opened its door to free enterprise and foreign investment. Containerisation played an important role in opening these markets by providing an efficient freight transportation system.*
>
> '50 Years of Containerisation', *US Journal of Commerce*[1]

Two documents from the end of 1989 provide an insight into the thinking of Maersk Line's management at the time. The first was a McKinsey report entitled 'Challenges in the 1990s'. Flemming Jacobs summarised the report in a note to Mærsk Mc-Kinney Møller and the A.P. Moller Group leadership: to win in the coming years 'superior analytical skills would be essential; strong operational expertise would represent a necessary base platform; wide strategic flexibility would be needed; financial freedom would be required, with aggressiveness and a strong bias for action'.[2]

The second was a short memo from Jacobs to Mærsk Mc-Kinney Møller and Ib Kruse. In it, he proposed the creation of a 'vision' for Maersk Line to build on the existing product differentiation and to guide the global organisation over the next few years.[3] Jacobs cited intense competition from the Korean carriers as well as the Chinese COSCO, the reduced effectiveness of the conferences and the fact that none of the carriers was in a position to be a price leader.

His proposal read:

It is our vision to develop a basis for Maersk Line to become a global market leader and a low-cost provider with a truly dominant position in the world containerised trades, to enable effective pricing control and decisively distance Maersk from any viable competition and create significant barriers to entry.

Jacobs added that he believed now was the right time to do so, with the objective of becoming 'the IBM of our industry' (IBM had a market share of over 30 per cent in the integrated solutions segment).

Figure 7.1 Flemming Jacobs, shown here thanking the godmother of the *Dirch Mærsk* in 1996, was instrumental in setting up containerised services in Maersk Line. Jacobs started his career with A.P. Moller – Maersk in 1960 and was part of the original team in Maersk Container Line. He became CEO of Maersk Line in 1986, when the 'old' Maersk Line and the 'new' Maersk Container Line were merged.

Jacobs' view was that more or less daily departures would be needed in the main trades. At the time there were weekly services (twice-weekly on the Trans Pacific service) and he calculated that it would cost \$5.6–7.5 billion and take 15–20 years to increase this to three or four departures per week. Along the way, existing ships would need to be replaced so the process could take even longer – and was anyway too slow.

His alternative proposal was the acquisition of three or four competitors. Targets included APL, Sea-Land, OOCL, Evergreen and NedLloyd. The sums involved would not be dissimilar to the costs of extending services and replacing ships. His idea was not necessarily to integrate the companies into Maersk Line, but to use their existing strengths – Sea-Land's terminals globally, APL's land transport in the United States and NedLloyd's land transport in Europe – to complement the total.

Finally, he proposed a small team consisting of himself, Per Jørgensen and Michael Fiorini should investigate further and report back by April 1990. Building on the changes implemented earlier and the growing self-confidence derived from having established Maersk Line as a major player in the container market, these two documents can be said to summarise the thoughts that would guide Maersk Line's development, formally and informally, for many of the next 15 years or so.

Was this another major turning point in Maersk Line's development? It was never formalised as strategy. However, Maersk Line did pursue many of the ideas presented in these documents and exploited many of the opportunities the developing business presented.

The container terminal strategy

In his role as head of Maersk Line's Traffic and Operations Department, Vagn Lehd Møller was also busy. In a letter sent to the main Maersk Line offices towards the end of 1989, he summarised the status of the department and said:

the constant increased demand and opportunities for improving efficiency and the search for the exploration of ever smaller competitive margins, requires that Maersk Line establishes a strategy to develop container terminals and streamline terminal operations based on the experience gained worldwide.[4]

The letter designated a team consisting of himself, Bjarne Kolbo Nielsen, Jørgen Engell and Jörg Schuster to review terminal-related issues, learn from them and coordinate projects, while providing local management with assistance when such projects were being developed. The objective was to develop terminals that ensured the fastest possible loading and discharging of vessels, the fastest, most efficient customer service and the lowest possible long-term costs.

A key driver was the desire to have control over day-to-day operations and Maersk Line's operational destiny. A similar philosophy was evident in Sea-Land, but not yet in most of the other significant carriers.

Conference versus non-conference

In February 1990, Flemming Jacobs commissioned an analysis of Maersk Line's involvement in conferences. For many years a faithful conference supporter and member, provided the conference in question was reasonably effective, Maersk Line's management was becoming more sceptical.

The list of concerns included:

- The right of independent action with ten days' notice in the trades to and from the US where the concept was being misused as a sales tool. No lengthening of the notice period was in sight.

- The tendency of lines to go after short-sighted capacity development plans rather than long-term rate increases.
- The lack of commitment in many carriers when, despite management's agreement to increase rates, these were not followed through at the operational and sales levels.
- Some lines' apparent disregard for other lines' views, even at conference meetings, even when agreement seemed to be in place.

The list was extensive and included an analysis of customer feedback and the conferences' inability to compete effectively with the outsiders.[5] Finally, Jacobs summarised Maersk Line's dilemma clearly. On the one hand, conferences were becoming less and less effective. On the other, calculations showed that for a number of reasons, driven mainly by capacity constraints and rate reductions, Maersk Line's overall results would be $100–120 million lower than forecast if the line operated as an outsider.

The conclusion which was supported by management, was to remain in conferences where there was a good chance they would function reasonably effectively and to do everything to make that happen. Where that was not possible, to work to create rate agreements with simple structures and low costs and for meetings to be at top-management level, to ensure the best possible levels of commitment. Flemming Jacobs' final statement reiterated the importance of Maersk Line achieving a strong position in the main trades so that it could set the rates for others to follow.[6]

Cost-efficiency, 1990

As part of the 1989 budget process for 1990, another cost-efficiency drive was initiated. The target set was an overall reduction of 5 per cent on budgeted operational expenses as a step to enable Maersk Line to achieve 16 per cent return on investment.[7] Cost-efficiency teams visited and worked with the management in each of the more significant countries to identify cost reduction opportunities as 'cutting expenses is the only way to improve our bottom line'.[8] Major cost items were taken to pieces to identify opportunities for improvement. Feedering costs globally amounted to $376 million, while container leasing costs and positioning of empty equipment costs were also substantial and were thus targeted, while the United States was also asked to investigate lower-cost alternatives to their double-stack train operation. Since June 1985 this had been running from Tacoma to Chicago and the East Coast using some 160 double-stack railcars at a cost of some $80 million a year.

Figure 7.2 The *Adrian Mærsk*, which inaugurated Maersk Line's containerised service in September 1975. The garage for roll-on–roll-off cargo was added in 1984 before the ship was deployed on the Asia–Middle East service.

What only a ship owner can do

In September 1990, following the Iraqi invasion of Kuwait on 2 August and the build-up to Operation Desert Storm, Mærsk Mc-Kinney Møller made the unilateral decision to offer garage space on two of Maersk Line's combined roll-on–roll-off (RO-RO) container ships to the US authorities, free of charge. While the Middle East Container Line (MECL) was left with a hole in its capacity, the US Military Sea Lift Command was highly appreciative.

On their normal schedule, the *Adrian Mærsk* and *Albert Mærsk* left Charleston, North Carolina for Dammam in Saudi Arabia in October 1990, with a large portion of non-paying cargo, while on a commercial basis and in competition with other carriers, Maersk Line made four more sailings from North America and four sailings from Saudi Arabia to the United States. As time went on, further commercial voyages were chartered in using the same ships, which were ideally suited for the movement of the cargoes needed to support Desert Storm.[9]

Commercial developments, P&O and Sea-Land

The markets in the main trades were poor and the results for 1990 were not looking positive. Erik Møller-Nielsen was given the task of improving results over the next three years, with the proviso that 'we should not continue with things, just because we always have'.[10] He did so by taking singularly different directions and approaches.

One was noted in the A.P. Moller Board minutes for June 1990. With effect from March 1991, when the TRIO consortia agreement with the Japanese and Hapag Lloyd expired in the Europe–Far East–Europe trade, Maersk Line would work in partnership in this trade with P&O of the UK. The agreement was for the next four to five years, and during that period both parties would explore other opportunities together. The operating agreement was signed on 11 July 1990.

In its 1991 yearbook, *Containerisation International* noted this agreement and wrote 'Maersk's deal with P&O has quite a sacrificial ring, not lightly entered into as a temporary thing. Logically, this pair could now join others and build up an unbeatably competitive pattern of *daily* service calls.'[11]

In February 1990, Alex Mandl, CEO of Sea-Land, had visited Copenhagen. As always when visitors were expected, briefing material had been drawn up by Maersk Line. This summarised the status of Maersk's relations with the visitor's company, pinpointing business issues and/or opportunities that would be of interest to both parties. At the time, Sea-Land was once again pioneering containerisation, this time in the former Soviet Union, now dispersed into 15 newly independent states of which Russia was the dominant power. Sea-Land was deeply involved with the Trans-Siberian railway bridge between Asia and Europe, while actively supporting the Desert Storm build-up by providing a service from the United States to Saudi Arabia.

In September 1990, Ib Kruse had dinner with Alex Mandl, and as a result, Flemming Jacobs and Erik Møller-Nielsen studied how a cooperative agreement between Maersk Line and Sea-Land might also be made operational. Later that month, the A.P. Moller Board was told about a new agreement with P&O and Sea-Land, covering the Trans Atlantic, where P&O and Sea-Land would each load, in both directions, on the Maersk Line Trans Atlantic sailings.

Meanwhile, in November, a connecting carrier agreement was made with Lauritzen Reefers to ship up to 50 reefers per sailing from Chile to Long Beach, with Maersk Line on-carrying the containers for delivery in Asia.[12] The main commodities included grapes, stone fruit and fish.

It might appear that these developments compromised Maersk Line's independence and freedom to act. However, that is not the perception of those who were directly involved at the time. It could also be

Box 7.1 Other significant developments

Before we move on from 1990, it is also worth noting some other developments.

In the Trans Pacific, the Federal Maritime Commission (FMC) was strengthening the role of the Neutral Body, resulting in fines of over $18 million to six Asian carriers.

In Europe, in June 1990, the Danish East Asiatic Company bought out ScanDutch.

Also in Europe, Brian Allen, Director General of the FEFC, reported on 'unfriendly correspondence' with Mr Temple Lang of DG IV (the European Union's Competition Directorate) on several aspects of the FEFC's meetings and the stabilisation meetings the FEFC was trying to hold with some of the outsiders.

In Maersk Line Copenhagen, a reorganisation had Michael Hassing managing the Europe–Far East services while Jørgen Harling took over the Trans Atlantic and Lars Michael Jensen, the Middle East Container Line (MECL).

Continuing his efforts to focus on improving the bottom line, Erik Møller-Nielsen set up a project team to replace the old system of calculating the net revenue from a container (known as the 'minima' system) with a new, more sophisticated system with an improved analytical capability.

In 1990, Vagn Lehd Møller had taken over as Managing Director of Mercantile as Flemming Jacobs moved from his role as CEO of Maersk Line and Mercantile, to run The Maersk Company Limited in London. This was a substantial ship-owning operation as well as a diverse business in tankers, drilling, supply ships, oil exploration and aviation, as well as being agents for Maersk Line and Mercantile in the UK.

A couple of years later, Flemming Jacobs moved again to become Regional Managing Director for Maersk in Asia, based in Singapore. In late 1996 he moved back to Copenhagen, promoted to Partner in the A.P. Moller Group with effect from 1 January 1997.

argued that these developments slowed decision-making; with partners involved, more consultation was needed before decisions could be made. In each case, however, these agreements were based on both carrier partners putting forward 'win–win' proposals by providing more sailings, greater shipping capacity, greater flexibility and more trade expansion opportunities – which meant that their customers were winners, too.

Another visitor that year was Reiner Gohlke, Director General of Deutsche Bahn (DB), the German state railway. Maersk Line was already spending about $10 million per year with DB, distributing containers across Germany; now the purpose of his visit was to discuss the practical issues of operating container trains cross-border in Europe.

Building a new business: Mercantile

In Chapter 4 we left Mercantile as a small independent consolidator with about 85 staff worldwide, working in Asia mainly for US importers, with a few small customers developing into Europe and loading essentially all shipments on Maersk Line. Some saw Mercantile as a potential 'cargo trap', a way of tying the customer closer to Maersk Line and thereby increasing the barriers to exit. Others saw its development as a supply chain-related business opportunity in its own right that would also provide A.P. Moller with a differentiated set of products. Both Sea-Land and APL were working separately towards similar ends, with varying degrees of investment, while ScanDutch was providing some of its Scandinavian customers with quite sophisticated consolidation services. P&O and NYK of Japan were thinking along similar lines.

Towards the end of 1988, a small team chaired by Martin Skaanild with Niels Kim Balling, Poul Bjerre, Jørgen Harling and Michael Lauridsen began evaluating the concept called Maersk Materials Management (3M).[13] This proposed a computer-supported logistics system that would allow 'Maersk Line to expand its role in the transportation and logistics chain from supplier to ultimate receiver and thereby actively participate on a profitable basis also in all the land based logistics and distribution facets'.[14]

The planning was driven by the comments of people like Rune Svenson, President of Volvo Transport Corporation, who stated in an interview with *SeaTrade Business Review* in November 1988:

The industries of the 1990s will demand and force the integration of the various links in the transportation chain, and the time when shipping lines, land transport organisations and ports could work independently will be gone.[15]

Across the Atlantic, Tony Reed, Corporate Transportation Manager at Payless Cashways Inc., was quoted as saying:

There are plenty of carriers that think 'point to point', but few who have grasped the idea of smoothing the path of cargo over a logistical chain utilising systems expertise – including the use of EDI – so that the cargo arrives in the right condition, at the right place, at the right time, with the consignee.[16]

However, the 3M committee also recognised that not all of Maersk Line's customers would want or be able to make effective use of such integrated logistics. The 3M concept was therefore put forward in February 1989 as a three-product, segmented approach to the market, of which the Maersk Triple Star Logistics Service was the prime product.[17]

A small team was set up to test the Triple Star Logistics service: 'A few customers should be selected to whom the concept can be presented, gaining experience for a fine-tuning and possible improvement to the products.'[18] Integrated by IT, it would effectively allow goods to be 'pulled' through the logistics and transport pipeline with optimal efficiency. Possible target customers included Apple Computer, Kodak, Liz Claiborne (who did become an early Mercantile client) and, interestingly enough, Meldisco, a company we will shortly meet in more detail.

While Henk Rootliep, Chairman of NedLloyd Group NV, indicated that they 'might' invest in a global logistics network, Timothy Rhein, President of American President Lines (APL) was unequivocal. In an interview at the Containerisation and Intermodal Institute in Oakland, California on 10 June 1988, he stated:

Through the use of advanced logistics analysis and computer systems, a single carrier can plan and control the entire movement of a shipment ... We can also provide customers with up-to-the-minute tracking and financial information related to their shipments and we can help in managing the logistics of distributing our customers' merchandise through the pre- and post-production stages.[19]

In this interview, Tim Rhein touched on one of the most important parallel developments that has supported and complemented the development of container shipping as a low-cost, reliable facilitator of globalisation – developments in technology and communications.

As companies' logistics and supply chain competences developed in the 1980s and 1990s and became more sophisticated, a focus on inventory, inventory-related costs and inventory management became the order of the day for many. Visibility, provided by technology and communications tools, supplied with data from carriers, among others, became a must-have for the growing number of companies trading more and more globally. The importance Maersk attached to technological support is illustrated in Box 7.2.

Box 7.2 Maersk Information Technology Support (MITS)

Successful implementation of a tailor-made Triple Star package, satisfying the logistical needs of customers, depends heavily upon a timely and accurate flow of information.

A system monitoring and controlling the information flow will be the main component in the MITS programme, with the following features:

- MITS will relate and reflect the status of all activities in the total flow of materials from automated placement of the order to final delivery against a 'planned' schedule.

Box 7.2 (cont.)

- At specified events, the system will trigger reports to relevant parties.
- The system will accumulate information 'upstream' and 'downstream'.
- Information will be available for measuring of process performance.
- Customers will be able to query the system using a wide variety of criteria.

Electronic data interchange
Information technology permits different computer networks with different hardware and communications protocols to share logistics information among customers, sub-contractors and carriers. Standards still remain to be established.

Communications (MCS)
Customers can access MCS for exchange of time-sensitive information from suppliers, carriers and agents.

International InCom
An international version of Maersk Data's InCom Service (Information Communication) would add value to the IT package.

Administrative systems
Requirements for development of administrative support systems have not been established yet.

Future IT features
Maersk may at a later stage decide to develop or acquire dedicated software packages for selected customers for in-house use.[20] When MITS eventually went live, it was initially known as Log*IT A; once it was operating successfully, its name was changed to Log*IT.

The only issue that the committee could not fully resolve concerned the 1984 US Shipping Act, which 'did not embrace activities beyond traditional intermodal transportation' and where 3M 'as a part of Maersk would be operating in "uncharted territory" and any co-mingling of activities would, therefore, theoretically be attached with some legal uncertainties.'[21] A structure was therefore proposed whereby 3M would be set up as a completely separate division from Maersk Line, to handle global contracts with customers, and appointing Mercantile as its agent and operating contractor in each of the appropriate localities.

After review by a number of senior managers around the world, all were in agreement that a small team should test the concept.

APM Logistics Management A/S

Accordingly, a small team was put together at the end of 1989. It was led by Jørgen Theisen Schmidt, who was brought back from his role as country manager for Thailand, where he was replaced by Peter Miller.[22] Reporting to Flemming Jacobs, the team's first task was to consider and develop a business plan that would realistically provide the real-life tests the committee had recommended. To maintain the legally required distance from Maersk Line, an independent company, APM Logistics Management A/S, was formed to be the global contracting partner. This company would then sub-contract the actual work to the local Mercantile office for execution.

At the end of 1989, Jørgen Theisen Schmidt wrote to all the main Maersk offices outlining the roles and responsibilities of the small team, essentially saying that if anyone approached them asking about supply chain management, the team would be very interested to know.

The business plan was developed during the first few months of 1990 under the direction of Yim Choong Chow, previously Managing Director of Maersk Line in Malaysia, who was on assignment to Copenhagen. The plan set out to find two to three medium-sized, relatively low-risk retailing customers operating on the Trans Pacific with whom to pilot the concept.

Meanwhile the team was learning about the concepts from, among others, Professor Douglas Lambert, then at the University of South Florida, an expert in supply chain and partner-shipping, as well as in understanding stock keeping units (SKUs) and calculating and managing inventory costs. These were very new areas for the team, and required them to collect facts and make calculations in ways they had never foreseen.

Per Starup Johansen, responsible for the design and development of the technical computer platform that would support the business idea, was working with Alain Kornhauser, Professor of Operations Research at Princeton, while the development work was to be carried out by Maersk Data. The newest member of the team, Chris Jephson, who had previously been running Maersk Line and Mercantile in the UK, arrived in Copenhagen at the beginning of March 1990.

In April, a letter arrived at Maersk Hong Kong from a Boston-based consultant, Temple, Barker and Sloane (TBS), requesting a meeting that month to discuss supply chain opportunities. Remembering Jørgen Theisen Schmidt's appeal, Henrik Zeuthen, Managing Director of Maersk in Hong Kong, forwarded it to Copenhagen. The meeting was attended by Henrik Zeuthen, Lars Reno Jakobsen and Paul Lo – both senior executives of Maersk Line Hong Kong – and Chris Jephson. The visitors were represented by a senior TBS consultant, Dr Bob House, and a mysterious person who just listened while questions were posed and Maersk replied. It seemed to go well but Maersk remained none the wiser about the identity of the potential client on whose behalf the questions were being asked.

Confirmation that Maersk's answers had at least been acceptable came shortly afterwards when a second meeting in Hong Kong was requested for May. The process was similar to the first – lots of questions posed by TBS on behalf of a third party, with an audience this time of two unidentified listeners. At the end of the session, while making it clear they were holding discussions with several other possible providers, these two attendees identified themselves as Bob Huth, Chief Financial Officer, and Shahid Quraeshi, Financial Controller, of the US-based Melville Corporation.

The Melville Corporation

At the time, the Melville Corporation was relatively unknown, yet it comprised the third largest retail group in the United States, operating through 14 different retail outlet names, seven of which imported goods: Wilsons Leather Goods; Chess King, a clothing retailer; Consumer Value Stores (CVS), a major, broadly ranged pharmaceutical retailer; Kay Bee Toy, a major toy retailer; Marshalls, a discount clothing retailer; Meldisco, a major footwear retailer; and Thom McAn, a specialist footwear retailer.

In July, Maersk was asked to tender for the business and the next few weeks were characterised by feverish activity. Proposals were drafted, calculations made and re-made. Mercantile's platform, MODS (Mercantile's Operations and Documentation System), was reviewed for enhancements and development of the new technical platform, the prototype Log*IT A, was pushed forward.

The proposal to Melville was delivered on 17 August 1990, three days ahead of the deadline. Melville was in a hurry. Some substantial financial improvement opportunities had been identified across the group by TBS, one of which was synergies across the importing divisions that could be obtained from a systematic approach to managing their supply chains.

The Melville Corporation was looking for an integrated logistics solution, based on a long-term, mutually beneficial, partnership to drive down the total cost of sourcing product from the Far East, while improving reliability and speed of the supply chain. All services were to be bound together by information systems accessible by all divisions at Melville locations in the United States and Far East, and capable of managing information at a purchase order number level, supporting tracking, tracing and historical movement analysis for all purchase orders and segregating one division's information from another while permitting corporate overview of all activity. They would include single electronic billing for all services per shipment, at an item level.[23]

The bids were narrowed down to a choice between Maersk and Sea-Land. After some significant discussions, telephone conferences and meetings, with Bob Huth, Shahid Quraeshi and Bob House visiting Copenhagen to meet Maersk management on more than one occasion, the decision went to Maersk.

Asked some months later on what basis the decision had been made, Bob Huth commented that Maersk's prices were slightly higher than Sea-Land's, but he believed that the chemistry was better and would be all-important for the partnership relationship that was envisaged. Shortly after the decision was taken, Bob House moved from his role as Consulting Principal at TBS to become Vice President of Logistics for Melville. The contract was signed by both parties in Copenhagen at the end of 1990.

Implementation

In retrospect, the venture with Melville may seem questionable. The combination of a small, untried and untested organisation (Mercantile), a technical platform still in the early stages of development and new concepts of integrated supply chains, SKUs, items and purchase orders (at least from a liner shipping perspective) might have given rise for concerns.

However, there were precedents for such steps into the unknown in Maersk's history. In the early 1940s, A. P. Møller recalled the formation of the Steamship Company of 1912:

> The start of the company was the purchase of two rather antiquated ships for DKK 300,000. To pay for the ships, a bank demonstrated its confidence in me by giving the company a loan of DKK 275,000 against a mortgage on the ships and my personal guarantee. The share capital was set at DKK 50,000, of which I personally subscribed DKK 40,000, and against these shares I borrowed a further DKK 25,000. People who go only by the rule book, of which there are many these days, me included, would no doubt think such a start reckless, even indeed the work of a mad-man, yet there was method in my madness.[24]

The Melville contract allowed no room for faintheartedness. It might have been a much bigger and more complex arrangement than the original business plan anticipated, but Maersk had a product and a customer who was willing to pay for it, so there was no looking back. Per Johansen from the team and Per Steffen Hansen from Maersk Data had three months to get Log*IT A and then Log*IT off the ground, with initial delivery made in January 1991. Although it had been built on proven technology from IBM, creating accurate transport plans that could be attached to

Figure 7.3 A warehouse in an unidentified Asian location. All individual items are placed on pallets and can easily be consolidated into a container for shipment.

each purchase order, sometimes at item level, was immensely complex. Critical elements in the process were connecting the correct 'ready for shipment at origin dates' with the relevant 'exportable' (i.e. customs cleared at origin) date and the desired 'delivery date at destination', as well as the intervening checkpoints.

Further complexity was added when Melville asked for the largest importing division, Meldisco, which retailed its footwear through all the K-Mart stores, to be first to migrate in order not to miss the 'back to school' import flows in August 1991. Melville's forecast showed planned imports of 8,462 TEU of goods, originating mainly from Hong Kong, Taiwan, Korea, Indonesia and Shenzhen in South China. The 3M team set about the project planning preparations, organising meetings with the Melville divisions, Melville Corporate, Mercantile and Maersk Line.

Supplied with the latest personal computers from Toshiba (each weighing about 4kg), which could be plugged into any office or hotel telephone point, allowing access to Maersk's Communications System (MCS) e-mail, the team travelled extensively in the United States and Asia. Their immediate objectives were to explain, develop, enhance, educate and prepare the Mercantile organisations for what was to come, including employing extra people where needed.

As the process developed, the workload became overwhelming. Jim Dorrian, President of Mercantile Inc. in the United States, was challenged to expand his small team quickly enough. As so many of the Melville divisions required meetings, planning and development at the same time, the United States-based team was strengthened with temporary support from Copenhagen: Michael Christensen, Peter Verner Kristensen and Lene Borgen. The chemistry in which Melville had put its faith held, despite the extreme pressure and some major challenges that tested the commitment and the partnership approach on both sides. Ultimately, the Melville volumes that season exceeded 11,000 TEU and came mainly from China, rather than the expected origins.

Despite this, the migrations were brought under control[25] and Mercantile started to deliver on its commitments and in August 1991, Poul Bjerre, who had been an original 3M team member, took over the role of Melville Account and Project Manager to be based in the United States for the next couple of years, although he also continued to travel extensively.[26]

An unexpected ending

All good things come to an end, but the end of the partnership with Melville came as a surprise to many. In October 1995, the Melville Corporation announced a dramatic restructuring programme. The market had expected some radical changes, but not the total spin-off that actually took place. The outcome was the creation of three separate, independent companies in pharmaceuticals, footwear and toys. Other divisions were sold off and ultimately Melville itself ceased to exist.

With effect from May 1996, the supply chain management agreement was terminated and agreements had to be made with each of the independent companies. Thanks to the close relationships that had been established, Mercantile and Maersk Line were able to maintain their operating agreements for several years after the Melville Corporation formally closed.

As Bob House wrote later, the partnership had moved over 600 million units of product with a retail value of approximately $4.8 billion. The goods had been consolidated at 38 origin points and delivered to 39 distribution centres at a cost of some $246.5 million. A comprehensive information system controlled product movement at the purchase order line level developing an activity based plan specifying the routing, timing and cost of more than 268,000 purchase order lines representing over 83,000 unique purchase orders. A total of 3.9 million cubic metres (CBM) of cargo were moved by ocean and air freight accounting for approximately 69,500 40-foot container movements.[27]

House's comprehensive report was 'designed to permit the "New Melville" organisations and Mercantile to more rapidly achieve success in the new partnerships by building on the successes of the past and avoiding the difficulties that retard progress'. It addressed the key roles, the challenges of how best to achieve the objectives of the programme, regulatory constraints, the role of information technology and data quality, and concluded that 'despite the problems, the partnership achieved considerable success'.

Finally, it reviewed the structure of the contract, where a productivity-sharing agreement had been put in place. In comparison to the 1993–1994 base data, 1995 costs were reduced by 12 per cent and on-time delivery achieved 96.6 per cent on 9,226 containers. The report concluded:

'The clarity and relative simplicity of the productivity measurement system allowed both Mercantile and Melville to focus on the two critical issues in international logistics: costs and reliability.'

Shortly after Flemming Jacobs' promotion to Partner in the A.P. Moller Group was announced in late 1996, Bob House, who had moved on to become Vice President of Logistics at K-Mart after Melville's closure, wrote to congratulate him. In his letter he said:

Your vision and willingness to support our efforts at Melville produced the single most outstanding logistics system that has been developed. Looking at what was accomplished at Melville from my new perspective at K-Mart, has shown me how far advanced our two firms were. The productivity measurement system that we jointly installed is so far ahead, that it will take us up to three years to get to the position where Melville was in 1994.[28]

But what had it done for Maersk?

The volumes alone, of which some 70–80 per cent moved on Maersk Line and with higher than average contribution, boosted Maersk Line's ability to mix cargo in a reasonably strong Far East to US market. One lesson for Mercantile was that shipping line economics differed greatly. With shipments originating from many different Asian factories and destined for many different US distribution centres (DCs), carriers were keen to balance their inbound and outbound container flows to the best extent possible, to minimise costs and improve profitability. Consequently, as Mercantile's discussions with the carriers became more data driven, within the working agreement with Melville, some specific corridors were found to be attractive to one carrier while other corridors were attractive to others.

Through extraordinary effort by people too numerous to mention, particularly throughout Asia, but also in the United States, Mercantile was now firmly established, with substantially stronger capabilities in both areas but particularly in the newly expanding factory to the world – China. The organisation also had much stronger income streams based on the Melville volumes.

Most important of all, Maersk now had a solid differentiator firmly in place relative to its competition: a design and roll-out methodology and a proven technical IT platform that were unique for their time. Both had been tried and tested, delivered value to the parties involved and could now be taken to market to other clients. And there was now a small but growing team of experienced people who had the confidence to carry the concept further into the market. Maersk had an unmatchable competitive advantage in international supply chain management on which it would continue to build.

At the beginning of 1995, following a reorganisation of the overall Maersk Line structure, Vagn Lehd Møller, head of Mercantile and Logistics, reported to Ib Kruse, CEO of the Maersk Line function. With a small team in Copenhagen responsible for the strategy, sales coordination and systems, they were now supporting a business of some 34 offices globally and a staff of over 600. By the end of 1996, this had risen to 780. Mercantile was growing up.

Parallel to Maersk Line, Mercantile implemented a regional structure in mid 1995, creating centres in Europe led by Peder Winther, North America with Henning Bach Nielsen and in Singapore under John Ewing, and made significant investments in bar-coding (over $1 million in Asia alone), EDI processes and systems enhancement.[29] A new opportunity, warehousing and distribution, was investigated and towards the end of 1995, a 15,000 square metre warehouse was acquired in Gothenburg, Sweden, while a similar project got under way in Jakarta, Indonesia. These developments were to stimulate similar ventures in many other parts of the world, not always as profitable as management would have wished.

In June 1996, Vagn Lehd Møller wrote to the offices, summarising developments. Mercantile's mission was 'to generate business to Maersk Line by attracting clients to the Group, who could not otherwise be obtained unless they were offered a wide scope of services optimising the supply chain, in a one entry point scenario'.[30]

In 1995, Mercantile, as its largest customer, had provided Maersk Line with over 9 per cent of its Far East to Europe liftings, some 5 per cent of its Europe to Far East liftings and nearly 11 per cent of its Far East to United States liftings. Mercantile's main competition came from other carrier-based operators, such as American Consolidation Service (ACS, of APL), Buyers Consolidators (of Sea-Land) and also from companies such as UPS Worldwide Logistics, Kuehne + Nagel and Fritz Companies.

An article in *KLM Cargo Magazine* in October 1996, under the heading 'Shipping Channels', made a detailed four-page comparison of Buyers Consolidators, Mercantile Consolidators and P&O's approach through their newly created P&O Global Logistics organisation and concluded 'customers are moving in a particular direction – if you do not go with them, they will not be your customers for very long'.

Shipping partners: the relationship with P&O and Sea-Land

In March 1991, Maersk Line's agreement with P&O was to provide two sailings per week in each direction on the Europe–Far East service, on the basis of 'mutuality and equality in service, slot capacity, size and status in the trade'.[31] The following month, Alex Mandl, Chairman and CEO of Sea-Land, issued a press release about his company's new relationship with Maersk Line:

[Our] agreement reflects a high level of cooperation between Sea-Land and Maersk. Over the past few months the two carriers have worked intensively to develop a mutually beneficial vessel sharing agreement.[32]

From 1 May 1991, in cooperation with Sea-Land, Maersk Line would offer five weekly sailings in each direction on the Far East–United States trades, as well as enhanced intra-Asia services. Mandl's press release listed a number of service highlights that the combined operation would provide, including 104 port calls per week in North America and Asia, direct Tokyo to Oakland services and direct Yokohama to Tacoma services (each with 8-day transits), direct Hong Kong to Long Beach services (12-day transit) and Singapore to the US West Coast (16-day service). The extensive feeder coverage of Southeast Asia was also summarised.

In September 1991, cooperation with Sea-Land was extended to cover the Far East/Arabian-Persian Gulf trades. At the end of October that year, Vagn Lehd Møller recommended to management that P&O join the vessel-sharing agreement that Maersk Line was operating in these trades with Sea-Land, with effect from June 1992. The service would then be upgraded from four to six ships, with Maersk Line supplying four ships and Sea-Land and P&O one ship each.[33]

Towards the end of November 1991, Vagn Lehd Møller also proposed that the cooperation with P&O in the Far East–Europe trade be extended to a joint third weekly service (known as a string) where Maersk Line would supply approximately 60 per cent of the capacity and P&O 40 per cent. The plan would cover capacity needs through 1993 and would have beneficial effects on Maersk Line's market shares not only between North Europe and the Far East, but also in the Arabian-Persian Gulf, Mediterranean and North Africa markets. The bottom line result would be improved while the extra service would generate a return on investment of between 16 and 18 per cent. This was also approved.

On 20 December 1991, Vagn Lehd Møller summarised the initial findings of a committee that had been reviewing Maersk Line's tonnage requirements up to the year 2000. He was in agreement with its broad recommendations, based on an expected trade growth of 6–7 per cent per year in all the main trades except the Trans Atlantic. A consequence of this was that as from 1993–1994, Maersk Line, even with the vessel-sharing agreements now in place, would face capacity shortages, particularly in the Europe–Far East and Trans Pacific trades.

The plan required 'redeployment of existing Maersk Line tonnage plus the injection of significant additional capacity to protect Maersk Line's market position'.[34] Buried in the paper on page 6 is a paragraph that mentions:

A design group with representatives from A.P. Moller and the Lindø yard has developed a 6,000 TEU vessel with the following preliminary main particulars: Length overall: 311 metres, Beam (width): 42.4 metres, Deadweight: 68,000 tons, Speed: 24.6 knots. The ship yard had indicated that they could deliver two such ships in 1995, three in 1996 and four in 1997.

These would be the first post-Panamax ships, too large to transit the Panama Canal. Maersk Line was demonstrating leadership in the industry by optimising its presence in its main trades through relationships with prominent partners and proposing the development of innovative and significantly competitive ships.

The optimistic tone in the paper perhaps reflected the improving economic situation. An International Monetary Fund (IMF) report projected a 2.8 per cent rise in world output for 1992 (compared to 0.9 per cent in 1991 and 2.2 per cent in 1990), helped by the ending of the Gulf War. The same analysis also suggested a rise in world trade volume of 5 per cent in 1992, compared to 0.6 per cent in 1991 and 4.3 per cent in 1990.[35]

Containerisation International's yearbook for 1992 gives some interesting insight into the profitability of the industry. Quoting a report by Booz-Allen and Hamilton from 1991, they noted that

return on assets in 1991 of US ocean carriers was well below two per cent with only the automotive, banking and electronics industries performing worse out of 23 sectors surveyed. The same report also showed that for the ocean liner industry at large the average pre-tax return on assets for the five year period 1985 to 1989

Figure 7.4 Like all other ships before her, the post-Panamax container ship *Regina Mærsk* was the immediate result of the collaboration between Maersk Line operations staff, who defined the specifications based on commercial requirements, the naval architects and technicians of A.P. Moller – Maersk's Technical Organisation, and their counterparts at the Odense Steel Shipyard. The *Regina Mærsk* was the world's largest container ship and very important to both its owner and the shipyard.

was only 1.4 per cent. This compared with a still modest but nonetheless sounder 4.6 per cent in 1979 to 1982.[36]

While the numbers in Maersk Line Finance's analysis (see Box 12.1) are not directly comparable with the Booz-Allen analysis, it would appear that Maersk Line was generally doing better than the market place.

Partnerships on land

Back in 1990, Per Flemming Christensen had proposed a cooperation agreement between Maersk Line, the Maersk-owned SKANDI rail swap-body operator, Danish State Railways, Deutsche Bahn (the German state-owned railway company) and Inter-Container, a company based in Switzerland that coordinated cross-border container trains in Europe. The objective was to develop full container trains.[37] Although it did not get off the ground at the time, the idea would not go away: running full container trains was seen as a major operational and customer service enhancement, as well as a cost-saving opportunity.

Levinson describes the early development in the railroad transport of containers, which took off on both sides of the Atlantic at the time of the first international shipments of standard containers in 1966.[38] Maersk Line made its first major agreement when a pure Maersk Line train was introduced between Tacoma in the US Northwest and Chicago in 1985.

In October 1991, Palle Weidlich, at that time head of Maersk Line's Equipment, Intermodal and Capacity Management team in Copenhagen, summarised the opportunity for Maersk. About 55 per cent of Maersk Lines' intermodal movements in Germany were by rail, and this level could potentially be achieved in other European countries. He anticipated that Maersk Line would move about 231,000 FFE by rail that year, while SKANDI would have about 27,000 movements. Weidlich proposed that a small team, comprising himself, Niels Vallø Christiansen and Günther Clasen from Maersk Line Hamburg, initiate discussions with the state railway companies to establish what might be needed in terms of rolling stock and engines. His proposal was approved.

The basis for this development was two-fold. First, the tariff barriers between the member states of the European Economic Community (EEC) were lifted in 1992. Second, Transport 2000, a new transport policy for Europe, was under development and included a new rail directive that in principle allowed private rail companies to operate private block trains nationally and between European states. Weidlich maintained: 'We need an efficient rail operation with Maersk-controlled daily trains between key ports and key Maersk-owned inland terminals. This can be combined with SKANDI and Norfolk Line.'[39]

Towards the end of 1992, a new team, Inter-European Transport, was established with its objective 'to become a factor in profitable corridors within Europe by selling inter-European transportation as a separate and fully fledged Maersk Line service'. Although concerned mainly with container movements by sea in and around European waters, both on feeders and the main line vessels serving Europe, the existence of such a team meant more attention was paid to the opportunities to move goods and containers by other means, including barge and rail.

And in 1994, a separate company called European Rail Shuttle (ERS) would be formed, initially in partnership with Sea-Land and P&O, with the 1999 acquisition of Sea-Land by Maersk, it was then run as a joint venture, and from 2006 and the acquisition of PONL, as a 100 per cent Maersk Line owned subsidiary.

By 2008 ERS was moving over 700,000 TEU annually by rail, deploying 18 of its own locomotives and buying in another 50 per cent of its traction,

Figure 7.5 Skandi trailers on rail waggons.

with over 1,000 rail wagons in its fleet. ERS was by then expanding into more peripheral European countries such as Bulgaria. Its 2009 budget proposal was to continue that expansion; however, the global economic slowdown at that time forced significant changes in its strategy, initially to a heavy focus on its core markets and on its profitability.

Developments in the reefer business

We last touched on the reefer business in Chapter 5, where Maersk Line was very much in discovery mode and considering entry into the Australian and New Zealand markets, with their extensive export volumes of meat and fruit.

In response to a general enquiry from Mærsk Mc-Kinney Møller about recent developments in this business area, Vagn Lehd Møller had initiated a study team with representatives from the United States, Europe and Asia to 'ensure that we cover all aspects of the reefer business ... and to review possible enhancements to further cement our position as leader'. In September 1991, Vagn Lehd Møller summarised the mid-year reefer developments and noted that in most trades, Maersk Line's market shares were solid and the volumes were growing faster than the general cargo market. He was concerned to ensure that Maersk Line would have enough equipment available for the coming year or so. The team reported in the

Box 7.3 Techniques for preserving perishable cargo

Pre-transit treatment

Pre-cooling	For many commodities the most important pre-transit treatment is the rapid removal of field heat from the product prior to loading.
Bactericides	As an added precaution, chemical treatments are often applied to fruit and vegetables to prevent infections and reduce the incidence of disease.
Fungicides	See bactericides.
Waxing	Wax is applied to certain fruit and vegetables to reduce moisture loss, thereby reducing wilting and shrivelling. Waxing also increases sales appeal.
Fumigation	Fumigants can be applied to specific commodities to control disease and insects.
Biological	A number of new products have been developed in recent years that slow down the ripening process of fruit.

Transit environment

Temperature	Refrigeration has long been recognised as the prime factor for maintaining quality.
Modified or controlled atmospheres	These are only supplements to refrigeration and cannot substitute for the proper use of refrigeration.
Nitrogen	Liquid nitrogen or nitrogen-rich atmospheres can be excellent for temperature control or preservation of fruit and produce; however, these cannot be used universally as they can induce adverse reactions in some commodities, such as citrus fruits.
Ventilation	Under certain circumstances, this can be a satisfactory substitute for refrigeration, as precise temperature control is not required. The ambient temperature of the ventilating air must be within the range of temperatures under which the fruit can survive for the period of transportation, plus time required for shelf life. Ventilating air must reach all the fruit or at least sufficient to ensure removal of noxious gases and heat from respiration. Air velocity must be enough to cool the fruit when needed, but not so great that it dehydrates the fruit. Ventilating air should have high relative humidity, preferably 85–90 per cent, the higher the better.

Special requirements for commodities

Dairy	Butter is extremely susceptible to taint.
Citrus	Biphenyl, which is used as a fungicide on citrus fruit, may impart odours to other commodities.
Limes	Do not hold below 7°C (45°F) for longer than about two weeks.

Box 7.3 (cont.)

Oranges and tangerines	Compatibility depends on the source. Florida or Texas-grown oranges are shipped at 0–4°C (40°F), but California and Arizona-grown oranges are shipped at 4–7°C (44°F).
Bananas	The carrying temperature is 12–13°C (54–55°F). Bananas give off ethylene gas and in order to retard ripening this must be expelled as quickly as possible.
Deciduous fruit	Apples and pears taint other cargoes and should be stowed away from meat, butter, cheese, flour, etc. CO_2 content should be kept below 2 per cent. Ethylene production can be high.
Grapes	Compatible with other crops only if the grapes are not fumigated with sulphur dioxide (SO_2) and if no chemicals that release SO_2 are included in packages.

Source: Maersk Line's Reefer Report, April 1986.

middle of October 1991 and its recommendation was to take up existing purchase options and to review the status again towards the end of that year, when there would be a further purchase option available. The purchases were agreed.

In a file note for the end of 1991 closing of accounts, Henrik Mauritzen of the Claims Department noted that Maersk Line's reefers were equipped with the most advanced technology, including micro-processor controlled machinery and humidity control and that an Operational Reefer Efficiency section was visiting the main reefer areas on a regular basis to ensure high performance. With special training in place for the ships' officers and electricians, his summary made positive reading from a claims perspective with less damage, and many fewer claims. Overall, Maersk Line was well positioned in its markets, and was a strong leader in many of the reefer trades.

Maintaining market shares to 2000

At the end of January 1992, Vagn Lehd Møller addressed a memo on a number of issues facing the business to Per Jørgensen in Japan, Ted Ruhly in the US and Flemming Jacobs in Singapore. On the Trans Atlantic, there was a need for rationalisation by the withdrawal of capacity, and work was moving forward with both P&O and Sea-Land to achieve this. On the MECL, where Maersk Line was not working with Sea-Land but was coordinating with P&O, Sea-Land had recently implemented a fortnightly service and was likely to want to upgrade that at some point. As Maersk Line was full, and P&O needed more space, there were some possibilities for cooperation, but these had yet to be explored. On the Far East–Europe service, the third string with P&O was progressing as planned. The threat was Sea-Land's overt intention to enter this trade, building on its existing cooperation with NorAsia Line and possibly with Hyundai of Korea. Both P&O and Maersk Line had so far rejected Sea-Land's approaches, but the latter's determination to enter the trade required consideration of a number of options, including taking a tough line with Sea-Land, if necessary.

Meanwhile, the committee that had been reviewing the need for the nine post-Panamax ships submitted its report, which Vagn Lehd Møller summarised to Mærsk Mc-Kinney Møller, Jess Søderberg and Ib Kruse on 3 February 1992. The conclusion, supported by data on market developments from TBS[40] in the United States, was favourable, although the situation was highly competitive and an influx of new ships was expected, with Asian and European owners actively placing orders.

Maersk Line was the third largest global carrier, with about 10 per cent of the market, after Sea-Land with 11 per cent and Evergreen with 12 per cent. Allowing for the known orders of new ships and the trade growth projected both internally and externally from TBS, the 1992–1993 capacity requirements were in place. But, the period 1994–1996 would require Maersk Line to charter in up to ten ships of between 1,650 and 2,400 TEU, and the period 1997–2000 would require not only the nine new ships but an additional five chartered ships in order to protect Maersk Line's market shares.

The memo is also interesting for its argumentation on the post-Panamax ships:

- Diminishing growth to the US Northeast coast ports from Asia, relative to the California region.
- All current Maersk Line ships can proceed through the Panama Canal, so capacity on that route will not be short.
- Only 9 per cent of the global deep-sea trades proceed through the Panama Canal.
- We should not limit the dimensions of all future vessels to the Panama restrictions from a commercial and operational point of view.
- By employing such post-Panamax container vessels we will reduce our slot costs by an estimated 15 per cent as compared with operating M-class ships.[41]

The memo concluded: 'The deployment described in this report appears to be both practical and economical and should be pursued.'

Mærsk Mc-Kinney Møller's reaction to the estimated 15 per cent slot cost differential was to ask how it could be increased to 30 per cent. The decision was not yet made, but it was getting closer. Towards the end of March 1992, Vagn Lehd Møller was able to go back to Mærsk Mc-Kinney Møller, Jess Søderberg and Ib Kruse with a detailed calculation showing that the proposed post-Panamax would have 30 per cent lower slot costs than the existing L-class ships and 21 per cent lower than the new M-class vessels. A good-enough result.

The 1990s: a summary

The growth of information and communications technologies, plus the arrival of early social networking tools, marked the genesis during this period of what was to become known as the knowledge economy. In 1990, there were about 11 million mobile phone subscriptions worldwide; by 2012 this had risen to six billion. But developments were not stable globally. Financial crises in the emerging markets of Mexico, Russia and Brazil led to the IMF making emergency loans to many of these countries.[42]

The devaluation of the Thai baht in 1997 triggered a regional economic crisis that spread across Asia and into Russia, with generally falling stock markets and in Russia a devaluation that led to the suspension of currency trading when the rouble lost about 40 per cent of its value against the German mark. The shock of these crises and the effects of the terms of the IMF loans ultimately drove the countries of East Asia in particular to build up foreign currency reserve holdings, exacerbating trade imbalances in the first decade of the twenty-first century. In the meantime, in 1999, a number of countries in Europe adopted a common currency: the euro.[43]

Containerisation International looked back in their 1990 yearbook and characterised the container transportation industry as 'momentous, as the pace of change accelerated and fierce competition between carriers was maintained … Generally the next decade will be like the one which preceded it – intensely dynamic.'[44]

Some of the factors *Containerisation International* believed would shape the industry in the decade included:

- slightly lower growth in major arterial routes, but intra-European expansion due to the opening up of Eastern Europe;
- further global economic unification;
- sustained demand for even bigger container ships and feeders;
- differentiation between large, global operators with high service packages and smaller niche players;

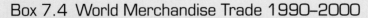

Box 7.4 World Merchandise Trade 1990–2000

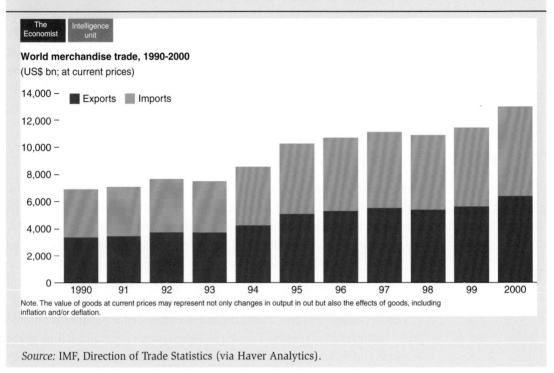

World merchandise trade, 1990-2000
(US$ bn; at current prices)

■ Exports ▨ Imports

Note. The value of goods at current prices may represent not only changes in output in out but also the effects of goods, including inflation and/or deflation.

Source: IMF, Direction of Trade Statistics (via Haver Analytics).

- further growth and refinement of electronic information networks and systems;
- the ending of the conference system as presently constituted on major east/west trade routes;
- the demise of close-knit, jointly marketed consortia;
- increasing awareness of environmental considerations.[45]

Most of these predictions were to prove prescient. Did 'differentiation between large, global operators with high service packages and smaller niche players' really occur? One could argue both for and against. One that did not develop as projected was 'the demise of close-knit, jointly marketed consortia'. While the existing consortia of the time were to go through a number of major permutations, with lines leaving and others joining and some closing altogether, as well as undergoing substantial operational as well as name changes, some close-knit consortia are still with us today in 2013.

Containerisation International also noted the emergence of 'an elite deliberately positioned to supply companies' global distribution needs', identifying Maersk, Sea-Land, APL, NYK and P&O Containers as members.[46]

This chapter opened with a reference to two forward-looking papers, the McKinsey 'Challenges for the 1990s' and Flemming Jacobs' 'Vision' paper. The latter paper summarised growth options for Maersk Line as it entered the 1990s. Maersk Line saw continuing opportunities to build on the growth that had already been achieved. Volumes had risen from 130,000 FFE in 1981 to over one million FFE by 1994. Turnover that year also broke $3.5 billion for the first time, up from $100 million in 1975, just 20 years earlier. While there had been a few years with poor returns, Box 12.1 also indicates that the last ten years had still provided a number of good years from a 'return on investment' perspective, with particularly good results in 1991, 1992 and 1993. Expansion could be continued.

A selection of important developments: 1990–1994

Political

- 1990 Iraq invades Kuwait, leading to the first Gulf war. A US-led military campaign sees Iraq withdraw in February 1991.[47]
- 1991 The Warsaw Pact, a defence alliance between the Communist regimes of the Soviet Union and Eastern Europe, is dissolved.[48] Mr Gorbachev resigns and the USSR is dissolved, leading to the formation of the Commonwealth of Independent States (CIS).[49]
- 1991 War begins in Yugoslavia.[50]
- 1991 In South Africa, apartheid laws are repealed. Nelson Mandela is elected president of the African National Congress (ANC).[51] The country's first democratic elections will take place in 1994.[52]
- 1993 Israel and the Palestine Liberation Organisation (PLO) sign the Oslo peace accords.[53]
- 1994 Around 800,000 Rwandans are killed in a genocide. Tutsi soldiers from the Rwandan Patriotic Front (RPF) take control of the capital, Kigali, driving 2m Hutus into Zaire.[54]

Economic

- Early 1990s The collapse of the Soviet Union and the end of the cold war spur a period of globalisation and economic liberalisation across the world.[55]
- Early 1990s Japan enters the "Lost Decade": growth stagnates and a previously accumulated asset bubble deflates.[56]
- Early 1990s Regional trade agreements gain momentum. Between 1990 and 1999, the World Trade Organization (WTO) will be notified of 87 regional trade agreements.[57]
- 1991 Brazil, Argentina, Uruguay, Paraguay and later Chile, sign the Southern Cone Customs Union (Mercosur) trade pact.[58]
- 1991 Economic reforms to lower tariffs, open the economy to foreign firms and liberalise markets are launched in India.[59]
- 1993 The US, Canada and Mexico sign the North American Free Trade Agreement (NAFTA). NAFTA will come into force in 1994.[60]
- 1994 The Free Trade Area of the Americas is proposed,[61] but the proposal was later abandoned.[62]
- 1994 The Uruguay Round establishes the WTO to oversee and liberalise global trade.[63]

Social

- 1990 McDonald's opens its first restaurant in China. By 2008 the company will have 960 restaurants in China and 60,000 employees.[64]
- 1991 Mainland Chinese are allowed to travel abroad as tourists for the first time under communist rule. Travel is restricted to several Asian countries. By 2010, 57m Chinese tourists will travel abroad annually.[65]

- 1992 MP3s – digitally compressed music files – are created, allowing sharing of music across the Internet. This will ignite significant controversy, as record labels fight for the right to control their intellectual property.[66]
- 1993 The first World Telecommunication Standardization Conference takes place in Helsinki.[67]

Technological

- 1990 The National Aeronautics and Space Administration (NASA) launches the Hubble space telescope.[68]
- 1991 The first commercial food-irradiation plant is opened[69] and irradiated fruit and vegetables appear on the market in the US. The process increases shelf life and kills insects.[70]
- 1991 A Finnish Global System for Mobile Communications (GSM) operator, Radiolinja, launches second-generation wireless telephone networks (2G) using digital technology. 2G introduces data on phones, including text messaging.[71]
- 1993 Scientists clone human embryos.[72]
- 1994 Carrier Corporation introduces EverFresh, the first totally integrated controlled-atmosphere container system for *reefer applications*, in order to carry perishable freight.[73]

Legal

- 1992 US president, George H.W. Bush, signs into law the allowance of the commercial use of the Internet, previously owned and exclusively used by the US government.[74]
- 1992 The Australian High Court, at the conclusion of a court case commonly known as *Mabo*, declares that Australia was not a *terra nullius* (a land without owners) when Britain asserted sovereignty in 1788, enabling indigenous Australians to reclaim land rights.[75]
- 1994 The Trade-Related Aspects of Intellectual Property Rights (TRIPS) agreement negotiated in the 1986–94 Uruguay Round introduces intellectual property rules into the multilateral trading system.[76]
- 1994 The creation of the WTO leads to the suspension of Article 301 of the 1974 US Trade Act "Super 301", which authorises the investigation of the trading practices of an entire country and the right of the US to impose penalties unilaterally.[77]

Environmental

- 1991 The Canada-US Agreement on Air Quality is signed in an attempt to harmonise approaches and policies related to *acid rain*. The agreement commits both countries to reducing their sulphur dioxide emission levels by 50% by the year 2000.[78]
- 1992 The Convention on Biological Diversity is signed.[79]
- 1992 China's National People's Congress approves the construction of the Three Gorges Dam, the world's largest in terms of capacity.[80]
- 1992 The Rio Earth Summit leads to the adoption of Agenda 21, a wide-ranging blueprint for action to achieve sustainable development.[81]
- 1994 The Eurotunnel is opened, connecting the UK to the European mainland.[82]

Merchandise trade by country

Global population: 5.3bn

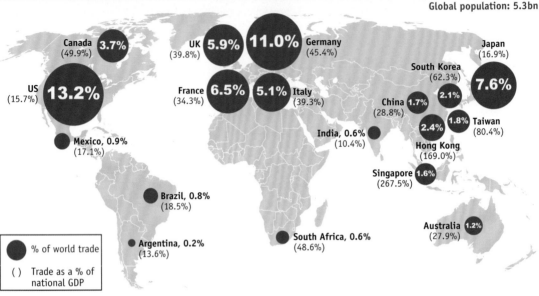

Canada (49.9%) 3.7%

UK (39.8%) 5.9%

Germany (45.4%) 11.0%

Japan (16.9%) 7.6%

South Korea (62.3%) 2.1%

US (15.7%) 13.2%

France (34.3%) 6.5%

Italy (39.3%) 5.1%

China (28.8%) 1.7%

Taiwan (80.4%) 1.8%

Mexico, 0.9% (17.1%)

India, 0.6% (10.4%)

Hong Kong (169.0%) 2.4%

Brazil, 0.8% (18.5%)

Singapore (267.5%) 1.6%

Argentina, 0.2% (13.6%)

South Africa, 0.6% (48.6%)

Australia (27.9%) 1.2%

● % of world trade

( ) Trade as a % of national GDP

Note. The map is based on January 2013 boundaries. Trade is based on merchandise exports and imports.
Sources: The Economist Intelligence Unit (EIU) calculations using trade data from IMF, *Direction of Trade Statistics* (via Haver Analytics) and GDP data from EIU. Population data from UN (via Haver Analytics).

World merchandise exports

US$ trn (at 2005 prices)

0.4	0.6	0.8	1.2	1.8	2.3	3.0	3.3	4.4				
1950	1955	1960	1965	1970	1975	1980	1985	1990	1995	2000	2005	2010

Note. World exports have been rebased to 2005 constant prices using world export volumes from the World Trade Organization (WTO).
Source: EIU calculations using WTO data.

World exports of selected commodities

US$ bn (at 2005 prices)

■ Fruit, nuts and vegetables ■ Meat and fish ■ Dairy products ■ Computers and televisions
■ Motor vehicles ■ Clothing ■ Footwear

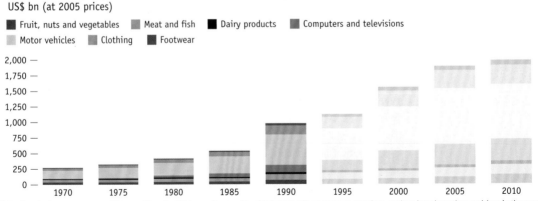

Note. In order to compare commodities over time, the EIU has made a number of judgment calls on category groupings, as there have been three revisions in the way that UN commodity data are classified. The data have also been rebased to 2005 constant prices using world export prices from the WTO. The motor vehicles category refers to road motor vehicles, including cycles, trailers, and parts and accessories; clothing includes headgear, excludes travel goods and handbags.
Source: EIU estimates using UN Comtrade, *DESA/UNSD* and WTO data.

Merchandise trade by country

Global population: 5.7bn

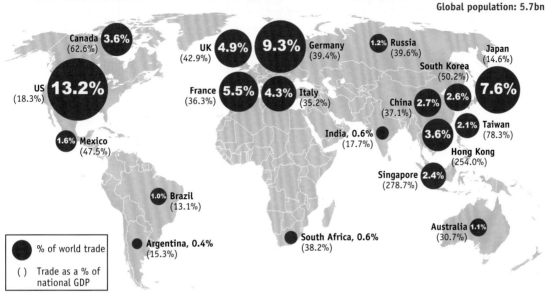

Canada **3.6%** (62.6%)

UK **4.9%** (42.9%)

9.3% Germany (39.4%)

1.2% Russia (39.6%)

Japan (14.6%)

South Korea (50.2%)

US **13.2%** (18.3%)

France **5.5%** (36.3%)

4.3% Italy (35.2%)

China **2.7%** (37.1%)

2.6%

7.6%

2.1% Taiwan (78.3%)

1.6% Mexico (47.5%)

India, 0.6% (17.7%)

3.6%

Hong Kong (254.0%)

1.0% Brazil (13.1%)

Singapore **2.4%** (278.7%)

Argentina, 0.4% (15.3%)

South Africa, 0.6% (38.2%)

Australia **1.1%** (30.7%)

⬤ % of world trade

( ) Trade as a % of national GDP

Note. The map is based on January 2013 boundaries. Trade is based on merchandise exports and imports.
Sources: The Economist Intelligence Unit (EIU) calculations using trade data from IMF, *Direction of Trade Statistics* (via Haver Analytics) and GDP data from EIU. Population data from UN (via Haver Analytics).

World merchandise exports

US$ trn (at 2005 prices)

0.4	0.6	0.8	1.2	1.8	2.3	3.0	3.3	4.4	5.8			
1950	1955	1960	1965	1970	1975	1980	1985	1990	1995	2000	2005	2010

Note. World exports have been rebased to 2005 constant prices using world export volumes from the World Trade Organization (WTO).
Source: EIU calculations using WTO data.

World exports of selected commodities

US$ bn (at 2005 prices)

■ Fruit, nuts and vegetables ■ Meat and fish ■ Dairy products ■ Computers and televisions
■ Motor vehicles ■ Clothing ■ Footwear

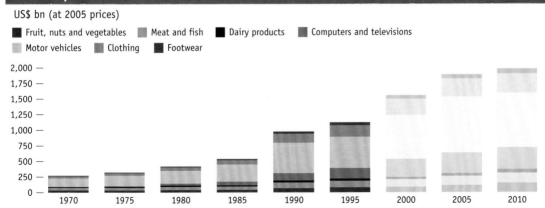

Note. In order to compare commodities over time, the EIU has made a number of judgment calls on category groupings, as there have been three revisions in the way that UN commodity data are classified. The data have also been rebased to 2005 constant prices using world export prices from the WTO. The motor vehicles category refers to road motor vehicles, including cycles, trailers, and parts and accessories; clothing includes headgear, excludes travel goods and handbags.
Source: EIU estimates using UN Comtrade, *DESA/UNSD* and WTO data.

The Acquisition Trail
(1992–1998)

8

> *The more we do, the more remains to be done.*
> Ingvar Kamprad, founder of IKEA

Close, but not quite

At the beginning of 1991 a fax had been received by Maersk Line's management from the Danish East Asiatic Company (EAC), announcing that from 1 January 1992 it would be operating a joint weekly service between Asia and Europe with Ben Line of Edinburgh, under the name EAC-Ben Line. There would be seven ships on the service, four provided by EAC and three by Ben Line.

On 1 May 1992 Hans Henrik Sørensen reviewed Maersk Line's needs for capacity up to the year 2000 and increased the need for chartered ships from five to nine to cover the period 1997–2000. His conclusion was that it would be 'unrealistic to charter these vessels, therefore we have to investigate possible purchase options'. Maersk Line had in the past looked into several acquisition possibilities but none of these had materialised. Now, 'an acquisition possibility that would be in conformity with our strategy and where the present owners might be willing to sell their container vessels would be: EAC and Ben'.[1]

Sørensen went on to summarise their set up: EAC had two 4,000-TEU, 24-knot ships (built in 1990) and four 2,800-TEU ships (built 1972–1973); Ben Line had three 3,000-TEU, 23-knot ships, also built over the latter period. Sørensen estimated that the nine ships could provide the needed capacity and at a potentially acceptable price.

But would EAC-Ben Line want to sell? EAC had been founded in 1897 and had developed into a major shipping and trading company with extensive global interests, primarily in Asia. While its shipping interests had declined, its trading activities were still extensive. Sørensen believed that when ScanDutch had broken up as a consortium and EAC-Ben had taken its place, its load factors had fallen substantially. Although

Figure 8.1 Still in the colours of the Danish East Asiatic Company (EAC), but with the distinct Maersk blue and a white seven-pointed star on the funnel, the *Alsia* was renamed *Munkebo Mærsk* following the acquisition in 1993.

container volumes had improved, his evaluation still showed a likely operating loss.

In view of the age of some of their ships, Sørensen hypothesised that 'EAC might find it more attractive to sell their vessels now and invest their money in other divisions'. Despite their age, he concluded that, with good maintenance, the ships should be able to continue trading through to the year 2000.

An informal and strictly confidential lunch meeting in May 1992 brought to light EAC's understanding that it would never become a global carrier. It was concerned about the need for greater tonnage and its agency functions in the Far East; several of these made notable contributions to the results of the local EAC trading companies. Pulling out of transport would hurt the overall result of its trading divisions.

If EAC were to sell, then in addition to the nine ships, Maersk would have to buy its containers, the office in Sevenoaks in the UK, from which the operation was managed, and take over about 130 staff. Three other services would be included in the package: West Australia to the Far East, East Australia to Japan and Korea, and Vietnam.

In early July 1992, Vagn Lehd Møller summarised Maersk's internal investigations to Mærsk Mc-Kinney Møller and Ib Kruse and suggested that Maersk go back to EAC with an expression of interest. He attached a list of the main assumptions for the financial calculations, which showed a return on investment of 12 per cent in 1993 and some 19.8 per cent for the period 1994–1997. The paper included a plan of how the ships could be best deployed and the estimated net result if agreement was reached and an initial implementation plan, and it recommended that discussions continue with EAC.

Later in July, Ib Kruse and Michael Fiorini, head of Maersk's Finance Department, met Karsten Stock Andresen of EAC for dinner at Ib Kruse's home outside Copenhagen. A number of issues – differences of opinion on possible takeover dates and price, the complexity of the existing Maersk Line arrangements with P&OCL and Sea-Land – led Ib Kruse to conclude 'We are a long way from each other.'[2] And so the matter lapsed.

Box 8.1 Developments with competition

Trans Atlantic: Alternative vessel-sharing arrangements were being explored and Martin Lundberg, CEO of Bil Spedition of Sweden and owners of Atlantic Container Line (ACL), visited Copenhagen in January 1992. Later that year, a visit was paid to one of the ACL ships to evaluate its capabilities.

Orient Overseas Container Line (OOCL) had been through an aggressive rationalisation programme in the late 1980s to resolve its debt crisis. C. H. Tung of OOCL visited Copenhagen in February 1992. An extensive Maersk Line analysis evaluated the possibility of acquiring OOCL as well as what could be learned from what OOCL had been through.

Regional Container Lines, in intra-Asian trades, were buying new buildings from Hanjin Heavy Industries in Korea. The ships' draft allowed loading of 1,060 TEU, compared to Maersk Line's ships of 920 TEU, an important edge in serving Bangkok, where a bar limited available water depth.

The FEFC: in May 1992, a European Stabilisation Agreement was made with Evergreen and filed with the EU, following the success of the Trans Pacific Stabilisation Agreement (TSA). In September the Trans Atlantic Agreement (TAA) followed. The prime motive was to drive rates up from the unremunerative levels by capping container capacity. The TSA and TAA were approved by the Federal Maritime Commission (FMC), but the Directorate General for Competition (DGIV) in Brussels was not going to be so helpful.

ACL, as Chairman of the TAA, raised serious concerns about the European Union's approach to liner shipping. Following the European Maritime Law Organisation

Box 8.1 (cont.)

Conference in London in October 1992, ACL proposed that member lines should 'engage in a cooperative effort to counter the approach'.[3]

The Soviet Union and Yugoslavia broke up between 1991 and 1992. The former USSR fleet was disbanded and allocated to Russia and the Ukraine. The former Yugoslav fleet was retained mainly by Croatian companies.[4] The Swiss fleet also increased by 46 per cent, largely due to Mediterranean Shipping Company's purchases of second-hand tonnage.

In April, negotiations with P&OCL concluded a Trans Atlantic vessel-sharing agreement and in May announced a new joint Maersk Line and P&OCL service between Europe and the Middle East, with weekly coverage of Jeddah and Dubai and feeder connections to the Gulf, India and Pakistan.

Sea-Land's desire to enter the Europe–Far East trades continued and in May 1992 John Clancey, President of Sea-Land, wrote to Vagn Lehd Møller that 'after a great deal of thought and deliberation', Sea-Land had decided it had no alternative but to launch the joint venture with Nor-Asia Line. Despite this, a new Maersk Line/Sea-Land agreement to continue cooperation on the North Atlantic was put in place in December.

If at first you don't succeed . . .

Maersk did not have to wait long. A file note from Jess Søderberg on Tuesday, 23 March 1993 to his fellow Partners, Mærsk Mc-Kinney Møller, Ib Kruse and Per Jørgensen (who had been promoted to Partner on 8 March), summarised a meeting requested by Michael Fiorini (now Managing Director of EAC) that had taken place the previous day. Fiorini wanted to know if A.P. Moller would be interested in taking over EAC's liner service and equipment, either in part or in whole. EAC was also in discussions with American President Lines (APL), but Fiorini did not expect this to lead to an agreement.

Jess Søderberg, after consulting his A.P. Moller Partners and taking legal advice, responded by asking EAC to specify what they wanted to sell and to give a realistic price indication. He also asked EAC to stop negotiating with APL and requested a letter from APL confirming that EAC was 'free of any obligations regarding any letter of intent or other tentative agreements, verbally or in writing'.[5] On 24 March, Fiorini wrote to Søderberg, confirming that APL had terminated negotiations and attached a copy of a letter from John Lillie, Chairman of President Companies Limited, confirming the end of the negotiations, outlining exactly what was on offer and proposing a price of about $253 million.

Fiorini requested that the takeover be expedited. He proposed that meetings to finalise the details should take place that same day. Fiorini needed

Figure 8.2 Per Jørgensen was involved in A.P. Moller – Maersk and indeed in world trade for well over 50 years, taking an active part in Maersk Line's development from a regional break-bulk liner operator to a global container transport provider.

to have clarification before EAC's annual general meeting now only four short days away. Following a brief meeting between Jess Søderberg and Michael Fiorini on the morning of Thursday 25 March, when the general terms were agreed, a team of specialists worked around the clock until Monday morning, where the final papers were signed.

And so the first of Maersk Line's acquisitions of the 1990s was put in place. But it brought far more than the additional tonnage needed. It marked what has been described as 'the great leap forward . . . in 1993 when Maersk took over EAC's remaining container fleet (the EAC-Ben Line) they thus became the world's largest container shipping company'.[6]

Box 8.2 Australia and New Zealand (Oceania)

Australia

Settled by aboriginals at least 40,000 years ago, the land was claimed for Great Britain in 1770 by Captain James Cook. The six colonies federated as the Commonwealth of Australia in 1901.

The world's biggest island with the world's largest cattle station (some 34,000 km^2, larger than Belgium), it is also the smallest and driest inhabited continent. With approximately ten times as many sheep as people, three people per square kilometre, roughly 89 per cent of its 21.7 million people today live in urban areas.[7]

Australia has a strong economy with a per capita GDP on a par with major European economies. The economy has fared relatively well during the global economic slowdown.

Box 8.2 (cont.)

Solid export prices for both raw materials (coal, iron ore, alumina), particularly to China, as well as for agricultural products (meat, wool, dairy products, wine) shipped to most of the world, have helped to maintain GDP growth.[8]

Maersk Line in Australia opened its head office in Sydney in 1993, and has branch offices in Adelaide, Brisbane, Freemantle and Melbourne. Damco in Australia operates from offices in Brisbane, Melbourne and Sydney.

New Zealand

New Zealand lies approximately 1,500 km east of Australia. Settled by Polynesians in the thirteenth century, New Zealand became a British colony in 1841, the first country to have universal suffrage (1893) and a Dominion in 1907. Its population at the end of 2012 was estimated to be 4.45 million.[9]

New Zealand's economic development, based on agricultural products, suffered significantly in the 1980s after Great Britain joined the European Union in 1973. Since then, New Zealand has transformed its economy to a liberalised free-trade economy and has broadened its export markets.

New Zealand remains vulnerable to international commodity prices as some 24 per cent of its output is in agricultural products such as dairy products, meat, wool, fruit and fish.[10]

Maersk Line New Zealand operates from its offices in Auckland, as does Damco New Zealand.

At last, Maersk Line would be able to offer services to and from Australia, serving both the East and West Australian markets. Søren Houman was appointed as manager for these services, based initially in Copenhagen with a team on the ground in Australia. In addition, EAC had been developing two interesting services in Southeast Asia, one serving Ho Chi Minh City in Vietnam and one serving Cambodia, both new areas for Maersk Line and areas that were to become fast-growing business opportunities. A second team, based in Vietnam, was responsible for that integration process. The platform was there to be built on and that is exactly what happened. The former EAC service network in Southeast Asia was to form the basis for a new stand-alone container activity, MCC Transport.

These were dramatic days, yet the deal was not celebrated; EAC and the A.P. Moller Group were the largest and best-known companies in Denmark, had been fierce competitors in shipping for the best part of the twentieth century and, despite all reservations, it was viewed with a certain sadness that EAC had to pull out of the liner business.

YOUR INTRA-ASIA PARTNER

Figure 8.3 The MCC logo.

Box 8.3 MCC Transport: 'your intra-Asia partner'

MCC Transport, based in Singapore as a ship owner and operator of intra-Asia container services, was initiated by Maersk Line following the EAC acquisition in 1993. Its origins date back to 1988, when EAC bought a local container operator. Although it took a few years to develop significantly, the business gained momentum with the move of Maersk Line from the port of Singapore to Tanjong Pelepas in Malaysia in 2000, and in 2005 the various intra-Asian services were merged into one company under the MCC Transport banner.

MCC Transport operates container ships in one of the world's largest markets for containerised transport, estimated in 2013 to be close to ten million FFE (20 million TEU) and one where the IMF estimates GDP growth to be between 3.1 and 9.6 per cent per year.

Headquartered in Singapore, MCC Transport operates between ports in Bangladesh, Cambodia, Indonesia, Malaysia, Myanmar, the Philippines, Singapore, Thailand, Vietnam, China, eastern Russia, Hong Kong, South Korea and Taiwan. Since 2010, MCC Transport has issued bills of lading in its own name on all these trades.

In 2011, MCC Transport's turnover exceeded $1 billion and it handled over 1.5 million FFE (some three million TEU). By 2012, MCC Transport had approximately 500 employees, operated some 60 ships, made about 170 port calls per week and was serving over 3,500 inter-Asian corridors.

MCC Transport's role as both a feeder operator and a ship operator in its own right has become seen as a cornerstone to Maersk Line's overall strategy for the future, with the vision 'to position A. P. Moller-Maersk as a significant and profitable player in the Intra Asia market.'[11]

Source: Material from MCC Transport, 2012.

Only three months later, Jess Søderberg took over the corner office in the A.P. Moller headquarters, as Mærsk Mc-Kinney Møller stepped down as CEO of the A.P. Moller Group.

Into South America

A Maersk tramp ship had called at South American ports in 1913, and the *Anna Mærsk* was the first Maersk ship to pass through the Panama Canal in 1917, but South America had never been a focal area for Maersk's shipping activities. Maersk had also been in the reefer trades in the late 1930s, but had refrained from investing in specialised reefer tonnage after the Second World War.

A. P. Møller was hesitant 'because I or my organisation do not know enough about refrigeration'.[12] An attempt to enter the trade with new tonnage built at the Odense Steel Shipyard in 1961–1964 proved too difficult as Maersk lacked size, experience and customer contacts. The ships were chartered to

Figure 8.4 In 1913, four years before *Anna Mærsk* passed through the Panama Canal, the first Maersk ship to do so, *Laura Mærsk* had performed three other firsts for the trampers in the Maersk fleet: the first Atlantic crossing and the first calls to both South and North America.

experts in the field and so Maersk did not have a background in the most important trades with South America – perishable fruit and vegetables.

This period was also characterised by a flurry of memos from Erik Møller-Nielsen, Thorkild Olesen, head of Projects in Maersk Line, and others to Maersk management proposing expansion projects as Maersk Line extended its reach further and further out into the corners of the world.[13] One, dated early 1992, summarised the situation in South America and was initiated jointly by Erik Møller-Nielsen and Peter Spiller, who had moved back to Maersk Line in the US from Copenhagen in 1971. That same year, Spiller had visited South America with the Danish Ambassador Toyberg-Frandsen, and generated a substantial report covering the key countries. However, because of strong legislation in place at the time protecting national flag shipping lines from competition, the opportunity was put to one side.

Further studies, particularly of the Caribbean area, had taken place in 1985 and 1988, but these were also shelved. The impact of the debt defaults on the development of these economies in the early to mid 1980s can be clearly seen in Box 8.4. But, by 1992, the flag preference limitations were disappearing and the opportunity looked ripe for development.

Olesen and Spiller's memo of February 1992 provided a positive overview of visits to Chile, Ecuador and Peru, all of which were undergoing political and economic changes. Chile was seen as the 'economic locomotive of the area' due to its relative stability, competitiveness and sound

Box 8.4 Proportion of world merchandise trade of selected countries in Latin America, 1970–2010 (Argentina, Brazil and Mexico)

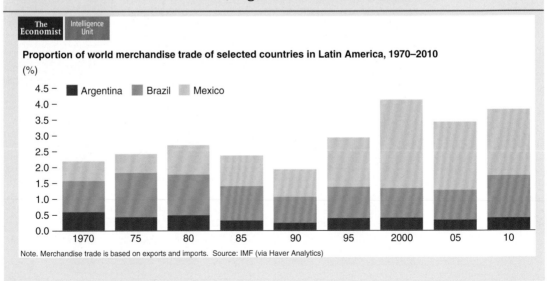

The Economist Intelligence Unit

Proportion of world merchandise trade of selected countries in Latin America, 1970–2010

(%)

Argentina   Brazil   Mexico

Note. Merchandise trade is based on exports and imports. Source: IMF (via Haver Analytics)

economic policies. Its seven different climatic regions meant that its sea-sonal agricultural cycle was generally opposite to those of the principal consumer markets in the Northern Hemisphere, giving it important marketing opportunities.

Olesen and Spiller were to establish the costs, risks and feasibility of Maersk Line running a fortnightly service between US Atlantic ports and the west coast of South America. The team visited the ports and also talked to a number of potential customers:

We visited a major fruit exporter who in no uncertain terms invited Maersk Line to participate in their seasonal movements ... Past good experience with shipments to Japan had convinced shippers that the reefer container (porthole concept disliked), was here to stay and would eventually capture the market.[14]

Box 8.5 South America

Robbert Jan van Trooijen, now Maersk Line's Regional Managing Director for South America with overall responsibility for the region, having been in the area in the 1990s with NedLloyd, commented on his impressions on returning there:

Twenty years of international commerce ... When I worked there in the early 1990s, there were essentially three brands of cars, Ford, GM and Volkswagen. It was unthinkable to have Toyota, or Hyundai or Kia cars on the road. Now it is Chinese cars, Korean cars, Samsung flat screens, etc., so the markets have really opened up.

For example, Brazilians have access to affordable outside products – in the early 1990s, that was much more difficult.

Shipping has made the difference there, to ensure there are affordable, available products. That is a clear example of the cultural change that has helped to create a new middle class.

The most challenging aspect of running a business in the area is the economic volatility. But, we have been in the region for many years. We have experienced people who have been through volatile changes before, so I believe we are very resilient when it comes to managing change.[15]

South America consists of Argentina, Bolivia, Brazil, Chile, Colombia, Ecuador, French Guiana, Guyana, Paraguay, Peru, Suriname, Uruguay and Venezuela. With a population of about 400 million, per capita GDP in 2008 ranged from $3,900 in Guyana to $10,100 in Brazil and $14,900 in Chile.

Maersk Line and Damco have been active in South America since the early 1990s, each operating through offices in eight countries there. APM Terminals operates a number of terminals, including Buenos Aires in Argentina, Pecem and Itajai in Brazil and a major new development at Callao in Peru, which is scheduled to be operational in 2015.

Maersk Line's planned transit times were seen to be 'very competitive in the trades to/from the US, Europe and from the Far East', while a great deal of material was collected on which the calculations of service viability could be made with some confidence. The region was not seen as a major financial opportunity at the time, but it was considered important to establish a solid presence.

In view of the positive calculations, the Andean Team recommended that negotiations be concluded with the reefer shippers and with the Dole Food Company Inc. (already a major client in other trades) for a share of their movements as well as contracting the needed tonnage, so that the service could commence from October 1992.[16]

That plan was approved and Erik Møller-Nielsen was appointed to head the start-up process.

The mission of the Andean service, developed in late 1992, was to operate with a service level superior to the existing carriers, attracting profitable cargo and generating economies of scale to ensure a positive result for the line and at least 16 per cent return on investment if own vessels are eventually deployed ... Be independent in terms of conference membership while maintaining comparable rate levels and possible talking agreements with competition.[17]

Maersk Santiago inaugurated Maersk Line's service to the west coast of South America when it called at Arica in Chile on 26 January 1993. Thorkild Olesen's review in June 1993 concluded that after six months of actual operation, bookings had already reached budget levels by March and accumulated bookings had reached ratio 100 by mid-May (the plan had been significantly more conservative). By the end of 1993, bookings as well as the estimated net result were well ahead of plan.

With the reefer season starting in December, Olesen was keen to plan the 1994 deployment of tonnage and proposed that the opportunity was there to upgrade to a weekly service and 'leave competition far behind' (the best competitor was offering a ten-day service). Such a development would also provide better flexibility, faster turn-around of containers and a number of other savings opportunities.

New offices, new services, new systems

Writing in *Containerisation International*'s 1994 yearbook, Jane Boyes commented:

As 1993 drew to a close, the future of those companies involved in providing container transport services seemed to hinge on two massive opportunities or challenges: securing cost advantage and satisfying the needs of customers. The consensus is that failure to seize either or both will ultimately condemn carriers to commercial oblivion in a trading environment that each year becomes ever more competitive. With virtually all routes containerised the opportunities for growth are now primarily a function of an expansion in world trade.[18]

Box 8.6 World container traffic by country, 1991

Country	1991 TEU	Country	1991 TEU
United States	15,728,396	Sweden	493,349
Japan	8,623,643	Pakistan	468,829
Singapore	6,354,000	New Zealand	457,779
Hong Kong	6,161,912	Portugal	437,762
Taiwan	6,126,570	Turkey	401,228
UK	4,072,915	Denmark	394,992
Netherlands	3,846,460	Canary Islands	362,665
Germany	3,511,413	Mexico	344,494
South Korea	2,694,115	Eire	339,071
Spain	2,154,611	Cyprus	328,520
Belgium	2,090,044	Finland	276,269
United Arab Emirates	2,073,125	Panama	233,450
Italy	1,716,232	Argentina	221,000
Australia	1,672,963	Nigeria	210,144
Puerto Rico	1,619,366	Chile	207,671
France	1,590,270	Malta	207,636
China	1,505,837	Honduras	190,100
Philippines	1,463,223	Iceland	186,346
Canada	1,410,482	Morocco	185,838
Thailand	1,170,697	Norway	179,750
Indonesia	1,156,265	Cote d'Ivoire	179,501
Malaysia	1,074,295	Jamaica	164,636
Saudi Arabia	1,044,661	Oman	156,439
South Africa	862,420	Guam	145,795

Box 8.6 (cont.)

India	679,114	Windward Islands	139,533
Sri Lanka	669,489	Kenya	135,541
Brazil	623,446	Colombia	135,157
Egypt	565,858	Poland	132,586
Greece	548,944	Lebanon	131,175
Israel	530,399	Qatar	129,753
Other countries			2,182,564
World total			93,100,738

Source: Containerisation International Yearbook 1993, page 6, © 1997, reproduced with the permission of Lloyds List Group.

Although Jane Boyes might exaggerate the status of globalisation in terms of container shipping coverage, Box 8.6 does illustrate her point, and she clearly predicted some of the key developments that would play out in the coming years. Containerisation could be said to be moving towards becoming a commodity where the lowest container slot costs would become a key driver of economic survival. As a McKinsey report of 2012 observed, 'price is the primary buying factor in transportation. While operators will and should continue to seek out niches, they should also be realistic: there is no way around being very cost-efficient and lean.'[19]

Olesen's small project team reviewed and recommended one project after another during these months, motivated by Maersk Line's interest in establishing an early presence in an area's economic development. An additional aim of extending the coverage on the existing main line services was to spread the risk of being too dependent on the main markets with high levels of competition.

Maersk Line's Project Office was busy.[20] Maersk Line was firmly established in the main east–west trade routes of the Pacific, Asia–Europe and across the Atlantic and was now taking steps to offer improved coverage of the north–south trades and local feeder routes. And so were its competitors. To illustrate the range of development, 1992 had seen Maersk Line open offices in St Petersburg and Moscow in Russia, Xiamen in China, Agadir in Morocco, Leixoes in Portugal, Gdynia and Lodz in Poland, Laem Chabang in Thailand, Bamako in Mali, Tehran in Iran, Dubai City in the UAE, Kuwait City in Kuwait, Johannesburg in South Africa, Panama City in

Figure 8.5 When entering a Maersk Line office anywhere in the world, you would be met (and still will be) by a uniform design. However, some offices succeeded in making the most of the rules, or even bending them a little, and Singapore stands out.

Panama, Lima in Peru and Santiago in Chile, while 1993 saw 24 new offices opened and Maersk Line entering nine new countries.

As the larger manufacturers and exporters in an increasingly globalised world strove to expand their activities into new markets, the shipping companies were positioning themselves to take advantage of these opportunities by offering low-cost, efficient shipping – something C. C. Tung of OOCL had described as 'the vital link to world trade'. It was a learning experience to understand that to the world's largest retailer, the two containers of goods it was buying from Nicaragua were just as critical as the 10,000 containers it was shipping from Hong Kong, and that it expected a comparable service capability from these new markets.

While all this was going on, the 1993 plans for electronic data processing had developed and included an integrated booking system that automatically validated bookings of dangerous cargoes against a dangerous cargo acceptance system, new releases of a marketing system, and links to the *Journal of Commerce*, bringing the applications closer to the needs of the business and its customers.

A major step forward was the full implementation of a customer service system that 'greatly increased customer satisfaction with Maersk Line's documentation'.[21] A new equipment management system was also scheduled to enter service in 1993.[22]

> The benefits will be a closer control of transportation costs plus an integrated information flow from the initial freight quotation all the way through the delivery to the customer, giving Maersk Line a total overview of the full transportation process and its associated costs.[23]

In an innovative approach in early 1995, Ole Larsen, responsible for all Maersk Line systems, took steps to focus the global organisation on the importance of data quality. Supported by Ib Kruse, this focus was addressed through the establishment of local super-users at the office or country level. The super-users role was to work locally to establish root-cause analyses and to implement training on a work-process basis rather than the more traditional approach of pure systems training.

Out in the world, 1995 saw the founding of Amazon.com and, shortly after, eBay, both major steps in the development of e-commerce solutions. They were followed in 1998 by Google, a search and data-organising engine that by 2011 would average some 620 million visitors per day.

The end of the affair

In Chapter 7 we described the early stages of vessel-sharing agreements with P&OCL and Sea-Land. Both agreements were based on a concept of equality. One consequence of the EAC-Ben Line acquisition impacted the relationship with P&OCL: from being a 50–50 relationship, the acquisition now tipped the balance in Maersk Line's favour. This was not an immediate issue and the relationships continued to develop. In May 1993, an agreement was made with both P&OCL and Sea-Land to cooperate on the United States to Mediterranean and the Arabian-Persian Gulf trades.

In his book *Trusted Partners*, Jordan D. Lewis interviewed a number of Maersk Line and Sea-Land people on how the relationship had developed over time. His thesis was that 'alliances' are based on trust, and he defined an alliance as 'cooperation between groups that produces better results than can be gained from a transaction … An alliance must stay ahead of the market by making continuing advances.'[24] Dick Murphy, at that time Corporate Marketing and Chief Commercial Officer of Sea-Land, was quoted as saying, 'We would not have our results without trust. It is the cornerstone of our relationship.'[25] And Ron Sforza of Sea-Land, talking about his working relationship with Jesper Kjædegaard of Maersk Line, said, 'We have helped each other understand the realities within our respective organisations.'[26]

Box 8.7 Comparative financial results, Sea-Land and Maersk Line, 1993

	Sea-Land 1993 total ($ million)	Maersk Line 1993 total ($ million)
Revenue	3,246	3,320
Operating costs including depreciation	−3,053	−3,165
Depreciation	127	228
Operating income before depreciation	320	383
Lease commitments	238	109
Operating income before leases	558	492
Investment cost price	4,052	3,440
Return on investment	13.8%	14.3%

Note: The lease commitments in Sea-Land relate to their vessels, while Maersk Line operates with leases only on containers. Investment cost price on Sea-Land's leased assets are based on depreciation over 16.67 years with 7.5 per cent interest (equal to Maersk Line).

Source: Memo, 7 December 1994, Maersk Line Business Development.

Lewis observes:

A typical plan, like the one developed by Sea-Land and Maersk, specifies that at every level individuals should resolve their own problems according to what best serves their mutual objectives ... Questions that cannot be decided at lower levels go to the alliance steering committee. Since no one in either firm wants that to happen, there is a sense of urgency to resolve them before quarterly committee meetings. John Clancey and Ib Kruse, the carriers' CEOs, are the last resort.[27]

Lewis also elaborates on what he calls 'working with discordant structures' and is clearly impressed with the fact that

not only are they major rivals, but their structures and operating philosophies are vastly different. Despite their enormous differences, the two companies not only have surpassed their ambitious cost-reduction targets, but keep bettering them, and have greatly increased their service frequency and geographic coverage.[28]

From the Maersk perspective, it is unfortunate that while analysing this alliance, Lewis did not look at the parallel alliance Maersk Line was operating with P&OCL. The contrast might have been revealing. In the summer of 1993, P&OCL requested that the two parties develop a global agreement that would allow P&OCL to enter the Trans Pacific trade, the original trade in which Maersk Line had started in 1928, and which was its first to be containerised, in 1975.

No agreement was reached. The market from Asia to the ports of southern California, in particular, was seeing strong growth, and the carriers were expanding in response. Hanjin Line of Korea and NYK of Japan had both expanded since 1992 and were planning additional capacity. So were the outsiders, COSCO of China and Hyundai of Korea. The consensus in Copenhagen was that there was no need to see P&OCL enter the trade: it was crowded enough already.

Efforts continued to draft a new agreement during 1994. P&OCL asked for it to be extended to the end of 2000, and a compromise was reached to extend it to the end of 1999. A number of meetings took place in the middle of 1994 between Palle Juhl and Vagn Lehd Møller from Maersk and Robert Woods and Michael Seymour from P&OCL to resolve a number of trade- and capacity-related issues – but one item was clearly a challenge.

On 11 May 1994, Robert Woods wrote to Per Jørgensen in Copenhagen:

I am concerned that we appear to have reached an impasse on the issue of providing both parties with the opportunity to grow. Whilst there is no dispute about the general principles, we are finding it difficult to agree their practical implementation at least as far as they relate to P&O.[29]

Both sides continued to try to find solutions. Palle Juhl's and Erik Møller-Nielsen's memo to Ib Kruse of December 1994 summarised the issues. The first related to Maersk Line's plan to substitute the existing L-class ships on the Europe–Far East service, first with the M-class and later the new C-4800 ships. In the draft agreement, these ships, like the new P&OCL ships, were termed 4,000-TEU ships; but they were known to have a capacity of 4,800 TEU. Their actual capacity was in fact going to be somewhat larger (the K-class ships' capacity was in excess of 6,000 TEU) and this would only serve to exacerbate the Maersk/P&OCL imbalance.

The second concerned P&OCL's Europe–Far East capacity. Without it, Maersk Line would only be able to operate sailings twice each week, compared to the existing four, and this would compare poorly with the Hapag Lloyd/NYK services of three per week and the three per week services to be offered by the NedLloyd/MOSK/MISC/OOCL/APL service planned for 1996. However, the really critical issue was the Trans Pacific, where P&OCL had decided they needed to become a factor and where

Figure 8.6 One of the original six K-class post-Panamax container ships delivered from the Odense Steel Shipyard in 1996–1997, *Kate Mærsk*'s real capacity was a well-guarded secret for many years.

Maersk Line saw a trade already over-tonnaged with no room for yet another significant player.

Discussions continued, including the exchange of a number of letters between Lord Sterling of P&O and Mærsk Mc-Kinney Møller, but to no avail. At the very beginning of May 1995, a letter was received from P&OCL giving one year's notice of the cancellation of all existing agreements with Maersk Line, with effect from 5 May 1996.

Two tough years

Throughout 1994–1995, it was evident market pressures were combining to put pressure on Maersk Line's financial results. Maersk Line's capacity now totalled 403,000 TEU compared to Evergreen's 372,000 and Sea-Land's 322,000. Maersk Line was now represented in 233 cities in 70 countries. Of these some 200 were online, connected to the centralised computing and communications facilities.

Jess Søderberg had already expressed concerns about the complexity of Maersk Line's organisation in May 1994. A memo from Vagn Lehd Møller in early May had proposed separating Mercantile from Maersk Line; this would allow the former to operate independently and simplify Maersk

Line's structure. Jørgen Engell, at that time President of Maersk Inc. in the United States, had disagreed and the suggestion had not been pursued.

The same month, Jess Søderberg asked the PCG (Vagn Lehd Møller for Copenhagen, Jørgen Engell in New York representing the United States, Flemming Ipsen representing Europe and Africa and Flemming Jacobs for Asia) to focus all their efforts on addressing the losses in Maersk Line. In the summer, he elicited the support of consultants from McKinsey to create two task forces for this purpose.

In September 1994, a reorganisation was announced, to come into effect on 1 January 1995. The PCG, internally known as the Quartet, which Vagn Lehd Møller had proposed be scrapped, was replaced by the Business Development Council (BDC) with a wider membership. The principle of decentralised decision-making was re-confirmed. Erik Møller-Nielsen was made responsible for strategy, while the three Maersk Line regional managers in New York, Europe and Asia were to be responsible for managing the individual services. In addition, operational and financial controls were strengthened. Erik Møller-Nielsen, through the regional line managers, Jørgen Harling for Europe/Africa, Peter Frederiksen for Asia and the Middle East and Lars Reno Jakobsen for North and South America, was made directly responsible for driving a profit improvement plan (PIP) designed to improve the expected result for 1995.

Mærsk Mc-Kinney Møller supported the changes with a note dated 27 October 1994, emphasising his views on the importance of getting closer to Maersk Line's customers and improving competitiveness. He had regularly expressed concern as the organisation had grown from 4,000 to over 9,000, considering that continually asking the organisation to cut operational and staff costs was demotivating. Finally, he noted that the target for the business should really be a result of $200 million.

The PIP process was the most extensive of its kind to date. Workshops were held and every cost item taken to pieces to evaluate improvement opportunities and savings. The cooperation with Sea-Land and, while it lasted, P&OCL was to be focused on 'lowest cost' objectives. It was noted in mid 1995 that 'all carriers in the Asia/Europe trade are now losing money', so this was not just a Maersk Line issue.

In May 1995, Ib Kruse advised the three regional managers that the first four months' results showed no improvement and again asked that they personally focus on reducing operational costs. By September 1995, Ib Kruse was able to send some more encouraging messages as the full-year estimate was now back in the black. After much work and input from the PIP teams, substantial improvements had been put in place, and most of these were coming to fruition.

Box 8.8 Mærsk Mc-Kinney Møller's guidelines to ship owners and managers on the aims and concepts of the group

It is probably in response to the reorganisation process in late 1994 that Mærsk Mc-Kinney Møller was stimulated to think about establishing some fundamental ideas that would help to guide the A.P. Moller Group and its managers in the future. In his new role as Chairman, Mærsk Mc-Kinney Møller was no longer deeply involved in the company's day-to-day activities and was beginning to consider his and his father's legacy. In September 1994, he sent a confidential letter to the ship owners and managers around the world.

The letter began: 'With the uncertainties of life and death Mærsk Mc-Kinney Møller has set down on paper the attached guidelines for the future as well as for the present for executives and managers in the A.P. Moller Group'. It ended: 'You are requested in your doings and actions to always be instrumental in securing that these guidelines are complied with by everyone.'[30] The guidelines are reproduced below.

5 September 1994

Aims of the Group

Always   remember that the Group must be second to none, healthy, liquid, highly esteemed and profitable

Always   honour the name of A. P. Møller. Guard it. Protect its image. It must always be A1

Always   bear in mind the Group's historical background. A. P. Møller, his fundamental upright principles, his spirit, and those of Mærsk Mc-Kinney Møller

Always   remember to uphold the family origin of the Group. APM and MMM intended this, it will be beneficial, but it should not be overdone

Always   remember that a strong, viable, independent and preferably growing organisation abroad is absolutely essential

Concepts of the Group

Always   our word is our bond – our word must be trustworthy whether spoken or written

Always   remember that precise, correct and kind treatment of each customer is a prerequisite for the prosperity of our business. No detail too small, no effort too great

Always   demonstrate constant care in everything and everybody

Always   remember that no loss should hit us that can be avoided by constant and timely care

Always   have in mind that developments may be different from the expected – even suddenly – and have contingency measures ready for suitable response

Always   before committing the Group make sure that – especially larger – decisions have been, faulted, examined, reassessed and recalculated by someone other than the proposer

Always   guard the Group's purse – always avoid inessential expense

Always   act as if there were a crisis and the company was in a crisis

Always   give high priority to the training of personnel, white-collar and blue-collar, in Denmark and elsewhere. It is also important to always assure that preferably

Box 8.8 (cont.)

more than one good and qualified alternative candidate is available for all significant positions including one's own managerial level

Always   remember that it is essential for the individual companies abroad to be sufficiently financially sound so that they can borrow whatever is necessary for their business and its expansion in their own name without guarantees, letters of comfort, awareness or similar warrants from the parent company

Conduct of Managers

Always   be loyal to the organisation, to the A.P. Moller Group and to one another

Always   be frank with your management peers

Always   be communicative with each other and with your superiors

Always   consider the whole – do not give priority to your own area of responsibility at the expense of the whole

Always   be accessible, always thorough, always be scrupulous

Always   acknowledge and admit to oneself and others when developments take a wrong turn in order to rectify them without delay

Always   accept responsibility for decisions made – even when they prove to be wrong

Always   learn from your own faults and mistakes and make sure that others realise their faults and mistakes and learn from them

Always   bear in mind that our most valuable asset is our large, hard-working, competent and loyal staff and work force on land, at sea, in the air, in Denmark and wherever they might be

Always   be mindful of the responsibility for the many employees

Always   treat employees decently, including the retired. Decades of goodwill and inspiration can be broken easily, and lost very quickly. Their preservation is vital

Always   bear in mind that a manager in the A.P. Moller Group – in Denmark or in the world at large – should always be respected within the organisation, within the A.P. Moller Group, and in the community. He or she should always act as a leader, always be businesslike, be straightforward, polite, know languages, dress like a leader. He or she should never be boastful. Never have extravagant manners or habits

Always   remember that we are all sales people and that no one is too elevated or too fine to be a sales person

On 22 December 1995, Ib Kruse was able to write to the country managers around the world that

the many efforts you all have put into the PIP plans continue to contribute very positively to the performance of the Line. The result for 1995 will be a drastic improvement over 1994 and, most significantly, we will meet or slightly exceed the revised budget for 1995. The revised budget was ambitious, so to achieve it is a credit to everyone![31]

Ultimately, as can be seen in Box 12.1, the result was significantly better than expected.

These cost reduction efforts, as Mærsk Mc-Kinney Møller had envisaged, led to staff lay-offs in several parts of the world, something for which the paternalistic Maersk organisation had not been known. The Danish press noted with some shock that about ten members of staff had been laid off in Copenhagen. In Europe, plans were put in motion to merge the Dutch and Belgian organisations and thereby reduce overall headcount by 20 per cent. Tommy Thomsen, who had taken over as President of Maersk Inc. in the US, was working on a plan that would reduce costs by 25 per cent over the coming three years. Overall headcount globally would be reduced by 250–300 people, about 4 per cent of the total.

The partnership with Sea-Land

In February 1995, Erik Møller-Nielsen and Thorkild Olesen had put forward to Ib Kruse yet another joint operation with Sea-Land, this time between North Europe, Brazil and Argentina in conjunction with Transroll, a local Brazilian operator. Transit times to and from Europe would be fully competitive but not superior; however cargoes from the Far East, relayed over Algeciras, would arrive 6–12 days faster than the competition. The memo asked for authority to conclude negotiations with Sea-Land and Transroll and, on that basis, the service would be launched from mid May 1995.[32]

With the receipt of P&O's letter cancelling all agreements with effect from May 1996, a senior committee on future vessel-sharing agreements (VSAs) had immediately been put in place to review future arrangements. The members were Ib Kruse with Ted Ruhly and Tommy Thomsen for the US, Flemming Jacobs (Asia), Flemming Ipsen (Europe) and Erik Møller-Nielsen (Copenhagen). They concluded that operating alone would not allow Maersk Line to maintain its current market shares. The existing services with Sea-Land were generally satisfactory and no alternative partner was recommended. A meeting with Sea-Land had generated a draft note of understanding covering additional areas for cooperation; rationalisation and cost-efficiency opportunities could be maximised; and financially, the projections were 'approximately as if we had continued to operate with P&O but could be improved further'.[33]

On 17 May 1995, the committee recommended to Mærsk Mc-Kinney Møller and Jess Søderberg that Maersk Line should not go it alone but should move forward with Sea-Land. Mærsk Mc-Kinney Møller's response was to ask that any agreement to replace the one with P&OCL be 'solid, well thought through, profitable and capable of being presented to the press as a great solution'.[34] Work therefore continued with the drafting of a formal note of understanding with Sea-Land.

Ib Kruse and Sea-Land's CEO, John Clancey, held frequent telephone conversations to help get the agreement in place and planned that John Snow, Sea-Land's Chairman, would visit Copenhagen in June to sign the note of understanding. This was completed on 19 May 1995. A press release would be issued and within 90 days of his visit an acceptable agreement covering new areas of cooperation and rationalisation would be finalised. Combined, the business would have over 175 container ships and 500,000 containers and chassis at its disposal and would set new standards in the business.

At the A.P. Moller Board meeting later in May, Mærsk Mc-Kinney Møller and Ib Kruse briefed the Board and outlined the trades in which Maersk Line and Sea-Land were already cooperating, putting forward the recommendation that Maersk Line should build further on this platform with effect from May 1996. The Board duly gave its blessing. Interestingly, the paper also provides the first formal indication that CSX Corporation might be interested in selling Sea-Land.

At the end of August 1995, Erik Møller-Nielsen e-mailed all the main offices to announce the creation of five joint Maersk Line/Sea-Land teams to move the planning processes forward in detail. These were:

- Global fleet planning: Jesper Kjædegaard (Maersk) and Steve Rothberg (Sea-Land).
- Terminals: Arno Dimmling (Sea-Land) and Niels Vallø Christiansen (Maersk).
- Equipment: Jim Devine (Sea-Land) and Palle Weidlich (Maersk).
- Information technology: Bill Donovan (Sea-Land) and Ole Larsen (Maersk).
- Administration and finance: Tom Becker (Maersk) and Steve Rothberg (Sea-Land).

At the BDC in September 1995, Erik Møller-Nielsen reported that cooperation with P&OCL was, perhaps unsurprisingly, deteriorating, while that with Sea-Land was improving. Ib Kruse commented that the plan was to achieve 20 per cent more capacity, with no increase in operating costs.

Peter Spiller had worked closely with Erik Møller-Nielsen on developing and opening up South America and they had had a number of disagreements, mainly centred around Erik Møller-Nielsen's more conservative approach. Later, however, Spiller would describe Møller-Nielsen as

'a genius. There was nobody else in the world who could see the entire Maersk Line network in his head. He was a brilliant strategist. If Erik Møller-Nielsen brought to the Sea-Land integration process his amazing strategic ability and Dick Murphy [of Sea-Land] brought in his marketing ability, they were enormously complementary. They respected each other.'[35]

While the negotiations, detailed planning and implementation were all being put into place, a twist in the story was developing. Ib Kruse and John Clancey were building a close working relationship and in September 1995, in a private conversation, John Clancey mentioned that a possible restructuring of CSX Corporation might lead to a change in the ownership of Sea-Land. Ib Kruse indicated Maersk's possible interest and set in motion an internal evaluation of such an acquisition.

In October and November 1995, discussions continued between John Snow (Sea-Land's Chairman), John Clancey and Ib Kruse, and a number of options were considered, the main driver being CSX's desire to invest further in its rail operations. Sea-Land's performance was also leading CSX to be under-valued by the market. Options included a management buy-out of Sea-Land, or Maersk buying 51 per cent of the company. Ib Kruse was concerned that any such option would complicate Sea-Land's ownership structure at a time when both sides were very keen to implement the new partnership arrangements.

Nearly a year later, in September 1996, John Clancey and Ib Kruse e-mailed both organisations' global management teams and encouraged them to do more together.[36] But the main message was one of real progress towards achieving the primary goal of 'providing the most comprehensive and best service network in the industry'. The challenging and deteriorating competitive environment required all to 'accelerate our efforts to also achieving the lowest costs in the industry'.[37]

The Maersk Line and Sea-Land developments were not happening in isolation, however. In *Containerisation International*'s 1996 yearbook Jane Boyes commented on the

massive concentration of power in the hands of a few carriers as the global alliances that were announced last year come into effect. Four mega-groupings had been announced:

- The Global Alliance of American President Line, Mitsui-OSK Lines, Orient Overseas Container Line, NedLloyd Lines plus Malaysian International Shipping Corporation (MISC).
- Maersk and Sea-Land.
- The Grand Alliance of Hapag-Lloyd, Neptune Orient Lines, Nippon Yusen Kaisha, and P&O Containers.
- Hanjin Shipping, DSR-Senator Line and Cho Yang Line.

Evergreen Line continues to operate in virtual solitary splendour and rapidly expanding COSCO Container Lines still operates in total isolation. Shippers fear that these new global pacts will seek to collude in rate fixing, although as 1995 drew to a close, aggressive price cutting rather than rate hikes, was the tendency.[38]

In September 1996, P&O and NedLloyd announced that they would merge with effect from 1 January 1997 under the name P&O NedLloyd Container Line (PONL). This created a significant amount of turbulence in the market, as NedLloyd was a member of the Global Alliance, while P&O was a member of another complex grouping, the Grand Alliance.

The alliance of Hanjin, DSR-Senator and Cho Yang Line announced in mid 1996, to start in mid 1997 and scheduled for completion by January 1998, was also undergoing development. Negotiations were taking place covering several route-by-route agreements, although again, other partners were involved in some trades such as the Mediterranean Shipping Company (MSC) with Norasia and Hyundai on the Europe–Asia route. And, to round off the year, in October 1996, CMA acquired the French state-owned carrier CGM.

The Maersk/Sea-Land alliance was the largest alliance according to *Containerisation International*'s 1997 yearbook, offering 380,000 TEU of slots. The only trades excluded from the agreement were Maersk Line's routes to and from Australasia and Africa.

Shipping deregulation

Things were changing daily, and the power and influence of shippers was growing. As Jane Boyes had written in the *Containerisation International* 1994 yearbook, 'with the conference system in terminal decline, there are few structures left to encourage price discipline within the industry'.[39] Elaborating on an earlier report by Mercer Management Consulting, Jane Boyes noted that,

> the main cause of shippers' poor perceptions of the industry was the conference system and in particular its inflexibility in terms of rate setting and contract negotiations ... [C]onferences prevented carriers from establishing close working relationships with their customers.

Mid 1995 was also a period of considerable change from a legislative perspective, on both sides of the Atlantic. In the United States, the House Budget Committee had proposed eliminating the FMC. In Brussels, while negotiations continued with the Commission and shippers to resolve the question of intermodal rate-making authority, Commissioner van Miert was talking seriously about removing intermodal authority from the members of the Trans Atlantic Conference Agreement (TACA).

An article in *American Shipper* in June 1995 quoted Rey Ortiz, International Transportation Manager of Du Pont, a major chemical company, as saying, 'the rules of 1994 need to change. We want a win-win situation for shippers and carriers.' One of his key concerns was TACA's 70–80 per cent market share, which was 'too high'. Du Pont had had no major problems with conferences until the emergence of super-conferences such as TACA.

US Maritime Administrator Albert J. Herberger was quoted in the same article as saying that it would be a serious mistake to allow the US maritime industry 'to be cast off in a stampede'.[40] The external discussions would continue throughout 1995 and beyond, only achieving clarity in 1998, but it was clear that the days of conferences were probably numbered and the anti-trust immunity that conferences had enjoyed was on the way out.

In the meantime, Flemming Jacobs and Tommy Thomsen were asked by the BDC to consider what changes would be needed, particularly to the sales organisation, to operate effectively in a deregulated environment. One outcome was the creation in 1996 of a global sales committee, chaired by Jesper Kjædegaard, with support from Lars Christiansen and representation from North America with Kurt McElroy and Henning Bach Nielsen. This team drove the first moves towards a 'global account based' sales organisation. The team proposed the appointment of senior sales people in relevant parts of the world to be tasked with negotiating large and global contracts with major customers, with the objective to commit 50–70 per cent of space through such contracts. To support this, a substantial training programme was launched, targeted at sales and customer services globally.

Duncan McGrath of Cargill Incorporated welcomed this development:

We were really impressed with how organised Maersk was in terms of account management and systems. It was a professional approach to what can be a not-so-professional business sometimes. Then when Maersk and Sea-Land got together, that further reinforced it.[41]

Other changes were also taking place. By 1995, ten of the top 20 container carriers were Asian and nearly 43 per cent of all container traffic globally moved through Asian ports. Trade between the countries of Asia was increasing rapidly as their economies developed. This growth was enhanced by component flows, with parts and semi-finished products moving between Asian countries for goods that would ultimately be assembled and exported to the United States or Europe. A report by Mercer Management Consulting predicted that 'between 1994 and 2000, intra-Asian trades would achieve compound annual growth rates of 9.1 per cent while the Europe/Asia and Trans Pacific routes seven per cent and 6.3 per cent respectively'.[42]

Containerisation International's Jane Boyes pointed to other changes:

The requirements of shippers include lower transport costs, consistent and reliable service, including information on the status of their shipments, and value-added elements which permit shippers in turn to provide better service to their own customers. Shippers are also rationalising the number of carriers they do business with and in many instances are seeking global, multi-trade partnerships with carriers.[43]

The emerging internet and enhanced communications technologies were beginning to influence daily work. Although not fully realised at the time, these were also beginning to erode a Maersk Line competitive advantage based on its proprietary global communications network.

A revolution in world trade

Box 8.9 The K-class ships

Maersk Line is always proud of its ships and, when time permits, new vessels are berthed at Langelinie Quay in Copenhagen, open to employees, invited guests and the public. So it was with the *Knud Mærsk* on its maiden voyage in May 1996, when the ship berthed for a total of seven days and was visited by shareholders, schools, customers from all over Europe, business connections and government officials. Over a weekend, more than 25,000 people braved the bad weather to visit the ship. The *Knud Mærsk* incorporated the most up-to-date technology and from a safety and environmental perspective a double hull and in-board fuel tanks.

Ib Kruse used the occasion to good effect, giving a short presentation about the revolution containerisation had made in shipping to members of the International Council of Containership Operators (the Box Club) invited to participate in the open days at Langelinie.

In 1973, 4 million TEU transported goods around the world. Ten years later, that figure had risen to 12 million – and ten years after that to 26 million, with about 95 per cent of all goods on liner services moved in containers.

Investments had been huge, totalling more than $65 billion, while customers had received improved services at lower freight costs: for example, the freight costs for moving a TV that cost Danish kroner 3,995 came down to Danish kroner 56.55; shipping a pair of Reebok sports shoes from Hong Kong to Denmark cost kroner 1.87; and transporting a Canon reflex camera costing kroner 3,395 from Japan to Denmark cost kroner 0.51.

Kruse then took the opportunity to ask his colleagues to help 'freight rates find a sustainable level and that this discussion can take place in open dialogue between ship-owners and customers'.[44]

Maersk Line's K-class and subsequent ship particulars all built at Odense steel shipyard, Denmark

Names	*Regina, Knud, Kate, Karen, Katrine, Kirsten Mærsk*
Built	1996–1997
LOA	318 metres × 43 metres
TDW	90,456 tons deadweight
TEU capacity	7,400 TEU

Box 8.9 (cont.)

Maersk Line's S-class ship particulars

Names	*Sovereign, Susan, Sally, Sine, Svendborg, Sofie, Svend, Sorø, Skagen Mærsk*
Built	1997–1999
LOA	347 metres × 43 metres
TDW	104,750 tons deadweight
TEU capacity	8,160 TEU

Maersk Line's C-class ship particulars

Names	*Clifford, Cornelius, A P Møller, Caroline, Carsten, Chastine, Charlotte, Cornelia, Columbine, Clementine Mærsk*
Built	1999–2002
LOA	347 metres × 43 metres
TDW	104,750 tons deadweight
TEU capacity	8,160–8,650 TEU

Maersk Line's A-class ships particulars

Names	*Axel, Anna, Arnold, Arthur, Adrian, Albert Mærsk*
Built	2003–2004
LOA	352 metres × 43 metres
TDW	109,700 tons deadweight
TEU capacity	8,272 TEU

Maersk Line's G-class ship particulars

Names	*Gudrun, Grete, Gunvor, Gjertrud, Gerd, Georg Mærsk*
Built	2005–2006
LOA	367 metres × 43 metres
TDW	115,000 tons deadweight
TEU capacity	9,074 TEU

Maersk Line's M-class ship particulars

Names	*Marit, Mette, Margrethe, Mathilde, Maren, Marchen Mærsk*
Built	2008–2009
LOA	367 metres × 43 metres
TDW	114,700 tons deadweight
TEU capacity	9,038 TEU

Maersk Line's PS-class ship particulars

Names	*Emma, Estelle, Eleonora, Evelyn, Ebba, Elly, Edith, Eugen Mærsk*
Built	2006–2008

Box 8.9 (cont.)

LOA	398 metres × 56 metres
TDW	156,900–158,200 tons deadweight
TEU capacity	15,500 TEU

Figure 8.7 Her Majesty Queen Margrethe II and His Royal Highness the Prince Consort Henrik were the guests of honour *par excellence* when *Knud Mærsk* visited Copenhagen in 1996. Captain Henrik Solmer explained the details while the always attentive Mærsk Mc-Kinney Møller observed proceedings.

In his letter to the countries in December 1996, summing up the year, Ib Kruse was able to report:

We have emphasised and paid attention to the customer. We strive to deliver quality. We are active in most of the important trade lanes of the world and we have expanded our coverage during 1996. Most importantly, Maersk Line is profitable! ... The service network operated jointly with Sea-Land was put in place with more direct ports and/or higher frequency; services on North and South America were rationalised into better products; and Europe/ECSA enhanced with a fixed weekly schedule and larger vessels. The Middle East service was extended from Singapore to Japan while Maersk Line increased capacity and improved coverage of West Africa and the Eastern Mediterranean including Egypt and the Lebanon.

While rates deteriorated on some of the main trades, the PIP process had significantly reduced Maersk Line's unit costs per FFE compared to 1995 costs giving substantial savings. While bunker costs had increased sharply to $118 per ton (up from about $65 only five years earlier), the message was 'there are still many opportunities where we can jointly [with Sea-Land] take costs out of the system'.

Looking forward to 1997, Kruse noted that coverage of South Africa would improve. From early 1997, a new service to and from Europe would be established and Maersk Line's own ships would be operating, providing slots between Asia, South Africa and South America. The reefer container fleet was growing at roughly double the rate of growth of the general containerised trade. Asian importers were now controlling some 70–80 per cent of reefer movements from the US and Europe and strengthened sales efforts were needed to ensure Maersk Lines' position was protected. Additional services to New Zealand and South Africa were expected to help Maersk Line grow in the reefer segment.

On the systems front, Kruse confirmed that significant investments would continue to be made to improve relations with customers and to bring down administrative costs. A critical success factor was the focus on establishing common standards on which future systems could be based, initiated through a Business Process Improvement effort involving some 2,400 Maersk Line staff globally. This was a pre-requisite for the visualisation and later implementation of a major new end-to-end customer service system, GCSS.[45]

Finally, Ib Kruse noted that 1997 was starting at a much lower level of activity compared to 1996 and described the prognosis as 'unsatisfactory'. The focus was to be on improving the performance of the Trans Pacific and Europe–Far East services in particular, as well as further cost reduction and launched a team to overhaul these two services through restructuring and rationalisation. Meanwhile, the regional management organisations were to drive a more general PIP: 'It is the same old story – we just have to improve once more. The driving force behind efforts everywhere should be URGENCY.'[46]

In a follow-up letter in April 1997, Ib Kruse asked the organisation 'not to build any fat into the monthly estimates. When we can deal with the bare facts we are more likely to make the right decisions as we go along.' The Asian financial crisis was beginning to bite and the new year was not shaping up well.

In response to growth and opportunities, the three Maersk Line regions (Europe, North America and Asia) were broken down further with the creation of two new regions, South America and Africa, on 1 April 1997.

Maersk Line had increased the order for 1,100 TEU feeder vessels being built in Taiwan from six to ten and the order for the K-class container ships from Lindø now amounted to 15, of which five had been delivered. Kruse's letter warned:

Maersk Line's expansion is watched keenly by competition. Maersk Line is a leader and is growing. Never be arrogant. We need friends to make things go our way in conferences, rate agreements, pricing issues and legislative matters.[47]

Despite all the challenges, the list of developments implemented in 1997 is substantial and includes:

- Implementation of a fortnightly service from Europe to South Africa and Namibia.
- A fortnightly service between Singapore and New Zealand.
- A direct US flag service from the US East Coast and Gulf to the Mediterranean.
- A fortnightly East Africa service covering Kenya and Tanzania, extended later to cover Mozambique and South Africa and then upgraded to weekly with calls at Mombasa and Dar Es Salam.
- The introduction of 'super-reefers', catering mainly to Japanese fish importers.
- Direct services between Asia, South Africa and the east coast of South America, provided by a VSA with the Good Hope Express Consortium.
- Extension of the South Africa service to serve Luanda in Angola, and then to link to Portugal, providing a direct Portugal/Luanda connection.
- Enhanced coverage of the East Mediterranean by introducing two Maersk feeders serving Gioia Tauro in Italy and Turkey on a weekly basis.
- Launch of a direct Europe–Canada service with three ice-class ships.
- Upgrade of the Europe and US to east coast South America services with larger and faster ships, once Transroll left the VSA.
- Weekly Andean and Californian services to South America.[48]
- 26 new offices across Europe, Africa, China, Asia and South America, with a further 24 planned for 1998.

While 1998 was not going to be a good year, despite all the efforts to cut operational and administrative costs, the productivity gains achieved by the organisation were going to be substantial with, for example, each salesperson handling 50 per cent more FFE in 1998 when compared to 1995.

9

1999 A Year of Developments and Acquisitions

Containerisation was growing, it was exciting, we were really led by a lot of shrewd, tough, smart people. You know, we had no capital, nothing really behind us except our own energy. There was no model for us to follow. It was interesting, stimulating and exciting.

John Clancey, President of Sea-Land[1]

Writing in *Containerisation International*'s 1997 yearbook, John Fossey started his article by stating:

The container liner industry appears to be heading for the rocks. With no appreciable pick-up in the level of scrappage, with freight rates in the major trades lower in real terms than they were 10, even 20 years ago in some cases, and with trading volumes likely to grow by eight per cent a year at best to the end of the decade, how can the industry genuinely support a record order book equivalent to 22 per cent of the existing fleet?[2]

With market volumes growing at about 8 per cent a year and a number of development opportunities still in front of it, Maersk Line's plan was to grow by about 10 per cent a year for the next three years and thereafter with the market. The target was for Maersk Line to be achieving a weekly turnover of $100 million, or a minimum annual turnover of $5 billion, by December 1998, while from 1999 growth was to be organic. The vessel-sharing agreement (VSA) with Sea-Land was considered important, but to ensure long-term operational viability, separate plans were also being made by each service to be able to develop independently of the VSA, if necessary.

Meanwhile, costs were to be cut by 3–4 per cent per year over the same period. The VSA with Sea-Land was expected to reduce costs in 1997 by $100 million, while optimising and rationalising terminal operations with Sea-Land, together with increased throughput per terminal, would bring unit costs down even further.

By now, Maersk Line owned and/or operated some ten terminals globally and had also invested in several other terminals on its network.[3]

Figure 9.1 The port of Salalah is a product of containerisation and indeed globalisation; the first steps towards changing the local port into today's major trans-shipment terminal were taken in 1996.

Plans were afoot to buy or invest in a terminal at Rotterdam and a total of 11 other terminals in different parts of the world. The operating philosophy remained to control Maersk's destiny through ownership and to ensure that the best services and prices were obtained at each key facility. However, one change was made: the Terminal Planning and Implementation Group was redirected to focus on global operational and cost-efficiency issues and to ensure that best-practice learning was shared across facilities. Container terminal investments had reached an amount large enough to be clearly visible on the balance sheet.

Meanwhile, a business process improvement programme was being rolled out with the objective that the overseas offices should be able to handle double the 1997 volumes with the same headcount by the year 2000. On top of this, potential 'Year 2000' (Y2K) issues were receiving priority attention.

To support the business plan, some 74 ships, plus chartered ships, would be needed by the end of 1999. Seven K-class vessels were currently on order in addition to six 2,500–3,000-TEU ships with 700 reefer plugs specifically for the Europe–South American east coast trade. A number of ships of 2,000–2,500 TEU would be needed for the Europe–South Africa, Australia–New Zealand and US West Coast–South American west coast services. A review of the market in Israel and the Black Sea area identified both as potential opportunities for penetration.[4]

The European Commission and Trans Atlantic Conference Agreement (TACA)

As we saw in Chapter 8, trouble had been brewing for some time between the EC and TACA. Although the ship owners involved were following developments with the Commission, events were beginning to move quickly. In October 1997, Karel van Miert, the Competition Commissioner and head of Directorate General IV (DGIV) of the Commission, made a speech in which he indicated that he wanted to impose fines on TACA members for jointly agreeing rates in the Trans Atlantic trade. At about the same time, Jean-François Pons of DGIV used a meeting of the European Shippers Council in Barcelona to discuss a paper entitled 'After TACA'.

Alarmed by these developments, Ib Kruse organised a meeting between the Commission and a number of other relevant ship owners in Brussels on 22 January 1998. The two main areas of contention were intermodal rate-making authority and service contracts. The meeting led to a working group being formed to resolve the issues.[5] Working with Knud Pontoppidan, head of External Relations and Shipping Policy Coordinator in the A.P. Moller Group, and Torben Petterson, Maersk Line's head of Conference Affairs, good progress was made in creating a set of guidelines that were to provide lines with a 'modus vivendi' until resolution of the competition rules for shipping. On 11 February, after an initial meeting between Knud Pontoppidan and Jean-François Pons, the feeling was that a 'good, open and concrete dialogue' was being established. An article in the *Journal of Commerce* on 9 February reported the Commission as indicating 'there may be room for compromise'.

But there was not. In June 1998, information was received that fines were going to be imposed on TACA members. Despite this, the working group and the ship owners continued constructive and open negotiations with DGIV to find solutions.

Internally in Maersk Line, a paper in June 1998 summarised the situation and reflected a growing confidence in Maersk Line's position in the market and the industry:

The framework for conferences will change dramatically with the passing of the new Shipping Act in the US and the EU decisions in the TACA case. Conference authority over individual service contracts will disappear. The objective for a

Maersk Line change should be a strengthening of our position where we take advantage of our global customer facing organisation, sales force, IT platform and operational capabilities.

The paper's conclusion was firmly in line with a position of independence:[6]

'We should not be drawn into further activity on a collision course with authorities and we should be prepared to go independent if others will not join with us.'[7]

A further meeting of 'interested lines' took place in Brussels on 2 July and agreed to seek a new meeting with Commissioner van Miert, hoping to find areas of compromise but also preparing for the worst. Some progress was made and in a letter to Kruse on 2 October 1998, van Miert complimented the owners on the 'improved, constructive and open way negotiations are progressing'. Nevertheless, the fines were imposed on the 15 carriers involved and totalled nearly ECU273 million, the Commission taking the position that in forming the TACA Conference, the lines had abused a 'collective dominant position' relative to competition rules.

The penalty was ultimately waived on 30 September 2003, following an appeal by the carriers to the Court of First Instance in Luxembourg – the largest appeal in history, according to DGIV, consisting of about 1,000 pages – but the story of deregulation does not end there. In April 1999 the new US Shipping Act (the Ocean Shipping Reform Act of 1998) came into force, largely deregulating shipping in the United States. A consequence of this was that the existing agreements (Asia North America Eastbound Rate Agreement (ANERA) and the Transpacific Westbound Rate Agreement (TWRA)) were replaced by two stabilisation agreements.[8] In Europe, the process rolled on until 2006, when the Commission repealed the underlying EEC regulation 4056/86 that granted conferences anti-trust immunity, with effect from 2008.

Mercantile: on a mission

Mercantile was continuing its fast-track growth, despite the turbulence caused by the Asian economic crisis. At the end of 1996, Vagn Lehd Møller moved from Copenhagen to become Managing Director of Maersk in Benelux. His role as Managing Director of Mercantile was taken over by Søren Brandt.

Before his departure, Vagn Lehd Møller proposed a mission, objectives and strategy for Mercantile, agreed by Ib Kruse. Its preamble read:

Mercantile is an independent organisation operating worldwide through locally incorporated companies and engaged in satisfying customers' expectations in respect of competitive international export and import services.[9]

The year 1996 had been a good one for Mercantile, with the supply chain penetration of Karstadt-Neckermann's volumes to Germany from Vietnam and Yantian in China; the nomination by Disney Stores of the United States; and the nomination by Sony of the Mercantile warehouse in Algeciras as a distribution centre for their traffic to North and West Africa.

During 1997, a supply chain and product-visibility project with Mattel called 'I Can See Clearly Now' was to become significant, with volumes being moved primarily with Maersk Line via two hubs: Singapore for Southeast Asia shipments and Yantian for South China volumes. Work with Mattel involved not just the UK, but also its operations in Holland, France, Italy and Spain. The objective was simple enough – 'to ensure the right product was in the right distribution centre in Europe, at the right time' – and was driven by the availability of timely and accurate electronic information.[10] And reliable shipping services.

As an indicator of the importance of maintaining multiple relationships with major customers, during 1997, Anders Moberg, IKEA Group President, visited the A.P. Moller headquarters and had lunch with senior executives. Moberg was very complimentary about the overall relationship, despite his team's negotiations for the 1998 global service contract having just broken down with Maersk Line only days before. While this was a set-back for both IKEA and Maersk Line, Mercantile's relationship with IKEA continued to strengthen and at the next negotiation, assisted in allowing the liner relationship to be quickly rebuilt and a new agreement successfully put in place.

Mercantile's bar-coding investment in Asia, initiated in 1995, was proving its worth in providing clients with detailed information in an accurate and automated manner. Carton-level content information was captured at origin and related directly to the relevant purchase order in Mercantile's systems; the customer had full access to the information, enabling real-time supply chain decision-making.

In 1997 two major new clients for supply chain services were brought on board, Reebok and Federated Department Stores, involving movements for Macy's, Bloomingdales, Burdines, Sterns and other store groups. This was a major capture from ACS, American President Lines' consolidator, and was facilitated by Mercantile North America's acquisition of the Hudd trans-loading operation in California.

Trans-loading operations can be quite simple. In Hudd's case, however, the operation for Federated Department Store Group was complex and sophisticated. Using the inbound electronic information sent by Mercantile from Asia to both the customer and to Hudd prior to the containers' arrival on the US West Coast, the customer would transmit carton-level and sometimes item-level distribution data to Hudd electronically.

Figure 9.2 The warehouse operation at Hudd in Los Angeles. Operations were increasingly automated with the introduction of information technology, the bar code and the bar code scanner.

Hudd would strip the inbound container on arrival and scan the bar code on each carton. The cartons would flow through the facility on conveyor belts to arrive at the right outbound door. At each outbound door (the facility had about 50 doors on each side of the building), a 53-foot road trailer would receive the cartons and would take them on to their final distribution, the relevant city store or local distribution centre. The operation was fast and provided the customer with daily replenishment of the specific items needed to maintain desired stock levels in its stores.

Supply chain management had come a long way since the original term was coined back in 1982, thanks to the extraordinary advances in information technology, which Professor Martin Christopher identified as

a major driver of modern practice in supply chain management ... [W]e've always talked about the need to connect and extend visibility upstream and downstream. The thing that has made it possible is information technology and related communications technology. There is no question that it has made the globalisation of supply chains a practical proposition.[11]

The acquisition of Hudd became a major business opportunity for the North American Mercantile organisation as well as for Maersk Line volumes. Based on this model, Walmart requested a similar trans-load facility to be built in Suffolk, Virginia. This was to be a 120-door, 40-acre facility operated by Hudd. At the time, Walmart was importing some 100,000 FFE a year directly in its own name. Its objective was to increase direct sourcing to 250,000 FFE and facilities such as Suffolk would be needed to support the logistics management of such substantially increased flows. The Suffolk facility was ready for operation by 1 January 2000 and was quickly followed by another, a leased facility in Seattle. Each facility had estimated throughputs of about 13,000 FFE per year.

In China, pressure from the US government had generated two operating licences for freight forwarding, one for Buyers Consolidators of Sea-Land and one for American Consolidation Services of APL. Not to be outdone, very shortly thereafter Sir Leon Brittan, Trade Commissioner at the EU, used his considerable negotiating powers to obtain parallel operating licences for two European companies and Mercantile was awarded a licence with P&O Global Logistics. Mercantile China Limited was rapidly incorporated with its head office in Shanghai and branch offices in Tianjin, Qingdao, Shenzhen, Guangzhou, Xiamen and Shenyang.

Meanwhile, the success of the warehouse investments in Gothenburg and Jakarta, referred to in Chapter 7, were capped when in 1998, Mercantile Sweden made a six-year agreement with IKEA to manage one of their major, technically advanced facilities, at Torsvik. Most of IKEA's warehouses were managed internally. This agreement gave both parties the chance to benchmark global best practices.

By the end of 1997, Mercantile was operating through some 90 offices in 40 countries and employed over 800 staff. About 65 per cent of volumes were moving on Maersk Line, a total of some 53,000 FFE. Mercantile was continuing its 30 per cent annual growth trajectory with work for Toys R Us, Walmart, K-Mart and others. The operating committee overseeing the development consisted of Søren Brandt and Chris Jephson in Copenhagen, John Ewing for Asia in Singapore, Peder Winther for Europe and Les Carmichael for North America. A year later, at the end of 1998, Mercantile had grown to some 109 offices and 1,255 staff.[12]

Filling in the gaps

Within Maersk, significant changes were taking place. Flemming Jacobs had resigned as Partner and head of Maersk Tankers on 1 May 1999 to join Neptune Orient Lines in Singapore as their chief executive. On the same

Figure 9.3 Knud E. Stubkjær became the Maersk Line CEO in 1999. He came to A.P. Moller – Maersk in 1977 and worked in a great variety of positions in Maersk Line in Europe and Asia as well as in Norfolk Line, before being promoted to Partner in 1999.

day, Knud Stubkjær, who had returned to Copenhagen in early 1998 to run Maersk Line following the tragically early death of Erik Møller-Nielsen on 29 January 1998, was promoted to Partner.

Since 1996, Per Jørgensen had held management responsibility for the development of three major up and coming areas: namely China, India and Africa. Over the years he had spearheaded Maersk into these areas, both in his role as working Chairman but also as a senior manager with a deep knowledge of the Far East and the vision to see the potential of these areas. Per Jørgensen's 33-year Asian career had started back in 1959 when he was stationed in Bangkok and had involved periods in India, Indonesia, Hong Kong and Japan before he returned to Copenhagen as a Partner. His knowledge was put to effective use both in supporting the development of strong local organisations, as well as in having substantial investments approved and implemented in these areas. His address book of top-level contacts across these three areas in particular must have been worth ten times its weight in gold. Although he retired from these roles in 2007, he remained active as an advisor and in 2012 was still Chairman of one Maersk company in India.

A direct outcome was the strengthening of management focus on these emerging markets, including Latin America, which provided Maersk Line with the early platforms on which to develop and build services not just in the traditional east–west and north–south trades, but also the newer, and fast-developing south–south trades.

In the meantime, the Maersk Line Projects team continued to investigate new business opportunities. The nature of their proposals was changing: in the past they had focused on significant opportunities such as Oceania, Africa and South America; now their projects were smaller, tightly focused on profitable ventures to fill the gaps in Maersk Line's service capability. As an example, legislation in Spain liberalising local trades led to a project that added connections to both Madeira and the islands of the Azores, while the Maersk Line organisation in Portugal was strengthened so that sales, operations and customer service could support the coverage of Angola, part of the new services which would be ready to start by July 1999.

One project that did not succeed was a service called FLEXCON. The concept was to assist the customers with containers, break-bulk and project cargoes by serving the US East Coast, US Gulf and Gulf of Mexico to the countries of West Africa. Target customers in the United States were mainly the oil industry and the freight forwarders that supported it. Shipments were moving to relatively undeveloped parts of West Africa, and frequently involved heavy-lift shipments, often with out-of-gauge requirements. In addition, project management capabilities would be offered at destination.

Søren Skou, who was running the service, wrote to Knud Stubkjær in December 1998 that progress was not going according to plan: there was civil unrest in Nigeria, so volumes were substantially down. A month later, he wrote again to recommend closing the service. Short-term profitability was not going to be achieved, despite a number of alternative ideas for improvement.[13]

Preparing for deregulation

Continuing the global focus on cost reductions, but also preparing for changes in the way the industry was structured, Maersk Inc.'s management in the United States reviewed their customer service arrangements and concluded that better quality customer services could be provided if such services were consolidated into five centres, rather than each of the 30 offices handling its own. This was implemented during 1999.

Towards the end of 1998, a small committee involving the key overseas offices had evaluated the risks and opportunities in the coming deregulated environment. Its recommendations were broad and included Maersk Line's need to handle the seasonal contracting process on a customer agreement basis rather than based on conference requirements. Systems would also be needed to handle fulfilment of the Federal Maritime Commission (FMC) and European Union regulations as well as the bid process and contract management. Maersk Line's own tariff structure would also need to be in place for all services.

A key message was the need for flexibility so that Maersk Line could respond quickly and effectively to the needs of the market place – not just its traditional shipper and consignee relationships, but also the growing influence of the freight forwarders. The Committee concluded that

the organisation possesses the core strengths to grow in a deregulated environment. We must act quickly to align our organisation to obtain the best results. We must communicate the vision consistently ... and anticipate our customers' questions. They want to understand how we will structure our group to serve their needs and make it easier to do business with Maersk Line globally.[14]

Box 9.1 The Ocean Shipping Reform Act (OSRA) 1998

Completed in 1998 to become effective on 1 May 1999, the effects of the Act were reviewed by the FMC in June 2000. The objectives of the Act were to produce a more market-driven shipping industry, and the initial report provided preliminary indications, from the FMC's perspective, that this was happening.

The FMC review noted that:

- Shippers were negotiating one-on-one contracts with carriers.
- The terms were seen to be confidential.
- The number of conferences was declining.
- Independent action on a rate was reduced from ten days' to five days' notice.
- Tariffs were no longer to be filed with the FMC, but carriers were obliged to 'make tariffs available electronically to any person, without time, quantity or other limitation'.
- Discussion agreements, which are prohibited from imposing binding commitments on members, were prevalent.
- Rates and services were increasingly being driven by market forces.
- Freight forwarders and NVOCCs were to be licensed.

Between May 1999 and May 2000, 46,035 service contracts and 95,627 amendments had been registered with the FMC's online system, most of which were individual agreements. Of these, 75 per cent were signed by the beneficial cargo owner, 20 per cent by freight forwarders and 5 per cent by shipper associations.

In 1997 there had been 32 conference agreements registered, whereas by 2000 there were only 22.

Source: The Ocean Shipping Reform Act: An Interim Status Report, the FMC, June 2000.

The main elements of the recommendations were acted on quickly through the BDC.

Dick McGregor, Vice President, Northern Asia, for Sea-Land in the late 1990s, recollected an aggressive rate action taken by Maersk Line. He approached Michael Hassing, Maersk Line's Manager for Japan, to ask 'What have you done?' He was met with the response 'We've taken it in the interest of Maersk Line.' 'That crystallised what Maersk was seeking to do. They were casting off being a participant in the Kabuki[15] and saying "We're striking out on our own".'[16]

Systems developments

The new millennium was still three years away, but the organisation was very serious about identifying and eliminating any issues in Maersk Line's systems related to the Y2K threat. Meanwhile, a Global Information Council (GIC), chaired by Ole Larsen, was overseeing systems development work, while the new platform for sales and customer service, GCSS, remained the key focus area, scheduled to deliver Release 1 in December 1998.

The pressure mounts

In his letter to the Maersk Line country managers in July 1998, Ib Kruse wrote, 'I wish I could write you on a more optimistic note [but] the Asian crisis is biting deeper and wider and has impact all over our business.' However, there was also good news, like the opening of seven new services and a number of service enhancements:

'a lot for the organisation to digest and manage, and it is a credit to the Maersk Line staff that they with great enthusiasm have taken on this challenge'. Nevertheless, results from some services were dragging the consolidated result to an 'unsatisfactory' level: 'We are at a watershed . . . find ways to reduce costs, think alternatives, re-address and be determined. Don't ask IF it can be done, but how, then do it – today.'[17]

The monthly accounts for August 1998, reviewed by Knud Stubkjær, now CEO of Maersk Line, showed a result, after improvements and risks, at about half the previous year's result.[18] Ultimately, the year-end net result would not reach that level.

Later that month, Knud Stubkjær sent out the 1999 budget guidelines to the offices and stated that:

1999 in particular, but also the coming years, promise to be at least as challenging . . . Our foremost aim is to be profitable. Growth in business volumes on account of lower rates will not achieve our aim, and 1999 will have to prove that rate restoration can be achieved while growing at the same time.

Headcount in Maersk Line Copenhagen was to be reduced by about 10 per cent, while Asia, Europe, Africa, South America and North America saw similar levels of reduction, with global headcount reduced by more than 600.

Overall, rates in 1998, driven by the state of the market, had fallen by over $600 per FFE, equivalent to wiping $1 billion off Maersk Line's turnover. July and January PIP teams reviewed each service to ensure they were optimised and several services were cut back.[19]

Volumes out of South America were impacted significantly by an extended periodic climatic phenomenon known as El Niño which impacted the export of refrigerated products and which was later estimated to have taken some $7 million off Maersk Line's expected result for the year.

Box 9.2 Reefers: a customer's story

To get a customer's view of the refrigerated products industry, we talked with Christian Peter Løth, Purchasing Manager in Dansk Supermarked (DS), a retail chain operating with three different formats in four countries in Scandinavia and Northern Europe, retailing through over 1,200 stores, and a division within the A.P. Moller – Maersk Group.

Working with a 'field to fork' concept, DS have a short list of key criteria when buying direct. These include the use of an ethical code of conduct, a focus on food safety, ensuring that they control the voyage and thereby also know the history of the product, the provision of short lead-times (field to shop), while looking for high quality at a good price. To do this, their approach is to be 'better informed about the market and better informed about our customers'.[20]

Global container logistics has made it possible to source not just fish and meat products, but also fruit from all around the world and has enabled growers to sell their products outside their local markets.

DS import, over the varying seasons, for example pomelo and garlic from China, baby corn from Thailand, grapes from India, beans, oranges, lemons, apples and grapes from southern Africa, grapefruit from Florida, pineapples and bananas from the Caribbean, with a range of products including avocados, blueberries, lemons, grapes and bananas from South America.

A large part of DS's cool products sourcing is made direct with the producers, in contrast to only a few years ago. The advantages, such as better control, better information on market developments and more knowledge on the state of harvests, have provided for fresher products, improved food safety and savings.

DS provided an example of the movement of bananas from Ecuador and Costa Rica to Denmark; in each case, the shelf-life of a banana once arrived in Europe and ripened is

Box 9.2 (cont.)

about four days. As Thomas Eskesen of Maersk Line's reefer team noted about the banana trade in general, 'that is probably the biggest change we have seen in terms of our products because the banana customers are the most demanding'.[21]

From DS's perspective, the international cold chain is of growing importance with, for example, salads now also moving this way. Top of the agenda is compliance with food safety, to ensure the customer receives a better buying experience and to reduce loss due to wastage. That requires investments in cooling warehouses and logistics, but also in process visibility to ensure transport connections and hand-over points work smoothly and required temperatures are maintained throughout. The ability of the carrier to control the whole chain and deliver punctually are critical success factors for the business.

Safmarine

In early November 1998, the South African Minister of Trade and Industry, Alexander Erwin, visited Copenhagen as part of a trip to Europe, and met the management of the A.P. Moller Group. On 10 November, Barings Bank offered the South African carrier Safmarine for sale to a number of interested parties and a few days later, Howard Boyd, CEO of Safmarine, headed a small team that visited Copenhagen to meet and sound out the Maersk management.

On 27 November, Jørgen Engell and Søren Skou put together a memo summarising Maersk's views, concluding that 'an acquisition of Safmarine Container Line would have significant strategic value to Maersk Line'.[22] The memo looked at Safmarine's liner services, bulk and reefer businesses and identified several strengths, including its strong market position and brand name in Africa; its position similar to Maersk Line in the Europe to West Africa trades; a well-educated and competent organisation; consistent profitability and earnings growth.

Synergies and network rationalisation opportunities between the two businesses were expected to be over $150 million. There were several other advantages in such an acquisition. Maersk Line would achieve an improved cost position by loading on larger Safmarine ships, and in the longer term would be able to employ larger tonnage with lower operating costs. The improved volumes in West and South Africa would allow economies of scale on land-based operations. The joint organisation would also be significantly enhanced in South and East Africa, reinforcing Maersk Line's already strong position in West Africa. These advantages also meant

Figure 9.4 One of Safmarine's *Great Whites* in front of Cape Town's magnificent Table Mountain.

there were several competitors for Safmarine, among them P&O NedLloyd and Mediterranean Shipping Company (MSC).

On 1 December 1998, Jess Søderberg, Knud Stubkjær and Lars Reno Jakobsen flew to Cape Town for meetings with Safmarine. The following day, Jørgen Engell, head of A.P. Moller's Finance Department, supported by lawyers Holman, Fenwick and Willan in London, sent them a draft of a non-binding initial offer for Safmarine with an indicative price, subject to 'due diligence'. Due diligence needed to take place, and a final offer to be developed, approved and submitted by 17 December. Final negotiations would take place in January and February 1999, when the deal would be closed.

A task force led by Jørgen Engell and Søren Skou was put together. On 4 January 1999, Ib Kruse flew to Tampa, Florida, to seek the advice of Alistair McMillan, a former senior executive from South Africa with intimate connections in the country. On 15 January, Alexander Erwin called Ib Kruse to indicate his government's interest in A.P. Moller's acquisition of Safmarine, although as the bidding process was under way, Ib Kruse was unable to comment.

On 30 January, a Memo of Understanding was concluded on the purchase of Safmarine's liner business (excluding the bulk and reefer activities) for $394 million, and on 5 February Ib Kruse was able to call

Alexander Erwin and say that, subject to Board approval, negotiations could be completed. The deal was concluded on 10 February 1999.

A key element of the post-acquisition strategy was to retain the Safmarine name and the instantly recognisable white livery of the ships in order to build on the strong brand image and powerful 'close to the customer' culture that Safmarine had established over the years. Knud Stubkjær recalled: 'Safmarine had an extremely strong brand, an extremely strong presence, in certain markets, not least in South Africa. It was an extremely proud team and we wanted to maintain that. And we actually found out that Maersk did not always do everything the best way. There were some best practices that we could share in both directions.'[23]

Box 9.3 Safmarine since 1999

Since 1999 Safmarine, like Maersk Line and others in the container shipping industry, has experienced the ups and downs associated with that industry.

As Michael Benson, Regional Director of Interbrand, a brand specialist, noted in the fiftieth issue of Safmarine's in-house magazine, *Navigator*, 'brand leaders capture what is special about their offering, convey it to the desired audience and allow customers to experience it. Safmarine has focused on the experience it delivers customers and your customers speak highly of the interactions they have with you. The brand experience is heavily reliant on the people that ultimately serve the customer – you.'[24]

Grant Daly, CEO of Safmarine, writing in the same issue of *Navigator*, said:

2012 was a year of milestones and change for Safmarine. But what has not changed is how we as Safmariners continue to engage with our customers in the Safmarine way.

We have strengthened our position as a valuable contributor to the A.P. Moller – Maersk Group's container business.

We have demonstrated that we will go that extra mile for our customers.

We have successfully delivered on the initiatives that would return us to profitability in the short term and have embarked on a journey that will position us for long-term sustainable profitability.

We have defined and launched our Customer Value Proposition, which will enable us to consistently and coherently deliver the Safmarine brand to our customers, knowing what they expect from us.

The consistently strong message received through our Customer Experience Survey – that people can and do make a difference – is a testament to Safmarine being on the right track.'[25]

Emphasising the long-term importance of sustained maritime training to support the development of shipping and maritime competences across Africa, in 2003 the Maersk Group donated funds for the creation of a South African Maritime Training Academy, not just for South Africa, but for the use of all countries in the African region.

Sea-Land

In March 1999, Vagn Lehd Møller delivered a paper on an 'Acquisition/ Expansion Strategy for Maersk Line', which Ib Kruse forwarded to Mærsk Mc-Kinney Møller, Jess Søderberg, Knud Stubkjær and Eivind Kolding, then Chief Financial Officer of the A.P. Moller Group, for discussion. The premise was deregulation and the likely ending of anti-trust immunity over the next few years. Vagn Lehd Møller's paper was informed by the findings of Maersk Line's marketing team, which had been looking into both the acquisition of APL by Neptune Orient Line of Singapore and the 1997 merger between P&O and NedLloyd, to ascertain what went right and wrong, what impact the mergers had had on market shares, customer retention and other aspects of their businesses.

Ten years earlier, at the end of 1989, Flemming Jacobs had proposed two alternatives to growth, by organic development or through acquisition of competitors. In the intervening decade, most effort had gone into organic development, an approach that was generally preferred by Maersk's management. Now, however, Vagn Lehd Møller was proposing that Maersk Line needed to develop a more active, conscious and aggressive growth strategy. Although the company could survive alone, it would not be able to obtain the critical mass needed to provide competitive, low-cost operations. The indications were that Sea-Land was going to be sold, in which case it was unlikely to be an alliance partner after 2001. Meanwhile, industry consolidation would continue and Maersk Line needed to be at the forefront, before others 'take away the opportunities'.

He had looked in depth into about 30 existing carriers and recommended the acquisition of one or two major competitors. His paper also noted that it was 'essential to control' the container terminal business, 'this important and in the future, expected scarce, cost element of our operation'.[26]

In fact, negotiations for the acquisition of Sea-Land had already begun. In January 1999, Vagn Lehd Møller had written a note under the code name Project Sailor, summarising the effects on Maersk Line's network and operation if Sea-Land were to be bought by another company. While the acquisition of Safmarine had represented a good strategic fit, Sea-Land was beginning to be seen as a must-have. As early as 1995, as we saw in

Figure 9.5 Ib Kruse spent more than 50 years with A.P. Moller – Maersk. He was the first CEO of Maersk Container Line and his last – and lasting – impact on the organisation included the significant acquisitions of Safmarine and Sea-Land in 1999. The oil and gas exploration and production activities should have a special mention among Ib Kruse's many other responsibilities – but the list is much longer.

Chapter 8, CSX Corporation had given discreet signals that it might be prepared to sell Sea-Land. In March 1998, in conversation with John Snow, Ib Kruse indicated that if CSX ever wanted to sell, Maersk might be interested. Meanwhile, the project group had continued to monitor Sea-Land's results quarter by quarter, identifying both the similarities and differences between the two companies. In August, John Snow indicated to Ib Kruse that CSX was reviewing its ownership of Sea-Land and later that month, the project group sent Kruse an internal paper headed 'Why we might acquire Sea-Land', which included valuation calculations.

Vagn Lehd Møller continued to work through an acquisition plan, developing a detailed outline of what would need to happen if Project Sailor went forward. This was summarised for Maersk Line's centre managers and key overseas office managers so that they would be ready to set up work-groups to manage all the aspects of such a complex acquisition.

On 15 February, Maersk Line made a board-approved offer to John Snow for the acquisition of Sea-Land. However, the following day all discussions were put on hold due to differences in the valuation of Sea-Land. But, as Ib Kruse remembers, one thing had been established: 'It was important to John Snow in parting with Sea-Land, that they should have a good home and that's a very important expression.'[27]

Reviewing Sea-Land's 1998 results, a loss of $64 million, Henning Knust, Maersk Line's head of Finance, noted that John Snow now referred to the Asian economic turmoil as having put Sea-Land and the industry into the worst situation for two to three decades and provided 'dismal operating conditions'. John Snow saw this, combined with the practical effects of deregulation, as putting the whole industry in jeopardy. These elements combined to finally persuade CSX Corporation that the time was right to divest itself of Sea-Land.

Meanwhile, preparations were being made elsewhere. On 16 July, Ib Kruse finalised arrangements with J. P. Morgan and HSBC for funding of $1 billion, and also headed an extensive presentation of Project Sailor to the A.P. Moller Boards. The necessary consent was given and on 21 July, the acquisition contract was signed.

Due diligence was worked out in parallel with the practical preparations for the takeover of ships, offices and staff during the autumn of 1999 and when the final approvals from the authorities were received on 10 December, Project Sailor was completed. Three days later, a press release announced the new brand Maersk-Sealand – 'a signal to all our customers, not least the new ones, that we intend to provide a service drawing on the best from the two organisations', as it was expressed in the in-house *Mærsk Post* magazine.

The strategy had been to acquire Sea-Land's assets, rather than the organisation. While substantial effort was put into retaining key people, the numbers that joined the new organisation were limited.

Dick Murphy had been Senior Vice President at Sea-Land and was a key driver of the VSA arrangements between Sea-Land and Maersk Line. As Senior Vice President of Maersk-Sealand and a member of the steering committee that integrated the two businesses, he was clear:

First and foremost, it started at the top. If Kruse and Clancey were not prepared to provide their full support, the VSA would not have succeeded. Sea-Land knew that Maersk had the best fleet and it was only going to get better and Maersk knew that Sea-Land was a superior terminal operator in cost and productivity but also realised that Sea-Land had unique customer relations.[28]

If the VSA had not succeeded then the acquisition would never have gone forward, so the combination of operational success and a close working relationship at the top were two cornerstones on which the acquisition was built.

Dick McGregor, by then Vice President of Global Sales for Sea-Land and later Maersk-Sealand until his retirement in 2007, commented:

We heard at the time of the acquisition, and that came from Tommy [Thomsen] and Knud [Stubkjær], one of the things Maersk wanted to gain and learn from Sea-Land was how to be more effective in sales. Sea-Land grew up on a sales platform.

Maersk, of course, grew up as ship-owners. The importance was focused on the product. If we have the product, the customers will come.[29]

The difference in sales approach was illustrated by Nick Taro, who held various sales positions with Sea-Land between 1972 and 1992: 'It was a very aggressive environment in Sea-Land. A lot of focus on sales. You had to meet your quotas, the tolerance level for failure was virtually zero.'[30]

Flemming Jacobs, in his new position in Singapore, had a different perspective on the acquisition and on sales: 'To me at APL, it was the best thing that could happen because it confused the market with respect to what Maersk was and who was running it.'[31]

That possible confusion was not going to last for long. Starting in September 1999 and continuing until March 2000, detailed reports from the regions to Merger Management updated the integration status of the new company. By February 2000, Vagn Lehd Møller and Jesper Kjædegaard were able to summarise the lessons learned. In parallel, positive reports were received from Mercantile on the integration with Buyers Consolidators, a business that had been acquired as part of the Sea-Land deal.

A host of items had needed addressing, from the handling of US Government cargoes to relations with the Trans-Siberian Railway in Russia; slot charter arrangements and VSA arrangements with P&O NedLloyd; and the need to meet Federal Maritime Commission and European Union legislative requirements. Then there were claims issues, equipment management, systems integration (including Y2K issues) and ownership and flag arrangements for the Sea-Land ships. Meanwhile, Sea-Land staff and customer retention programmes needed to be managed at the local level.

The integrated Maersk-Sealand business

The numbers compiled in April 2000 to be able to incorporate the effects of the Safmarine and Sea-Land acquisitions make interesting reading. All the numbers – for the integrated liner services and other related activities (including the global agencies, the terminals and Mercantile) – took a substantial jump.[32]

The market outlook globally was in recovery mode, with containerised growth reaching over 5 per cent for both 1999 and 2000. In the United States, the economy was buoyant, while the European area was expected to achieve high growth due to the weakness of the euro, robust consumer spending and rising real disposable incomes. Eastern Europe and Russia had both shown improved economic activities and Japan's GDP was expected to rise by 1.6 per cent in 2000, compared to 0.3 per cent in 1999.

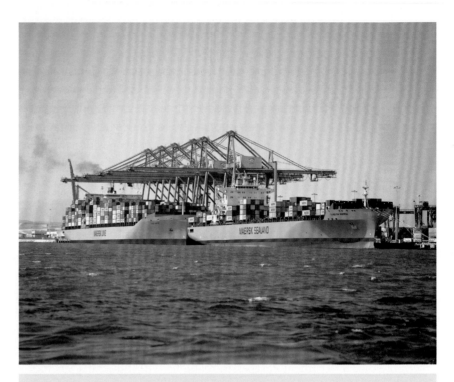

Figure 9.6 The Maersk Blue is the base and the white seven-pointed star is on both funnels, but the brand name is different. The *Glasgow Mærsk* was one of the first ships to have the new Maersk-Sealand brand painted on the hull in 2000.

China remained a strong growth area, particularly after its accession to the World Trade Organization (WTO) in 2001, while across the rest of Asia, increasing domestic demand plus robust demand from other global markets was expected to benefit the area.

Latin America, with the exception of Mexico and Peru, had seen negative GDP growth in 1999. However, the last quarter of 1999 had seen improved momentum and the region was expected to grow by about 3.9 per cent in 2000. A note of caution was sounded that the region would remain vulnerable to global credit conditions and commodity prices.

From a competitive position, Maersk-Sealand led the way but more consolidation had also taken place: Canadian Pacific purchased the outstanding 50 per cent of its joint venture Americana Ships from TMM of Mexico, which withdrew from container shipping. Compania Sudamericana de Vabores (CSAV) of Chile took over two small local South American carriers, while Hamburg Süd purchased South Pacific Container Line, Transroll and Crowley American Transport's South American services.

Box 9.4 Maersk-Sealand's market shares 1999–2000

	1999	2000		1999	2000
Far East–United States	6.5	11.2	South America southbound	9.9	15.3
United States–Far East	7.6	12.0	South America northbound	7.5	13.8
United States–Europe	8.8	12.7	West Africa southbound	21.1	22.2
Europe–United States	7.1	13.7	West Africa northbound	14.7	20.2
United States–Middle East	11.6	20.9	Middle East–Far East	10.6	12.3
Mediterranean–United States	9.2	15.6	Far East–Middle East	13.4	13.1
Europe–Far East	8.7	12.1	Intra Asia	3.9	3.5
Far East–Europe	9.2	13.4	Intra Europe	2.4	3.6

Source: Maersk Line Revised Budget 2000–2004, 7 April 2000, A.P. Moller – Maersk archives.

Finally, the Bolloré Group, owners of Delmas, a French-based container operator specialising in serving West Africa, acquired OT Africa Line.

Overall, the supply and demand situation was relatively positive, with a net increase of container ship tonnage of 4.9 per cent in 1999; this was expected to increase again to 9.8 per cent in 2000, with roughly the same growth in 2001.

Maersk-Sealand was now also the largest reefer operator. The reefer trade was expected to show growth of 5.8 per cent to reach 58.6 million tons in 2000, with the main growth coming in the frozen goods segment. Maersk-Sealand's particular strengths were in the fish, meat and deciduous fruit markets. Maersk-Sealand was substantially the market leader for specialised and high-technology reefer equipment, such as controlled atmosphere, high humidity or super-reefers. This area was expected to continue to see good growth. Conversely, Maersk-Sealand's participation in the largest trade, bananas, which were traditionally carried by reefer ships, would only reach 1.8 per cent.

From an operational perspective, the merged business was now working 250 container vessels with a capacity of about 600,000 TEU. Managing a container fleet of that size is not without its own challenges. Nick Taro recollected an event that clearly represents an owner's perspective. Shortly after the acquisition of Sea-Land, Mærsk Mc-Kinney Møller was on a visit to New York and driving out of the Newark, New Jersey terminal, he saw a Maersk container whose condition was not to his liking.

He had the driver stop the car, took down the container number and gave it to me and said, 'I want you to take this out of service. That is my name on the side of that container and I don't want to see containers ever look like that one.[33]'

While bunker costs in 1998 had been down to $75 per ton, these increased to $112 per ton in 1999 and were expected to reach $135 in 2000. With the combined fleet, total costs for bunkers were expected to rise from $229 million in 1998 to $626 million in 2000.

On the information technology side, the decision was made to run the newly merged business on Maersk Line's systems, much to the chagrin of many in Sea-Land, who believed its systems were sound and whose new system, DYMES (dynamic yield management for Sea-Land), had been seen as a potential game changer.

The costs of the network and systems that bound the whole business together were also growing, with the main growth coming from business applications and technical infrastructure developments.

The global network capacity had also been expanded and nearly all offices now had at least a 64 kilobit line. The main activities planned for 2000 were to use the internet to present Maersk-Sealand's customers with the definitive website for container shipping and to complete three releases of GCSS. Finally, it was also noted that productivity per staff member had increased by 82 per cent over the period 1998–2000.

The expected result for 2000 was seen as acceptable; however, calculations showed the sensitivity of the business to relatively small changes, for example, a 1 per cent reduction in volumes would reduce the result by about $30 million. A perennial risk was a weakening of the US dollar against other currencies where the A.P. Moller Group accounts were in Danish kroner, whereas the Maersk Line business was conducted in US dollars.

In January 2000 Dick McGregor presented some global sales observations to the BDC, comparing Sea-Land and Maersk Line. The recommendation was for 'a more integrated, enterprise-based customer strategy that will leverage all of our capabilities to achieve the most long-term profitable result'.[34] The material included a challenging article on successful and less successful approaches to partner-shipping entitled 'So You Think You Want a Partner?'[35] The presentation was well received and in due course led to the development of a Global Sales programme that Dick McGregor then implemented and managed for Maersk-Sealand.

That same month, Vagn Lehd Møller wrote to Knud Stubkjær outlining possible further acquisition targets. Maersk-Sealand's growth strategy was now firmly geared to acquisition.

Ib Kruse, reflecting on the Sea-Land acquisition, observed:

It gave strategic advantages. In the United States, our organisation had to have offices all over the country, but the flow of cargo was really too low to support that high cost, so by acquiring Sea-Land, we got blood into our system so that we could afford the right organisation. Also important was the network of Sea-Land. By acquiring, we immediately got into Costa Rica, Guatemala, the Dominican Republic, Honduras and others. The same applied to South America. From one day to the next, we were a factor there. We could really spread our wings.[36]

Looking back on his time in management in Sea-Land and later as Chairman of Maersk Inc. in the United States, John Clancey reflected:

Even though Maersk was late into the game, they certainly were pioneers in a lot of what they did on the ship side. What Maersk accomplished was providing in every shipping country in the world an opportunity to participate in global trade. Facili-tated it, improved it, certainly reduced pilferage to almost zero, improved transit times. You know the only two carriers in the world that cared about on-time delivery were Maersk and Sea-Land, and Maersk continue to do it and do it very, very well. I think the company is really never given credit for what it has done to improve the livelihoods and the well-being of people around the world.[37]

On 8 May 2000, Kruse, the steady hand who had guided and managed the development of Maersk Line since 1974, retired as Partner in A.P. Moller after more than 50 years in the Maersk organisation. While Kruse denied to the last that there had been a strategy for Maersk Line, insisting that 'opportunities just developed', Knud Stubkjær thought very differently: 'I think Ib had the strategy in his head and actually had the fantastic capability of being able to implement it without needing to write it down and still keep the troops aligned behind it.'[38]

A selection of important developments: 1995–1999

Political

- 1995 The Dayton Peace Accords end a three-year war in the Balkans.[39]
- 1997 Russia and Chechnya sign a peace treaty in an attempt to normalise relations after an armed conflict that lasted from 1994–96.[40]
- 1997 China resumes sovereignty over Hong Kong, the culmination of a transition process started in 1984 with the Sino-British Joint Declaration.[41]
- 1998 The Indonesian president, Suharto, steps down after 32 years in power.[42] Elections will be held in 1999, the first free elections since 1955.[43]
- 1998 Northern Ireland acquires a fragile peace when the Good Friday Agreement is signed.[44]
- 1998 Al-Qaeda bombs US embassies in Kenya and Tanzania, killing 213 people. The US retaliates with air strikes against perceived terrorist sites in Afghanistan and Sudan.[45]
- 1999 The North Atlantic Treaty Organization (NATO) launches an airstrike against Yugoslavia to halt army actions against ethnic Albanians in Kosovo.[46] NATO forces mistakenly bomb the Chinese embassy in Belgrade, Serbia.[47]

Economic

- Mid 1990s Globalisation, the growth of information and communications technologies (ICT), and nascent social-networking tools spur the development of the *knowledge economy*.[48]
- Late 1990s Financial crises break out in emerging economies, including Mexico, several East Asian countries, Russia and Brazil.[49]
- 1995 A futures trader, Nick Leeson, is jailed for a US$1.4bn fraud that leads to the collapse of merchant bank, Barings.[50]
- 1997 A devaluation of the Thai currency triggers a regional economic crisis. Asian currencies and stock markets plunge, creating an economic crisis in the region.[51]
- 1998 Russian markets fall in response to the Asian crisis. The central bank allows currency devaluation. The rouble plummets and trade in the currency is suspended as it loses around 40% of its value against the German mark.[52]

Social

- Late 1990s The communications revolution continues. In 1990 there are 11m mobile phone subscribers worldwide.[53] By 2012 mobile subscriptions will reach 6bn.[54]
- Late 1990s Supermarkets grow rapidly in Asia. In 1990 Korea, Taiwan and Philippines see supermarkets account for 10% of sales. By 2003 this will increase to 50–60%.[55]
- 1995 E-commerce begins to develop, with the founding of Amazon.com.[56]
- 1996 A satellite channel, Al Jazeera, is launched in Doha, Qatar. Al Jazeera will launch an English-language news channel in 2006.[57]
- 1998 Larry Page and Sergey Brin rename their data-organising and search engine company Google.[58] The search engine will average 620m daily visitors in 2011.[59]

Technological

- 1996 The *digital versatile disc* (DVD) is released. It has the size of a regular compact disc (CD), but is able to contain ten times the information, making it viable for the distribution of digitally encoded movies.[60]
- 1997 Scientists in Scotland announce the birth of Dolly the sheep, the world's first successfully cloned mammal.[61]
- 1997 Biologists isolate human embryonic stem cells.[62] Embryonic stem cells can generate all cell types in the body and are considered to be able to generate healthy tissue to replace tissue damaged by either trauma or disease.[63]

Legal

- 1995 The Schengen Agreement comes into force, allowing the free movement of people within a number of countries in Europe (Belgium, France, Germany, Luxembourg, the Netherlands, Portugal and Spain).[64] Other European countries will join in the late 1990s and early 2000s.[65]
- 1995 The World Trade Organization (WTO) Agreement on the Application of Sanitary and Phytosanitary Measures (SPS Agreement) is signed. This agreement structures member states' policies relating to food safety, animal and plant health, and imported pests and diseases.[66]
- 1997 The Convention on the Prohibition of the Use, Stockpiling, Production and Transfer of Anti-Personnel Mines bans land mines designed for use against humans.[67]
- 1998 The UN establishes the International Criminal Court (ICC) to investigate and try individuals, including political and military leaders, for the most serious international crimes: genocide, crimes against humanity and war crimes.[68]

Environmental

- 1995 Fears for the environment grow as an extended periodic climatic phenomenon altering temperatures and air pressure – known as "El Niño" – creates extreme weather conditions globally.[69]
- 1995 The Intergovernmental Panel on Climate Change finds evidence of a discernible human influence on climate.[70]
- 1996 The World Health Organization (WHO) calls for a global phasing out of leaded gasoline.[71]
- 1997 The Kyoto Protocol is signed by the US government and 121 other nations, but it is not ratified by the US Congress. The protocol has binding targets for 37 industrialised countries and the EU for reducing greenhouse gas (GHG) emissions. It will come into force in 2005.[72]

10 Into the New Millennium (2000–2005)

> *Other companies, such as Hutchison and Sea-Land Services, probably saw this a little bit earlier than the Maersk Group, but the need for highly efficient and quality port infrastructure has become more and more evident. The journey was not a revolution, it was an evolution. It has taken since 2004 to really establish APM Terminals as an independent business with its own portfolio of customers and with its own individual branding.*
>
> Kim Fejfer, President of APM Terminals[1]

Getting to Year 2000

As so often, *Containerisation International* provided a commentary on the sector in its 1997 yearbook. Jane Boyes wrote:

It was unsatisfactory bottom lines and disgruntled shareholders, which pushed P&O and NedLloyd into each other's arms, rather than a desire to provide shippers with better service. The largest portion of PONL's yearly cost savings, some USD 130 million, will be made on staff and overheads. The industry wisdom was that the global operating alliances should ultimately produce savings of approximately USD 100 per TEU moved per year. The question which has yet to be answered is, are they delivering this?

One alliance which might have the best chance of realising such economies, is the largest grouping of all, that between Denmark's Maersk Line and Sea-Land Service, of the USA. According to John Clancey, President and CEO of Sea-Land, each partner is anticipating annualised savings of USD 100 million by 1998.

In the same article, she went on to say that

the problem is not lack of growth in revenues overall, which rise inevitably each year as a function of annual container trade increases in the order of seven per cent to eight per cent, but rather a consistent erosion of per box revenues. There has been a decline of as much as 60 per cent in real terms per unit revenues in certain key East/West trades since the mid-1970s. Collectively, the industry seems to be unable to reverse the debilitating price erosion which has characterised it for so long, hence the emphasis on costs.

Figure 10.1 The Maersk Line brand was introduced in 1928 when the first sailings took place on the Panama Line. Following the acquisition of Sea-Land, the brand was changed to Maersk-Sealand, but still in conjunction with the well-known white seven-pointed star. Just out of the Maersk Container Industry factory, these new reefer containers clearly show off the new identity.

Concluding, she suggested that 'the only real beneficiaries continue to be the carriers' customers who frequently find they are pushing on an open door when it comes to negotiating rate decreases'.[2] Containerisation is fundamentally a commoditised industry and as scale is all-important, consolidation would continue.

And indeed it did, throughout the late 1990s, with the take-over in 1997 of American President Lines (APL) by Neptune Orient Line (NOL) of Singapore. Canadian Pacific's CP Ships acquired Cast Line (a Trans Atlantic and Canadian carrier), Lykes Lines of the US Gulf and Contship Container Lines, to join Canada Maritime. Prices, with very few exceptions, continued to fall, but despite the growing Asian financial crisis, there were signs of optimism with few orders for new ships and a significant increase in the number of old container ships being scrapped.

A note in the *Containerisation International Yearbook 1998* tracks the rise of a relatively unknown company, Mediterranean Shipping

Company (MSC) where 'over the past five years, MSC's slot count has mushroomed from 35,531 TEU in 1992 to 154,100 TEU in 1997'.[3] By the end of 1998, this had increased further to 220,745 TEU and MSC ranked fourth after P&O NedLloyd (250,858 TEU), Evergreen (280,237 TEU) and Maersk Line (346,123 TEU) in terms of capacity offered to the global market. MSC had become one of the fastest-growing container operators, with its fleet expansion programme based largely on second-hand tonnage.

The tone of the 1999 *Containerisation International Yearbook* was, however, rather dismal:

Carrier profitability showed no sign of improving and consolidation, either through takeovers or mergers, continued. In addition, there appeared to be no end in sight to the consequences of Asia's economic meltdown on the container business, while the top 20 largest carriers now account for 53 per cent of the world's container carrying capacity. Ten years ago, their share was just over 37 per cent.[4]

Was this the period when container shipping became seen as a commodity? Or had that happened earlier and was the realisation only just sinking in? While trade was growing, rates had fallen and uncertainty prevailed about legislative developments that were fundamental to the way container shipping operated. It is noticeable that in the literature covering the industry in this period, the focus is on cost reductions and then more cost reductions, so that slot costs provided to the trade were as low and as competitive as possible.[5]

Tim Harris, previously Managing Director of both P&O Cruises and P&O Containers, was quite clear that

the old idea that your customer would stick to you because of service became commoditised. The original service, setting it up, building ports, making it work, after 15 years, people got used to that and they said, 'What's the price?' So you had commoditisation, particularly people like Evergreen and the classic commoditiser now, MSC. And that was linked to the rise of the forwarders, the Kuehne + Nagels and others who were able to get very cheap, excellently run services for next to nothing.[6]

The freight forwarder and other intermediaries that could provide the beneficial cargo owner, the customer, with full-service capabilities were rising fast. As Tim Harris put it, 'clever people like Kuehne + Nagel ... decided that control of the customer was more important than control of the steel.' Carriers, whose sales organisations tended to focus on larger customers, might find it interesting to know that the invoiced turnover in Box 10.1 is generated from customers whose average business with Kuehne + Nagel is about 150 TEU per year.

Box 10.1 Kuehne + Nagel key figures, 1985–2010

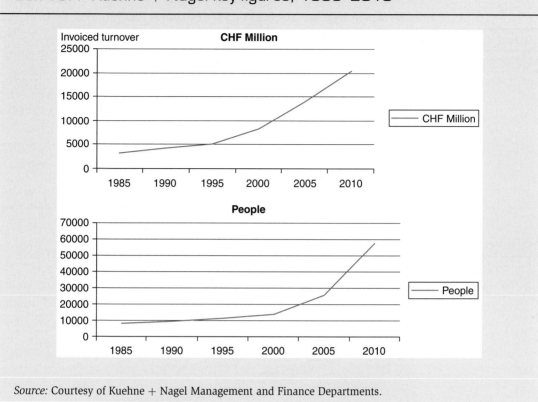

Source: Courtesy of Kuehne + Nagel Management and Finance Departments.

Maersk Line: the integrator?

Despite the fact that Ib Kruse had formally retired in May 2000, Vagn Lehd Møller summarised the progress of the Sea-Land integration to him that July. He concluded that the Merger Management team had completed its role. Ib Kruse agreed and forwarded the memo to Mærsk Mc-Kinney Møller and Jess Søderberg, with the suggestion that a Container Business Executive Board be formed, to be chaired by Ib Kruse and consisting of John Clancey and Knud Stubkjær.

The Container Business Executive Board oversaw activities in Maersk-Sealand, Safmarine, Mercantile, the terminals business and the local agencies around the world. For a number of years, the Container Business, referred to internally as the CB, was regarded as one business with these different components. The Sea-Land integration was progressing well. The main customers were being closely monitored to ensure retention was achieved.

Once the integration was completed, the Container Business Executive Board was disbanded, while the coordination of the newly integrated business was made the responsibility of the Container Business Committee (CBC). John Clancey became chairman of Maersk Inc. in the United States.

Bunker prices had risen from $81 per ton in 1998 to $112 in 1999 and $163 per ton in 2000. That amounted to an extra bunker bill of over $240 million. To reduce bunker costs, a study was conducted on slow steaming.

In April 2000, Knud Stubkjær, initiated a Global Logistics Study, asking a small team consisting of Søren Toft Madsen (Maersk-Sealand), Diederich Blom (Norfolk Line), Jesper Bramming (Finance) and Chris Jephson (Maersk Logistics) to provide an overview of the development options available across the business. The study recommended that the business move further towards assuming an 'integrator' role as a way of differentiating Maersk:

Logistics will be the gateway to freight. Building and successfully marketing integrated logistics services will be key to maintaining client ownership and participating in the most profitable supply chain management services.[7]

The consultants PricewaterhouseCoopers (PwC) had provided a rule of thumb that approximately 10 per cent of the GDP of developed markets could be attributed to logistics costs. Global GDP in 2000 was $31 trillion, so the PWC data suggested that the logistics market was in the order of $3 trillion, with 20 per cent of all logistics spend outsourced and growing at about

Figure 10.2 Maersk Logistics, formerly Mercantile and now Damco, expanded the integrated logistics services business.

15 per cent per year. The conclusion was that integrated logistics represented an attractive business opportunity and that the A.P. Moller Group was well positioned to capture a large and profitable share of the market.

That September, Deutsche Post announced its takeover of DHL, adding to its existing shareholding by buying shares from Japan Air Lines and from DHL's existing management and shareholders. In October, United Parcels Service (UPS) announced an increase of 9.7 per cent in its 1999 revenues, to $7.4 billion, with an operating profit of $1.16 billion, up 17.3 per cent on the previous year. Both companies were seen as positioning themselves in the global logistics marketplace.

Towards the end of September, Knud Stubkjær recommended to Jess Søderberg that further work be undertaken on four possible business areas where potential had been identified. The teams were formed in mid-October and final reports, including responses to questions, were to be ready by 15 February 2001.

Presentations were given to the CBC at the end of January 2001 and further discussions led up to a final presentation towards the end of

Box 10.2 Growth potential for Maersk Logistics, 2001

The Global Logistics Study Group, meeting in mid 2000, defined the following:

- Global GDP: $31 trillion[8]

Logistics spend was seen as approximately 10 per cent of global GDP.

- Logistics spend: $3 trillion[9]

GDP was expected to grow by 3–4 per cent per year. Logistics spending was seen as likely to grow faster at 4–5 per cent per year.

The outsourced[10] share of logistics spend was estimated at about 20 per cent, and was growing at about 15–20 per cent per year.

This generated an outsourced logistics market in 2000 of about $600 billion, growing to about $1,200 billion by 2005.

The rationale behind outsourcing was taken from another report:

Companies across all industry sectors will outsource more of their logistics activities to transport and logistics companies … As shippers integrate their supply chains, they are outsourcing more of their logistics processes. This development will also affect the scope and complexity of the partnerships between shippers and transport and logistics companies.[11]

The report proposed a series of recommendations to be implemented to build the capabilities of Maersk Line and Maersk Logistics to allow exploitation of this opportunity.

February. After much internal debate, Maersk Logistics was given the go-ahead to implement an aggressive growth strategy. Based on both organic growth and acquisitions, the strategy was to expand globally in four key activity areas: airfreight services, warehousing and distribution services, freight forwarding and integrated logistics.

A globalising economy

The *Containerisation International Yearbook 2000* noted that the world container fleet passed six million TEU capacity towards the end of 1999 and that the number of post-Panamax ships now totalled 68, with a further 61 on order. Maersk Line's acquisition of Sea-Land was seen as substantial, but it was only one in a succession of 43 mergers and acquisitions over the previous five years.

The improving market had led to some rate increases in the Asia–Europe and Asia–US trades, but rates in the outbound direction in both trades fell, while the continuing influence of the Asian economic crisis on operating costs were clearly stated in a Drewry Shipping Consultants' report that estimated positioning and repositioning costs for empty containers at $11.8 billion for 1998, or 15.3 per cent of industry income for that year.[12]

Some things were moving in the right direction. Foreign direct investment flows (FDI) were growing significantly, a strong indicator of the growth in globalisation and the integration of countries into the world economy. The number of countries with an inward FDI in excess of $10 billion reached 50 in 2000, of which 24 were developing countries, up from 17 in 1985, when only 7 were developing countries.

In 2001, the Doha Round of trade liberalisation discussions, including the Doha Development Agenda, was launched, with a key objective to make trade rules fairer for developing countries. That same year, China joined the World Trade Organisation after 15 years of negotiations. China's merchandise exports would rise from $266 billion in 2001 to $1.9 trillion by 2011 (at current market prices), by which time it had become known as 'the factory to the world'.

Other developments of note were to be found in the US. President George W. Bush continued an initiative of the Clinton administration that encouraged home ownership, a strategy that would ultimately inflate a housing bubble. This, combined with increased US borrowing to support wars in Iraq and Afghanistan, was raising the US budget deficit to record heights. The Ocean Shipping Reform Act (OSRA) of 1998 had been implemented but the effects had not yet materialised significantly. This was supposed to usher in an era of greater partnerships between carriers and customers, by the provision of confidential contracts with greater emphasis on service

Box 10.3 Top 25 recipients by inward direct investment flows, 2005–2011

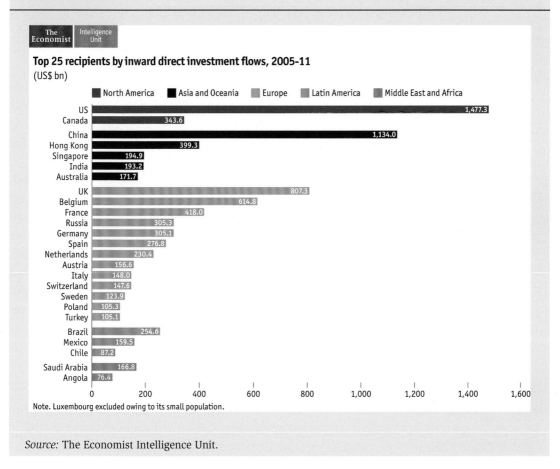

Top 25 recipients by inward direct investment flows, 2005-11
(US$ bn)

Legend: North America | Asia and Oceania | Europe | Latin America | Middle East and Africa

US	1,477.3
Canada	343.6
China	1,134.0
Hong Kong	399.3
Singapore	194.9
India	193.2
Australia	171.7
UK	807.3
Belgium	614.8
France	418.0
Russia	305.3
Germany	305.1
Spain	276.8
Netherlands	230.4
Austria	156.6
Italy	148.0
Switzerland	147.6
Sweden	123.9
Poland	105.3
Turkey	105.1
Brazil	254.6
Mexico	159.5
Chile	87.2
Saudi Arabia	166.8
Angola	76.4

Note. Luxembourg excluded owing to its small population.

Source: The Economist Intelligence Unit.

and less on price and to facilitate discussions about more strategic issues such as logistics services and integrated transport chains.

Another new business

In May 2000, Peder Søndergaard, then heading Maersk-Sealand's Terminals and Intermodal Department in Copenhagen, reviewed the terminals situation for the CBC. He suggested that Maersk-Sealand was missing an opportunity to generate income and reduce costs by servicing third-party carriers. Maersk was the third largest terminal operator in the world, although not recognised as such, but there was an opportunity to change perceptions. Søndergaard recommended that Terminals should be set up as an independent profit centre with active sales and marketing support.

By 2000 Maersk-Sealand had 20 facilities around the world, including newer terminals such as Pier 400 in Los Angeles and in Port Elizabeth, New Jersey as well as Rotterdam, Yantian in China, Algeciras in Spain and Felixstowe, UK. The very latest was the new connecting point in Tanjong Pelepas in Malaysia, just across the water from Singapore, where Maersk-Sealand had moved that autumn. The total investment that Maersk had made in terminals by now amounted to $1.11 billion.

Peder Søndergaard's recommendation was accepted, but debate continued over a name for the activity until, in February 2001, Tommy Thomsen suggested APM Terminals as it 'signals the desired differentiation from Maersk-Sealand while still identifying the activity as part of the A.P. Moller Group'.

This was accepted by Mærsk Mc-Kinney Møller and Jess Søderberg and, although already passed, 1 January 2001 was chosen as the official starting date for the new company. APM Terminals was also given permission to use the Maersk star logo, but without using the word Maersk in its name. And, in 2004 APM Terminals moved its headquarters away from Denmark to operate as a separate business entity within the group, with its head office in The Hague, Netherlands.[13] An aggressive expansion plan was put forward in February 2002, involving investments of up to $1.6 billion over the next few years.

Box 10.4 Port of Tanjung Pelepas, Malaysia

Situated on the Straits of Johor in Southern Malaysia, to the north of the port of Singapore, the port of Tanjung Pelepas was opened in October 1999. By 2011 the port ranked 18th globally in container throughput, with 7.5 million TEU, handling an estimated eight million TEU in 2012.

The port is managed by APM Terminals, which owns 30 per cent. Malaysian-based utilities and infrastructure group Malaysian Mining Corporation owns a 70 per cent majority share.

In 2011, Maersk Line accounted for 80 per cent of the port's throughput, with Evergreen as the other main user. Other carriers operating at the terminal include Korean-based Hanjin Shipping and the Japanese Mitsui-OSK Line. Over 90 per cent of the port's throughput relates to trans-shipment containers.

The port area includes an industrial and commercial duty free zone. The port is currently engaged in a $434 million expansion programme that will add 2 berths to the existing 3.6 km of quay as well as 8 super-post-Panamax cranes and 32 rubber-tyred gantry cranes. The expansion will increase the Port's annual capacity to about 10.5 million TEU.

Tanjung Pelepas has been nominated as the most productive port in the region, averaging 34 gross moves per hour.

Figure 10.3 Some of the 24 super post-Panamax gantry cranes at APM Terminals Port of Tanjung Pelepas servicing some of the largest container ships of the world.

Box 10.5 APM Terminals 2001–2013

Maersk has been involved in terminal management since 1951, when the Brigantine Terminal Corporation was formed in New York to operate two leased terminals in Brooklyn. Later in 1958, Moller Steamship Company leased Pier 11 in Brooklyn to handle the pallet and semi-container ships on the Panama service. This operation continued until 1975 when, with the arrival of the first container ships, the operation was moved to Berth 51 in Port Newark, New Jersey.

In 1986, Maersk Line's terminal at Algeciras, Spain was opened and between then and 1999, terminals in Denmark, Japan, the United States, Thailand, Taiwan and Oman were added. With the acquisition of Sea-Land in 1999, Maersk Line became a major terminal operator.

By February 2013 APM Terminals was operating in 68 countries and had some 25,000 employees. Operations spanned 62 terminals, with 7 new projects under way as well as 14 expansion projects, plus the operation of more than 170 inland service locations. Turnover was $4.8 billion and APM Terminals was serving over 60 shipping companies. Throughput was in excess of 35.4 million TEU.

APM Terminals is proud of its achievements over the last 12 years and in particular of its efforts to achieve a safe working environment and improve its carbon footprint.

APM Terminals is also leading the way with innovative solutions. The new Maasvlakte II terminal uses automated guided vehicles that increase productivity by between 25 and 50 per cent over conventional terminal designs.

Box 10.5 (cont.)

APM Terminals development timeline

2002

- Terminal throughput of 14.3 million TEU.
- Opened Pier 400, Los Angeles, the world's largest proprietary terminal.
- Signed joint venture to develop Port of Luanda, Angola.

2003

- Terminal throughput of 16.7 million TEU.
- 49 per cent share in Shanghai East Container Terminal, China.

2004

- APM Terminals moves headquarters to Holland.
- Terminal throughput exceeds 20 million TEU.

2005

- Turnover of $1.5 billion.
- Opens terminal at Itajai, Brazil.
- Acquires majority shares in Port Pipavav, India.

2006

- Turnover exceeds $2 billion.
- Named 'Best Global Terminal Operator' by *Containerisation International*.
- Assumes control of Apapa Container Terminal, Nigeria.
- Assumes control of Mina Salman Port, Bahrain.
- Opens terminal at Zeebrugge, Belgium.
- Opens terminal at Mumbai, India.

2007

- Financial results reported as an independent business within the group.
- Turnover exceeds $2.5 billion.
- Terminal throughput exceeds 30 million TEU.
- Opens terminal at Tangier, Morocco.
- Opens terminal at Portsmouth, Virginia; largest private terminal in the US.

2008

- Turnover exceeds $3.1 billion.
- Terminal throughput exceeds 34 million TEU.
- Opens terminal at Mobile, Alabama.
- Assumes control of Port of Pecém, Brazil.

2009

- Opens new Bahrain Gateway terminal.

Box 10.5 (cont.)

- Part of consortium to develop Pointe-Noire, Republic of the Congo.
- Non-A.P. Moller – Maersk business accounts for 42 per cent of turnover.
- Named 'Port Operator of the Year' by *Lloyds List*.

2010

- Inland Service Group is added to APM Terminals' portfolio.
- Acquires 50 per cent of Terminal Portuário in Santos, Brazil.
- Starts development of Port of Santos, Brazil.
- Signs concession for operating Monrovia Freeport, Liberia.

2011

- Concession to develop Moín Container Terminal, Costa Rica.
- Concession to develop Terminal Muelle Norte, Port of Callao, Peru.
- Purchases majority share in Seaport Poti, Georgia.
- Concession to operate Skandia Container Terminal, Gothenburg, Sweden.
- Concession for a new terminal at Lázaro Cárdenas, Mexico.

2012

- Purchases a controlling interest in Global Ports, Russia and the Baltics.
- Opens container terminal at Wilhelmshaven, Germany.
- Cooperation agreement to enlarge the Meishan Terminal at Ningbo, China.
- Operational management of inland terminal at Mombasa, Kenya, acquired.
- Named 'Port Operator of the Year' by *Lloyds List* and 'Terminal Operator of the Year' by *Containerisation International*.

2013

- Signs agreement to develop and operate new port at Izmir, Turkey.

Figure 10.4 The APM Terminals logo.

Box 10.6 The world's top ten container ports 1990–2010

1990			2000			2005			2010		
Rank	Port	Thousand TEU	Rank	Port	Thousand TEU	Rank	Port	Thousand TEU	Rank	Port	Thousand TEU
1	Singapore	6,354	1	Hong Kong	18,100	1	Singapore	23,192	1	Shanghai	29,069
2	Hong Kong	6,162	2	Singapore	17,040	2	Hong Kong	22,427	2	Singapore	28,431
3	Kaohsiung	3,913	3	Busan	7,540	3	Shanghai	18,084	3	Hong Kong	23,699
4	Rotterdam	3,766	4	Kaohsiung	7,426	4	Shenzhen	16,197	4	Shenzhen	22,510
5	Busan	2,694	5	Rotterdam	6,275	5	Busan	11,843	5	Busan	14,194
6	Kobe	2,635	6	Shanghai	5,613	6	Kaohsiung	9,471	6	Ningbo	13,144
7	Hamburg	2,189	7	Los Angeles	4,879	7	Rotterdam	9,300	7	Guangzhou	12,560
8	Los Angeles	2,038	8	Long Beach	4,601	8	Hamburg	8,088	8	Qingdao	12,012
9	Keelung	2,005	9	Hamburg	4,248	9	Dubai	7,619	9	Dubai	11,600
10	New York/ New Jersey	1,865	10	Antwerp	4,082	10	Los Angeles	7,485	10	Rotterdam	11,145

Source: Containerisation International Yearbooks for 1993, 2002, 2007, 2012, © 1993, 2002, 2007, 2012, reproduced with the permission of Lloyds List Group.

Developments in technology

When the Maersk-Sealand finance managers' meeting took place in September 2000, the main discussion was around the delivery of a new system, originally (before the Sea-Land integration) known as Maersk Line's Invoicing System (MLIS). Designed to create one global invoicing and accounts receivable system, it was innovative and based on a standard Oracle platform, with bespoke items tailored to Maersk-Sealand.

However, the big push was in another direction: e-commerce, a relatively new development. This opened up tremendous opportunities for ocean carriers and their customers. *Containerisation International* reported:

It is clearly perceived that IT is the key to not only dealing more effectively with customers, but also creating more efficient internal structures within companies, allowing better management of vital information on costs as well as revenues. The announcement in late October 2000, that a group of five major European-headquartered carriers had joined forces to create and financially support a neutral transportation portal on the internet, under the working name of INTTRA, was particularly significant.[14]

Thomas Eskesen, at that time head of Maersk Line's e-commerce team, commented:

we started with a blank sheet of paper. We spent a lot of time with customers such as Carrefour and Wal-Mart, trying to understand what their e-commerce strategies were, and out of that came this radical thing, that customers were not looking for proprietary e-commerce solutions, they didn't want websites, they wanted an industry portal. And so, INTTRA came about.[15]

Reorganisation at Maersk-Sealand

Neither 2001 nor 2002 were to be good years as over-capacity combined with poor economic developments generally was to plague the business. World GDP growth in 2001 was a negative 3.7 per cent, while 2002 saw a recovery to 4.3 per cent growth, but this was still low when compared to the recent past. The situation was made all the worse by the attacks on the World Trade Center in New York and the Pentagon in Washington on 11 September 2001, which led to the beginning of the 'war on terror'.

That summer, Tommy Thomsen, until then President of Maersk Inc. in the United States, was promoted to Partner, handing the North American role over to Thomas Thune Andersen, who moved from his role as Managing Director for The Maersk Company Limited in the UK. Tommy Thomsen moved back to Copenhagen and was made joint CEO of Maersk-Sealand with Knud Stubkjær. The two were to share the responsibility and

Figure 10.5 Tommy Thomsen was co-CEO of Maersk-Sealand 2001–2006. He joined A.P. Moller – Maersk in 1978 and became CEO of Maersk Tankers in 1991. From 1995 to 2001 Tommy Thomsen was President and CEO of Maersk Inc. and responsible for Maersk Line's activities in North America, Central America and the Caribbean, before returning to Copenhagen as Partner as from 1 July 2001.

workload of pulling the business back to profitability. Maersk had never tried dual leadership before. At the time, it seemed natural to organise that way, with two people overseeing the portfolio of activities, bearing in mind the size of the business following the 1999 acquisitions.

Knud Stubkjær's role was to focus on Line Management, with a Chief Commercial Officer covering Sales and Customer Focus, Business Development, Reefer and Regulatory Affairs; a Chief Operations Officer encompassing Vessel Operations, Service Delivery, Equipment Management and Operations Management, as well as a Chief Information Officer responsible for a series of major projects including e-commerce initiatives; and a Chief Financial Officer responsible for Finance and Management Information Systems.

Tommy Thomsen was to focus on the global organisation through six regional managers, Bjarne Hansen (Asia), Jesper Kjædegaard (West and Central Asia), Thomas Thune Andersen (North and Central America), Michael Hassing (Europe), Lars Reno Jakobsen (Africa) and Kim Gadegaard (South America). In addition, as Partner, he was responsible for the subsidiary companies, Maersk Logistics, headed by Søren Brandt, APM Terminals, headed by Peder Søndergaard and Maersk Tankers, headed by Søren Skou.

The container shipping scene

Meanwhile, a new trend had been noted. This was for carriers operating vessels off balance sheet on long-term charters, which had facilitated the growth of German and Greek tramp-owners specialising in the management of container ships. Conti-Reederei, Claus-Peter Offen and ER Shiffahrt of Germany, and Greek companies Costamare and Danaos, were particularly active.

Consolidation had continued with P&O NedLloyd acquiring the UK's Harrison Line and US-based Farrell Lines, CP Ships taking control of Americana Ships and Christensen Canadian African Lines, and CSAV of Chile buying Norasia. By 2000, the top 20 carriers controlled 76 per cent of all container slots in service.

MSC's expansion continued with the receipt of its first new-building, one of ultimately fifteen 6,750 TEU post-Panamax ships, some of which were to be owned by Conti-Reedererei, while Hapag Lloyd ordered four 7,500 TEU ships from Hyundai in Korea, the largest vessels yet ordered in terms of official capacity. An article in the *Containerisation International Yearbook 2001* ended by saying it remained to be seen 'whether this influx of new tonnage can be safely absorbed into the market without an impact on supply and demand'.[16]

This was quite prophetic: the 2002 yearbook started with the statement, 'Acute over-capacity, fuelled by a continuous injection of new buildings coupled with declining growth in cargo volumes, ensured that the year would end negatively for most ocean carriers.' The South Korean carrier Cho Yang Line was forced into bankruptcy by its creditors. Large, modern container ships were laid up as a number of entire routes were slimmed down by closing strings by, among others, CMA CGM, China Shipping, the New World Alliance (APL, Hyundai and MOSK Line), the Grand Alliance and Maersk-Sealand.

Jane Boyes wrote:

The extent of the crisis facing the providers of container liner services in 2002 cannot be overstated. As a consequence, it is likely that there will be major reorganisation within the industry over the next 12 months.[17]

The WTO expected growth in world merchandise trade to slow to only 2 per cent in 2001 compared to 12 per cent in 2000 and 'even this growth is not assured given the present great uncertainties about economic and trade developments'.[18]

There was a recession in Japan and the United States, during which the dot-com bubble burst, growth slowed in Europe and Asia, excluding China, and a total of over 1.5 million TEU of new capacity was on order for delivery over the next two years. Senator Lines of Germany cut back its services substantially, while Trans-Pacific Lines ceased operations and CP Ships acquired Italia di Navigazione, the container liner company of the Italian d'Amico Group.

While US consumers showed remarkable resilience by continuing to spend, and the NASDAQ stock exchange peaked at 5,132 on 10 March 2000, by November 2002 the Federal Reserve in the United States needed to reduce interest rates by 0.5 per cent to 'an historic low of 1.25 per cent' to bolster confidence.

With a threatened dock strike on the US West Coast and the decision in the United States to start requiring manifest information to be electronically transmitted to US Customs 24 hours before a container consigned to the United States could be loaded on the vessel, delays and disruptions were of real concern, despite full understanding of the need for tighter security after the tragic events of 9/11.

The StarLight strategy

In October 2002, A.P. Moller's liner operations (consisting of Maersk-Sealand, Safmarine and the recently acquired Torm Line of Denmark) operated a fleet of 312 ships with a capacity of 773,931 TEU and with 98,536 TEU of capacity on order – in total, about twice the size of the second largest carrier, which was now MSC, with 413,814 TEU of capacity and 93,050 TEU on order.[19]

The year 2001 had seen a net loss in Maersk-Sealand, despite a turnover of just under $9 billion. The 2002 business plan put forward by Peter Frederiksen and Vagn Lehd Møller did not show significant improvement.

While the income from other CB activities – Safmarine, agency offices, Maersk Logistics, etc. – was substantial, it was not enough to turn the result into an acceptable return on investment.

The expected result, 'unsatisfactory as it is, is a reflection of the present market situation, where high tonnage growth and stagnant markets have driven freight rates to unsustainable levels in major trades'.[20] Despite a slightly more positive note on trade growth in 2003, it was not believed to be enough to absorb the capacity available and the 2003 expected result was also forecast as a loss. Ultimately, both years would show significantly better results, but they were still in the future.

While many of the smaller trades were continuing to do reasonably well, the problem was clearly the major trades, with the Far East to Europe trade

Box 10.7 Maersk-Sealand average freight rates, 1995–2002 per FFE

| | US dollars per FFE | | | |
	Dry	Reefer	Average	000 FFE handled
Actual 1995	3.259	5.206	3.485	1.051
Actual 1996	3.026	5.128	3.285	1.157
Actual 1997	2.663	4.874	2.919	1.401
Actual 1998	2.529	4.480	2.753	1.567
Actual 1999	2.408	3.933	2.593	1.886
Actual 2000	2.460	3.909	2.610	3.100
Estimated 2001	2.334	3.890	2.502	3.240
November 2001	2.202	3.858	2.397	–
Budget 2002	2.140	3.786	2.322	3.475

Source: Maersk-Sealand 2002–6 Budget, Centre Finance, 12 November 2001.

leading the way with losses, followed closely by the Trans Pacific, the Trans Atlantic and the Middle East markets.

A meeting of the CBC at the beginning of 2002 identified a wide range of issues and concerns about Maersk-Sealand's existing strategy and ability to confront the poor operating environment. McKinsey, Accenture and Bain & Co were approached by the joint CEOs for assistance and on 17 April, Bain & Co was retained to assist the turnaround process. A series of 14 workstreams were formed to address specific areas of the business under the project name StarLight. The plan was to complete the initial review by the end of June 2002.

The starting point was a structural review of Maersk-Sealand, Maersk Logistics and APM Terminals. Prices for ocean freight had dropped by 20 per cent since the previous year, while a further 30 per cent increase in container capacity was expected. Maersk-Sealand's global market share was about 12 per cent and it was the market leader – but such shares were generally unable to influence either the market or rate levels.

Knud Stubkjær was as direct as always:

We needed to take a completely new, a fresh look at our strategic direction. We had been through a period of market turmoil, and we were not in control of our own destiny, because while you can control some parts of your activities, other parts are controlled externally by competition, for instance, or pricing.[21]

Immediate efforts were focused on profit hunting, using many of the traditional cost-saving approaches to improve results. But the problems were deeper and as this became clearer, so the focus shifted to addressing more fundamental issues, such as the commoditisation of the industry and Maersk-Sealand's continuing ability to differentiate – with a long list of initiatives to be agreed and prioritised.

A StarLight Steering Committee meeting in May focused on the concept of route profitability, while discussions also covered measurement of customer profitability and the implications for both APM Terminals and Maersk Logistics of the initial ideas coming out of the workstreams. A more detailed management-level workshop was held in June, with Knud Stubkjær, Tommy Thomsen, Peter Frederiksen (Maersk-Sealand's Chief Commercial Officer), Flemming Frost (representing Maersk Logistics), and Soren Toft Madsen (Knud Stubkjær's assistant) supported by Bain.

The outcome was a clear agreement on ways of achieving improved profitability in certain specific and critical trades under the banner headline 'A New Dimension in Shipping', while the acquisition of P&O NedLloyd was posited as providing the best way of achieving a clear leadership position in the market place.

The StarLight workshops produced a new and very clear vision for Maersk-Sealand from which the title of this book is derived. It also led to the creation of a mission statement and a three-pronged approach to the future based on improving profitability, requiring tonnage deployment to support and sustain the strategy; cost leadership, with the focus on back to basics; and finally on having the best customer proposition based on the integration of the sales forces, market segmentation and key client teams.

Box 10.8 The StarLight strategy

The StarLight strategy provided a clear roadmap for how Maersk-Sealand, Maersk Logistics and APM Terminals and other adjacent businesses should be sustainably and profitably grown.

Recommendations were:

- Create a true industry leader in the Line by focusing on clear route profitability in the main routes, providing the best proposition to our customers and driving cost leadership throughout the business.
- Build a profitable Logistics business that leverages and reinforces the Line.
- Develop a profitable, independent Terminals business with strong strategic links to the Line.
- Organise container-related transportation as one business, to provide a low-cost organisational platform, enabling the strategy to be successfully implemented.

Box 10.8 (cont.)

Issues and opportunities were:

- The industry has struggled to meet its cost of capital.
- Additional capacity is creating the worst capacity situation for 20 years.
- Continued price erosion is expected in the long term.
- Scale matters, but relative scale is what drives cost and product leadership.
- Under an acquisition scenario, leadership could be built in the majority of routes.
- Leadership positions provide the opportunity to improve product offerings.
- Alliances improve the product, but only generate 50 per cent of the savings.
- Bain experience shows that leaders earn superior returns.
- Logistics: leverage the Line by offering value-added services; deepen relationships with strategic clients; exit airfreight.
- Terminals: develop as a stand-alone business; strong strategic position with Maersk-Sealand; create one Terminals team to drive best practice, recommend investments and manage local budgets.

Organisational:

- Merge Line and Logistics sales into a key account and specialist sales organisation.
- Move back-office processes to shared service centres.
- Consolidate country structures into about 15 areas reporting to Copenhagen.
- Empower area management with authority and accountability for all countries in their area and focus them on customers.
- Clarify the roles of centre, area and country management.

Knud Stubkjær, looking back on the StarLight efforts, saw that this was 'probably the first time that Maersk had called it a formal, written-down strategy. I think that the strategy was very strong and I think it was the right strategy. But as with any strategy, it is always a matter of being able to execute it.'

Claus Hemmingsen agreed:

The whole notion around improving profitability was that to gain a powerful position in some trades, you had to accept that we would decline in other trades. We remained in all trades.'[22]

A key element in the strategy required Maersk-Sealand to use its leadership position in certain trades to generate cost advantages over competition and, as Knud Stubkjær put it:

Box 10.9 The Container Business vision and mission, 2002

Vision

We create opportunities in global commerce.

Mission

We will fulfil our mission by:

- Truly understanding our clients and their business.
- Offering second-to-none transportation solutions.
- Being profitable – and delivering sustainable profitable growth.
- Continuously reducing costs and increasing efficiency.
- Offering our colleagues personal growth and a motivating place to work.
- Being innovative.
- Being good corporate citizens.

---

when competition starts to push the price, then you will always be able to compete and you will always be the last one not to make money. But, that was a difficult one when in your culture, in your blood, it's difficult to take it upon yourself to reduce a rate without being asked to do so!

The regional structure that had been in place for a number of years and which had grown from the original three regions – North America, Asia and Europe – had expanded to include Africa and South America, now changed fundamentally. The Maersk-Sealand world was divided into 17 areas, each of which reported to Tommy Thomsen, in addition to the existing subsidiary companies, Maersk Logistics and APM Terminals.

The plan also recommended that Maersk Logistics' focus on providing integrated logistics solutions to customers should be strengthened and that activity itself be grown to a $1 billion turnover business. Another recommendation was to break down the barriers between Maersk-Sealand and Maersk Logistics and by doing so provide customers with a single point of contact to the business.

Maersk-Sealand was also to put increased effort into analysing and understanding its customer base and to creating a segmentation model that allowed for a more effective and efficient provision of sales and customer service effort, customer by customer. A key driver was to be Maersk-Sealand's ability to understand whether a customer required personal, face-to-face attention, or coverage by telephone sales or, alternatively, via the rapidly expanding and user-friendly e-commerce channels.

Finally, the plan was to build up a small number of service centres in low-cost, competent Asian countries to which, for example, documentation and other back-office support functions could be off-shored. An extensive report from 2001 by PA Consulting on the role of shared service centres was also particularly influential.

In the meantime, Thorkild Olesen's project team continued to look into projects to reduce operating costs, increase margins, improve port coverage and reduce investments, all with the objective of finding ways to improve the bottom-line result.

In September 2002, Maersk-Sealand acquired the liner services of the Danish Torm Line. Negotiations had been active in 2001 but had been broken off due to disagreement about the price. That was resolved in September 2002, and the project team also became involved in the integration of Torm Line's services between the US Gulf and US East Coast to West Africa into Maersk-Sealand.

Security-related issues came to the fore globally in 2002. In January, Admiral James Loy, Commandant of the US Coast Guard, proposed that US inspectors be given authority to inspect cargo containers at origin, putting the onus on overseas authorities to strengthen their security measures. In May, Vagn Lehd Møller wrote to the main offices outlining the pending legislation in North America and the start of the Customs Trade Partnership Against Terrorism (C-TPAT) programme, which Maersk-Sealand, Safmarine and Maersk Logistics were supporting fully via the World Shipping Council (WSC).

Box 10.10 The World Shipping Council (WSC)

Members of the WSC represent about 90 per cent of the global liner vessel capacity. Formed in 2000, originally to interface with the US government on behalf of the liner shipping community, after the 9/11 attacks it expanded its coverage to build close working relations with the European Commission and international organisations related to maritime commerce. The WSC opened an office in Brussels in 2007 to support the industry's efforts with the European Commission.

Today, its range of activities includes trade, security and customs initiatives, as well as environmental issues, supporting the establishment of effective and uniform standards.

In 2009, the WSC was granted Consultative Status at the International Maritime Organisation (IMO), supporting the development of safety, security, environmental and other maritime regulatory matters.

Source: WSC website, www.worldshipping.org (accessed 4 March 2013).

In June, Vagn Lehd Møller visited Washington to meet Commissioner Bonner who was driving much of the legislation at that time. The G8 meeting that month was headlined as 'Shipping security takes G8 limelight'. The key issue from Maersk-Sealand's perspective was to work with the authorities as closely as possible to ensure, on the one hand, that whatever steps were being taken were as feasible and effective as possible, and, on the other, that they would minimise disruption to the flow of goods and could be implemented at reasonable cost.

On 11 July 2002, the US authorities finalised plans for C-TPAT and on 15 July Maersk-Sealand and Safmarine were among the first carriers to sign up for participation. When US Customs opened the process up for freight forwarders on 26 August, Maersk Logistics was again one of the first to apply to the programme. Meanwhile, other legislation was getting under way in the form of a Port Security Bill, a Smart and Secure Trade Lane initiative and a new set of Vessel Security Rules.

On 1 November, US Customs released their requirements for the 24-hour Advanced Manifest Rules. These required information on all containers that were destined for the United States or might transit it (for example, en route to Canada or Mexico) to be electronically transmitted to US Customs 24 hours in advance of the container being loaded onto the ship at origin, so that any suspicious container could be rejected prior to loading. While this could have been a major threat to trade and supply chains involving the United States, sufficient dialogue and consultation with the industry had taken place that, although it was a scramble to meet the deadlines, most carriers were able to deliver within the implementation deadline set by US Customs.

The process was not, however, completely foolproof. In September 2003, on the second anniversary of 9/11, ABC News shipped a container of severely depleted uranium from Jakarta, Indonesia to New York, via Maersk-Sealand and it was delivered, undetected. The publicity surrounding this event raised further awareness of the risks relating to shipping containers and this led to further steps to tighten processes, including the development and testing of new ways to scan containers.

In January 2005, the European Commission published a paper on supply chain security, which ultimately led to the establishment of similar advanced information requirements, which are now operational in many parts of the world.

Containerisation International's yearbook for 2004, looking back on 2003, was optimistic. Despite an enormous volume of new tonnage on order (675,025 TEU in 2004, a further 715,691 TEU in 2005 and many of the ships for 2006 delivery being in the 7,500–8,000 TEU class), the

Figure 10.6 Shortly after delivery from the Odense Steel Shipyard, *Albert Mærsk* passed Kronborg Castle in Elsinore on its way to Copenhagen. Around 35,000 people visited the ship on a series of 'open ship' days in August–September 2004.

China effect, with double-digit trade growth, was driving improved ship utilisation and increasing rate levels in many trades.

This rapid growth actually created capacity shortages in 2002 and into 2003. Despite the launch of new services, rates rose and carriers started to move away from annual contracts with their customers towards quarterly contracts.[23] By the end of 2003, the top 20 container carriers controlled some 83.7 per cent of global capacity. Maersk-Sealand was now operating 328 vessels, with 30 more ships on order. MSC had increased the size of its fleet by 75 per cent over the previous two years and was planning to narrow the gap between it and Maersk-Sealand even further.[24]

In Maersk-Sealand, with results improving and the key elements of the StarLight strategy being implemented, acquisitions were back on the table and in March 2003 Vagn Lehd Møller and Knud Stubkjær spent some time considering the options available for a possible acquisition of P&O NedLloyd.

By now, Maersk had been in the container business nearly 30 years and was moving over 4 million FFE a year covering most parts of the world. Despite the poor results in 2001 and 2002, turnover in 2003 would break $11 billion for the first time and the net result, both before and after interest and depreciation, would be at record levels and would only improve further in 2004. World trade was roughly ten times larger than in 1975 when Maersk Line's first container service was started. Trade growth as measured by global merchandise was strong and was expected to continue to be so.

A note of caution was sounded at the beginning of 2004. John M. Nielsen and Michael Laursen (now Maersk-Sealand's CIO) reported delays to the critical MGM project. This project consisted of three main parts: MARS, a core element designed to handle customer contracting, was delayed; GCSS, the customer service and sales module, was proving to be more complex than originally expected; while MLIS, the invoicing system, was operational.

Reaching the customer

One of the focus areas in the StarLight strategy was customer confusion. Maersk was operating in so many environments (Maersk-Sealand, Maersk Logistics, Hudd in the United States and MCC Transport in Asia, as well as in trucking and in other transport-related activities) that customer contacts were seen by some as uncoordinated, with the same customers being approached by more than one of these entities.

The StarLight solution was to combine the sales organisations of these varied activities into one sales organisation that would have the ability and knowledge to sell across the businesses, so that one Maersk sales person became the customer's single point of contact. Conceptually simple, the concept was subject to many complexities.

Substantial effort was put into training the global sales force through the Star Training Process, which was launched in the middle of 2003. This focused on identifying the required competences in sales, particularly sales management, and then addressing these through a combination of face-to-face and automated learning. The programme carried the key concepts and messages around the world.

The consequences of the merger of the sales forces have remained somewhat controversial within Maersk over the years, as opinions vary as to the benefits and issues. While the implications for Maersk-Sealand would generally be seen as positive, Søren Brandt as Managing Director of Maersk Logistics recollects:

the biggest challenge was clearly the close tie to Maersk-Sealand where the Logistics country managers reported to the local Maersk-Sealand country managers. Depending on how firmly they believed in the concept, the logistics business could grow or fall. That was difficult to manage on a global basis.[25]

Developing the integrated sales organisation, which consisted mainly of successful liner sales people, many with over ten years' experience, and helping them to understand and to sell not just sea-freight, but also air-freight, warehousing, customs clearance services and complex supply chain management services was never going to be easy. The interest was there, as it was exciting; but when faced with a sophisticated customer, too often the sales call reverted to 'what I know best' – in this case sea-freight services.

Supporting this effort, Maersk-Sealand's 2003 key focus areas listed its first item as 'Implement Key Account Management and the integrated sales approach (including Maersk Logistics) for large customers'.

From Maersk Logistics' perspective, however, a lot was going right. Søren Brandt recollected:

> As far as I remember, when we merged with Sealand Logistics, we doubled the size of the company. With DSL, we added another third and that took us fairly high up in the ranks of our peers.[26]

In the United States, Maersk Logistics acquired DSL Star Express in 2001 and with it, a major entry into Walmart's business.

In the *Containerisation International Yearbook 1988*, DSL had been described as 'a major NVOCC (non-vessel operating common carrier) in the Trans Pacific trade where it ships as many as 15,000 FFE to 20,000 FFE a year under its own bills of lading, and influences the movement of a similar number of FFE on carrier bills of lading'.[27]

At the time, DSL was handling some 80–90 per cent of all of Walmart's international business, so it was an opportunity that in volume terms had a similar effect on Maersk Logistics' capabilities and global coverage that the Melville contract had earlier had on Mercantile. In addition, DSL brought expertise and specific competences that allowed Maersk Logistics to continue to develop. Over the period 1990 to 2004, Maersk Logistics grew from the original 85 staff in Mercantile to over 6,000 staff and achieved net results of up to about $50 million.

The integration of Buyers Consolidators, renamed Sea-Land Logistics just before the acquisition of Sea-Land by A.P Moller in 1999, brought with it some major US clients such as Target Stores, Home Depot, Lowes and others. Meanwhile in Europe, Peder Winter, Maersk Logistics Regional Manager, working with Maersk-Sealand, identified the UK market as having high potential for integrated supply chain management.

With a small team consisting of Maersk Logistics and Maersk-Sealand people, he began a campaign to penetrate that market. Active support was provided from Maersk Logistics in Asia, in particular the substantial strengthening of Maersk Logistics, capabilities in China under Steffen

Schiottz-Christensen. Kingfisher, with its main companies Woolworths and B&Q, were among the first UK clients, with Marks and Spencer, Walmart's UK affiliate Asda, Halfords, Grattans and Disney Stores following.

A major client to come to Maersk at this time was the sports goods manufacturer Nike. For Nike, Maersk-Sealand and Maersk Logistics, the decision to work together was strategic and took time to put in place. Once agreed, it was critically important that it was successful. To that end, regular planning and review meetings were established at a management level, both senior management as well as operational, and at the local level where the agreed plans were executed. The first management-level meeting between Nike, Maersk-Sealand and Maersk Logistics was held in Copenhagen in October 2001. Mærsk Mc-Kinney Møller did something very rare: he invited the joint teams to his house just north of Copenhagen. John Isbell, previously Director of Corporate Delivery Logistics for Nike, who had been instrumental in setting up the new relationship, recollected the evening:

He did so because we are an American company and it was right after the 9/11 attack on the World Trade Center. It was a thank you by Mr Møller to America, which had provided him with shelter to run the Maersk business during World War II.

Looking back at events in 2001 from December 2012, John Isbell recalled:

The initial contract negotiation I led with Maersk covered both logistics and ocean. We called it a bundled service agreement and I think it was an industry first. The Nike–Maersk partnership was based on trust and while we had some issues over the years, the partnership held strong. The annual meeting was a coming together of two companies that enjoyed each other's friendship and respected each company's business. We got business done and then celebrated another year of outstanding partnership. Nike pushed Maersk-Sealand and Maersk Logistics to be innovative in terms of services and service agreements, and Maersk rose to the occasion each time, and Nike benefited from Maersk's commitment to service excellence.

I believe we had the only multi-year ocean contract where rates were determined by a formula based on set rules. It lasted from 2004 to 2008, during which time we never renegotiated rates as we let the formula determine the rates for the transpacific and Asia–Europe trade. I think it remains an industry first.[28]

Nike's Inbound Vendor and Network Transportation Manager, Frans Smit, reviewing more than ten years of Nike's relationship with Maersk in 2012, saw the developments as owing a great deal to the increase in professionalism, understanding and knowledge:

If you could have done the things we know now, in those days, we would have saved an enormous amount. A simple thing like container fill rate has increased by more than 12 per cent! And, what we are working on right now – Dynamic Flow Control – where Damco is so integrated in our process, I have the feeling they understand the process even better than I do![29]

Global service centres

In 2004, after nearly ten years developing Maersk Logistics, Søren Brandt was thinking about new prospects. He told Tommy Thomsen, his manager, that 'if the job of running the service centres ever becomes available, I would like to be considered for it because I think this could be really, really interesting and the potential is so enormous'.[30] A few weeks later, Claus Hemmingsen, who had the job at the time and was moving on to become CEO of APM Terminals, called Brandt and asked, 'Did you really mean it? Because the job is actually there, right now.' Although filling the job had to go through the normal procedures, Søren Brandt became Managing Director of the global service centre organisation shortly afterwards, handing over the role of running Maersk Logistics to Henrik Ramskov, who moved from Singapore to Copenhagen.

Since the Sea-Land acquisition in 1999, Maersk-Sealand had been operating service centres in Manila, the Philippines, Mumbai in India, Guangzhou in China and a small facility in Costa Rica. The main role of these centres, which had around 1,400 staff, was administrative and a serious discussion had taken place about closing them down. While some did not agree (Thomas Dyrbye and Hanne B. Sørensen, both in Mumbai, in particular), it was Bain, as part of StarLight, who identified these facilities as providing great infrastructure and an opportunity to reduce costs by moving some transactional processing work to them. Claus Hemmingsen had been tasked with getting this set up as independent entities right from the start. The key was the need for the centres to be able to serve the entire geography of Maersk-Sealand.

Bain's statistics made the opportunities clear: 'back-office consolidation' would move current staff out of the countries, producing a reduction in headcount and total savings of about $100 million.[31] It would also be 'a huge undertaking' and some critical steps would need to be taken to achieve the strategy from a purely organisational perspective. These included:

- changing the mindset from industry custodian to industry leader;
- manically chasing a lowest cost position;
- refocusing local managers;
- delayering and consolidating to cut costs;
- upgrading IT systems.

Moving swiftly from theoretical, high-level strategy to the challenges of front-line execution, as Søren Brandt outlined:

There were local bill of lading processes that had developed over a long time with specific customers, in specific countries with specific 'standard operating procedures', whereas today there is basically one global standard process.[32]

It would require a major change in the way the Maersk-Sealand organisation worked and a substantial effort to bring 'process management' and lean thinking successfully into the Maersk-Sealand organisation.

The China effect and outsourcing

The *Containerisation International Yearbook 2005*, looking at 2004, continued to be optimistic and pointed out that 'the shift to outsource manufacturing to China is structural rather than cyclical and is here to stay'. Its analysis was supported by UBS Investment Research in a report that highlighted four trends:

1 To remain competitive, companies would have no choice but to reduce production costs by relocating to China.
2 Chinese exports would continue to become more high-value items, electronics and automotive parts.
3 The end of textile and clothing quotas would boost apparel from China to both Europe and the United States.
4 Europe would follow the United States in outsourcing to China and this could lead to annual container volume growth of 15 per cent a year in the coming years.

However, while volumes were expected to show significant growth, the Trans Pacific and Far East–Europe trades were about to receive 'a massive influx of new tonnage, especially vessels with capacities in excess of 6,000 TEU'.[33]

By now Maersk-Sealand was operating 345 ships with a capacity exceeding 900,000 TEU and had 78 new container vessels of various sizes on order for delivery over the next five years. Speculation was rife that the dimensions of the newly launched *Albert Mærsk*, officially rated at 6,600 TEU, indicated it was more likely to have an operating capacity of 8,500 to 9,000 TEU. Meanwhile, MSC was also growing and was now operating 237 ships with a total capacity of 618,000 TEU. Further speculation focused on who might buy the first 12,000 TEU ships; *Containerisation International* believed this 'would probably be Asian liner operators'.[34]

Writing in the 2006 yearbook, however, John Fossey noted a number of challenges facing the industry. Rates to the United States and Europe out of Asia were weakening; the European Commission was continuing to push hard for the end of anti-trust immunity for liner shipping conferences; and port infrastructure was under pressure with the high growth in container volumes of recent years. The biggest concern was over the 'bulge in new tonnage deliveries over the next two years', with 1.2 million TEU scheduled to enter service in 2006 and another 1.4 million TEU coming on stream in 2007. *Containerisation International* was concerned to note that 'there is evidence to suggest that the boost given to world trade by China joining the World Trade Organization (WTO) in November 2001 is slowing'.[35]

Box 10.11 The 'Asian Tigers'

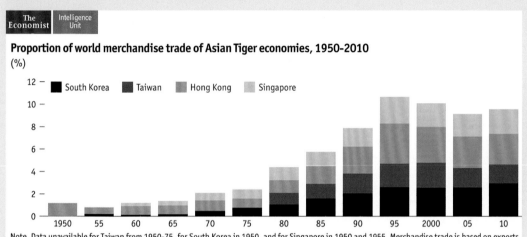

Proportion of world merchandise trade of Asian Tiger economies, 1950-2010
(%)

Note. Data unavailable for Taiwan from 1950-75, for South Korea in 1950, and for Singapore in 1950 and 1955. Merchandise trade is based on exports and imports.
Source: The Economist Intelligence Unit calculations using IMF, *Direction of Trade Statistics* (via Haver Analytics) and Ministry of Finance for Taiwan.

The graph above illustrates several significant points; one is the obvious rapid economic rise of the four countries in terms of their import and export growth; another is the rise of Hong Kong, not only related to its own economy, but also as the gateway to and from China, starting in the late 1980s and continuing today, although at a slower pace as China's trade now moves by a multitude of ports (See Box 5.11 and the development of Li & Fung). A third point is the rise of South Korea, which did not have the benefits of Hong Kong's China connections. By 2010 South Korea had the largest export/import trade of the four areas.

In 1997, Maersk Line had introduced the concept of global sales, which was to focus on its larger clients. This was quite timely as the large Korean companies had recently started to move goods under their own brands (for example, LG, Hyundai and Samsung) and the establishment of production facilities outside Korea required them to find shipping lines that had global coverage and were able to help them with cross-trade business.

The automobile industry was one of Korea's major growth industries in the 1980s, when it started to export to the North American market. Automobile exports saw substantial growth until 1988, when exports totalled 576,000 units, of which 480,000

Box 10.11 (cont.)

(83.3 per cent) were sent to the United States. Over time, Korea grew into one of the world's largest automobile producers, ranking fifth behind the United States, China, Germany and Japan. At the same time, the automobile industry drove the growth of associated industries such as machinery, metalwork (including white goods) and domestic electronics.

The help Maersk Line provided these companies at an earlier stage, by handling their production line equipment, among other things, led to it becoming a significant carrier for them, and provided the opportunity to handle their finished products – for example, from Mexico to Panama.

In 2009 Korea became the 24th country in the Development Aid Committee of the OECD and the first ever case of a country moving from aid-receiving to aid-giving. In 2011, Korea became the ninth country with total trade exceeding $1 trillion, at $1.16 trillion. Exports were $556 billion – the economy was still heavily export-driven, with a dependency of almost 50 per cent.

A selection of important developments: 2000–2004

Political

- 2001 On September 11th, terrorists attack the World Trade Center in New York and the Pentagon, causing nearly 3,000 deaths.[36] This event will lead to the beginning of the "war on terror", a series of US-led military operations against the Taliban and Al-Qaeda.[37]
- 2001 The US and Russia meet final START I requirements, completing the largest arms reduction in history.[38]
- 2002 Bombings occur in the tourist district of Kuta in the Indonesian island of Bali. The attack, the deadliest act of terrorism in the history of Indonesia, kills 202 people and is the work of Jamaah Islamiah, an al-Qaeda affiliate.[39]
- 2004 US administrator, Paul Bremer, hands over power to an interim Iraqi government under prime minister Iyad Allawi.[40]
- 2004 The European Union (EU) expands to 25 countries, its largest single expansion in terms of territory, number of states and population. New joiners include Cyprus, the Czech Republic, Estonia, Hungary, Latvia, Lithuania, Malta, Poland, Slovakia and Slovenia.[41]

Economic

- Early 2000s With the US economy booming, US president, George W. Bush, continues an initiative of the Clinton administration to encourage home ownership, inflating a housing bubble.[42] Increased borrowing, combined with US spending on the wars in Iraq and Afghanistan, raise the US budget deficit.[43]
- 2000 As more countries integrate into the global economy, foreign direct investment (FDI) flows increase. The number of countries with an inward FDI stock in excess of US$10bn reaches 50 (24 of them are developing countries), compared with only 17 (seven developing) in 1985.[44]
- 2000 The *dot-com bubble* bursts. The NASDAQ stock exchange peaks at 5,132 points on March 10th.[45] The same day a decade later, the NASDAQ will be trading at 2,358.[46]
- 2001 The Doha Round – including the Doha Development Agenda – is launched. The intent of the round is to make trade rules fairer for developing countries, but negotiations stall.[47]
- 2001 China joins the WTO after 15 years of negotiations.[48] Chinese annual merchandise exports will rise from US$266bn in 2001 to US$1.9trn in 2011 (at current market prices).[49]
- 2002 Euro coins and banknotes are introduced in the 12 participating EU member countries.[50]

Social

- 2000 The Millennium Development Goals are established.[51]

- 2001 Wikipedia, a free online and co-operatively edited encyclopaedia, goes online. From 20,000 content pages at the end of its first year,[52] by 2012 it will host over 4m.[53]
- 2003 The National Aeronautics and Space Association (NASA) determines the age of the universe to be 13.7bn years.[54]
- 2004 Google Earth makes general as well as 3D satellite imagery of the world accessible to the general public.[55]
- 2004 The *Opportunity* exploration rover finds evidence of water on Mars, underlining the possibility of conditions on the planet that could have been conducive to life.[56]
- 2004 Facebook launches, highlighting the development of Web 2.0, where social interaction adds a dimension to information. By 2010 Facebook will have 350m members.[57]

Technological

- 2000–04 Africa produces nearly 70,000 scientific publications or 1.8% of the world's research. In comparison, India produces 2.4% and Latin America 3.5%. Research in Africa is concentrated in just two countries – South Africa and Egypt – accounting for 50% of the continent's publications.[58]
- 2003 The Human Genome Project deciphers the genetic blueprints of humans. A 13-year project, it will allow for the sequencing of human chromosomes.[59]
- 2003 A thermal-imaging thermometer which automatically checks the temperature of air travellers as they step off the plane is used to combat the Severe Acute Respiratory Syndrome (SARS) global pandemic.[60]

Legal

- 2001 The Council of Europe adopts an international cybercrime treaty, the first treaty addressing criminal offences committed over the Internet.[61]
- 2003 The UN Convention against Corruption is adopted.[62]
- 2004 In the wake of the September 11th 2001 attacks, the International Ship and Port Facility Security Code (ISPS Code) is introduced by the International Maritime Organization (IMO).[63]

Environmental

- 2001 The Clean Development Mechanism (CDM) – a market-based offset mechanism for emissions – begins operating: tradable credits are awarded for emissions reductions on a project-by-project basis and the resulting credits are purchased by firms or governments under an obligation to reduce emissions.[64]
- 2003 EU legislation restricting the use of hazardous substances in electrical and electronic equipment and promoting the collection and recycling of such equipment comes into force.[65]
- 2004 A tsunami kills an estimated 226,000 people in 13 countries across Asia and leaves 5m without homes or food and water.[66]

Merchandise trade by country

Global population: 6.1bn

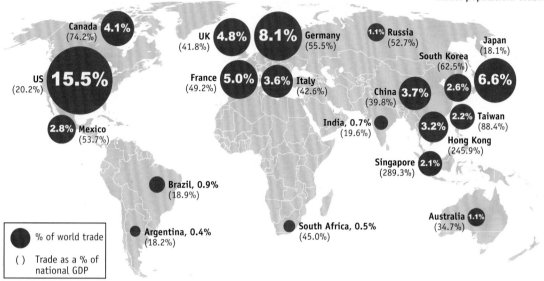

Canada 4.1% (74.2%)

US 15.5% (20.2%)

2.8% Mexico (53.7%)

UK 4.8% (41.8%)

8.1% Germany (55.5%)

France 5.0% (49.2%)

3.6% Italy (42.6%)

1.1% Russia (52.7%)

Japan (18.1%)

South Korea (62.5%)

2.6%

6.6%

China 3.7% (39.8%)

India, 0.7% (19.6%)

3.2%

2.2% Taiwan (88.4%)

Hong Kong (245.9%)

Singapore 2.1% (289.3%)

Brazil, 0.9% (18.9%)

Argentina, 0.4% (18.2%)

South Africa, 0.5% (45.0%)

Australia 1.1% (34.7%)

● % of world trade

( ) Trade as a % of national GDP

Note. The map is based on January 2013 boundaries. Trade is based on merchandise exports and imports.
Sources: The Economist Intelligence Unit (EIU) calculations using trade data from IMF, *Direction of Trade Statistics* (via Haver Analytics) and GDP data from EIU. Population data from UN (via Haver Analytics).

World merchandise exports

US$ trn (at 2005 prices)

0.4	0.6	0.8	1.2	1.8	2.3	3.0	3.3	4.4	5.8	8.2		
1950	1955	1960	1965	1970	1975	1980	1985	1990	1995	2000	2005	2010

Note. World exports have been rebased to 2005 constant prices using world export volumes from the World Trade Organization (WTO).
Source: EIU calculations using WTO data.

World exports of selected commodities

US$ bn (at 2005 prices)

■ Fruit, nuts and vegetables ■ Meat and fish ■ Dairy products ■ Computers and televisions
■ Motor vehicles ■ Clothing ■ Footwear

2,000 —
1,750 —
1,500 —
1,250 —
1,000 —
750 —
500 —
250 —
0 —

1970   1975   1980   1985   1990   1995   2000   2005   2010

Note. In order to compare commodities over time, the EIU has made a number of judgment calls on category groupings, as there have been three revisions in the way that UN commodity data are classified. The data have also been rebased to 2005 constant prices using world export prices from the WTO. The motor vehicles category refers to road motor vehicles, including cycles, trailers, and parts and accessories; clothing includes headgear, excludes travel goods and handbags.
Source: EIU estimates using UN Comtrade, *DESA/UNSD* and WTO data.

2005

Merchandise trade by country

Global population: 6.5bn

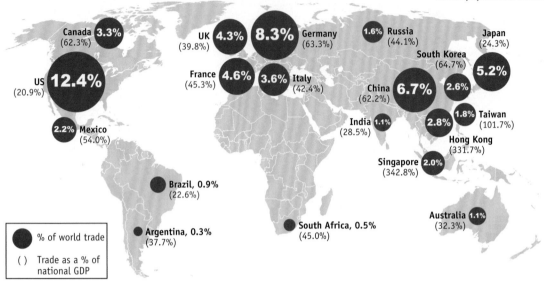

Canada **3.3%** (62.3%)

UK **4.3%** **8.3%** Germany (63.3%)

(39.8%)

1.6% Russia (44.1%)

Japan (24.3%)

South Korea (64.7%)

5.2%

US **12.4%** (20.9%)

France **4.6%** **3.6%** Italy (45.3%) (42.4%)

China **6.7%** (62.2%)

2.6%

2.2% Mexico (54.0%)

India **1.1%** (28.5%)

2.8%

1.8% Taiwan (101.7%)

Hong Kong (331.7%)

Brazil, **0.9%** (22.6%)

Singapore **2.0%** (342.8%)

Australia **1.1%** (32.3%)

Argentina, **0.3%** (37.7%)

South Africa, **0.5%** (45.0%)

⬤ % of world trade

( ) Trade as a % of national GDP

Note. The map is based on January 2013 boundaries. Trade is based on merchandise exports and imports.
Sources: The Economist Intelligence Unit (EIU) calculations using trade data from IMF, *Direction of Trade Statistics* (via Haver Analytics) and GDP data from EIU. Population data from UN (via Haver Analytics).

World merchandise exports

US$ trn (at 2005 prices)

0.4	0.6	0.8	1.2	1.8	2.3	3.0	3.3	4.4	5.8	8.2	10.4	
1950	1955	1960	1965	1970	1975	1980	1985	1990	1995	2000	2005	2010

Note. World exports have been rebased to 2005 constant prices using world export volumes from the World Trade Organization (WTO).
Source: EIU calculations using WTO data.

World exports of selected commodities

US$ bn (at 2005 prices)

■ Fruit, nuts and vegetables ■ Meat and fish ■ Dairy products ■ Computers and televisions

■ Motor vehicles ■ Clothing ■ Footwear

```
2,000 —
1,750 —
1,500 —
1,250 —
1,000 —
  750 —
  500 —
  250 —
    0 —
        1970   1975   1980   1985   1990   1995   2000   2005   2010
```

Note. In order to compare commodities over time, the EIU has made a number of judgment calls on category groupings, as there have been three revisions in the way that UN commodity data are classified. The data have also been rebased to 2005 constant prices using world export prices from the WTO. The motor vehicles category refers to road motor vehicles, including cycles, trailers, and parts and accessories; clothing includes headgear, excludes travel goods and handbags.
Source: EIU estimates using UN Comtrade, *DESA/UNSD* and WTO data.

11

P&O NedLloyd (2005–2007)

A Contentious Acquisition

The merged company will enjoy the critical mass of an alliance, and the ability to differentiate itself by simply being the only carrier big enough to operate entirely on its own.

A. Donovan and J. Bonney, *The Box that Changed the World*, 2006[1]

The first decade of the twenty-first century was turbulent for many, in many different parts of the world and in many different ways. In 2005 the US housing market peaked and the asset bubble that had financed so much of the power of the consumer to keep global markets buoyant started to collapse. On a more positive note, that year the International Monetary Fund approved 100 per cent debt relief for 19 countries under the Multilateral Debt Relief Initiative. The amount involved was relatively small, some $3.3 billion, but a positive step had been taken.

That same year, 2005, the Multi-Fibre Agreement, which had imposed quantitative restrictions on textile movements, particularly from Asia and the less developed areas of the world, came to an end after a long phase-out period. The China effect was beginning to be significant; China's share of global textile exports to the US and Europe, 17 per cent in 2005, would rise to 40 per cent by 2010.

Reviewing 2005 in *Containerisation International*'s 2006 yearbook, John Fossey wrote:

The container liner shipping industry achieved a highly profitable performance, with 2005's interim results and projected figures on a par with and in several cases, even better than 2004. However, there is evidence to suggest that profit margins are coming under pressure, that freight rates are weakening and the overall supply/demand balance is softening.[2]

A year later, reviewing 2006 in the 2007 yearbook, Fossey reported that:

the seriousness of the situation was clearly seen from various ocean carriers' 2006 interim financial results, with Maersk Line, Hapag Lloyd and Evergreen Marine all posting losses. The three Japanese operators (NYK Line, Mitsui OSK Lines and K Line) also reported deficits in their liner shipping activities for the period April–end September 2006 ... On the demand front, 2007 and 2008 are fraught with uncertainty with the pace of global trade growth expected to slow. Although freight rate forecasts are extremely difficult to make, it is likely that on a global basis there will be an overall decrease of anywhere between five per cent and 10 per cent in average revenue per TEU in 2007.[3]

By 2007, the Western world would be rapidly moving towards recession, with US sub-prime mortgage debt reaching levels that would oblige the US administration to intervene to rescue the Federal National Mortgage Association ('Fannie Mae') and the Federal Home Loan Mortgage Corporation ('Freddie Mac') from collapse, as well as the giant debt insurer AIG. The following year, the collapse of Lehman Brothers would lead to banking mergers and the partial nationalisation of banks.

Between 2008 and 2011, the global economy slowed significantly. The compound annual GDP growth dropped from 2.9 per cent per year during the period 2004–2007 to 1.1 per cent for the period 2008–2011. Unemployment rates rose substantially in the United States and later in Europe, reaching the highest levels seen in decades.

As the European sovereign debt crisis hit, particularly in Greece, Ireland, Italy, Spain and Portugal, significant pressure was put on the European Union and the euro, leading to one rescue package after another being implemented as politicians and their advisors sought to find policies that would turn their economies round without incurring even more debt.

On a more positive note, Russia, the last major economic power not to be a member, was admitted to the World Trade Organization after 19 years of negotiations – although no immediate major boost to the world economy was predicted to accompany Russia's membership, unlike China's accession.

Maersk-Sealand developments and global service centres

The year 2004 was a good year for Maersk-Sealand, with overall profits in excess of $1 billion and many things going the right way. The major new MGM system, which integrated MARS, GCSS and MLIS, was moving forward, designed to provide a comprehensive set of tools for use across the global organisation. Apart from some delays, the main concern was around the system's growing complexity.

The objective of the bundled system was for the global organisation to be able to work in one, seamless, end-to-end process that could support workflow management, the elimination of re-work and in particular eliminate errors when one part of the organisation handed a shipment over for completion to a destination organisation or an intermediate office, where trans-shipment took place.

Figure 11.1 By 2012 more than 12,000 employees in the service centres in Pune, India, and four other locations in Asia supported the Maersk business units. More than 8,000 were occupied servicing Maersk Line and its customers.

Claus Hemmingsen, then head of Maersk-Sealand's Service Delivery organisation, considered the development of the global service centres (GSCs) was progressing well. Phase one, the movement of some of Maersk-Sealand's documentation to the service centres, was sufficiently far advanced that phase two could now be considered. This would involve the transfer of elements of Maersk-Sealand's finance and accounting activities, some further customer service back-office work, as well as some human resources (HR) and information systems (IS) work. However, he was concerned about the readiness of the new MGM system to support the process. His recollection of the discussions was direct and to the point:

The CBC was firm, we will need the savings. We will fix the issues and we will make our way through. And we did make our way through, but it was not always pretty. I think Søren Brandt took over then and it was only a couple of years later that the systems really started to provide the functionality and the quality needed. Of course, today the story is entirely different.[4]

At the end of 2004, things did not look quite so bright. In August, Claus Hemmingsen briefed Knud Stubkjær and Tommy Thomsen on some service delivery issues in the Mediterranean region, and in September invoicing issues brought complaints from the Gap Stores and others. At the end of that month, the service delivery score in the management scorecard was at a low of 71 per cent.[5]

Claus Hemmingsen commented: 'that was when "service delivery" as a term really entered the liner business. Our responsibilities increased from just providing documentation services to also having process ownership and so we got some traction with the thinking in 2004.'[6]

Claus Hemmingsen got the support he needed to set up a task force to address the issues. He was able to report back to the CBC on 31 December on the status of the plan addressing specific tasks in the centre and the areas, the clarification of the roles of service delivery compared to customer services and sales and on measuring the impact of the tasks as they were implemented.

It is clear that many of the issues were closely linked to the new area structure that Maersk-Sealand was in the process of implementing. The world was being divided into 17 areas where each area management team would consolidate many of the activities from the country-level organisations, gaining economies of scale in, for example, accounting.

There were therefore a wide range of issues, relating to roles, responsibilities and authority levels. A meeting of the stakeholders in November 2004 set further work in motion. That work would be the foundation for many of the functional changes that would take place over the coming years.

Vagn Lehd Møller also faced some challenges that November, when he summarised an analysis of vessel schedules compared to the pro-forma plans and had to report that the ships were on time only 81 per cent of the time, due to a combination of higher levels of container movements and lower levels of productivity than planned. Plans were put in place to bring the ships back on track and on schedule.

Søren Brandt remembered clearly some of the challenges that required major efforts to correct when he took over the global service centre organisation from Claus Hemmingsen in 2005 and the heated discussions of the time, where the growing need for standardisation and centralisation of such fundamental activities was not yet clear to the global organisation. In the many and varied country and local offices in particular, management naturally felt something akin to a loss of control of their business when transferring these critical document-related activities to a service centre hundreds, if not thousands, of kilometres away.

Søren Brandt was also very clear about what drove the constructive turnaround in the GSCs' fortunes:

First, we acquired [P&O NedLloyd], who had three service centres, two in India and one in China, so we doubled the organisation's size overnight. Second, we also had to move all of the PONL business on to our systems platform.

The possible acquisition of P&O NedLloyd (PONL), to which Brandt referred, had been a proposition since the late 1990s but had not got off the ground. Now, in 2005, that possibility was to become a reality.

The P&O NedLloyd acquisition: PONL's perspective

Back in 1995, two of the most respected shipping companies, P&O Containers Limited of the UK and NedLloyd Lines of Holland, had merged to create PONL. Both companies had traditions dating back over many years, P&O's to 1837. NedLloyd had been formed from the amalgamation in 1970 of four Dutch shipping companies, the oldest of which dated back to 1870.

Both P&O and NedLloyd had been flag carriers for their respective merchant fleets for many of those years. Both companies had been under pressure from financial markets and shareholders to improve their profitability; neither had been able to maintain the needed order book for new ships and had fallen behind the competition. The merger of P&O and NedLloyd, when it came, was very much one of equals. By making use of, among others, German KG ship-leasing arrangements, over time the new company was able to turn a defensive merger into an offensive position in the market place. Aided by a relatively strong market with little new capacity coming into it, the overriding objective of that merger was to keep all the freight.

Tim Harris, Managing Director of P&O Cruises and P&O Containers, commented:

The Dutch were very good partners. They went into it with great good will and tried very hard to make it work. They had very considerable expertise. The liner business is a very challenging business but the people in it are in my experience, very competent. The Dutch were probably operationally stronger than the British.[7]

By all accounts, Tim Harris, who had been with P&O since the 1980s was considered 'a very good CEO ... who although a "Brit" and coming from the P&O side of the business, was seen as neutral by the Dutch and was certainly seen as a very tough guy by the Brits'.[8] However, he was not to be there for long as differences of opinion with Lord Sterling on the future of the P&O Group led him to leave in 2000. His role was taken first by the experienced insider, Robert Woods, and then by Philip Green, an experienced executive from outside the shipping industry.

Green quickly made an impression, establishing that 'it is all about the customers, it is all about developing and growing the business and performing better than your peer group'.[9] He focused the organisation on improving its relative financial performance through a campaign called Bridging the Gap so that the company could be listed through an IPO.

Jeremy Nixon, who was with PONL at the time and joined Maersk-Sealand at the acquisition, recalled: 'We had all become shareholders and rather naively, we thought that was it! But, of course the minute we became listed, we then became a target.' Tim Smith, PONL's Regional Director for Asia Pacific, recollected:

I got a message in Hong Kong on the Saturday from Philip Green saying, 'You need to get to London for Monday. Please be there.' That Monday morning we all walked into the board room and Philip gave us the news that we had been bought! We were all completely dumbfounded! He then pulled back the sliding doors at the end of the room and there were Tommy [Thomsen] and Knud [Stubkjær]! We had a few hours with them and then I got back on the plane that night and flew back to Hong Kong so that I could brief everybody the next day. Quite an experience!

Continuing the story, Jeremy Nixon said:

I think Philip Green and probably one or two others at the top were aware that the offer had been made. I think it was a very good offer so that there wasn't going to be much negotiation over it; it was a question of rightfully accepting it on behalf of the shareholders. But the wind really got knocked out of our sails. Maersk had probably been one of our biggest competitors, we had fought toe-to-toe in the East–West and North–South trades.

Robbert van Trooijen, at that time working in PONL in London and later Managing Director of Maersk Line in South America, thought that as things had been going so much better for PONL, Philip Green was about to announce an acquisition of their own, maybe of APL: 'It was very different from what we expected would happen that day. It was an interesting day, that's for sure.'[10]

Jeremy Nixon remembered that:

Knud and Tommy ... immediately went on a very effective charm offensive. They indicated that 'We believe in this industry, we believe in PONL and we want to make one and one equal to two. We want to keep as many staff as possible because we want to keep growing the business.' It was a very positive period in the business and it made a lot of sense.

However, one of the key issues with the PONL integration was MGM: 'the fundamental problem was that the Maersk systems were not ready'.

PONL had also recently completed a major global effort on process management and standardisation and had been building a new end-to-end system, Focus Four, which directly supported their global processes and did what MGM aspired to. There were discussions about taking PONL's Focus Four on board, but Maersk's IT management was concerned about two issues. First, there were doubts about Focus Four's scalability to handle the total volumes of the combined business. Second, as well as integrating the PONL staff into the Maersk set up, a large part of the existing global organisation would have to be trained on a fundamentally new system. The risk was deemed too large, and despite its known shortcomings, the decision was to stay with MGM.

Lucas Vos, at that time part of PONL's Dutch management and who later worked with Søren Brandt on the integration of the service centres, has said that these platforms (Focus Four) were built for PONL to double in size, so scalability should not have been a deciding factor:

Focus was kept as simple as possible and yet it worked, and the right judges of that are clearly, at the end of the day, our customers, and they experienced PONL as being one of the most customer-oriented companies out there.[11]

Vos pointed to another aspect that was also identified by Tim Smith, namely that there was a belief that by combining the two companies, the offer would be irresistible to the market place. Vos suggested that in as complex an integration as this, some customer losses would be expected and the end result would probably be '$1 + 1 = 1.8$'. In this case, however, there was a widespread belief that the end products would be so much better than the competition, that 'the $1 + 1$ would achieve a result closer to 2.3. And that took me by surprise.'[12]

Lucas Vos compared the comparatively recent and successful P&O and NedLloyd integration with the PONL and Maersk-Sealand integration. In the former, 'the immediate focus was on how to maintain the business and make sure that in the eyes of our customers, this became a success'. In the latter 'the eyes were not on that. It wasn't as clear and as pronounced that this is also beneficial for our customers'.

Tim Smith was more direct:

It was a takeover, a situation where we followed the Maersk organisation structure, the network, the IT systems, processes, all of that. One very good thing was it happened very fast. Probably it was less effective than the PONL integration because what good things there were from P&O and NedLloyd were not really taken into account and I think quite a lot of them were lost.[13]

Lucas Vos also touched on another element on Maersk-Sealand's side:

The big difference for me on the sales side was that PONL was truly busy with what's important for customers, not being bothered about being different, just providing good service. I think that with Maersk-Sealand, [it was a case of] 'We know the ideal way of shipping and as a customer, why don't you adapt your processes around that?', not realising that at the end of the day, customers would end up with two sets of processes, one for Maersk-Sealand and one for the rest.

Jeremy Nixon recalled the first year of his tenure with Maersk Line:

I remember having some of those key client management meetings with some very senior clients in Copenhagen with Knud and Tommy and some of the others and we would take an absolute beating from this or that client. Knud and Tommy were fantastic at taking the heat; I mean, in cricketing terms it was like going against the fastest bowler in the world and having to keep dodging while these bouncers kept coming through and doing it with incredible integrity and professionalism. But, you know, when we all came out of those meetings, we were just absolutely shattered.

According to Nixon, issues of tradition and culture did not receive a great deal of attention at the time, but may have had significant 'under the radar' impact:

If you look at NedLloyd and P&O, these were two very traditional, almost colonial shipping companies. Steeped in history, P&O back to the days when half the atlas was pink, these two companies had gradually gobbled up and consolidated local and national shipping companies and brands. This was also their weakness, the

Figure 11.2 The P&O NedLloyd logo on a container on top of another container with another former brand name in the container industry. Maersk Line decided early to repaint the containers only as they were brought in for refurbishment in order to minimise the environmental and cost impacts.

colonial trading mentality, built around conferences, trading rights, whereas Maersk Line didn't really come with that baggage ... Once we had been accepted as management, we were saying, 'You have got to keep those guys', and, 'This person's critical to that customer', and you know, we kept the great majority of the staff and certainly on the customer service and sales side ...

There were a lot of us, including myself who were very committed to coming over to Maersk Line and who would have stayed on long-term if the industry situation had been more favourable. No one could foresee the kind of problems we were going to get into in 2007 and 2008. There were so many moving parts in the integration.[14]

The P&O NedLloyd acquisition: Maersk-Sealand's perspective

While 2004 and 2005 had been good and profitable years for Maersk-Sealand, 2006 produced a substantial loss of nearly $600 million at a time before the market had turned significantly negative.

The strategy on PONL was quite clear. As Knud Stubkjær commented:

It was underpinned through our existing StarLight strategy and everything in that acquisition was actually right. Could we have picked a better time? Yes, we could. Had we managed to do it a couple of years earlier when it was on the drawing board, it would have been fantastic, timing-wise, but that is hindsight. Everyone was favourable to this, both at the Board and at senior management level.

Eivind Kolding, then the A.P. Moller – Maersk Group's Chief Financial Officer, concurred:

I was quite involved in the business case, the negotiation and closing the deal. It was a big acquisition and we needed to discuss that with the Board and they supported it because it actually made a lot of sense. The synergies from combining PONL and Maersk-Sealand were tremendous. That was a very strong business case. We got the mandate to pursue it, we engaged bankers, especially since it was publicly quoted, so Goldman Sachs dealt with those matters. When you buy a publicly quoted company, there is a very limited amount of due diligence you can do but we knew the company well ... So, I went to London with Knud Stubkjær and we knocked on Philip Green's door and said that we had this interesting offer for them. I don't recall exactly what the levels were, but let's say we were indicating a [share price] level of 50, and I think we ended up at 57 or something like that. What was exciting was whether we got sufficient support for our offer. The rule in the Netherlands was that only if we had 95 per cent support [from the shareholders] could we squeeze out the rest. We got 95 point something.[15]

Maersk Line's first acquisition had been the rights of Companie Maritime Belge and Chargeurs Réunis in 1987. The purchase of PONL was the sixth and all the intervening acquisitions, small and large, had represented major changes in Maersk-Sealand's development as a company. Eivind Kolding reflected on Mærsk Mc-Kinney Møller's views of acquisition:

He was never keen on [them]. He was very cautious, I would not say sceptical, but quite reluctant when it came early on to the acquisition of Sea-Land. This was not his style of business. He was used to organic growth but this was buying companies. He saw that as a kind of disease you saw in any other industry and he felt it was sort of a contagious disease now also coming into shipping. It was not part of his DNA to go in that direction.

The overall management team led by Jess Søderberg acknowledged these concerns, and the decision to move ahead with the acquisitions was made with due respect for this fundamental change in the company's way of doing business.

The readiness of MGM and its core element, GCSS, to be the platform that would be used to run the consolidated business, as PONL's Jeremy Nixon and Lucas Vos indicated, was a major issue for the acquisition. A memo dated 27 May 2005 addressed to the PONL Implementation Group from Maersk-Sealand's CIO, Michael Laursen, on behalf of the global IS organisation, clearly spelled out the opportunity offered by PONL's Focus Four system, but also pointed to three major risks of which the first was of prime concern: switching over to Focus Four would mean that 'basically all systems and processes currently in place in Maersk-Sealand would have to be replaced ... and probably our entire e-commerce suite. This would be an enormous and very risky implementation, clearly much larger than Maersk-Sealand's MGM implementation.' The challenge was that MGM was still not ready for extensive use. While parts of the functionality were up and running, it would in reality take two more years before the main elements were all in place and the global organisation trained in how to use it effectively.

Eivind Kolding clarified the scale of the issue from his perspective:

I think it was obvious to choose the Maersk platform, because at least that had worked until that point and we knew what we had. The problem was that we were in this transition of MGM so our platform was not stable. And that was given quite clearly from the leadership of Maersk-Sealand, a requirement – 'You have to finish MGM by February 2006. You will be ready and we will put PONL on.' We overestimated our capabilities in what we could do IT-wise, so our systems were simply not ready for the additional volume. That was not why we lost a lot of money, but that was why our reputation was hurt a lot ... and you can imagine an organisation occupied with integration and getting the organisation right, a lot of new colleagues and so on, and at the same time, this avalanche of customers complaining about this, that and the other that didn't work. Reputation-wise, that was a big blow to Maersk.[16]

John Nielsen, at that time a senior colleague of Michael Laursen, added another perspective:

It was not because the system didn't work because it was exactly the same system as the day before. But you had 10,000 unskilled users, a lot of organisational changes with organisations being put together, so a lot more mistakes were made.[17] And we did not have a fully developed platform.[18]

Another element that has been less talked about, but which complicated working practices across the global organisation, was that Maersk-Sealand was in the early stages of implementing a new global financial system, SAP R3, known internally as the FACT project. Hanne B. Sørensen (at that time head of the FACT Project) and her substantial team were working heroically to manage this ultra-complex global project, which was ultimately to act as the base platform to revolutionise management information across the Maersk-Sealand business. However, at the time it was another element of complexity in which a large part of the organisation was involved.

Knud Stubkjær explained:

I think it was absolutely right to do [the FACT project] at the same time, as we had a number of other major projects going on inside Maersk-Sealand that went deep into our DNA, in a way, like the IT systems and so on. But ultimately these turned out to be a challenge that was too big for us to handle ... that cost us some significant reputational damage and that was not good.[19]

Eivind Kolding referred to the loss that Maersk-Sealand Line made in 2006:

the original business case anticipated we would scale down the network. There were huge synergies in the network. The intention was that we would amalgamate the two networks, probably scale down by the tune of 10 per cent of the fleet because then we would really have had something that was very, very efficient. And at a much better cost. But we did not scale down. I don't think that was flagged anywhere. On the contrary, we expected to be able to grow the business and actually even take market share. It was relatively good times for the liner industry in 2005, 2006 and 2007 so Maersk-Sealand felt that we could just continue our growth path irrespective of this big acquisition.

Jeremy Nixon's earlier reference to the integration process having so many 'moving parts' was very much to the point. A major joint integration team was established in Copenhagen, with a subsidiary team in London focusing on systems, working from a common integration plan that ran to many pages. In each of the areas around the world, similar work plans were being used, coordinated through the 17 area managers and their teams.

The first order of the day was to obtain the required percentage of shares in PONL to ensure that the acquisition could actually happen. Agreement with the PONL Board was reached on 10 May, with a public announcement of the intended acquisition on 11 May, one day before the PONL annual general meeting.

For everything to move forward the approval of the competition authorities was also required. In Europe contact with the EU's Directorate General IV (DGIV) was established on 18 May and approval received in late June. The United States, Australia, New Zealand and South Africa were all approached during the same week and approvals were received by mid August. A number of other countries had similar requirements, including Bulgaria, Brazil, Israel, Romania, Korea, Turkey, Canada, Mexico and Venezuela. Ultimately, approval was received from all.

While this was pending, only historical information could be exchanged between the parties and while internal planning could be pursued in Maersk-Sealand, the delay in being able to talk seriously about the future and make joint plans about, for example, offices, people, ships and the network, inevitably created uncertainty.

There were also other elements that required attention, such as union discussions and works council meetings. There were legal hurdles, too, where Maersk was obliged to divest certain operations because of a perceived 'dominant position' by the EU regulators. Although the prices obtained for these divestments were positive, all required manpower and time.

The overall process of integration took some six months, with a go-live date of March 2006, fast for an integration of two companies of this size. But, as Rob van Trooijen noted, 'if you have an integration period that drags out, then employees get jittery, customers don't know and competition has a field day because the first thing they do is target the joint customers. Customer and employee retention was very much on the forefront.'

In line with the StarLight strategy and the aspiration to achieve improved profitability in key routes, Maersk-Sealand's slot capacity was now more than twice that of the second-place carrier, Mediterranean Shipping Company (MSC), and more than three times that of CMA CGM in third place, which should have provided significant economies of scale.

The *Containerisation International Yearbook 2008* noted that 'Maersk Line remained in pole position with an operational fleet of 1.7 million TEU. This was equivalent to 16.2 per cent of world cellular capacity.'[20]

The acquisition meant that from operating some 350 ships, the network fleet now exceeded 600. Jørgen Harling commented:

Of course we had established a network that covered the world, but it is not a static network. It is something that we need to keep alive, and that we need to continue to tweak and to optimise so that we make sure that we do not sit on a lot of fixed expenses. And, it really is a lot of expenses because once we have crafted the

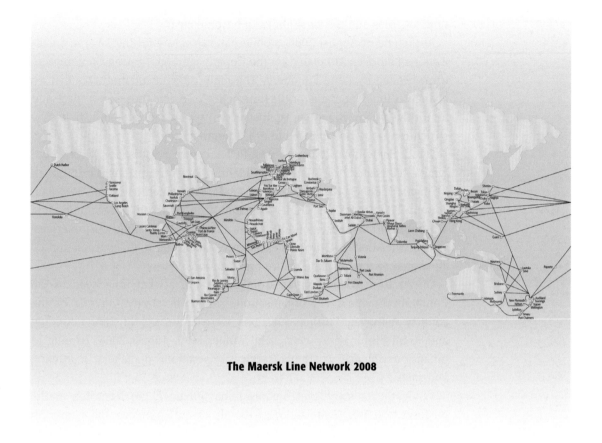

The Maersk Line Network 2008

Figure 11.3 The advance of globalisation expressed in trade lanes between all world markets. By 2008, following the acquisitions of the previous 15 years, Maersk Line was present on a truly global scale.

network, we have accounted for more than 80 per cent of Maersk-Sealand's expenses.[21]

Harling makes this 'tweaking' sound relatively easy, but in reality this required a substantial re-thinking and ultimately a scaling back to avoid serious under-utilisation of the network's assets.

In contrast to the acquisitions of EAC, Safmarine, Sea-Land and Torm Line, where the focus was mainly on acquiring the assets of the companies (ships and terminals), most of the PONL people were to join Maersk-Sealand, a deliberate approach to strengthen the organisation at a time when the 'war on talent' was beginning to make itself felt. However, both companies had offices in most of the key cities; these needed to be rationalised and people selected and organised to handle their future roles. In 2005 Maersk-Sealand had had approximately 22,000 people; this number had now grown to 35,000. Layers and complexity had been added as it took time for roles and responsibilities to become clear.

At the end of August 2004, a boilerplate structure for the 17 area organisations had been circulated by the Copenhagen-based Area Coordination team headed by Lotte Lundberg. The main recommendation was that no changes should be made for the time being 'to create the needed space and air for the organisation to grasp the current set-up and settle in to that'. The structure was to be reviewed in 6–12 months' time.[22]

On 22 September 2005, the post-PONL centre organisation workgroup, which consisted of Karsten Kildahl, Jesper Præstensgaard, Søren Laungaard, Robert Kledal and Adam Gade, sent a memo to Knud Stubkjær, Tommy Thomsen, Peter Frederiksen and Vagn Lehd Møller recommending a number of changes around 'decentralisation, marketing, customer service, service delivery, process excellence, reefer and route coordination',[23] all related to the area and centre organisations.

On 20 June 2006 a memo from Bill Allen, at that time head of the Container Business HR organisation, sought to clarify the role of the country manager. Further questions were addressed to Eivind Kolding and Knud Stubkjær by Vagn Lehd Møller on 1 August 2006, relating to process excellence, customer services, operations managers, marketing and sales.[24]

While the country-level organisations remained the front-line of the business, the area organisations were also growing in size and scope. On the one hand, Copenhagen was decentralising and delegating more responsibility to the areas, while the areas were also taking over and consolidating common activities from the front line offices, increasing the risk of complexity and decelerated decision-making.

And in Copenhagen, despite an excellent working relationship, the dual-CEO role shared by Knud Stubkjær and Tommy Thomsen was also complex to manage. When asked for his views on the concept of a dual CEO, Knud Stubkjær said simply: 'Don't.' He continued:

I think it is extremely difficult to make this a very powerful and successful position. However close we were together, however much we seemed to align our thought process, there will be grey areas and any ambiguity on strategic direction is always super-dangerous.[25]

On 12 February 2006, the name Maersk-Sealand, which had been the brand name since 2000, was changed back to Maersk Line. In an unrelated step, on 1 July 2006, Eivind Kolding, A.P. Moller – Maersk Chief Financial Officer, was appointed as a Partner in A.P. Moller. Shortly afterwards, Tommy Thomsen was made the Partner responsible for overseeing the development of APM Terminals and his part of the dual-CEO role for Maersk Line was filled by Eivind Kolding.

Reflecting on the PONL acquisition and its aftermath, Kolding, supporting Knud Stubkjær's earlier comments on the acquisition, commented:

> I still feel that, irrespective of the very challenging period in 2006 and 2007, it was the right thing to do. This was the acquisition that really put Maersk Line apart, and we got the synergies, but with a couple of years' delay, because what we did later under StreamLine and what others have done since, was really to capture the synergies that were there from the acquisition. We created a clear leadership position through that. And we have of course maintained that ever since.[26]

The subject of the PONL acquisition has remained contentious both within Maersk Line and elsewhere ever since it took place. Many of the people involved are still very active and have strong opinions on the subject. One of Mærsk Mc-Kinney Møller's favourite axioms was 'Always learn from our faults and mistakes.' It is clear that the learning from the acquisition and the costs involved, not just monetary, but in particular the careers that it cost, has been substantial.

The acquisition was undoubtedly a landmark and was in accordance with the StarLight strategy. It provided Maersk Line with a scale that would have been impossible to achieve quickly through organic growth. It provided a platform in the global service centres that Maersk Line has since been able to build on substantially to achieve low-cost operations and improved customer service. It also injected new blood into the organisation, both in diversity and in culture. It can also be said that the implications of the acquisition continue to rumble through Maersk Line, and to some degree the industry as a whole, exacerbated by the recession and subsequent slow growth in the Western economies.

Perhaps the last word on the PONL acquisition should be Claus Hemmingsen's reflection:

> One of the things I never forgot after just having been appointed a Partner was something that Jess Søderberg said in a meeting: 'Let us question past decisions in the right way, because past decisions were taken under past circumstances. It is always difficult to then say later, we should have done or should not have done – it is actually not the point, because unless you can put yourself exactly in the circumstances, you cannot really judge the decision.'[27]

A bright spot: *Emma Mærsk*

In a generally pessimistic article in the *Containerisation International Yearbook 2007*, John Fossey noted:

> Significantly, during the summer of 2006, Maersk took delivery of the *Emma Mærsk*, a new mega post-Panamax ship officially rated by the carrier as being able to load

Figure 11.4 More than 10,000 people came to see the world's then largest container ship, *Emma Mærsk*, being manoeuvred out of the Odense Fjord for its sea trials. In the background the next ship in the series of eight can be seen under the Odense Steel Shipyard crane.

11,000 TEU, but in reality more likely to have a capacity of 13,800 TEU. Potentially, this move has taken Maersk's operating economies of scale to a new level.[28]

In fact, the new ship's real capacity was about 15,550 TEU, which just goes to show how challenging capacity discussions can be.

Captain Henrik Solmer, the senior and most experienced captain in Maersk's container fleet, who had served on container ships since the *Adrian Mærsk* back in 1977, was asked to participate in the planning for the ships. Nearing retirement, he did not imagine that he would then be asked to take command of what he described as

the best ship I had ever sailed on, without a doubt. I felt very honoured and excited when I was asked to take *Emma* out on her maiden voyage ... The whole crew had been living and working together for months before we took her out, focused on intense training with both the soft human side and the very important technical side, all resulting in a fantastic team ... She is a vessel equipped with state-of-the-art equipment, with the world's largest engine and was the largest and fastest container ship. We knew we would get the whole world's attention from day one and it proved to be a fantastic experience to be her Master to the Far East and back to Europe.[29]

Maersk Line had ordered eight ships in the Emma class, all to be built at the Odense Steel Shipyard. In the midst of the turbulence of the PONL

Figure 11.5 In Hong Kong, *Emma Mærsk* called at Modern Terminals in 2006, just as *Adrian Mærsk* did on Maersk Line's first containerised service in 1975. However, the capacity of the ship was nearly ten times larger.

acquisition and the slowing world economy, it was a great boost to morale for the entire organisation to have eight of the largest ships in the world delivered to its business. For a moment, the increasingly customer-focused organisation got a glimpse of the ship owner perspective of the business; the central role of the ship, both as an effective money earner and certainly as a symbol of the company's activities.

The *Emma Mærsk* and its seven sisters became the pride of Maersk Line and their crews' performance deserves a great deal of credit for keeping spirits up at a difficult time in the business.

12 A New Strategy (2008–2013)

StreamLINE and Beyond

> *For shipping, all stands and falls with worldwide macroeconomic conditions.*
>
> UNCTAD, *Review of Maritime Transport*, 2011[1]

The A.P. Moller – Maersk Group made its first loss ever in 2009, after 104 years in business. Maersk Line's loss of $2.1 billion was highly influential in the group's overall loss of $1 billion, highlighting the close connection between the macroeconomic state of the world and shipping – in this case container shipping.

More formally, the A.P. Moller – Maersk Group's Annual Report stated that:

2009 was a challenging year in which most of the world was, to a greater or lesser extent, affected by the financial and economic crisis ... Consumption and investments slowed down dramatically, with a negative impact on world trade.

Maersk Line's loss reflected 'the tough market conditions with falling freight rates and volumes'. The immediate effect of the significantly changed supply and demand situation was a dramatic decline in turnover of some $8 billion from 2008 to 2009.

Maersk Line's turnover as a business had grown over 600 per cent in the ten years between 1997 and 2007, to about $26 billion. A further $2 billion would be added in 2008. Maersk Line was now a massive business and turning its result around to consistent profitability was not going to be a short-term activity.

The business plan for the period 2007–2011, prepared towards the end of 2006, reflected much of the complexity following the acquisition of P&O NedLloyd (PONL). With weakening freight rates compounding the issues, cash flow from operations was not expected to be sufficient to cover investments and interest-bearing debt. Each of the individual services had its strategy and plan to improve, as well as analyses of what went right and what went wrong in the acquisition process from their perspective – summaries to learn from.

Box 12.1 Maersk Line key numbers 1974–2013

	1974	1975	1976	1977	1978	1979	1980	1981	1982	1983
Maersk Line turnover ($ million)	N/A	100.5	178.0	236.8	312.7	338.4	418.2	545.7	589.5	590.4
Net result *before* interest & depreciation ($ million)	N/A	−4.6	23.7	43.7	85.7	82.6	60.0	70.3	69.5	49.6
Net result *after* interest & depreciation ($ million)	N/A	N/A	N/A	N/A	N/A	N/A	N/A	N/A	N/A	N/A
ROI (net result *before* interest & depreciation / cost price) (%)	N/A	N/A	N/A	N/A	N/A	N/A	N/A	N/A	9.5	8.2
Bunkers cost per ton ($)	N/A	60	91	N/A	64	98	N/A	N/A	N/A	N/A
Full containers carried ('000 TEU)	N/A	N/A	N/A	N/A	N/A	N/A	N/A	260	277	300
Staff globally (excluding seafarers)	N/A	N/A	N/A	N/A	1,500	N/A	N/A	N/A	N/A	N/A
$ / Danish Kroner exchange rate (end year)	6.1	5.6	6.0	6.0	5.5	5.3	6.1	7.1	8.4	8.4

Box 12.1 [cont.]

	1984	1985	1986	1987	1988	1989	1990	1991	1992	1993
Maersk Line turnover ($ million)	744.6	724.8	1,076.7	1,314.0	1,666.1	1,888.7	1,980.3	2,317.0	2,589.7	3,026.0
Net result *before* interest & depreciation ($ million)	115.4	87.0	57.2	84.2	101.2	89.7	45.8	202.4	236.4	264.1
Net result *after* interest & depreciation ($ million)	N/A	N/A	N/A	N/A	-4.8	-30.6	-96.6	-10.1	32.4	35.5
ROI (net result *before* interest & depreciation / cost price) (%)	16.3	10.8	6.3	8.7	11.1	7.7	4.7	12.9	12.5	13.0
Bunkers cost per ton ($)	N/A	N/A	N/A	N/A	N/A	N/A	N/A	65.0	75.0	N/A
Full containers carried ('000 TEU)	358	408	667	787	962	1,094	1,143	1,270	1,435	1,734
Staff globally (excluding seafarers)	N/A	N/A	N/A	N/A	N/A	N/A	5,927	6,306	6,801	7,563
$ / Danish Kroner exchange rate (end year)	9.9	11.8	9.1	7.3	6.8	7.6	6.2	6.4	6.0	6.5

Box 12.1 [cont.]

	1994	1995	1996	1997	1998	1999	2000	2001	2002	2003
Maersk Line turnover ($ million)	3,584.0	3,810.7	3,844.9	4,205.4	4,428.2	5,526.9	8,861.6	8,904.3	9,089.6	11,072.5
Net result *before* interest & depreciation ($ million)	187.9	323.9	404.7	441.9	412.9	586.9	744.7	560.6	821.8	1,287.0
Net result *after* interest & depreciation ($ million)	−69.5	98.5	139.2	141.6	58.6	155.3	152.6	−110.0	−32.1	339.6
ROI (net result *before* interest & depreciation / cost price) (%)	8.0	15.7	16.9	16.3	12.7	14.7	14.2	8.8	8.5	13.3
Bunkers cost per ton ($)	N/A	112.4	118.5	114.3	81.2	111.5	163.1	154.1	153.4	176.3
Full containers carried ('000 TEU)	2,154	2,119	2,311	2,825	3,144	4,253	6,736	6,983	7,512	8,275
Staff globally (excluding seafarers)	8,722	8,657	8,451	N/A	9,417	N/A	N/A	N/A	19,888	21,355
$ / Danish Kroner exchange rate (end year)	6.4	5.6	5.8	6.6	6.7	7.0	8.1	8.3	7.9	6.6

Box 12.1 [cont.]

	2004	2005	2006	2007	2008	2009	2010	2011	2012	2013*
Maersk Line turnover ($ million)	15,798.0	21,524.0	25,275.0	25,821.0	28,666.0	20,611.0	26,038.0	25,108.0	27,118.0	28,418*
Net result *before* interest & depreciation ($ million)	2,806.0	3,420.0	1,544.0	2,002.0	2,262.0	−144.0	4,602.0	1,009.0	2,179.0	N/A
Net result after tax ($ million)	1,513.0	1,278.0	−568.0	106.0	205.0	N/A	N/A	N/A	N/A	N/A
Segment result ($ million)	N/A	N/A	N/A	N/A	583.0	−2,088.0	2,642.0	−553.0	461.0	N/A
EBIT margin (used as a proxy for return on investments) (%)	11.2	8.0	0.5	3.1	3.4	−9.1	11.1	−1.9	1.9	N/A
Return on invested capital (net result before interest / invested capital) (%)	N/A	N/A	N/A	N/A	3.2	−11.2	15.4	−3.1	2.4	N/A
Bunkers cost per ton ($)	189.3	244.2	322.3	344.1	520.0	341.6	457.7	619.7	661.0	N/A

Box 12.1 [cont.]

Full containers carried ('000 TEU)	9,102	9,725	13,320	13,600	14,000	13,800	14,555	16,222	16,986	N/A
Staff globally YTD average (excl. seafarers and related activities)	N/A	N/A	N/A	N/A	25,768	22,967	23,653	25,124	26,291	N/A
$ / Danish Kroner exchange rate (end year)	6.0	6.0	5.9	5.4	5.1	5.4	5.6	5.4	5.8	

* Consensus estimate (Thomson-Reuters)

1975–2003 – numbers based on internal book close reports since no external reporting (2003 and 2004 external reports only in DKK)

1993, EAC (East Asiatic Company) container line activities were acquired in 1993

2000, Safmarine and Sealand were acquired in 1999 giving full impact from 2000

2004, 2007, 2011, restated figures as shown in subseqent annual report

2004–2012 – numbers based on external reports

2006, P&O NedLloyd impacting P&L from 2006 (acquisition Aug 2005 but only integrated during 2006)

Source: Maersk Line Finance Department & A. P. Moller-Maersk archives

It was clear that a further recovery plan was needed and such a major effort would require resources. Eivind Kolding and Knud Stubkjær launched phase one of the strategy formulation with Kim Hedegaard Sørensen and brought back Flemming Steen to be responsible for the subsequent strategy implementation. Steen had earlier been Finance Director in APM Terminals and, as he said later, 'I think Eivind knew me as a blunt and stubborn guy and that was why I was given the strategy job.'[2] Support was provided by a team hand-picked by Flemming Steen and Bill Allen (head of Maersk Line HR), who worked closely with a team from McKinsey.

The name given to the project, and subsequently to the new strategy was StreamLINE. Flemming Steen commented:

> We had around 45 Maersk Line people and 15 McKinsey. And we had the best people within specific areas that you could find. The amount of energy and skill in the room, I think, was enormous. It was one of the most fantastic experiences, but it was also one of those experiences you would not find in any other Danish company.

McKinsey in Denmark had started working closely with Maersk Line when the StreamLINE strategy was developed in late 2006. While impressed by the robustness of the diagnostics in the StarLight strategy, it was understood that there was a need to change direction in order to get back to profitability.

There were to be three main focus areas. The first was route profitability, where the focus on volume was not generating the desired results. Second, was the use of assets and asset turn, network design and use of vessels. Third, was improved clarity on Maersk Line's approach to freight forwarders and small customers.

The reliability and timeliness of management numbers was an area of concern. With the IT systems being introduced and a large acquisition still a focus area for the central and area management, good customer information was critical. The previous focus meant that the spotlight had been on numbers of containers to be moved rather than on profitability and 'what it meant to your bottom line', as Flemming Steen put it.

Bill Allen's focus was to support the new strategy by ensuring that the global performance management processes embedded both ownership and accountability into the organisation, and that talent management focused on becoming better at identifying, developing, deploying and retaining the best talent. The aim was to create a global organisation that could win in any marketplace.

Management changes

Since Tommy Thomsen's move away from Maersk Line to take partner responsibility for APM Terminals in 2006, Knud Stubkjær and Eivind Kolding had occupied the dual-CEO seats. In early 2007, while work in

Figure 12.1 Eivind Kolding started his career with A.P. Moller – Maersk in the Corporate Secretariat in 1989 and became head of Maersk Line Hong Kong in 1996. Having returned to Copenhagen, Kolding was the Group Chief Financial Officer 1998–2006. Eivind Kolding was made Partner in A.P. Moller – Maersk in 2006 and was CEO of Maersk Line 2006–2012, when he took over the position as CEO of Danske Bank, a leading financial institution in Denmark.

Maersk Line focused on the strategy review, A.P. Moller – Maersk's Chairman, Michael Pram Rasmussen, took steps to change the leadership setup, not only in Maersk Line, but also at Group level.

On 22 June 2007, a press release announced that Jess Søderberg, the Group CEO, would be retiring and be replaced from outside by Nils Smedegaard Andersen, the CEO of Carlsberg who had been a Board member of A.P. Moller – Maersk for two years. That announcement was enough to make the front pages of not only the Danish but also the international business press – but it did not stand alone.

The Chairman and the Board had decided to dismantle the dual CEO function in Maersk Line and informed the organisation and the public that Eivind Kolding was the new sole CEO. Both Knud Stubkjær and Tommy Thomsen were offered other positions in the group, but decided to leave. Others were also to leave.

Change, starting at the top

Eivind Kolding acknowledged that these management changes might have given rise to concerns about continuity:

I always endeavoured to make sure that the Board knew what was going on, to always be very honest about the problems and issues, but always to have a solution. All the way through, I never felt that I did not have the backing I needed, even in the difficult times in 2009.

Kolding continued the strategy review and established a new management team, named the Liner Management Board (LMB). Chaired by himself, the LMB consisted of Morten Engelstoft as Chief Operating Officer, Hanne B. Sørensen as Chief Commercial Officer, Lars Reno Jakobsen heading Network and Product, Lucas Vos heading Process Excellence and Information Technology, Bill Allen as head of Human Resources and Peter Rønnest Andersen as Chief Financial Officer.

Their first priority was to continue to address costs. The driving elements of the new strategy were costs and profitability and delivering a 5 percentage point higher EBIT (earnings before interest and tax) margin than Maersk Line's peer group.

Kolding's approach was to make everyone aware of the burning platform:

Despite all the problems in Maersk Line, the poor results, etc., there was still this kind of mentality that, Maersk Line, we are the best, we are number one. Many people did not see the need for change, even though it was staring us in the face. That was a very unpopular task internally, and externally, as people felt that they were part of a great story – which they had been.[3]

Another priority was to simplify the organisation so that management could focus on the key business drivers. Noting the success of the independent APM Terminals earlier in the decade, a process of separating Maersk Logistics and Damco from Maersk Line was initiated. The first steps had already been taken when Damco Sea & Air was acquired as part of P&O NedLloyd Logistics in 2006. The separation was completed in 2007 when the A.P. Moller – Maersk Group's logistics and forwarding activities were joined under the new brand name of Damco.

Figure 12.2 The Damco logo.

Box 12.2 Damco today

With the acquisition of PONL in 2006 came a new opportunity: Damco, a substantial freight forwarding activity within the PONL organisation.

When Maersk Logistics was established as an independent organisation within the A.P. Moller – Maersk Group in 2007, the forwarding activities of both Maersk Logistics and Damco, which was the larger and better established of the two companies, were merged under the Damco brand.

To give the company depth and strength in its operations as well as full independence, at the end of 2008 it was decided to merge the brands of Maersk Logistics and Damco into one organisation, which took the name Damco for all its global operations.

Damco today is a business with a turnover in excess of $3.3 billion (2012), some 10,800 employees and six core products:

- Ocean freight management.
- Air freight management.
- Inland transportation services.
- Warehousing and distribution services.
- Supply chain management.
- Supply chain development.

The business has been particularly innovative in its supply chain development activities and in delivering 'green' solutions, with a strong commitment to sustainability. With over 300 offices in more than 90 countries, Damco remains in fast-track growth mode, including appropriate acquisitions, and plans to continue that growth for several years to come. As part of that plan, the headquarters was moved to Holland in early 2013.

To further simplify Maersk Line's organisation and simultaneously develop an existing business opportunity, a new container shipping company was also formed in 2011. SeaGo Line was created to do with inter-European container movements what MCC Transport in Asia had done for inter-Asian container movements, with much success.

Change and simplification were also impacting the Maersk Line global organisation. The area organisations were being cut back from 17 areas to 8 regions. On average, their staff was reduced and their roles and responsibilities changed from running their area businesses to providing performance management, support and coaching to the front-line offices that were now grouped into some 54 clusters.

Those front-line offices, too, were being simplified, with as many functional tasks as possible removed to service centres so that the front line was focused on the main activities of selling, providing active customer care

Figure 12.3 The SeaGo Line logo.

Box 12.3 SeaGo Line

Formed in 2011 to focus exclusively on the inter-European market, SeaGo Line is a dedicated container operator serving some 40 countries that comprise the markets of Scandinavia, Russia and the Baltic countries, Northern Europe, the Mediterranean, North Africa and the Black Sea.

The initiative directly supports the European Union's efforts to move road-based traffic onto sea-based transport systems, creating a low-impact environmental approach with a reduced carbon footprint.

The services also provide those retailers and manufacturers who use near-market sourcing (as compared to the Far East, for example), with regular, reliable and frequent container capabilities and short transit times.

Services are tailor-made for the European market and offer a full range of equipment, including refrigerated units. By 2013, SeaGo Line was operating some 75 ships in its network. Service was based on a staff of about 300, with representation in 23 European countries.

and issue resolution. While management decisions were largely moved back to Copenhagen, all the back-office activities – document creation and handling, most accounting and invoicing and even some of the basic front-office functions – were also centralised, but in this case into the five

Table 12.1 Focusing the front-line offices

	January 2010	June 2012	
Service centres	4,643	8,232	Supporting Maersk Line only
Front-line offices	13,038	10,939	Includes liner operating centres

Source: Maersk Line HR, 8 January 2013.

global service centres, in Manila, the Philippines, Guangzhou in China (later moved to Chengdu) and India (Pune, Chennai and Mumbai).

The change was substantial and included some short-term overstaffing in the service centres to ensure that trained capacity was available to manage the transitions.

While Hanne B. Sørensen, Maersk Line's CCO, was travelling the world meeting and talking with customers, her other main responsibility was ensuring that the new slimmed-down regions were focused on their primary task – motivating the country clusters to focus on their customers and, in parallel, downsizing the offices by moving common activities to the global service centres in a structured and standardised way.[4]

Hanne B. Sørensen maintained that the lessons learned during her earlier experience as Area Manager for the East Mediterranean Area, with its many diverse cultures, could be used directly in the implementation of the StreamLINE goals: 'It is the sum of the small things that moves you',[5] the attention to detail when identifying the small problems in each process that in turn create comprehensive challenges for large operations.

Talking about the fundamental change that was driven into the sales organisation under the StreamLINE strategy, she said:

Sales went through a 180-degree swing, away from pure relationship selling to differentiation and value selling, an enormous change and very challenging. While some in sales loved it, others would not make it. But, in the end, it is a question of getting the balance right between relationships, differentiation and value.[6]

Another impactful development was communications. As Flemming Steen said: 'You need to accept that if you want to change something fundamentally, you are going to get unpopular.' To counter this concern, active communication to the whole organisation became the norm and was regular and consistent. Flemming Steen added:

We ran monthly surveys where we targeted people, saying 'What do you think about . . .?' on, I think it was 21 parameters and we could see immediately if it had an influence, but still I can say, looking back, that we communicated too little.[7]

Process excellence

A new organisation had been created consisting of a team dedicated to process excellence, working through business process owners in each of the business functions. Chaired by Lucas Vos, then head of Process Excellence, IT and the Service Centres, the Business Process Committee took over responsibility for the justification and prioritisation of IT projects and enhancements.

Over the next three to four years, this small team was to have major impact on IT projects and the effective implementation of standardised global processes that the systems under development would then be able to support. Such standardised global processes would also support the increasingly smooth transfer of front-line work to the service centres.

Change was also taking place in Operations. Returning to Copenhagen to take up his position as COO, having been Area Manager for Southeast Asia, Morten Engelstoft commented candidly:

> I need to be alert with the portfolio that I have and really understand what is impactful and what is not. When I first arrived, I did not have responsibility for the technical side of Maersk Line which I assumed a couple of years into my role. I did not have the responsibility for crewing that I assumed about a year later. Nor did I have responsibility for network design, which I assumed earlier this year.[8]

There were also a number of new initiatives under way to improve communications with the ships and their crews, focusing on their better integration into the business.

One major area to which Morten Engelstoft and his team turned their attention was the implementation of the eight liner operating centres (LOCs) around the world, responsible for the running of the ships and the related operations, their port calls and costs, on a daily basis:

> It is a complex network, but one where there is a lot of potential from figuring out better than the rest of the industry how to get competitive advantage from it ... Our numbers indicate that OOCL has managed to find a way consistently to be a stronger performer on many issues. There are a number of things we can learn from them, among others.[9]

Morten Engelstoft started his career as a trainee in Maersk Line in 1986 and spent most of his career away from Copenhagen. Looking outside the organisation for inspiration, knowledge sharing and learning was not at the top of a young trainee's education programme and he has had to change with the organisation. Indeed, he has been a leader in the shift towards a more open approach to managing the business.

Network and Product

Another new centre organisation, Network and Product, was headed by Lars Reno Jakobsen, today the A.P. Moller – Maersk Group's senior representative in Africa. Reno recalled his time running Maersk Line's Network and Product organisation in Copenhagen. This relatively small team was responsible for the design and management of each of the routes and strings that Maersk Line offered in each market and 'the greatest thing was to feel responsible for the bottom line',[10] the prime responsibility of each Route Manager.

Reno described his realisation that there are about 500 buttons one could press to get results, whereas in other industries the number was likely to be far fewer. This view was confirmed by others saying that it becomes critically important to think through what levers there are to differentiate, and in particular the cost structure of serving customers.

The 500 buttons might include, in no particular order, supply and demand balances, trade regulations, ship-related technology, communications and information management technologies, the history of how trade has been conducted, the people, the customers, the interaction between customers and Maersk people, ports and related technologies, capital costs or geography; but can also be as basic as port rotations, ship speeds, crane capacities and productivity, and the components used in the design of a product or service. How one pushes, pulls or turns those buttons creates the environment for the business.

As McKinsey pointed out, reliability is a differentiator for container shipping, as the only place in the whole supply chain where reliability was 50, 60 or 70 per cent was the shipping part. Reliability made sense to the customer, and if one can get reliability up, then costs can be taken out, a powerful combination.

In a 2010 edition of the *Mærsk Post*, Eivind Kolding was quoted as saying:

We are already the most reliable in the industry ... but being ranked as leader with a schedule reliability performance of 70 per cent highlights the unsophisticated nature of the industry. In the future, we are aiming for a game-changing 95 per cent on-time delivery performance. Such a dramatic increase in reliability would allow our customers significantly to reduce their inventory buffer and would increase our lead over our competitors.[11]

After several years in the pipeline, completion of the MGM project during 2007 was 'the most important activity' as this was 'the precondition for step change improvements in data quality and planned productivity.'[12]

Maersk Line was known to be good at implementing, but its ability to implement needed to change. The lack of patience in the Maersk Line organisation meant that it was natural to go from planning direct to implementation. However, to be truly effective, there should be a step between planning and implementing, where the concept is tested and hardwired within the organisation. This was identified as making the difference between driving deep change and devising a nice concept that worked in some places.

Looking back on StreamLINE in 2012, interviewees noted two areas where even more effort and urgency could have been applied. One was asset utilisation and the other management information: the reliability and timeliness of numbers are crucial when trying to make a business more profitable in a harsh business environment.

Kolding's team's efforts to make the organisation more externally focused were praised, as was the depth and strength of the talent base. Eivind Kolding, reflecting on Maersk Line's culture, agreed:

> The quality of the people and their attitude has been a great, great asset throughout. What has changed is that we have actually become more disciplined.[13]

An *annus horribilis*

By 2009 Maersk Line was already nearly two years into a major cost-cutting and product re-design process when the collapse of world trade occurred. Global trade volumes dropped by unprecedented levels of over 25 per cent on the major Asia–United States and Asia–Europe trades. These lost volumes were only marginally offset by more stable trade volumes within Asia and in the trade to Africa. Freight rates dropped by some 30 per cent and Maersk Line's top line collapsed by $8 billion while the bottom line, described so well by Eivind Kolding in the Prologue, descended to a loss of just over $2 billion.

John Fossey, in the *Containerisation International Yearbook 2009*, described the collapse: 'Up until July 2008, it seemed that the year would be one of modest increases. But then the wheels came off.' Writing in the *2010 Yearbook*, he said: '2009 was the worst year on record and the only one since the first containership sailed in 1956 that global container traffic actually fell.'[14]

Laid-up tonnage was

well over 500 ships aggregating between 840,000 and 1.2 million TEU. Several unlikely partnerships evolved, with Maersk and MSC working together in several trade lanes and Evergreen (of Taiwan) partnering China Shipping Container Lines on some Trans Pacific and Europe/Far East services. Another notable fact about 2009 was that it was the first year that Europe's liner trades were 'conference free'.

Box 12.4 World merchandise trade, 2005–2012

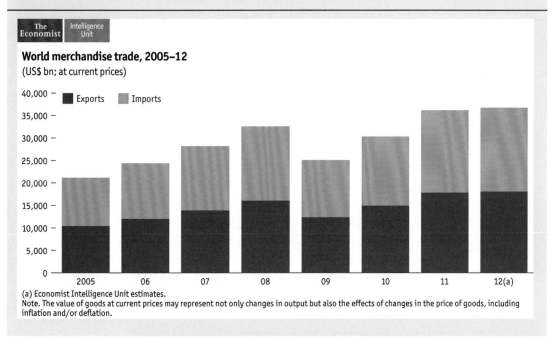

(a) Economist Intelligence Unit estimates.
Note. The value of goods at current prices may represent not only changes in output but also the effects of changes in the price of goods, including inflation and/or deflation.

Figure 12.4 A sign of the crisis and certainly not a situation any ship owner wants to be in. Five large container ships were laid up in Loch Striven on the Clyde in Scotland in 2009–2010.

Arguably this, combined with the global downturn caused more uncertainty in the market and exacerbated the collapse in freight rates.[15]

Reflecting on this *annus horribilis*, Eivind Kolding said:

However desperate it was, I still had the confidence that we would pull through. We knew that we were doing better than average, relatively speaking, but better than that, we had very strong backing. We were at the tipping point in the industry. If this had continued for, say, another six months, we would have lost an awful lot of money, but we would still be standing. Others would have fallen over.[16]

The next steps

By the middle of 2009, Eivind Kolding and his leadership team in the LMB were already planning the next steps in the StreamLINE strategy. The focus for the last two years had been on cost reductions. This was now changed to become very focused on the customer. The new priorities were to become our customers' first choice through ease of business, unmatched reliability and best environmental performance and to empower the organisation to deliver a superior customer experience – driven by continuous improvement and simplification.

To support this, a series of internal 'leaps' were set up. Each was to take part of Maersk Line's business and identify how to implement a quantum leap (as compared to incremental improvements), using some of the best and brightest from around the organisation worldwide. One such was related to the development of a new product, Daily Maersk, while another addressed sales effectiveness, the 180-degree swing that Hanne B. Sørensen referred to earlier. Another addressed improvements in bunker consumption, while yet another focused on improving operating processes between Maersk Line and the container terminals in key ports; another on making it as easy to ship by Maersk Line as it is, for example, to buy a book from Amazon.com.

Overall, there would be eight such efforts, some more successful than others. One that did move forward well and which, after about two years of planning, was to have substantial impact in 2011 in the Far East–Europe market, was Daily Maersk.

A roller-coaster year

2010 was a roller-coaster year, as John Fossey, writing in the *Containerisation International Yearbook 2011*, stated:

While 2009 was the worst year on record for the global container shipping industry, 2010 started off with one of its most robust turnarounds ever. Up to the mid-summer months, cargo volumes and port throughputs in most regions were up by double-digit levels on the corresponding period of 2009. Freight rates also climbed, jumping by between 30 per cent and 50 per cent on some corridors, such as the Trans Pacific, Asia–Europe and Asia–East Coast South America.[17]

Container capacity shortages, in particular for agricultural shipments out of the United States, became a politically sensitive issue, leading to deterioration in relations between carriers and shippers, as a key theme in President Barack Obama's national recovery plan to address the US budget deficit centred around encouraging exports. *Containerisation International* noted that while some 850,000 TEU of new capacity had been ordered from shipyards in 2008, the following year the total was 2,200 TEU – just two small ships.

Later in the same article John Fossey referred to Trond Westlie, Chief Financial Officer of the A.P. Moller – Maersk Group, who, when announcing the company's interim 2010 results, described the global economy as 'causing considerable uncertainty after the peak season ends'. Fossey ended the article with the statement: 'What is certain ... is that 2011 will be as challenging, if not more so, than the past two years because of the uncertainty.'

Generally, confidence in the recovery was fragile. Many people queried whether re-stocking, after a couple of years of heavy inventory cutbacks, was really sustainable. With all the restructuring and streamlining work that the global Maersk Line organisation had put in over the previous four years, Maersk Line was able to reap the benefits of the rise in container volumes and freight rates and turned its 2009 loss of over $2 billion to its best result ever, a profit of over $2.6 billion for 2010.

Eivind Kolding used his global management meeting – an intense workshop in November 2010 – to thank the organisation for all its hard work: 'After four years in crisis, we are out of the storm. You have done a fantastic job. We have fixed the basics ... now, I need your help again.'[18] The purpose of the workshop was to present a new, ambitious approach to build on the strengths of Maersk Line, create a streamlined global organisation of range and depth, with an unprecedented network of ships and services, a cost factor that was unmatchable by its competitors and a vision to 'be the undisputed leader in liner shipping'.

I felt we had fundamental issues in the liner business. The commoditisation, the price pressure, you *need* to do something to break out of that. For Maersk Line, it was really to try to make clear that we could differentiate ourselves in different aspects. We chose three:

- Unmatched reliability.
- Ease of business.
- Best environmental performance.

To reach out to customers primarily, you need to communicate. I felt that was the natural spot for Maersk Line to move in for the industry, but of course, also to benefit ourselves.[19]

The Triple Es: energy efficiency, environment and economy of scale

The next step in the plan came in February 2011 with a contract for new ships, signed in public by Nam Sang-tae, President and CEO of Daewoo Shipbuilding and Marine Engineering, and Eivind Kolding, representing Maersk Line. Primarily for competitive reasons, Maersk Line's order books and many other activities in the A.P. Moller – Maersk Group had traditionally been well-kept secrets, so the press conference in London that February was a huge step for the Maersk organisation and for Maersk Line in particular.

Not only was the number of ships on order announced, but also their real capacity. With 18,200 TEU, the Triple E ships would become the largest ships in the world when delivered in 2013 and onwards. It was even revealed that in addition to the contract for 10 ships signed that day, Maersk

Figure 12.5 A cross-section of the cargo hold of a Triple E ship under construction at the Daewoo Shipbuilding and Marine Engineering yard in Korea in early 2013. The dimensions are emphasised by the two people on bicycles.

Figure 12.6 The first of 20 Triple E ships nearing completion in the building dock. The ship was named *Mærsk Mc-Kinney Møller* in June 2013 by his daughter Ane Mærsk Mc-Kinney Uggla, chairman of the A.P. Møller and Chastine Mc-Kinney Møller Foundation, the owner of a controlling shareholding in A.P. Moller – Maersk.

Line had options for no fewer than 20 more of the same type of ship. The option was partly confirmed in June 2011 when a second batch of 10 ships was ordered.

The press conference also focused on the three Es in the ships' code name: energy efficiency, environment and economy of scale. To support the communication effort, a website www.worldslargestship.com was launched and Maersk Line's sustainability organisation set out to explain the many initiatives underway to fulfil the strategic goal of best environmental performance.

Another initiative was launched at a conference in Antwerp in June 2011 under the banner 'The New Normal', designed to re-shape the industry and differentiate Maersk Line from its competitors.

John Fossey of *Containerisation International* was among those who attended the launch and wrote in the 2012 yearbook that

in announcing the manifesto, Kolding stressed: 'This document has been based on feedback from our main customers and it highlights the need for better reliability, greater care to be taken over the environment and easier ways of doing business.'[20]

Box 12.5 Headlines from the Manifesto

The Manifesto was entitled, 'The New Normal: a manifesto for changing the way we think about shipping'. It challenged some of the basic tenets of the container shipping industry by suggesting that very little change had occurred in the 50 years since containerisation started.

Using a series of examples from other industries, such as the car industry, retail, music players and mobile phones, the Manifesto examined the risks to an industry and to the companies in it, of not changing to meet customers' needs. Two lessons were drawn:

1. 'Just because a business is established, it may only be a few years from being completely overtaken by new technology.'
2. 'Market and customer behavior is forcing companies never to lose sight of what customers really want – including the needs they are not even aware of.'

And three conclusions:

1. 'Getting cargo there on time. Reliability is the new rate war.' Cargo delivered on time enables customers to rationalise their internal processes and optimise their supply chains and inventories, saving hundreds of dollars per container.
2. 'Ease of business. Our complexity is a customer's challenge – and our opportunity.' Elaborated in five key areas from pricing and scheduling to availability, simple documentation, tracking and notifications.
3. 'Doing it with environmental excellence.' Shipping is the least polluting way to mass-move commercial goods around the world.

Illustrated with further examples from Disney and Nestlé, the Manifesto concluded by asking three questions:

1. What if we could guarantee that cargo would be on time, every time?
2. What if placing a shipping order was as easy as buying an airline ticket?
3. What if the shipping industry was known for beating environmental expectations, not struggling to meet them?

In response to each question, a number of positive outcomes was outlined, all from the perspective of the industry, but each with specific reference to the end-customer. A website, www.changingthewaywethinkaboutshipping.com, was available as a forum for debate across the industry.

On improving the ease of doing business, Kolding was quoted as saying:

Think of the revolution in aviation; 20 years ago you could hardly book an airline ticket without using a travel agent, but today there are hardly any intermediaries. It is far simpler and far more efficient and container shipping needs that too.

Box 12.6 Daily Maersk

After a great deal of planning and testing, in September 2011 a press release announced the start, on 24 October, of the upgraded container service covering Ningbo, Shanghai, Yantian in China and Tanjung Pelepas in Malaysia to Felixtowe, Rotterdam and Bremerhaven in Europe.

The concept was a daily cut-off at the same time every day, seven days per week, with the same transit time between each port. The objective was to provide customers with unmatched frequency and reliability – a giant ocean conveyor belt. The promise was backed up by monetary compensation should containers not arrive on time.

Using 70 ships, the service achieved 98 per cent on-time deliveries over the first year of its operation, covering over 200,000 containers. Environmental impact calculations indicated 13 per cent lower CO_2 emissions than the industry average on the route.

In November 2012 the service added two extra ports in the Far East, Jakarta in Indonesia and Laem Chabang in Thailand, both feedering containers to and from Tanjung Pelapas.

Initial customer reaction varied between sceptical and positive.

The industry's reaction, however, was significant, with CMA/CGM and Mediterranean Shipping Company quickly joining forces in a vessel-sharing agreement, initially for two years, to allow them to compete.

The Grand Alliance (Hapag Lloyd, NYK and OOCL) and the New World Alliance (APL, Hyundai and Mitsui-OSK) were also forced to respond and joined forces to create the new G6 Alliance with effect from March 2012.

The launch was followed in September 2011 by the launch of 'Daily Maersk', operating between specific ports in Asia and specific ports in Europe and providing guaranteed port-to-port reliability for customers using the service.

In October 2011, Hanne B. Sørensen and Eivind Kolding hosted a major workshop with about 150 commercial managers from the Maersk Line world. Held at BMW's modernistic conference centre in Munich, the theme was 'Changing the way we sell'. Planning for the workshop had started back in April that year, as this was to be a fundamental change in the way the commercial side of the business operated, right up to the regional Managing Directors.

The workshop included critical presentations by a number of customers, as well as experts from sales consultancies, supply chain management and companies whose reputations had been built on providing customers with superior, differentiated and effective customer focus. The reaction from those participating was a set of standing ovations.

Maersk Line's customer focus had come a very long way in the years since the acquisition of Sea-Land in 1999 and the January 2000 presentation by Dick McGregor, when he compared and contrasted Sea-Land and Maersk Line's sales approaches. As Hanne B. Sørensen commented, 'Maersk Line's earlier Sales Excellence work had prepared the way. The organisation was now mature enough, the workshop provided a step-by-step process and it had focused on the practical things that we can do.'[21] Eric Williams, head of Sales Excellence, explained: 'This is about creating markets for our customers or potentially opening new markets. That is what Maersk Line is also about.'[22]

Interviewed nearly a year later, Tom Sproat, Senior Vice President responsible for customer services and customer care in North America, noted a distinct difference across the business, 'the orientation of the entire company towards the customer. When I can own their problems, that's what they want. The good news is, customers like it, colleagues like it. That is what makes the difference.'[23]

Nils Smedegaard Andersen, A.P. Moller – Maersk Group CEO, who participated in part of the workshop, was sufficiently impressed to ask the team to adapt it and present it to the management of the other group divisions so that they could consider adopting some of the key elements for their businesses.

John Fossey's summary of the year in the *Containerisation International Yearbook 2012* recorded

a firm start, a soft middle and a weak end [for] the fortunes of the container shipping industry in 2011. By late summer, analysts' estimates of a rise in global container trades of 10 per cent in 2011 had been cut back to between seven and eight per cent.

He quoted Neil Dekker, Editor of Drewry Maritime Research, as saying:

We see no major improvement in the global supply/demand balance for the next five years, and the two million TEU that has been ordered since June last year, 80 per cent of which are for ships of at least 8,000 TEU, has already done the damage.

Fate lends a hand

Now, perhaps, a twist of fate intervened. An affiliated company to the A.P. Moller – Maersk Group is Danske Bank, historically one of the largest banks in Denmark. The connection between Danske Bank and Maersk goes back to the 1920s. Following a business scandal, the bank, at that time called Den Danske Landmandsbank, had collapsed in 1922–1923 and the Danish government stepped in to act as guarantors over a five-year period for all legitimate claims on the bank but when, in 1928, the government put forward a proposal to continue the running of the bank on a share capital of DKK 50 million to be supplied by the government alone, A. P. Møller criticised the scheme sharply, since he feared it would become permanent.[24]

The Minister for Trade at that time asked A. P. Møller to become Chairman of the bank, which he led until 1952. To support its restructuring, A. P. Møller and the Maersk shipping companies took some shareholding and, by 2003, the Maersk Group owned around 20 per cent of the bank. Between 1952 and 1989, Maersk did not have a representative on the Board of the bank until Jess Søderberg became a member, remaining until 1999. Eivind Kolding took a place on the Board from March 2001, acted as Deputy Chairman from 1 July 2003 and became Chairman on 27 March 2011.

Danske Bank's Managing Director, Peter Straarup, was due to retire in mid-February 2012. As Chairman of the bank, Eivind Kolding headed the search for his replacement until at a certain point the rest of the Board decided to take a closer look at Kolding himself as a potential candidate. On 19 December 2011, a press release announced that Eivind Kolding would take over the role from 15 February 2012 and that with effect from 16 January, Søren Skou, a Partner in A.P. Moller – Maersk since 2008 and

Figure 12.7 Maersk Line CEO Søren Skou began his career in shipping with Maersk Line in 1983. From 2001 until 2012 he was the CEO of Maersk Tankers and in that role was also part of the A.P. Moller – Maersk leadership team, a role he retains.

head of Maersk Tankers since 2001, would take over the role of CEO of Maersk Line. Today, the A.P. Moller – Maersk Chief Financial Officer, Trond Westlie, is the Group's representative on the Board of Danske Bank.

Søren Skou, who worked with Jørgen Engell on the initial analyses for the 1999 purchase of Safmarine, had grown up in the liner business between 1983 and 1996. Assistant in his early days to Knud Erik Møller-Nielsen, whom he described as 'a great thinker', he had also spent a couple of years working in Maersk Line in both New York and Beijing.

Interviewed on 21 August 2012, after he had been back in the Maersk Line business for some eight months, Søren Skou's comments were enlightening. Following the announcement,

I had about a month before I started and I spent that time really talking to as many people as I could about Maersk Line and what was going on. I had, of course, been a close bystander for quite a while, so I had a pretty good idea that there were some things in the culture that I was not going to like and at the very first meeting in the week I started, I gathered the top 50 in Maersk Line globally to have a discussion about what we were going to do. That first night, I gave an after-dinner speech and I talked only about culture. For me, that is really important. There was a famous American management thinker called Peter Drucker who had a saying, 'Culture eats strategy for breakfast' and I really believe that.[25]

Faced with another significant loss in 2011, the result of an intense price war that developed in the second half of the year, one of Søren Skou's first steps was to articulate a plan to turn that loss around. The first step was called 'Back to Black', a series of wide-ranging actions from slow steaming and super-slow steaming to ensuring that assets were both optimally and fully used or even laid up where necessary.

Maybe characteristically, Søren Skou commented on the rate war:

My analysis, which is not exactly shared by everybody in Maersk Line, is that we were a big part of the problem. Overall Maersk Line grew 11 per cent in 2011, while the market grew seven per cent. So, we were taking share big time, and were rolling out a new, really good product in Daily Maersk and I think that scared other market participants and the only weapon they had left was price.

He continued:

Maersk Line has a number of cultural strengths that are truly important and have been instrumental in bringing the company to where it is today. First and foremost is a very strong execution capability. If we decide to do something, and we are able to articulate what that thing is, we can also make it happen very, very fast. I am even more convinced now because if I look at what we have done with the Back to Black plan, I had no expectations that we would be able to execute on that as fast as we have. That ability to make it happen is really unique!

Further, we have, on an individual level, strong individual accountability, a willingness to engage in very constructive dialogue. And finally, over the recent years, we have developed quite a process orientation in the way we think about things, which is hugely important in a global networked business such as Maersk Line has developed into.

But, over the years, we have developed a culture that is much more growth and volume focused than profit focused. I am trying to drag Maersk Line back to the time where we thought this is actually a business, we have to make money, we have to create a decent return for our shareholders before we worry too much about how we can grow faster than the market.

I also believe that we have developed a certain amount of arrogance in the organisation, which comes from simply being the largest, having been successful for a long time. We think of ourselves as market leaders, but we have not been really acting as leaders. We have not been willing to lead the industry down a healthy path.

In the 1980s we were number five or six and we slowly caught up and over-took the rest but that mindset of having to beat the competition has stayed with us a long time. We never realised that we had come to the leadership point and now we have to change our mindset a bit. We have to lead the industry as opposed to beat the industry.

And on the organisational side, we had developed a lot of silo thinking and that we have to change. This is a very, very complex organisation to begin with. No matter how we draw the lines on an organogram, because of the global nature of the business, the networked nature of it, it is never going to be simple and if we do not have the right culture, it will quickly deteriorate to silo thinking and that is not helpful at all.

In selecting the global management team, we decided on three criteria:

- Focus – we want people who can focus on delivering results;
- Simplicity– we want to have people who can keep it simple; and
- Teamwork – no matter how you design the organisation, it is going to be complicated, a matrix-like organisation, so we want people who are naturally teamwork-oriented, who can rise above the formal structures and engage in a constructive manner with people in other functions.[26]

When asked how these three words – focus, simplicity, teamwork – related to the Maersk values, Søren Skou was very clear:

My reading of Mærsk Mc-Kinney Møller is that many of his achievements have been driven by an extreme degree of focus, really focusing on the results and serving the customer. He has been, more than anybody, one who has wanted to keep things simple, so I think these components are very much part of the way that I have experienced him operating with such great success over many, many years.

Talking about his plans for the future of Maersk Line, Skou was very direct:

I think what I really want to communicate in Maersk Line is that there are three goals for us: that we create an absolute return for our shareholders that is probably in the region of 10 per cent; that we create a relative return that is better than our competition; and that we grow the company with at least the market growth.

To achieve this, we have to finish the foundation, that is mainly our IT systems, global processes, organisation and culture. I don't think there is any organisation in the world that knows more about global trade than we do – we have just not figured out how to harness that knowledge and make it useful in our daily work.

We also have to optimise the network, but that is really about the whole cost side of the business. The LMB shares the view that cost leadership is the most sustainable type of competitive advantage in this industry. It means we have to get better asset turn or have less capacity relative to how many containers we load. And we have to manage for profit and that is about pricing and pricing capability. I do think we can take that significant step forward, getting better at having decision rules and understanding how our pricing impacts the market.

In that connection, the reefer market is hugely important to us, and our mindset has been that every reefer is gold, that this is a great business. But when you look at the investment, where a reefer is four to five times the cost of a dry container, plus the plugs and power on the ships, and the fuel bill for running the reefers, then the return on the reefer business is disappointing and we have to get our returns up. I think that on the reefer side, we may have to invest a little bit of market share in getting prices up, not a lot, as there is not a huge amount of excess reefer capacity out there. We have a good chance of making that business attractive again.

Box 12.7 Developments in reefers since the 1990s

In early 1992, Vagn Lehd Møller put forward a proposal to purchase 1,500 40-foot reefers to supplement the existing fleet. This order was to become the first commercial order for reefer units using CFC-free R 134a as a refrigerant, a major environmental step forward, as CFC was due to be phased out under international protocols over the coming years.

Since the mid 1990s one of Maersk Line's focus areas has been the reefer market, with plans to tailor its product to the individual customer, build up barriers to entry for competition and expand coverage to destinations including West Africa, South America, Oceania, Eastern Europe, northern Norway and others – in effect, providing global coverage.

Whether moving live lobsters under special conditions or tuna frozen to minus 60°C, and a host of products in between, from fresh strawberries, apples and kiwi-fruit, to meat, poultry and green vegetables, Maersk Line's reefers have developed to cover just about all the requirements customers have asked for. As Thomas Eskesen, Senior Director, Reefer Management, said, 'When you go to the emergent markets in, for example, Ecuador or Costa Rica, five years ago we would not have had a footprint, because it was all break-bulk. The effect of containerising has gone a lot quicker than we had anticipated.'[27] The most recent innovation has been the beginning of remote satellite tracking and monitoring of reefer equipment and its performance in essentially the same way in which a GPS operates.

Box 12.7 (cont.)

The challenge here, as with the business overall, has been to provide these services in a profitable way. With an investment of over \$1.9 billion in a reefer fleet of 105,000 FFE of reefers, each of them costing approximately four times that of building and running standard dry containers, in September 2012, Maersk Line announced a substantial price increase with effect from 1 January 2013 to bring this part of its business Back to Black.

To give an indication of the cost of putting produce in a fruit-bowl, the examples in Table 12.2 were developed with the relevant Maersk Line offices.

Table 12.2 Transport costs for fruit in your supermarket

Apples from New Zealand to Denmark		Oranges from California to Hong Kong	
Trucking, field to cold store/packing plant (estimate \$)	100	Trucking, field to cold store/packing plant (estimate \$)	200
Handling and packing (estimated \$)	200	Handling and packing (estimated \$)	300
Trucking, cold store/packing plant to port (average \$)	240	Trucking, cold store/packing plant to port (average \$)	950
2013 Ocean freight New Zealand to Denmark (actual \$)	8,900	2013 Ocean freight Los Angeles to Hong Kong (actual \$)	3,815
Destination trucking to cold store (estimated \$)	200	Destination trucking to cold store (estimated \$)	300
Total costs (\$)	9,640	Total costs (\$)	5,565
Number of cartons of apples per 40-foot reefer	1,076	Number of cartons of oranges per 40-foot reefer	960
Number of apples per carton	110	Number of oranges per carton (size 72)	72
Total apples per 40-foot reefer	118,360	Total oranges per 40-foot reefer	69,120
Estimated total costs per apple (US cents)	0.08	Estimated total costs per orange (US cents)	0.08

Source: Maersk Line

And the last battle is customer care, and that is about doing what we already do really well, keep repeating that and taking care of our customers. We have great customer satisfaction scores so we are serving our customers well. We have to get even better at that.[28]

Tim Harris, formerly CEO of P&O, has maintained an abiding interest in the industry. Speculating on the changes in Maersk Line in recent years, he said:

Box 12.8 Customer care

By the end of 2012, the Customer Care process had been rolled out to offices accounting for about 40 per cent of Maersk Line's global volumes.

The concept is focused on making shipping as easy as possible for the customer. That means providing the customer with a dedicated point of contact for all service-related matters and providing tools and processes that allow proactive handling of issues and exceptions. Customer service needs to be able to reach out with a solution instead of waiting for the customer to call with an issue.

As Tom Sproat, Senior Vice President of Customer Services and Customer Care in North America, outlined, 'we are unleashing the knowledge and motivation of our colleagues to focus their energies on the customer. There is nothing more satisfying than seeing the pride on a colleague's face after they receive a compliment from a customer.'

A survey at the end of 2012 of some 4,000 customers measured the ease of customer interaction and resolution. On a five-point scale where 1 represents the lowest effort and hence the best score, Maersk Line's performance achieved an improvement from 2.83 to 2.32, putting Maersk Line in the top quartile of business-to-business companies (the threshold is 2.48).

The process was enhanced early in 2013 with the launch of the Customer Charter. The charter articulates the minimum service standard that all Maersk Line's customers will experience. The measurements are global and aspirational; they cover:

- booking turn-time, within two hours;
- documentation accuracy and turn-time, within eight working hours;
- documentation amendment turn-time, within one hour;
- pre-arrival notification timeliness, 24 hours prior to ships' ETA;
- invoicing accuracy and dispute resolution within seven working days;
- access to Maersk Line's service agents, calls answered within 30 seconds;
- issue resolution, communication of planned resolution within 12 hours;
- schedule reliability, overall best in class.

A dedicated Customer Charter website is attached to MaerskLine.com and an app is available for Android, iPhone and iPad platforms so that customers are able to monitor developments. Updates are posted monthly.

This is why I am interested in Maersk Line, because when you play according to normal rules, it is a different game. In the 1990s it appeared to us [P&O] that you were playing according to a different rule book. The rule book was 'We take the money from this and we put it in that.' When you looked at Maersk Line, there were no numbers. You took a long-term view. You were very honourable, there was no dissembling, no cheating, you looked after your customers. A formidable, well-run operation but not driven by short-term returns to shareholders.

But, if you play by one rule book and you start to play by another rule book, the risk is that you will end up where I was in 1990. Return on capital is conventional. Your competitors like MSC, they don't have the same constraints. Whereas Maersk Line is increasingly putting itself into a position of transparency, talking to analysts, etc., where it is going to have to answer 'What is my shareholder return?' and that is the conundrum I was faced with.

Eastern stock markets appear to be slightly more prepared to take the ups and downs, so it may be that our Asian friends are cleverer at doing that. Western stock markets *hate* the liner business. As one analyst said to me, 'It is like poison, because the one thing that stock markets like is predictability.'[29]

The industry today is, of course, very different from the container industry of the 1990s and the business itself is substantially different, in size and complexity. Maersk Line operates in about 150 countries, many of which have developed a level of commercial and industrial sophistication that people could only dream of in the 1990s. It is a world of over 7 billion people (5.3 billion in 1990) where the global flows of raw materials, semi-finished and finished products are more than five times greater than in 1990 and where hundreds of millions of people, particularly in the developing world, have moved out of poverty into the middle class.

As such, the types of people needed to run and develop the business have also had to change. The young, Danish male of yesterday's Maersk Line is just as likely today to be a young Chinese, Indian or South American female. The training and development process today may use modern automated tools to embed basic core skills globally, but the commitment to long-term personal development remains as strong as ever. And from a management perspective, as McKinsey indicated, it is typically very difficult for large organisations to grow their management mindset at the same pace as the company, but it is also pivotal to getting it to work.

This is not to claim that the pressures on companies in the 1990s were any less, but the pressures today are perhaps more diverse. The market has a growing expectation of companies, particularly multinational companies, not just to deliver profits but also actively to demonstrate their positive contribution to, and role in, society. Financial transparency, environmental awareness and an active approach to corporate social responsibility are prerequisites for a company that aspires to be not only successful but also to be a leader in the industry in which it operates.

The challenge, as also touched on in the Epilogue, is to find the right mechanisms for the future. On the one hand, these must provide an environment where companies are prepared to continue the major investments that are needed to support the easy, efficient movement of the flow of goods around the world. On the other, they must be able to provide customers, exporters, importers and intermediaries with the reliable, frequent and low cost capabilities that they have come to expect. All parties involved might agree if the word 'stable' were added to these adjectives.

The next few years will tell if the story is coming full circle, with Søren Skou and his Maersk Line management team focusing on getting the basics of the business right on a globally consistent basis. As substantial customer input indicated during the Back to Black investigations, 'just focus on being good!', a statement not that far from 'Service, All the Way', an early Maersk Container Line aspiration.

A selection of important developments: 2005–2012

Political

- 2005 Iraq holds its first free parliamentary elections since 1958.[30]
- 2007 The European Union (EU) expands to 27 members with the admission of Romania and Bulgaria.[31]
- 2008 In response to the financial crisis, US president, George W. Bush, signs the Emergency Economic Stabilization Act, creating a US$700bn treasury fund to purchase failing bank assets.[32]
- 2008 Barack Obama is elected US president. He becomes the first African-American to be elected to this office.[33]
- 2011 The Arab Spring sees popular revolts in Tunisia, Egypt and Libya, leading to the deposition of autocratic leaders.[34] Protests occur in Bahrain and civil war ensues in Syria.[35]
- 2012 Following the previous year's nuclear power plant disaster at Fukushima, Japan approves a plan to phase out nuclear power in the long run.[36] Germany makes a similar decision in 2011, following the accident.[37]

Economic

- 2005 The World Customs Organization (WCO) adopts the Framework of Standards to Secure and Facilitate Global Trade (SAFE framework), with the objective of developing a global supply-chain standards framework.[38]
- 2005 The Multi-fibre Arrangement (MFA) – which imposes quantitative restrictions on textile imports – comes to an end.[39] China's share of global textile exports will rise from 17%[40] to 40% in 2010.[41]
- 2005 The IMF approves 100% debt relief totalling US$3.3bn under the Multilateral Debt Relief Initiative (MDRI) for 19 countries.[42]
- 2008 The collapse of Lehman Brothers leads to banking mergers to consolidate and deleverage debt and partial nationalisations of banks.[43]
- 2010 The European *sovereign debt crisis* gets underway, generating pressure on the euro. This will mark the beginning of negotiations to try to develop a longstanding rescue plan.[44]
- 2012 After 19 years of negotiations, Russia is admitted to the World Trade Organization (WTO), the last major economic power to be granted accession.[45]

Social

- Late 2000s Deaths from Acquired Immune Deficiency Syndrome (AIDS) begin to decline. Deaths decline from 2.2m in 2005 to 1.8m in 2010.[46]
- 2005 Steve Chen, Chad Hurley and Jawed Karim develop YouTube, an online video-sharing and viewing community. It will be sold to Google 18 months later for US$1.65bn.[47]

- 2009 The WTO declares the outbreak of the "swine flu" (H1N1 influenza), a pandemic.[48] This is the first infection since the Hong Kong flu of 1967–68 to receive this designation.[49]
- 2011 The world's population reaches 7bn,[50] up from just over 2.5bn in 1950.[51]
- 2011 Started in the US and spreading to many countries, the Occupy protest movement aims for a more equitable society.[52]
- 2012 The World Health Organization (WHO) classifies diesel exhaust as carcinogenic (cancer-causing).[53]
- 2012 With women participating for the first time for Saudi Arabia, Qatar and Brunei, this is the first Olympics where every nation has at least one female entrant.[54]

Technological

- 2007 The Apple iPhone is released. One of the first devices to bring Internet access, computing, a camera and mobile phone technology together in a portable device, it will be later complemented by the iPad, the first tablet computer.[55]
- 2009 The proton beam circulates for the first time in the Large Hadron Collider, the world's largest and highest-energy particle accelerator, at the European Organization for Nuclear Research (CERN) in Geneva.[56] This will allow scientists to verify the existence of the Higgs boson in 2012, also known as the *"god particle"*, a major discovery with regard to the creation of the universe.[57]
- 2011 There are an estimated 1.8 zettabytes of digital data (created and replicated) in the world. This is expected to grow to 7.9 zettabytes by 2015.[58]
- 2012 Capable of selectively soaking up carbon dioxide from the atmosphere, the chemical compound NOTT-202 is developed.[59]

Legal

- 2005 The Kyoto Protocol – adopted in 1997 by parties of the United Nations Framework Convention on Climate Change – enters into force.[60]
- 2009 The first trial at the International Criminal Court (ICC) is held.[61]

Environmental

- 2006 The National Aeronautics and Space Administration (NASA) finds Earth's overall temperature has reached its highest level in 12,000 years.[62]
- 2007 Arctic sea-ice cover falls to a record low of 4.14m sq km, equivalent to an area the size of five UKs. For the first time in recorded history, the Northwest Passage becomes open to ships without icebreakers.[63]
- 2011 A tsunami follows a magnitude-9.0 earthquake in Japan, killing more than 15,000 people and triggering the worst nuclear disaster since Chernobyl.[64]

2010

Merchandise trade by country

Global population: 6.9bn

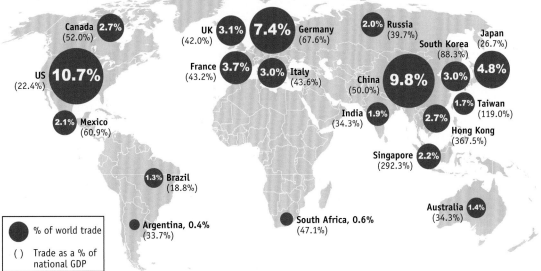

Canada 2.7% (52.0%)

UK 3.1% (42.0%) 7.4% Germany (67.6%)

Russia 2.0% (39.7%)

Japan (26.7%)

France 3.7% (43.2%) 3.0% Italy (43.6%)

South Korea (88.3%) 3.0%

4.8%

US 10.7% (22.4%)

China 9.8% (50.0%)

Taiwan 1.7% (119.0%)

India 1.9% (34.3%)

Hong Kong 2.7% (367.5%)

Mexico 2.1% (60.9%)

Singapore 2.2% (292.3%)

Brazil 1.3% (18.8%)

Australia 1.4% (34.3%)

Argentina, 0.4% (33.7%)

South Africa, 0.6% (47.1%)

● % of world trade

( ) Trade as a % of national GDP

Note. The map is based on January 2013 boundaries. Trade is based on merchandise exports and imports.
Sources: The Economist Intelligence Unit (EIU) calculations using trade data from IMF, *Direction of Trade Statistics* (via Haver Analytics) and GDP data from EIU. Population data from UN (via Haver Analytics).

World merchandise exports

US$ trn (at 2005 prices)

0.4	0.6	0.8	1.2	1.8	2.3	3.0	3.3	4.4	5.8	8.2	10.4	12.4
1950	1955	1960	1965	1970	1975	1980	1985	1990	1995	2000	2005	2010

Note. World exports have been rebased to 2005 constant prices using world export volumes from the World Trade Organization (WTO).
Source: EIU calculations using WTO data.

World exports of selected commodities

US$ bn (at 2005 prices)

■ Fruit, nuts and vegetables ■ Meat and fish ■ Dairy products ■ Computers and televisions
■ Motor vehicles ■ Clothing ■ Footwear

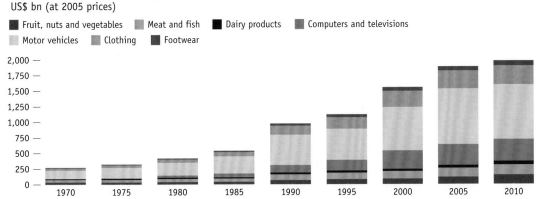

Note. In order to compare commodities over time, the EIU has made a number of judgment calls on category groupings, as there have been three revisions in the way that UN commodity data are classified. The data have also been rebased to 2005 constant prices using world export prices from the WTO. The motor vehicles category refers to road motor vehicles, including cycles, trailers, and parts and accessories; clothing includes headgear, excludes travel goods and handbags.
Source: EIU estimates using UN Comtrade, *DESA/UNSD* and WTO data.

Epilogue

> *There was not much new technology involved in the idea of moving a truck body off its wheels and onto a cargo vessel ... but ... without it, the tremendous expansion of world trade in the last 40 years – the fastest growth in any major economic activity ever recorded, could not possibly have taken place.*
>
> Peter Drucker[1]

Putting the economic development into perspective

In 1950, when one of the authors travelled as a young child by a British Overseas Aircraft Corporation flight (BOAC, the precursor to today's British Airways) from England to Jakarta in Indonesia, it took about five days to get there and was seen as a rare privilege. Flying in a four-engined, piston-driven Lockheed Constellation, known familiarly as the 'flying banana' because of its shape, the flights took place mainly during daylight hours, as little radar and few navigational aids existed at the time. Today, such travel is commonplace. Bali, in Indonesia, is a major tourist holiday resort for people from all over the world and flights to New Zealand from Europe, about as far as one can travel, take only 24 hours.

Maersk Line had been serving Indonesia regularly since 1929, and as part of expanding the liner network in Southeast Asia in the 1950s, Harrisons and Crossfield were appointed as agents in 1953. The liner services of the early 1950s, like the flights, were a very different story from those of 2013. Then, Maersk Line's ships, scheduled to arrive on a certain day rather than at a certain hour, berthed at quays in or near the city centre near the all-important infrastructure of roads and railways, rather than at terminals located far away, as today. The ships often stayed in port for days rather than hours, allowing time for gangs of longshoremen to unload or load the cargo, which consisted of many small boxes, bales and drums, rather than today's many large containers. It was a different world and, just as in the skies, the revolution in sea transport has changed the way we look at and live in a globalised world.

Similarly, since 1950, the world's import and export movements of merchandise have developed, at constant 2005 prices, from about

$400 billion to over $12 trillion. US merchandise imports and exports in 1950 accounted for about 19 per cent of world merchandise movements and totalled $19.4 billion. Despite the United States now accounting for only about 10 per cent of world merchandise movements, these are over 160 times greater than in 1950 at current market prices.

The UK, which in 1950 was the world's second-largest economy, representing about 13 per cent of such movements, was down to sixth place at 3 per cent by 2010, eclipsed by France (3.7 per cent), Japan (4.8 per cent), Germany (7.4 per cent) and China (9.8 per cent). Somewhere between 2014 and 2015, the Economist Intelligence Unit expects China to surge past the United States as world movements of merchandise exports exceed $15 trillion at 2005 prices. Meanwhile, countries such as Brazil, South Africa, Russia, India, Turkey and Indonesia have grown rapidly, and collectively are expected to account for at least 8 per cent of merchandise movements by 2015.

Economic development is generated by the sustained, concerted actions of policy-makers and communities promoting improved standards of living and economic health in a specific area, driving quantitative and qualitative changes in an economy. It covers a wide range of activities, including the development of human capital, critical infrastructure, competitiveness and environmental sustainability.

In this final chapter we will look at some of these developments, and at statements from a range of authorities that comment on current and possible future developments. We will also attempt to draw some conclusions, among others about the state of globalisation, some possible risks and opportunities at a macro and container shipping industry level – and finally about Maersk Line.

Global challenges and opportunities

The good news, as Mauro Guillén, Professor of International Management at the Wharton School in Pennsylvania, wrote, is that

there is evidence indicating that when countries grow economically and become incorporated into the global economy, poverty rates fall ... The global economy of the late twentieth century is driven by the increasing scale of technology, the surge of cross-border collaboration of firms along the value-added chain, and the cross-border integration of information flows.[2]

In the foreword of the 2011 UNCTAD Report, the Secretary General wrote:

Maritime transport is the backbone of international trade and a key engine driving globalisation. Around 80 per cent of global trade by volume and over

70 per cent by value is carried by sea and is handled by ports worldwide; these shares are even higher in the case of most developing countries.[3]

The report quoted Clarkson Research Services' statistics, showing that in 2011, global container trades amounted to some 151 million TEUs, a growth of about 7 per cent over 2010.

The UNCTAD report also discussed other structural changes that are occurring as economic development moves forward. China's move up the manufacturing value chain is providing commercial opportunities for countries such as Vietnam, Bangladesh and Indonesia. Re-shoring (the opposite of off-shoring) of some manufacturing back to Mexico and even to parts of North America is yet another structural change, as is China's policy of promoting greater domestic consumer spending, which presupposes some rebalancing of container flows. In a different direction, a review of competition laws in the report saw the United States' Federal Maritime Commission, as well as Singapore and Japan's competition authorities, all leaving container shipping's exemption from competition law in place for the time being. Europe, of course, finally eliminated this exemption in 2008.

A 2012 paper by the UK's Institute for Public Policy Research, 'The Third Wave of Globalisation', pointed to a number of positive and negative aspects of globalisation, in that it 'has helped to lift millions out of poverty. But, particularly financial globalisation and the impact that trade has on technological change has contributed to increased levels of inequality within countries.'[4] The paper noted that 'flows of goods and services, commodities, people, remittances and portfolio and direct investments are all on the increase between countries of the global south', and 'from 2001 to 2010 ... Brazil, China, India, Indonesia, Korea, Mexico, Russia and Turkey have contributed the same additional output to world GDP as the G7 group of rich countries.'[5]

The report also quoted a McKinsey paper of 2010, which estimated that spending by the expanding global middle class will increase from $6.9 trillion to $20 trillion during the next decade and that the middle-class market in Asia is already larger than that of North America and will surpass Europe in the coming years. To illustrate the development of wealth, according to the Hurun Report on the Global Rich for 2013, there were a total of 1,453 billionaires, with Asia leading at 608 (of which 317 are Chinese), North America has 440 (408 American) and Europe has 324. South America is represented with 49, while Africa and Oceania each has 17.[6]

Indicating yet another structural shift, figures from the World Bank indicate that the value of exports from developing countries to other developing countries (south–south trades) now exceed exports to the developed world (east–west trades) and 'it is forecast that by 2050,

60 per cent of exports from advanced Asia will go to emerging Asia, thus reinforcing the move eastwards and to south–south trades'.[7] The developing countries' share of world trade has climbed from 16 per cent in 1991 to 32 per cent in 2011, accelerating recently in percentage terms due to the recession in the developed world.

The United Nations' 2013 Human Development Report went one step further. Released on 14 March 2013, the press release stated

the rise of the South is radically reshaping the world of the 21st century, with developing nations driving economic growth, lifting hundreds of millions of people from poverty, and propelling billions more into a new global middle class.[8]

And, a recent *Economist* article on emerging markets indicated that 'together the emerging market countries have more than 1,000 firms with annual sales above USD 1 billion' and, later in the same article, 'emerging market multinationals are advancing on all fronts against their Western rivals', while 'for the rich world, such emerging giants represent opportunity and growth as well as competition and disruption ... Tata Group of India employs 45,000 people in Britain ... Wanxiang, a Chinese maker of car parts, employs 6,000 in America ... Huawei bought about USD 6.6 billion worth of parts from American companies in 2011.'[9]

Is the world truly globalised?

Pankaj Ghemawat of the IESE Business School pointed out in 2011 that there is still a long way to go if globalisation is to become truly global, rather than the 'semi-globalisation' he sees today. To illustrate the point, only 2 per cent of students are at universities outside their home countries; only 3 per cent of people live outside their country of birth; foreign direct investment accounts for only 9 per cent of all fixed investments and exports are equivalent to only 20 per cent of global GDP.[10]

Michael Shermer, writing the 'Skeptic' column in *Scientific American* magazine, picked up the same point and added that 'only 10–25 per cent of economic activity is international (and most of that is regional rather than global)'. Shermer also added, drawing on Ghemawat's research, that

two countries with a common language trade 42 per cent more on average than a similar pair of countries that lack that link. Countries sharing membership in a trade bloc (e.g. NAFTA), trade 47 per cent more than otherwise similar countries that lack such shared membership. A common currency (like the euro) increases trade by 114 per cent.[11]

In recent years, characterised by major trade deficits in some parts of the world and major trade surpluses in others, a debate has developed that illustrates just how complicated trade discussions can become. A short article in the *Economist* on 19 January 2013 noted:

China was the world's biggest exporter of electronic goods in 2009, but almost 40 per cent of its USD 467 billion worth of exports was first imported. Traditional measures of trade record gross flows of goods and services between countries, not how much value a country adds in producing goods and services for export. The general trend, though stalled slightly by the recent financial crisis, has seen a decline in the domestic value added component of all exports – which suggests that markets are becoming more interdependent.[12]

Box E1 expands on this theme.

Box E1 Estimating true value-added in trade

Summary of testimony before the US–China Economics and Security Review Commission Hearing on the Evolving US–China Trade and Investment Relationship, 14 June 2012.

When an American customer buys an iPhone from Apple's online store, the phone will be shipped from China and official trade statistics will record an export by China to the United States of about $200. The product is designed in California and contains components from Japan, Korea and elsewhere, although these will not show in trade statistics. The true Chinese value-added is in the order of $10, or 5 per cent of the recorded export value.

This illustrates the likelihood that the true Chinese trade surplus with the United States is probably 40 per cent smaller than is recorded in official statistics. Because a country's gross exports embed value-added from other countries, bilateral trade balances in value-added terms can be very different from the balance in gross trade terms.

Because China is a final assembler in a large number of global supply chains, and uses components from many other countries, its trade surplus with the US and EU countries in value-added terms is 41 per cent and 49 per cent, respectively, less than when measured in gross terms. Japan's trade surpluses are 40 per cent and 31 per cent larger, respectively, in value-added terms, as Japan exports parts and components to countries throughout Asia for final assembly and re-export to the United States and EU.[13]

Pascal Lamy, Director General of the World Trade Organization at that time, made the same point in a *Financial Times* article on 25 January 2011, where he also referred to the iPhone example and quoted an Asian Development Bank Institute report that showed the phone contributed $1.9 billion to the US trade deficit with China, whereas when measured in value added, those exports would only come to $73.5 million.

He commented, 'It no longer makes sense to think of trade in terms of "them" and "us" … If we are to debate something as important as trade imbalances, we should do it on the basis of numbers that reflect reality.'[14]

Whether globalisation is advanced or not remains an open question, but these and many other possible examples of structural change, interdependency and economic integration do indicate just how dynamic a world we live and work in. They may also help to illustrate the importance of understanding some of these macro-level dynamics when planning to invest for the future, from the perspective of the shipping industry and in attempting to manage successfully a business that operates globally within it.

The immediate future?

The UNCTAD Review of Maritime Transport for 2012 listed a number of risks and concerns with respect to the short-term developments in global merchandise trade:

- The World Trade Organization (WTO) pointed to a growth rate in global merchandise trade volumes of 'below the 6 per cent average recorded over the period 1990–2008'.
- 'A report by the International Chamber of Commerce (ICC) and the International Monetary Fund (IMF) ... expected trade finance in Asia to improve and only 16 per cent [of respondents] were optimistic about trade finance in Europe.'
- 'A surge in protectionist measures ... since mid-October 2011, 124 new restrictive measures have been recorded, affecting around 1.1 per cent of G20 merchandise imports.'[15]

During the 2013 World Economic Forum, a paper entitled 'Enabling Trade, Valuing Growth Opportunities' included in its foreword the statement: 'Increasing global trade is at the heart of igniting job growth, creating efficient and competitive markets and putting the global economy on a path of stable growth.'

The paper supported the reduction of tariff barriers, but pointed out that decreasing supply chain barriers to trade would increase world GDP by six times and suggested that

the global business community needs to be innovative and put forth best practices that can be coordinated among small and medium-sized businesses as well as large multinationals. In tandem, governments need to prioritise investments and ensure collaboration across countries, benefitting consumers through lower costs and more efficient global supply chains.[16]

The supply chain barriers identified in the paper included regulatory complexity, a lack of uniform global – and frequently even regional – customs rules, the use of paper-based documentation, the involvement of multiple government agencies, poor levels of information and communications technology, and more, all leading to challenges and delays preventing small and medium-sized businesses in particular from competing in the international import or export market place. The paper pointed to Singapore, whose 'strategic initiatives to reduce barriers have made it one of the most open economies in the world, placing it at the top of the Enabling Trade Index',[17] while Brazil, for example, is listed 127th out of 183 countries in the same World Bank ranking.

The next steps?

The World Economic Forum paper suggested that initiatives from both the global business community and governments would be required to move developments forward.

From a governmental perspective, the UK's Institute for Public Policy Research report listed six international recommendations, one of which stated that

the world has so far avoided a protectionist spiral of the kind seen in the 1930s ... To breathe life into the international trade agenda, we recommend that ... above all, the World Trade Organization (WTO) should be preserved as the preeminent forum for global trade rules and negotiations on future trade liberalisation.[18]

The UNCTAD Review of Maritime Transport for 2012 also suggested that 'eight years since their official start in 2004, the World Trade Organization (WTO) negotiations on Trade Facilitation may be close to delivering what could be the early – if not the only – harvest of the Doha Round'. The review highlighted the importance of finalising the Trade Facilitation agreement, saying, 'trade facilitation is increasingly seen as a rare success story ... and one of the very few areas where an agreement is within reach'.[19]

A recent leader in the *Economist* summarised some of the opportunities being promoted and under development by governments that would have substantial macro-economic impact. The *Economist* stated:

The three big barrier-bashing opportunities are the Trans Pacific Partnership, a free trade agreement that straddles the Pacific; an Atlantic spanning free-trade deal between America and the European Union; and a true single market in services within Europe. Each of these initiatives has recently moved from the politically fanciful to the just-about plausible, with serious progress possible over the next year or two. Each in isolation would improve confidence and increase prosperity. Together, they would transform the rich world's prospects.[20]

The word 'rich' relates specifically to the theme of that article, but as these items have been discussed more prominently in the media, many other reports have indicated that the impact on the world as a whole would be no less if that word were removed. As the United Nations stated in its paper 'World Economic Situation and Prospects, 2012', when talking specifically about high youth unemployment, 'a global employment deficit of 64 million jobs needs to be eliminated'.[21]

Creating opportunities

From a business perspective, Boxes E2–E4 provide brief illustrations of the type of innovation and investment that Maersk as a global business is making, illuminating the statement by Thomas Riber Knudsen, Area Managing Director for Maersk Line in Southeast Asia and Oceania, when he said 'the biggest foreign aid one can provide, is to allow people to get a job'.[22]

The three summaries provide different examples of where the transport and supply chain industries are working to overcome economic disadvantages caused by the lack of proper infrastructure, steps that will boost local, regional and ultimately global growth. Box E2 summarises an independent analysis of the impact of a new type of ship to serve markets in Africa. As the World Economic Forum paper suggested, the potential economic benefit to sub-Saharan African countries of improving trade facilitation halfway to global best practice would be a 63 per cent increase in exports, a 55 per cent increase in imports and a GDP bump of more than 9 per cent.

Such benefits would come on top of an already improved economic situation in much of Africa, as summarised in an article in the *Financial Times* in January 2013, which quoted the World Bank's development indicators as showing that African 'gross domestic product per person has risen every year since 2000, delivering a cumulative gain of more than a third'. The article also suggested that the standard numbers probably understate Africa's advance and illustrated other indicators of development, such as the rate of infant mortality, consumption and the move of subsistence farmers to jobs involving skills and tools.[23]

An article by Ngozi Okonjo-Iweala, Nigeria's Finance Minister, in the *Economist*'s 'The World in 2013', built on these positive developments, and among her projections suggested:

As Asia's economies slow and its wages rise, Africa will become the next preferred destination for labour-intensive manufacturing of products such as garments and shoes. Its large domestic market of 1.2 billion people will serve as a further attraction for low cost, light manufacturing.[24]

Box E3 is a summary of a study of the Indian banana trade, conducted by Maersk Line's sustainability team with support from independent

Box E2 Gearing West Africa for future growth

What are the links between intelligent vessel design, a port's productivity and a country's socio-economic development? A 2012 study conducted by Copenhagen Economics looked into the wider socio-economic impact of Maersk Line's investment in 22 new vessels designed to overcome the constraints in key West African ports and found measurable benefits for the ports, shippers and the wider West African economy.

West Africa is heavily dependent on international trade to stimulate development and alleviate poverty, yet West African ports are among the least efficient and most congested in the world. Dwell times – the time between a container being discharged and leaving the port – are nearly four times longer than those of Asian ports, and transport and logistics costs are among the highest in the world.

When the costs of trade are high, imported goods remain out of reach for many consumers, and the economy remains heavily dependent on commodity exports of oil and minerals.

To overcome these challenges, investments are needed to help reduce the cost of international trade in West Africa. Carrying 4,500 TEU, Maersk Line's WAFMAX (West Africa MAX) ships are the largest to serve the region. The vessels are designed to accommodate the lower drafts in West African ports and achieve increased productivity and economies of scale on the growing trade between Asia and West Africa.

As a result, the study found that the WAFMAX vessels will contribute to reducing the time the vessels are in port, thereby lowering transport and logistics costs and enabling an increasing flow of goods in and out of the region. Some of the key findings from the impact assessment in the ports of Tema (Ghana) and Apapa (Nigeria) include:

- The WAFMAX vessels are estimated to increase port productivity by up to 12 per cent in Tema and 20 per cent in Apapa.
- As a result of the increase in port productivity, the vessels are estimated to reduce the cost of shipping, inventory and logistics by about $80 million per annum in Tema and $131 million in Apapa. This, in turn, will enable increased trade flows worth an estimated $490 million (Tema) and $760 million (Apapa).
- The CO_2 footprint of the trade between Asia and West Africa will also be reduced. For each container so moved, the CO_2 footprint will be about 30 per cent lower than containers moved on industry-average vessels. The reduced waiting time in the ports as a result of these vessels also means reduced levels of sulphur emission, a pollutant with significant health implications.

Even with these ships, challenges remain in gearing West Africa for future growth. Capacity constraints at the ports, cumbersome customs procedures, widespread corruption and poor hinterland connectivity all contribute to driving up the costs of doing

Box E2 (cont.)

business in West Africa. Continued investments and collaborative efforts are critical to support the region's economic development and to provide the basis for future prosperity and poverty alleviation.

For more information, see www.Maersk.com/sustainability.

Source: Operations Sustainability, 'MAXimising West Africa's trade potential'.

Box E3 Indian bananas

Summary of a 2011 study by Maersk Line's sustainability team and consultants from AEHR and First Line.

Bananas are the world's favourite fruit and the fourth most important food crop after rice, wheat and maize.

India is the largest producer of bananas in the world, with 28 per cent of world production. Yet less that 0.1 per cent of Indian banana production is exported, in part due to lack of proper facilities for high-quality banana production and an effective cold chain.

The study found that the emerging banana export sector in India is contributing to driving important efficiencies on the ground, leading to improved yields and better quality. The Indian banana farmers involved in the export trade, many of whom are smallholder farmers living below the poverty line, now get more bananas out of each rupee invested, making the export sector an attractive economic alternative compared to the domestic market. Furthermore, with the help of refrigerated containers from quality service providers, Indian exporters are able to send their bananas across the long distances to ports with waste levels as low as 1–2 per cent.

As a result of these efficiencies in the emerging export sector, India was able to transport 3,000 containers to nearby markets in 2010 – and the potential to grow the sector is significant. The study estimated that if a mere 5 per cent of India's current banana acreage were used for exports the annual potential would be as high as 190,000 containers, which would make India one of the biggest global banana exporters. At this level, the Indian banana export sector would create some 96,000 jobs, support over 400,000 dependents and benefit some 34,600 smallholder farmers.[25]

However, the road to unlocking India's banana export potential is long and will require significant investments up- and downstream of the value chain, as well as collaboration between farmers, exporters, transportation providers, authorities and buyers. As the world population continues to grow, reaching a projected ten billion in 2050, so will the demand for bananas. Maersk Line is committed to exploring opportunities for supporting exporters in India and elsewhere, helping them to reach their full potential and deliver high-quality bananas to buyers in regional or global markets with minimum amounts of waste.

For more information, see www.Maersk.com/sustainability.

consultants. In areas of the world such as India, where substantial infrastructure investment is still ongoing, up to half of all transported fresh foods are wasted as the cold chains are still underdeveloped and inefficient and energy consumption is unnecessarily high, all leading to economic disadvantage.

This study illustrates the size of the opportunity if, for example, Indian banana exports were able to be developed from the 2011 level of 0.1 per cent of production to just 5 per cent of production and provides figures for potential jobs that could be created in the hinterland of India.

The final example (Box E4) is an impact assessment of Maersk activities in Brazil and is both broader and deeper. Conducted by the independent advisory body Copenhagen Economics and published in February 2013, this major report looks at Maersk's activities in Brazil from a macro-economic, value-added perspective as well as the additional effect of Maersk's activities in Brazil within transport/logistics and the off-shore sector in economic, social and environmental terms.

While China and India are two of the main developing countries because of their size today, Thomas Riber Knudsen, assessing the development opportunities in his area of Southeast Asia and Oceania in June 2012, said,

Box E4 Impact assessment of Maersk in Brazil

Maersk started operating in Brazil in 1977 when Maersk Supply Service contracted anchor-handling services to Petrobras, the Brazilian oil company.

In 2012 Maersk employed some 2,300 people in Brazil. This will rise to about 3,800 in 2013, when APM Terminals' new terminal at Santos is operational. In 2011, Maersk's turnover in Brazil was $1,287 million, procurement of goods and services was $373 million and taxes paid amounted to $135 million. Accumulated investments in Brazil amounted to $6.3 billion.

In total, the value-added of Maersk's direct, indirect and induced impacts is estimated to be around $1.7 billion, or nearly 0.1 per cent of Brazilian GDP in 2011, while the employment created is estimated to be around 48,200 persons ... Measured in broad terms, Maersk's container transport activities represent around two thirds of Maersk's total turnover in Brazil.[26]

Brazilian logistics costs are high, some 15–18 per cent of GNP, due mainly to the use of trucks rather than trains or coastal shipping. Trucking costs are 3–4 times higher than coastal shipping, with higher risks of theft and damage.

Mercosul, established in 1996, provides coastal container services. This became part of Maersk in 2006 and in 2011 moved 91,000 TEU, some 23 per cent of the cabotage market in Brazil.

Maersk Line started serving Brazil in 1994. Between 2011 and 2012 Maersk Line replaced many of the ships serving this area with 16 SAMMAX (South America MAXimum) ships.

Box E4 (cont.)

These have significantly improved port productivity and have led to a reduction in CO_2 levels of up to 30 per cent.

APM Terminals started in Brazil in 2002 via a leased facility at Itajai and in 2007 took full ownership of Terminals de Contêineres do Vale do Itajai and, since 2008, Ceará Terminal Operator at the Port of Pecém. APM Terminals, with its partner, Terminal Investment Limited, is currently expanding its presence in Brazil with a combined $1 billion investment in a new terminal in the Port of Santos, the largest port in Brazil.

APM Terminals Inland Services maximises use of rail to its eight inland off-dock terminals, reducing transport costs by 20 per cent and CO_2 emissions by almost 30 per cent.

Damco started in Brazil in 2002 and provides global logistics services, including airfreight, seafreight and customs clearance services.

For more information, see www.Maersk.com/sustainability

The interesting story for me is Indonesia with 250 million people, a lot of natural resources and a domestically driven economy. What is holding Indonesia back today is infrastructure and that is where the A.P. Moller – Maersk Group has a major role to play. In ten years time, Indonesia will be one of the G10s.[27]

It is clear that, despite the risks and concerns, the opportunities for the future have never been greater and that the role of low-cost, reliable container transport as a facilitator of the development of world trade remains a cornerstone of globalisation.

The challenges

As Peter Drucker and others whom we have cited in this book have indicated, without containerisation, the substantial growth in international trade over the last 40–50 years would not have been possible. Massive investments in ships, terminals and infrastructure, coupled with automation, have created opportunities globally to move goods in a safe, environmentally sustainable, reliable and low-cost way. Some outputs from this process have been the employment of thousands of people across the global industry and the provision of jobs in industries that would have struggled to survive without such access to world markets, thus helping to lift millions out of poverty.

The ability of shipping, and container shipping in particular, to continue to act as the facilitator of global merchandise trade is dependent on its ability to attract funds from shareholders and financial institutions. That ability has been significantly weakened in recent years, as growth in container ship capacity has been compounded by below-expected growth levels in global trade.

As this story of Maersk Line and the industry's development over the last 40 years illustrates, the lack of profitability is not necessarily a new phenomenon. What is relatively new is the length of time it has taken for the countries of the developed world, in particular, to return their economies to reasonable growth rates. While a return to growth would have a positive impact on the supply and demand balance related to global merchandise trades, a less positive feature is the apparent substantial reduction in the 'multiplier' effect. This, for many years, meant that global container volumes were growing at rates twice, three times or even more, the rate of global GDP growth. Some of the recent structural changes in global trade that we have touched on appear to have reduced or even eliminated this multiplier, so it is doubtful that such growth would result in any form of a return to the container volume growth of earlier years.

Bearing in mind the lifetime of a ship is generally 20–30 years, this will be important for the short-term future as well as for the longer term. The OECD projects that 'by 2050, world freight flows will be from two to four times above their 2010 levels, driven by flows outside OECD, where flows are expected to be between two and six times higher than in 2010'.[28]

The independent analysis of ROIC in Box E5 looked at the annual accounts for 67 companies, mainly the leaders in each field. It is clear that the main container carriers have substantially underperformed when compared to the other industries that make up most of the supply chain. This is perhaps not surprising when one considers that the ocean transport costs from Asia to Europe for a flat screen TV that retails at about $700 is about $4. Similarly, the transport costs for a pair of sports shoes are about 22 cents, an iPad about 10 cents and a T-shirt about 8 cents.[29] Results from the container carriers that have as of June 2013 posted their accounts for 2012 do not show any significant improvement.

In efforts to cut costs, a number of steps have been taken independently by industry leaders and others to ameliorate the supply and demand imbalances. An internal Maersk Line analysis for 2012 indicated that slow steaming took out some 2 per cent of global container ship capacity that year. The scrapping of older (and some not so old) container ships removed another estimated 2 per cent of capacity, while idling and the laying up of some ships removed a further 3 per cent. These actions were reasonably successful in balancing supply and demand, but it is questionable whether it will be possible for 2013 and 2014 to show similar such restraint.

Box E5 Average return on invested capital (ROIC) within the container
industry, 2006–2012

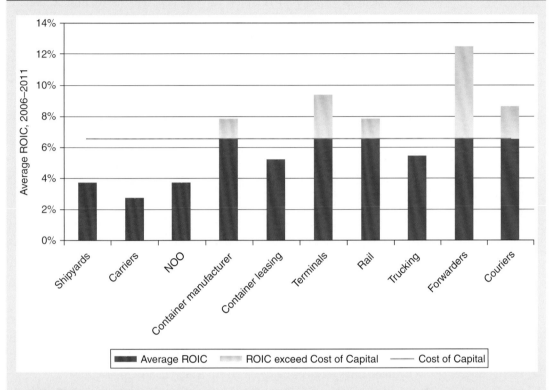

In this analysis, the cost of capital, at an average of 6.6 per cent, is for the packaging and container industry.

Source: SeaIntel Analysis

A booklet prepared for an internal Maersk Line management conference at the beginning of 2013 summarised the issues under the headline 'Creating value in global commerce – but not for shareholders' and began:

Over the past decades the shipping industry has had a great impact on the global economy by continuously offering better and cheaper transport solutions. Maersk's liner business has been right at the heart of this evolution creating value for both its customers and for global consumers. That value creation has unfortunately not led to satisfactory profits.

The booklet goes on to illustrate the size of the challenge, quoting a McKinsey study that concluded: 'The key industry challenge is how to make the industry profitable at lower levels of utilisation.'[30] A 2012 paper by the Boston Consulting Group[31] concurred: 'Carriers must apply a more disciplined mindset to their business [and] must be able to earn a profit when their utilisation rate is 70–80 per cent.'[32]

As discussed briefly in Chapter 12, the key will be to find a suitable mechanism for the future that will allow companies to continue to invest, to continue the innovation that has characterised the industry since its inception, and to provide services both at an acceptable cost and in a manner that customers will value and pay for. This has never been an easy balance to achieve, but, recalling the '500 buttons' that Lars Reno Jakobsen referred to in Chapter 12, for the sake of the industry and its ability to continue the facilitation of global trade, it must be possible. The implications for the world's continued successful economic growth and development are substantial.

Fundamental turning points

As we have progressed through this story, a number of turning points have been identified, building on a foundation of independence. Even as Maersk Line's business grew, it was on the basis of controlling its own destiny and, despite working tactically in vessel-sharing agreements for periods, rejecting offers to join consortia and thereby lose independence.

The first turning point was arguably made in about 1928, when A. P. Møller, in what must have been a momentous decision for a relatively small company in far-off Denmark, decided to put some of his ships into providing regularly scheduled liner services between North America and the Far East.

The second, over 40 years later, was the decision by Mærsk Mc-Kinney Møller to take the existing conventional and successful liner business into containers, with all the complexity, investments and challenges that that decision provided.

The third was the decision at the end of the 1980s to consider, and in due course to execute, a series of acquisitions that put Maersk Line on a growth curve that allowed it to become the largest container operator in the world.

Box E6 illustrates one way of looking at the impact of those acquisition decisions. While global merchandise exports are driven by macro-economic developments and Maersk Line's turnover is heavily dependent on freight rates that are driven by the markets in which it operates, the impact of the decisions to acquire Safmarine and Sea-Land in 1999 and P&O NedLloyd in 2005–6 can clearly be seen, supplementing the existing growth curve.

A fourth, the 2013 decision to enter into a cooperative operational agreement with two major competitors, MSC and CMA-CGM in the P3 alliance, appears as a radical departure and may be as innovative as any of those earlier decisions. The coming years will be as interesting to follow as the last 15 have been, with their acquisitions and economic turmoil. With questions around continuing market pressures, the need for scale economics and the life and/or death of differentiation, as well as the outcome of discussions with competition authorities in Europe, the United States and China, this development may prove to be both a fundamental departure from the past and the creation of a new approach to sustainable containerised liner services.

As we have touched on in this book, some fundamental components have supported the development over the 40 years covered in this book.

Little of this would have been relevant if the world had not been developing as it is economically; if the manufacturers, exporters and importers of the world had been content merely to produce for their local markets; if their customers had not been prepared to experiment and see diversity as an opportunity; if consumers were content with little or no

Box E6 World merchandise exports 1975–2012 and Maersk Line turnover

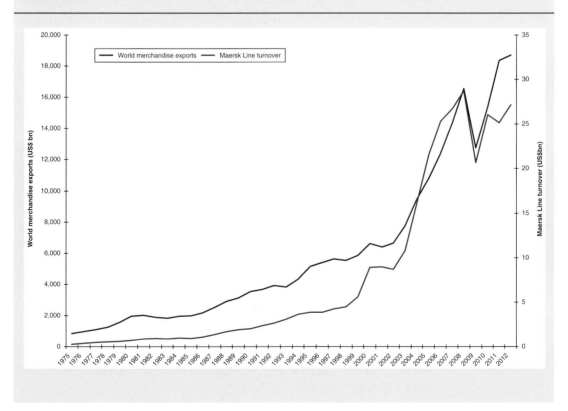

choice, rather than demanding variety and the ability to choose. Fortunately for this story, that has not been the case.

Given this growth in demand, it would be difficult to envisage this development without referring to the people involved. We have quoted some of them, both from within the Maersk Line business but also from outside. Unless you come from a shipping family or aspire to be a ship's Captain, as Tom Sproat in Maersk Line North America said, 'No one really grows up and says, "I'm going to be in shipping".' And yet, the industry, as well as Maersk Line specifically, has continuously been able to attract, retain and develop talent on a global scale, for both the ships and the offices, which has been fundamental to this development.

It is perhaps symptomatic of the impatience of Maersk people that an internal poll conducted in December 2012 showed about 40 per cent of the senior management globally believed that even more needs to be done to attract and cultivate the talent required for the business to continue to succeed.

Maersk Line's offices around the world were from the beginning a foundation on which both the global liner business as well as substantial other businesses have been, and continue to be, built. Box E4 provides an excellent example. Damco and APM Terminals are today major businesses in their own right. MCC Transport in Singapore, SeaGo Line in Copenhagen and Mercosul in Brazil are budding, relatively new regional container lines, while Safmarine continues to develop its business and its brand.

From the beginning of Maersk Container Line in 1973, the continuing commitment to quality equipment and service innovation and the aspiration to deliver a high-quality, on-time, reliable container service on a growing global scale has been fundamental to the operating philosophy on which the business has been built. This continues to be the case.

Behind all the Maersk Line-related developments has been one most important set of guiding principles, the A.P. Moller – Maersk values of constant care, humbleness, uprightness, our employees and our name. Embodied in the early organisation through the personal roles of A. P. Møller and Mærsk Mc-Kinney Møller, and subsequently articulated and embedded in the organisation for future generations, these principles will guide, support and inspire the business as it continues to develop in the future.

In 50 years, containerised shipping has grown from an innovative idea into a sophisticated system that, while invisible to the average person, can legitimately be said to have changed the world.[33]

We hope that this book has provided some insight into the role of low-cost, reliable container shipping as a major facilitator of change and development in the world.

Box E7 Container port traffic 1970, 1975, 1980

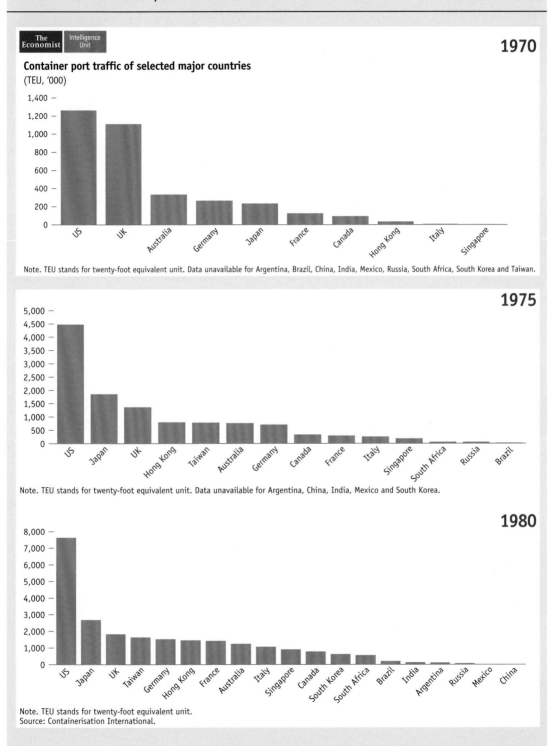

1970

The Economist Intelligence Unit

Container port traffic of selected major countries
(TEU, '000)

Note. TEU stands for twenty-foot equivalent unit. Data unavailable for Argentina, Brazil, China, India, Mexico, Russia, South Africa, South Korea and Taiwan.

1975

Note. TEU stands for twenty-foot equivalent unit. Data unavailable for Argentina, China, India, Mexico and South Korea.

1980

Note. TEU stands for twenty-foot equivalent unit.
Source: Containerisation International.

Box E8 Container port traffic 1985, 1990, 1995

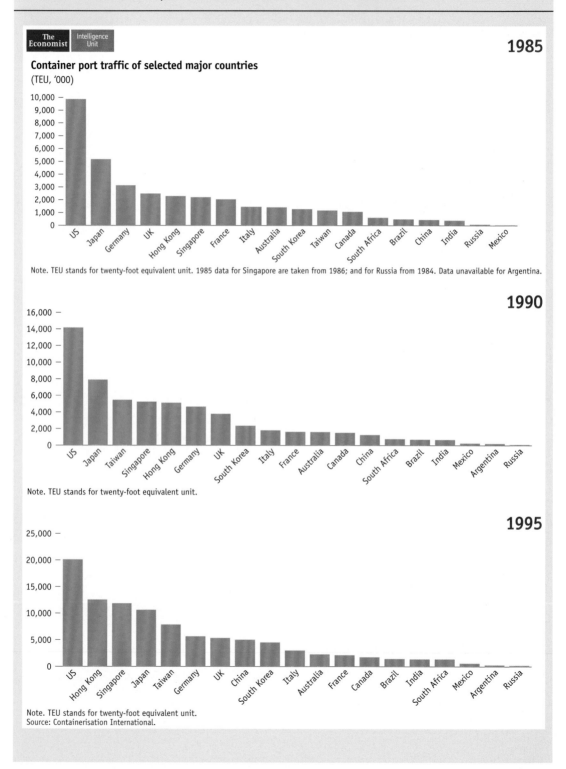

The Economist Intelligence Unit

1985

Container port traffic of selected major countries
(TEU, '000)

Note. TEU stands for twenty-foot equivalent unit. 1985 data for Singapore are taken from 1986; and for Russia from 1984. Data unavailable for Argentina.

1990

Note. TEU stands for twenty-foot equivalent unit.

1995

Note. TEU stands for twenty-foot equivalent unit.
Source: Containerisation International.

Box E9 Container port traffic 2000, 2005, 2010

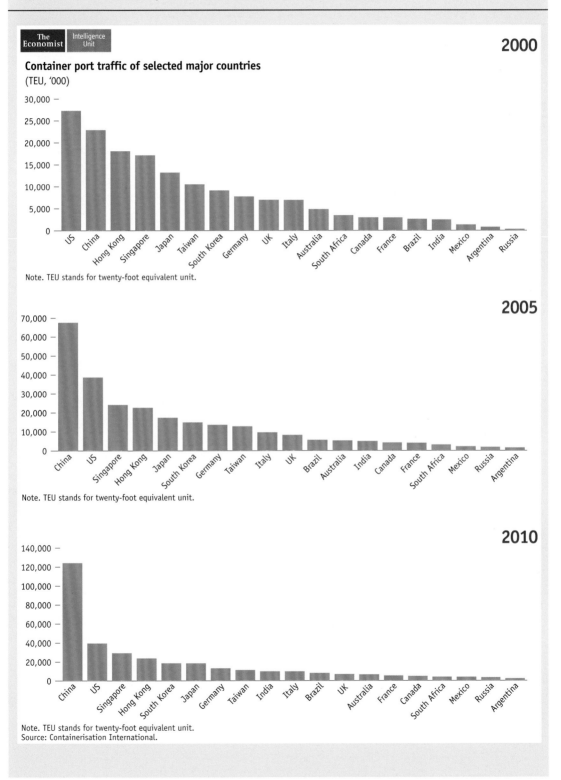

Notes and References

Prologue

1 F. Gilmore, *Brand Warriors: Corporate Leaders Share their Winning Strategies*, HarperCollins, 1999, p. 80.
2 Interview with Eivind Kolding at the Headquarters of Den Danske Bank, 7 September 2012.
3 Adolf Adrion, CEO of Hapag Lloyd, quoted in S. Ignarski, ed., *The Box, An Anthology Celebrating 50 Years of Containerisation*, The TT Club, 1996, p. 224.
4 M. Wendelboe Hansen, M. Greve, H. Schaumburg-Müller, *Container Shipping & Economic Development*, Copenhagen Business School Press, 2007, p. 10.

Chapter 1

1 O. Hornby, *'With Constant Care ...': A. P. Møller: Shipowner 1876–1965*, Schultz, 1988, pp. 110–18.
2 M. Stopford, *Maritime Economics*, 3rd edition, Routledge, 2009.
3 Stopford, p. 31.
4 For example, A. Riis, *Selandia: The World's First Oceangoing Diesel Vessel*, Nautilus Forlag, 2012; and F. A. Rasmussen, B. V. Rønne and H. C. Johansen, *Damp og diesel: Dansk søfarts historie 1920–1960*, Gyldendal, 2000.
5 A. A. Møller, H. Dethlefsen and H. C. Johansen, *Sejl og damp: Dansk søfarts historie 1870–1920*, Gyldendal, 1998.
6 Hornby, pp. 53–7.
7 Hornby, p. 286.
8 Hornby, p. 86.
9 G. Jones and J. Zeitlin, *The Oxford Handbook of Business History*, Oxford University Press, 2007.
10 Stopford, p. 37.
11 V. Rolls, *The Far Eastern Freight Conference 1879–2004*, Conference Administration Services, 2005, p. 28.
12 Hornby, p. 224.
13 M. Hahn-Pedersen, *A. P. Møller and the Danish Oil*, Schultz, 1999.
14 H. Morgen, *Dansk sukker i Østafrika*, Erhvervshistorisk Årbog, 2010.
15 *Mærsk Post*, February 2012.
16 www.maersk.com/Aboutus/Pages/OurValues.aspx (accessed 7 January 2013).
17 See http://investor.maersk.com/.
18 P. Boje, Ledere, *ledelse og organisation 1870–1972: Dansk industri efter 1870, Bind 5*, Odense Universitetsforlag, 1997, p. 28.
19 *Mærsk Post*, February 2012.

Chapter 2

1 M. Levinson, *The Box: How the Shipping Container Made the World Smaller and the World Economy Bigger*, Princeton University Press, 2006.

2 Levinson.

3 Levinson.

4 McKinsey & Co., *Containerization: Its Trends, Significance and Implications*, Report for the British Transport Docks Board, 1966.

5 www.abports.co.uk/Home/Company_History/ (accessed 7 January 2013).

6 F. Broeze, *The Globalisation of the Oceans: Containerisation from the 1950s to the Present*, International Maritime Economic History Association, 2002.

7 O. Hornby, '*With Constant Care ...' A. P. Møller: Shipowner 1876–1965*, Schultz, 1988, pp. 110–18.

8 Broeze, p. 60.

9 *Mærsk Post*, January 1971.

10 Interviews with Flemming Jacobs, 31 July 2012 and Poul Rasmussen, 25 September 2012.

11 Broeze, p. 50.

12 O. E. Allen, *The Box, An Anthology Celebrating 50 Years of Containerisation*, The TT Club, 1996, p. 224.

13 A.P. Moller – Maersk A/S, Annual Report 2012.

14 T. Larsen and F. Mortensen, *Mærsk Mc-Kinney Møller: The Danish Shipping Magnate*, Gyldendal Business, 2011, pp. 270–7.

Economist Intelligence Unit

15 United Nations: www.un.org/en/members/growth.shtml (accessed on 26 February 2013).

16 J. Young and J. Kent, *International relations since 1945* (Oxford: Oxford University Press, 2006): http://fdslive.oup.com/www.oup.com/orc/resources/politics/intro/young_kent/01student/timeline/timeline.pdf (accessed on 13 July 2012).

17 *The New York Times*: http://www.nytimes.com/1988/01/14/world/taiwan-at-a-glance.html (accessed on 13 July 2012).

18 History Today: www.historytoday.com/richard-cavendish/chinese-invade-tibet (accessed on 13 July 2012).

19 BBC: http://news.bbc.co.uk/onthisday/hi/dates/stories/january/26/newsid_3475000/3475569.stm (accessed on 15 July 2012).

20 US Department of State, Office of the Historian: http://history.state.gov/milestones/1945-1952/ANZUS (accessed on 13 July 2012).

21 Foreign Affairs: www.foreignaffairs.com/articles/66150/george-r-packard/the-united-states-japan-security-treaty-at-50 (accessed on 13 July 2012).

22 *Encyclopaedia Britannica*: www.britannica.com/EBchecked/topic/556523/Southeast-Asia-Treaty-Organization-SEATO (accessed on 15 July 2012).

23 *The Economist*: http://www.economist.com/blogs/freeexchange/2012/07/economic-history (accessed on 15 July 2012).

24 *The Economist*: http://www.economist.com/blogs/freeexchange/2012/07/economic-history (accessed on 15 July 2012).

25 G. Jones, *Multinationals and Global Capitalism: From the Nineteenth to the Twenty-First Century* (Oxford University Press, 2005). Excerpt available on Harvard Business School Working Knowledge: http://hbswk.hbs.edu/item/4961.html (accessed on 15 July 2012).

26 World Trade Organization. *World Trade Report 2008* (Geneva), p.22: http://www.wto.org/english/res_e/booksp_e/anrep_e/world_trade_report08_e.pdf (accessed on 14 July 2012).

27 World Trade Organization. *World Trade Report 2008* (Geneva), p. 15: http://www.wto.org/english/res_e/booksp_e/anrep_e/world_trade_report08_e.pdf (accessed on 14 July 2012).

28 Pearson Education: http://wps.pearsoncustom.com/wps/media/objects/2427/2486120/chap_assets/documents/doc34_3.html (accessed on 13 July 2012).

29 World Trade Organization. *World Trade Report 2008* (Geneva), p. 22: http://www.wto.org/english/res_e/booksp_e/anrep_e/world_trade_report08_e.pdf (accessed on 14 July 2012).

30 European Union: http://europa.eu/legislation_summaries/institutional_affairs/treaties/treaties_ecsc_en.htm (accessed on 15 July 2012).

31 United Nations: www.un.org/esa/population/publications/WUP2005/2005wup.htm (accessed on 17 July 2012).

32 M. Toossi, 'A century of change: the U.S. labor force, 1950–2050', *Monthly Labor Review* (May 2002): http://www.bls.gov/opub/mlr/2002/05/art2full.pdf (accessed on 17 July 2012).

33 *The World Book Encyclopaedia* (Chicago: World Book Inc., 2003), p. 119.

34 World Bank: http://siteresources.worldbank.org/INTPRH/Resources/GlobalFamilyPlanningRevolution.pdf (accessed on 15 July 2012).

35 BBC: http://news.bbc.co.uk/onthisday/hi/dates/stories/may/2/newsid_2480000/2480339.stm (accessed on 15 July 2012).

36 International Civil Aviation Organization: http://www.icao.int/safety/Documents/ICAO_State-of-Global-Safety_web_EN.pdf (accessed on 13 July 2012).

37 BBC: http://news.bbc.co.uk/onthisday/hi/dates/stories/may/29/newsid_2492000/2492683.stm (accessed on 14 July 2012).

38 *TIME*: http://time.com/time/magazine/article/0,9171,1893507,00.html (accessed on 13 July 2012).

39 Pacific Sea Air Cargo Services: www.psac.com.au/history-container-shipping/ (accessed on 17 July 2012).

40 R. Weston, '*UNIVAC: The Paul Revere of the Computer Revolution*', Virginia Tech: http://ei.cs.vt.edu/~history/UNIVAC.Weston.html (accessed on 17 July 2012).

41 Tetra Pak: http://www.tetrapak.com/about_tetra_pak/the_company/history/Pages/default.aspx (accessed on 17 July 2012).

42 Wessels Living History Farm: www.livinghistoryfarm.org/farminginthe50s/pests_01.html (accessed on 17 July 2012).

43 Science News: www.sciencenews.org/view/feature/id/339023/title/90th_Anniversary_Issue_Science_News_marks_a_milestone (accessed on 13 July 2012).

44 Gawker: http://gawker.com/5438083/this-day-in-history-the-first-color-television-broadcast (accessed on 14 July 2012).

45 United Nations: http://untreaty.un.org/ilc/texts/instruments/english/commentaries/7_1_1950.pdf (accessed on 14 July 2012).

46 World Customs Organization: http://www.wcoomd.org/home_about_us_auhistory.htm (accessed on 14 July 2012).

47 United Nations: http://www.un.org/womenwatch/directory/convention_political_rights_of_women_10741.htm (accessed on 13 July 2012).

48 International Institute of Refrigeration: //www.iifiir.org/medias/medias.aspx?INSTANCE = exploitation&PORTAL_ID = portal_model_instance__iif_mission_en.xml&SYNCMENU = MISSION&SETLANGUAGE = EN (accessed on 13 July 2012).

49 World Meteorological Organization: http://www.wmo.int/pages/about/index_en. html (accessed on 14 July 2012).

50 A. J. Haagen-Smit, 'A Lesson from the Smog Capital of the World', *Proceedings of the National Academy of Sciences*, vol. 67, No. 2 (October 1970), 887–897: –http:// www.arb.ca.gov/research/hsawards/a_lesson_from_the_smog_capital_of_world. pdf (accessed on 14 July 2012).

51 CIA World Factbook: https://www.cia.gov/library/publications/the-world-factbook/fields/2088.html (accessed on 14 July 2012).

52 BBC: http://news.bbc.co.uk/onthisday/hi/dates/stories/may/9/newsid_2519000/ 2519979.stm (accessed on 13 July 2012).

53 BBC: http://news.bbc.co.uk/onthisday/hi/dates/stories/may/9/newsid_2519000/ 2519979.stm (accessed on 13 July 2012).

54 The Jakarta Post: http://www.thejakartapost.com/news/2011/04/29/the-1955-bandung-conference-and-its-present-significance.html (accessed on 13 July 2012).

55 BBC: http://news.bbc.co.uk/onthisday/hi/dates/stories/july/26/newsid_2701000/ 2701603.stm (accessed on 13 July 2012).

56 BBC: http://news.bbc.co.uk/1/hi/world/americas/country_profiles/1231075.stm (accessed on 14 July 2012).

57 World Trade Organization, *World Trade Report 2008* (Geneva), p. 22: http://www. wto.org/english/res_e/booksp_e/anrep_e/world_trade_report08_e.pdf (accessed on 14 July 2012).

58 US Department of State, Office of the Historian: http://history.state.gov/ milestones/1953-1960/BerlinCrises (accessed on 14 July 2012).

59 J. Young and J. Kent, *International relations since 1945* (Oxford: Oxford University Press, 2006): http://www.oup.com/uk/orc/bin/9780198781646/01/student/ timeline/index.html (accessed on 14 July 2012).

60 Food and Agriculture Organization of the United Nations: http://www.fao.org/ docrep/x4400e/x4400e09.htm (accessed on 14 July 2012).

61 Food and Agriculture Organization of the United Nations: http://www.fao.org/ docrep/x4400e/x4400e09.htm (accessed on 14 July 2012).

62 J-P. Rodrigue, *The Geography of Transport Systems* (Routledge, 2009): http://people. hofstra.edu/geotrans/eng/ch4en/appl4en/ch4a2en.html (accessed on 14 July 2012).

63 Food and Agriculture Organization of the United Nations: http://www.fao.org/ docrep/x4400e/x4400e09.htm (accessed on 14 July 2012).

64 L. Bruno and S. Tenold, 'The basis for South Korea's ascent in the shipbuilding industry, 1970–90' (draft version; Norwegian School of Economics and Business Administration, 2010): http://www.ebha.org/ebha2010/code/media_168359_en. pdf (accessed on 13 July 2012).

65 BBC: http://news.bbc.co.uk/1/shared/spl/hi/asia_pac/02/china_party_congress/ china_ruling_party/key_people_events/html/great_leap_forward.stm (accessed on 14 July 2012).

66 Bank for International Settlements: http://www.bis.org/about/bretton_woods.htm (accessed on 14 July 2012).

67 World Trade Organization, *World Trade Report 2008* (Geneva), p.22: http://www. wto.org/english/res_e/booksp_e/anrep_e/world_trade_report08_e.pdf (accessed on 14 July 2012).

68 University of Leiden: http://www.let.leidenuniv.nl/history/migration/chapter8.html (accessed on 15 July 2012).

69 G. Mankiw and D. Weil, 'The baby boom, the baby bust, and the housing market', *Regional Science and Urban Economics*, vol. 19 (1989), 235–258: http://economics.harvard.edu/files/faculty/40_Baby_Boom.pdf (accessed on 15 July 2012).

70 B. Guyer, M. A. Freedman, D. M. Strobino, E. J. Sondik, 'Annual summary of vital statistics: trends in the health of Americans during the 20th century', *Pediatrics*, 106 (6) (December 2000), 1307–17: http://www.ncbi.nlm.nih.gov/pubmed/11099582 (accessed on 15 July 2012).

71 *Wired*: http://www.wired.com/thisdayintech/2010/10/1004first-transatlantic-jet-service-boac/ (accessed on 15 July 2012).

72 *Quality Digest*: http://www.qualitydigest.com/july03/columnists/smarash.shtml (accessed on 15 July 2012).

73 World Trade Organization, *World Trade Report 2008* (Geneva), p. 22: http://www.wto.org/english/res_e/booksp_e/anrep_e/world_trade_report08_e.pdf (accessed on 14 July 2012).

74 J-P. Rodrigue, *The Geography of Transport Systems* (Routledge, 2009): http://people.hofstra.edu/geotrans/eng/ch2en/conc2en/global_submarine_cable_network.html (accessed on 14 July 2012).

75 Thermo King, 20/40: http://www.thermoking.com/aboutus/tradepubs/2040/2040summer06.pdf (accessed on 15 July 2012).

76 BBC: http://news.bbc.co.uk/onthisday/hi/dates/stories/october/4/newsid_2685000/2685115.stm (accessed on 16 July 2012).

77 Container Transportation: http://www.container-transportation.com/malcolm-mclean.html (accessed on 16 July 2012).

78 The Nobel Prize: http://www.nobelprize.org/educational/physics/integrated_circuit/history/ (accessed on 16 July 2012).

79 Bloomberg: http://www.businessweek.com/2001/01_10/b3722003.htm (accessed on 16 July 2012).

80 International Maritime Organization: http://www.imo.org/KnowledgeCentre/ReferencesAndArchives/Pages/TheOriginsOfIMO.aspx#7c (accessed on 16 July 2012).

81 International Maritime Organization: http://www.imo.org/KnowledgeCentre/ReferencesAndArchives/Pages/TheOriginsOfIMO.aspx#7c (accessed on 16 July 2012).

82 *Wired*: http://www.wired.com/thisdayintech/2010/07/0729eisenhower-signs-nasa-act/ (accessed on 15 July 2012).

83 Food and Agriculture Organization of the United Nations: http://www.fao.org/docrep/x4400e/x4400e09.htm (accessed on 16 July 2012).

84 United Nations: http://untreaty.un.org/cod/diplomaticconferences/lawofthesea-1958/lawofthesea-1958.html (accessed on 15 July 2012).

85 Scripps Institution of Oceanography, UC San Diego: http://scrippsco2.ucsd.edu/sub_program_history/charles_david_keeling_biography.html (accessed on 15 July 2012).

86 BBC: http://news.bbc.co.uk/onthisday/hi/dates/stories/june/26/newsid_2988000/2988148.stm (accessed on 14 July 2012).

87 J. Young and J. Kent, *International relations since 1945* (Oxford: Oxford University Press, 2006): http://fdslive.oup.com/www.oup.com/orc/resources/politics/intro/young_kent/01student/timeline/timeline.pdf (accessed on 15 July 2012).

88 J. Young and J. Kent, *International relations since 1945* (Oxford: Oxford University Press, 2006): http://fdslive.oup.com/www.oup.com/orc/resources/politics/intro/young_kent/01student/timeline/timeline.pdf (accessed on 15 July 2012).

89 *Encyclopaedia Britannica*: http://www.britannica.com/EBchecked/topic/421810/Nuclear-Test-Ban- (accessed on 15 July 2012).

90 BBC: http://news.bbc.co.uk/onthisday/hi/dates/stories/may/25/newsid_2502000/2502771.stm (accessed on 16 July 2012).

91 J. Young and J. Kent, *International relations since 1945* (Oxford: Oxford University Press, 2006): http://fdslive.oup.com/www.oup.com/orc/resources/politics/intro/young_kent/01student/timeline/timeline.pdf (accessed on 16 July 2012).

92 S. Radelet, J. Sachs, and J. Lee, *Economic Growth in Asia* (Harvard Center for International Development, 1997): http://www.cid.harvard.edu/archive/hiid/papers/ecgasia.pdf (accessed on 16 July 2012).

93 World Trade Organization, *World Trade Report 2008* (Geneva), p.22: http://www.wto.org/english/res_e/booksp_e/anrep_e/world_trade_report08_e.pdf (accessed on 14 July 2012).

94 World Trade Organization, *World Trade Report 2008* (Geneva), p.22: http://www.wto.org/english/res_e/booksp_e/anrep_e/world_trade_report08_e.pdf (accessed on 14 July 2012).

95 World Trade Organization, *World Trade Report 2008* (Geneva), p.22: http://www.wto.org/english/res_e/booksp_e/anrep_e/world_trade_report08_e.pdf (accessed on 14 July 2012).

96 Bank for International Settlements: http://www.bis.org/about/history.htm (accessed on 16 July 2012).

97 United Nations Conference on Trade and Development: http://unctad.org/en/Pages/About%20UNCTAD/A-Brief-History-of-UNCTAD.aspx (accessed on 18 July 2012).

98 The Group of 77: http://www.g77.org/doc/ (accessed on 18 July 2012).

99 BBC: http://news.bbc.co.uk/1/hi/health/250337.stm (accessed on 18 July 2012).

100 Victorian Women's Trust: http://www.vwt.org.au/store/files/1322533344.pdf (accessed on 18 July 2012).

101 United Nations Children's Fund (UNICEF): http://www.unicef.org/sowc96/1960s.htm (accessed on 18 July 2012).

102 BBC: http://news.bbc.co.uk/onthisday/hi/dates/stories/june/12/newsid_3006000/3006437.stm (accessed on 18 July 2012).

103 US History: http://www.ushistory.org/us/56e.asp (accessed on 16 July 2012).

104 World Trade Organization, *World Trade Report 2008* (Geneva), p.22: http://www.wto.org/english/res_e/booksp_e/anrep_e/world_trade_report08_e.pdf (accessed on 14 July 2012).

105 *Science News*: www.sciencenews.org/view/feature/id/339023/title/90th_Anniversary_Issue_Science_News_marks_a_milestone (accessed on 19 July 2012).

106 World Shipping Council: http://www.worldshipping.org/about-the-industry/history-of-containerization/the-birth-of-intermodalism (accessed on 19 July 2012).

107 *Science News*: www.sciencenews.org/view/feature/id/339023/title/90th_Anniversary_Issue_Science_News_marks_a_milestone (accessed on 19 July 2012).

108 *Science News*: www.sciencenews.org/view/feature/id/339023/title/90th_Anniversary_Issue_Science_News_marks_a_milestone (accessed on 19 July 2012).

109 World Trade Organization, *World Trade Report 2008* (Geneva), p. 22: http://www.wto.org/english/res_e/booksp_e/anrep_e/world_trade_report08_e.pdf (accessed on 14 July 2012).

110 *Wired*: http://www.wired.com/thisdayintech/2010/07/0716mont-blanc-tunnel-opens/ (accessed on 19 July 2012).

111 H.M. Gladney, 'Perspectives on trustworthy information', *Digital Document Quarterly*, vol. 7, no. 3 (2008): http://www.hgladney.com/ddq_7_3.htm#_ednref17 (accessed on 19 July 2012).

112 CBC News: http://www.cbc.ca/news/canada/north/story/2010/07/01/north-first-nations-right-to-vote-60-years.html (accessed on 19 July 2012).

113 World Trade Organization: www.wto.org/english/thewto_e/coher_e/wto_codex_e.htm (accessed on 19 July 2012).

114 European Commission: http://ec.europa.eu/environment/pdf/50year/web/poster50_en.pdf (accessed on 19 July 2012).

115 WWF: http://www.wwf.org.uk/what_we_do/about_us/history/ (accessed on 19 July 2012).

116 PBS: http://www.pbs.org/wgbh/aso/databank/entries/dt62si.html (accessed on 19 July 2012).

Chapter 3

1 McKinsey & Company, Inc., *Discussion draft of a report 'Strengthening Corporate Return on Assets'*, 18 November 1968, Box 158006, A.P. Moller – Maersk archives.

2 O. Hornby, *'With Constant Care ...' A. P. Møller: Shipowner 1876–1965*, Schultz, 1988, p. 249.

3 McKinsey & Company Inc., *'A. P. Møller Organization Plan'*, July 1970, Box 112210.

4 P. Boje, Ledere, *Ledelse og organisation 1870–1972: Dansk industri efter 1870*, Bind 5, Odense Universitetsforlag, 1997.

5 Interview with Ib Kruse, 30 September 2010.

6 *'The Study of Containerisation Alternatives for the Maersk–Panama Lines'*, Stanford Research Institute, 1967.

7 A.P. Moller – Mærsk archives.

8 A.P. Moller – Mærsk archives.

9 Board meeting minutes, Steamship Company Svendborg, 17 April 1968.

10 C. Lund, *Nogle erindringer fra 50 år i Skibsfartens Tjeneste*, private publication, 1992, p. 105.

11 F. Broeze, *The Globalisation of the Oceans: Containerisation from the 1950s to the Present*, International Maritime Economic History Association, 2002, p. 44.

12 R. Gibney, *Containerisation International*, April 1976.

13 O. E. Allen, *The Box: An Anthology Celebrating 50 Years of Containerisation*, The TT Club, 1996, p. 19.

14 H. Sornn-Friese, R. T. Poulsen and M. Iversen, '"Knowing the Ropes": Capability Reconfiguration and Restructuring of the Danish Shipping Industry', in S. Tenold, M. J. Iversen and E. Lange, *Global Shipping in Small Nations: Nordic Experiences after 1960*, Palgrave Macmillan, 2012.

15 Board meeting minutes, Steamship Company Svendborg, 14 April 1971.

16 *Mærsk Post*, February 1999.

17 Interview with Poul Rasmussen, 25 September 2012.

18 Interview with Flemming Jacobs, 14 September 2012.

19 'Recommendation for Determining the Future Strategy for the USA/Far East Liner Services', 31 January 1973, Box 151747, A.P. Moller – Maersk archives.

20 'Preparations for Container Transport' is partly based on a brief dated 30 September 2010, written by Ib Kruse.

21 Interview with Flemming Jacobs, 31 July 2012.

22 Stanford Research Institute, 'Intermodal Containerization', 1972, p. 51.

23 Interview with Ib Kruse, 29 August 2012.

24 'Letter from N.J. Iversen to Moller Steamship Company, New York', 4 July 1973, Box 151811, A.P. Moller – Maersk archives.

25 Interview with Marna Nygaard, 2 July 2012.

26 Interview with Jørgen Harling, 11 September 2012.

27 Interview with Ib Kruse, 29 August 2012.

28 Box 112074, '. . . yet another pier . . .' refers to the inauguration in 1958 of Maersk Line's Pier 11 in Brooklyn.

29 Interview with Ib Kruse, 29 August 2012.

30 Broeze, p. 52.

Economist Intelligence Unit

31 J. Young and J. Kent, *International relations since 1945* (Oxford: Oxford University Press, 2006): http://fdslive.oup.com/www.oup.com/orc/resources/politics/intro/young_kent/01student/timeline/timeline.pdf (accessed on 13th July 2012).

32 BBC: http://www.bbc.co.uk/history/historic_figures/mao_zedong.shtml (accessed on 18th July 2012).

33 Association of Southeast Asian Nations: http://www.asean.org/1212.htm (accessed on 19th July 2012).

34 International Institute for Asian Studies: http://www.iias.nl/iiasn/24/general/24G4.html (accessed on 19th July 2012).

35 A. Mahizhnan, 'Smart cities: the Singapore case', *Cities*, vol. 16, no. 1 (1999), 13–18: http://www.spp.nus.edu.sg/ips/docs/pub/pa_Arun_Smart%20Cities%20The%20Singapore%20Case_99.pdf (accessed on 19th July 2012).

36 J. Young and J. Kent, *International relations since 1945* (Oxford: Oxford University Press, 2006): http://fdslive.oup.com/www.oup.com/orc/resources/politics/intro/young_kent/01student/timeline/timeline.pdf (accessed on 19th July 2012).

37 J. Young and J. Kent, *International relations since 1945* (Oxford: Oxford University Press, 2006): http://fdslive.oup.com/www.oup.com/orc/resources/politics/intro/young_kent/01student/timeline/timeline.pdf (accessed on 19th July 2012).

38 US Department of State, Office of the Historian: http://history.state.gov/milestones/1961–1968/NPT (accessed on 19th July 2012).

39 G. Jones, 'Multinational Strategies and Developing Countries in Historical Perspective', Working Paper 10–076, Harvard Business School (2010): http://www.hbs.edu/research/pdf/10–076.pdf (accessed on 18th July 2012).

40 S. Radelet, J. Sachs, and J. Lee, *Economic Growth in Asia* (Harvard Center for International Development, 1997): http://www.cid.harvard.edu/archive/hiid/papers/ecgasia.pdf (accessed on 16th July 2012).

41 World Trade Organization, *World Trade Report 2008* (Geneva), p. 22: http://www.wto.org/english/res_e/booksp_e/anrep_e/world_trade_report08_e.pdf (accessed on 14th July 2012).

42 World Trade Organization, *World Trade Report 2008* (Geneva), p. 22: http://www.wto.org/english/res_e/booksp_e/anrep_e/world_trade_report08_e.pdf (accessed on 14th July 2012).

43 United Nations Conference on Trade and Development: http://unctad.org/en/docs/ditc20082_en.pdf (accessed on 16th July 2012).

44 K. Hamada, *'Japan 1968: a reflection point during the era of the economic miracle'*, Center Discussion Paper No. 764 (1996), Economic Growth Center, Yale University: http://www.econ.yale.edu/growth_pdf/cdp764.pdf (accessed on 16th July 2012).

45 *Encyclopaedia Britannica*: http://www.britannica.com/EBchecked/topic/744592/Andean-Community (accessed on 17th July 2012).

46 History.com: http://www.history.com/this-day-in-history/unsafe-at-any-speed-hits-bookstores (accessed on 16th July 2012).

47 International Association for Food Protection: http://www.foodprotection.org/timeline/1960/ (accessed on 16th July 2012).

48 History.com: http://www.history.com/topics/1960s (accessed on 16th July 2012).

49 Stonewall: http://www.stonewall.org.uk/at_home/history_of_lesbian_gay_and_bisexual_equality/default.asp (accessed on 16th July 2012).

50 *Science News*: www.sciencenews.org/view/feature/id/339023/title/90th_Anniversary_Issue_Science_News_marks_a_milestone (accessed on 22nd July 2012).

51 *Science News*: www.sciencenews.org/view/feature/id/339023/title/90th_Anniversary_Issue_Science_News_marks_a_milestone (accessed on 16th July 2012).

52 *Wired*: http://www.wired.com/thisdayintech/2010/04/0419moores-law-published/ (accessed on 15th July 2012).

53 Intel: http://www.intel.com/content/www/us/en/silicon-innovations/moores-law-technology.html (accessed on 15th July 2012).

54 *Science News*: www.sciencenews.org/view/feature/id/339023/title/90th_Anniversary_Issue_Science_News_marks_a_milestone (accessed on 15th July 2012).

55 *The New York Times*: http://www.nytimes.com/2001/09/03/world/christiaan-barnard-78-surgeon-for-first-heart-transplant-dies.html?pagewanted = all (accessed on 16th July 2012).

56 *Encyclopaedia Britannica*: http://www.britannica.com/EBchecked/topic/745612/Defense-Advanced-Research-Projects-Agency-DARPA (accessed on 22nd July 2012).

57 International Maritime Organisation: http://www.imo.org/about/conventions/Pages/Home.aspx (accessed on 22nd July 2012).

58 Office of the High Commissioner for Human Rights: http://www2.ohchr.org/english/law/cescr.htm (accessed on 22nd July 2012).

59 World Intellectual Property Organization: http://www.wipo.int/about-ip/en/iprm/pdf/ch1.pdf (accessed on 20th July 2012).

60 Greenpeace: http://archive.greenpeace.org/comms/vrml/rw/text/ztextonly.html (accessed on 22nd July 2012).

61 National Oceanic and Atmospheric Administration: http://www.ncdc.noaa.gov/paleo/icecore/antarctica/byrd/byrd.html (accessed on 22nd July 2012).

62 United Nations Educational, Scientific and Cultural Organization: http://unesdoc.unesco.org/images/0014/001471/147152eo.pdf (accessed on 22nd July 2012).

63 *CIA World Factbook*: https://www.cia.gov/library/publications/the-world-factbook/
    fields/2088.html (accessed on 22nd July 2012).

64 Médecins Sans Frontières: http://www.msf.org.uk/about_history.aspx (accessed
    on 22nd July 2012).

65 J. Young and J. Kent, *International relations since 1945* (Oxford: Oxford University
    Press, 2006): http://fdslive.oup.com/www.oup.com/orc/resources/politics/intro/
    young_kent/01student/timeline/timeline.pdf (accessed on 22nd July 2012).

66 S. Winkler, *'Taiwan's UN Dilemma: To Be or Not To Be'*, Taiwan-U.S. Quarterly
    Analysis (June 2012), The Brookings Institution: http://www.brookings.edu/
    research/opinions/2012/06/20-taiwan-un-winkler (accessed on 22nd July
    2012).

67 J. Young and J. Kent, *International relations since 1945* (Oxford: Oxford University
    Press, 2006): http://fdslive.oup.com/www.oup.com/orc/resources/politics/intro/
    young_kent/01student/timeline/timeline.pdf (accessed on 22nd July 2012).

68 J. Young and J. Kent, *International relations since 1945* (Oxford: Oxford University
    Press, 2006): http://fdslive.oup.com/www.oup.com/orc/resources/politics/intro/
    young_kent/01student/timeline/timeline.pdf (accessed on 22nd July 2012).

69 BBC: http://news.bbc.co.uk/onthisday/hi/dates/stories/january/23/newsid_2506000/
    2506549.stm (accessed on 23rd July 2012).

70 G. Becker, 'What Latin America Owes to the "Chicago Boys"', *Hoover Digest*, no. 4
    (1997): http://www.hoover.org/publications/hoover-digest/article/7743 (accessed
    on 22nd July 2012).

71 *The Wall Street Journal*: http://online.wsj.com/article/SB1000142405311190400730
    4576494073418802358.html (accessed on 22nd July 2012).

72 NASDAQ: http://www.nasdaq.com/ (accessed on 22nd July 2012).

73 European Union: http://europa.eu/about-eu/eu-history/index_en.htm (accessed
    on 22 July 2012).

74 World Trade Organization: http://www.wto.org/english/thewto_e/whatis_e/tif_e/
    fact4_e.htm (accessed on 23rd July 2012).

75 BBC: http://news.bbc.co.uk/onthisday/hi/dates/stories/december/15/newsid_
    2559000/2559807.stm (accessed on 23rd July 2012).

76 University of Geneva: http://www.unige.ch/ses/ecopo/demelo/Cdrom/RIA/
    Readings/Trade_Blocs_Chap01.pdf (accessed on 23rd July 2012).

77 L. Bruno and S. Tenold, *'The basis for South Korea's ascent in the shipbuilding
    industry, 1970–90'* (draft version), Norwegian School of Economics and Business
    Administration (2010): http://www.ebha.org/ebha2010/code/media_168359_en.
    pdf (accessed on 23rd July 2012).

78 Southwest Airlines: http://www.southwest.com/html/about-southwest/history/
    fact-sheet.html (accessed on 23rd July 2012).

79 *Foreign Policy*: http://www.foreignpolicy.com/articles/2008/06/30/the_list_the_
    worlds_most_powerful_development_ngos (accessed on 23rd July 2012).

80 United Nations Children's Fund (UNICEF): http://www.unicef.org/sowc96/1970s.htm
    (accessed on 23rd July 2012).

81 United Nations Children's Fund (UNICEF): http://www.unicef.org/sowc96/1970s.htm
    (accessed on 23rd July 2012).

82 *Science News*: www.sciencenews.org/view/feature/id/339023/title/90[th]_
    Anniversary_Issue_Science_News_marks_a_milestone (accessed on 24th July 2012).

83 World Trade Organization, *World Trade Report 2008* (Geneva), p. 22: http://www.wto.org/english/res_e/booksp_e/anrep_e/world_trade_report08_e.pdf (accessed on 14th July 2012).

84 BBC: http://news.bbc.co.uk/1/hi/in_depth/sci_tech/2000/dot_life/1586229.stm (accessed on 24th July 2012).

85 Pingdom: http://royal.pingdom.com/2012/01/17/internet-2011-in-numbers/ (accessed on 24th July 2012).

86 BBC: http://news.bbc.co.uk/onthisday/hi/dates/stories/november/13/newsid_4101000/4101109.stm (accessed on 24th July 2012).

87 HP: http://www.hp.com/hpinfo/abouthp/histnfacts/museum/personalsystems/0023/ (accessed on 24th July 2012).

88 *Science News*: www.sciencenews.org/view/feature/id/339023/title/90th_Anniversary_Issue_Science_News_marks_a_milestone (accessed on 24th July 2012).

89 *The New York Times*: http://www.nytimes.com/1990/07/07/obituaries/n-c-wyeth-inventor-dies-at-78-developed-the-plastic-soda-bottle.html (accessed on 24th July 2012).

90 Sony: http://www.sony.net/SonyInfo/CorporateInfo/History/history.html (accessed on 24th July 2012).

91 *Encyclopaedia Britannica*: http://www.britannica.com/EBchecked/topic/260615/Helsinki-Accords (accessed on 24th July 2012).

92 Electronic Privacy Information Center (EPIC): http://epic.org/privacy/1974act/ (accessed on 24th July 2012).

93 United Nations Environment Programme: http://www.unep.org/Documents.Multilingual/Default.asp?DocumentID = 43&ArticleID = 3301&l = n (accessed on 24th July 2012).

94 European Union: http://www.eurunion.org/News/eunewsletters/EUFocus/2006/EUFocus-Environ.pdf (accessed on 24th July 2012).

95 *Science News*: www.sciencenews.org/view/feature/id/339023/title/90th_Anniversary_Issue_Science_News_marks_a_milestone (accessed on 24th July 2012).

96 Lloyd's Register of Shipping Annual Reports, 1967, 1968; Lloyd's Register of Shipping Statistical Tables, 1970.

Chapter 4

1 O. E. Allen, *The Box: An Anthology Celebrating 50 Years of Containerisation*, The TT Club, 1996, p. 14.

2 F. Broeze, *The Globalisation of the Oceans: Containerisation from the 1950s to the Present*, International Maritime Economic History Association, 2002, p. 65.

3 F. Jacobs, letter 5 January 1976, Box 151749, A.P. Moller – Maersk archives.

4 B. Riisager, letter 12 January 1976, Box 151749, A.P. Moller – Maersk archives.

5 Interview with Flemming Jacobs, 31 July 2012, A.P. Moller – Maersk archives.

6 Economist Intelligence Unit.

7 M. Levinson, *The Box: How the Shipping Container Made the World Smaller and the World Economy Bigger*, Princeton University Press, 2006, p. 96.

8 O. S. Johannesen, *Mærskflåden, Skibene i årene 1976–1990*, Editions Maritimes, pp. 116–17.

9 Johannesen, p. 196.

10 Each ship was backed into the dry dock, and cut in two. The forward section was then towed out, a newly constructed section some 14.3 metres long was welded to the stern section and then the forward section was re-welded to the new, longer aft section.

11 Johannesen, p. 200.

12 Broeze, p. 52.

13 Europe Project Presentation, 11 June 1980, section 8, Box 151957, A.P. Moller – Maersk archives.

14 The British lines held approximately 86 per cent of the Conference market into and out of the UK at that time.

15 The Trans Siberian Railway used feeder ships from Japan to Vladivostok from which containers moved by rail to Moscow and from there into the European hinterland.

16 Maersk Line Reports on Competition, 7 and 11 May 1981, Box 151877, A.P. Moller – Maersk archives.

17 Box 151963, A.P. Moller – Maersk archives.

18 J. Boyes, 'Maersk Lets its Mask Slip ... But Only Just', *Containerisation International*, January 1981, pp. 12–19.

19 A. P. Moller, letter to FEFC, 4 June 1981, Box 122002, A.P. Moller – Mærsk archives.

20 A. P. Moller, letter to FEFC, 4 June 1981, Box 122002, A.P. Moller – Mærsk archives.

21 V. Rolls, *The Far Eastern Freight Conference 1879–2004*, CAS, 2005.

22 *Containerisation International Yearbook 1983*, p. 8.

23 Rolls, p. 37.

24 J. Boyes, *Containerisation International*, January 1981, p. 12.

25 Internally in Maersk, the E-Class ships were known as Caroliners (cargo–RO-RO–liner ships. The official description would be multi-purpose vessel (MPV). Cargoes could include wheeled equipment, break-bulk cargo, cargoes in bulk and, of course, containers.

26 J. Boyes, *Containerisation International*, January 1981, p. 19.

27 O. Hornby, *'With Constant Care ...' A. P. Møller: Shipowner 1876–1965*, Schultz, 1988, p. 132.

28 Statements by Ib Kruse of Maersk Line in reply to questions from Mr. *Mitsuo Ikeda of Shipping and Trade News*, 1 October 1980, A.P. Moller – Maersk archives.

29 The Margaret Thatcher Foundation, www.margaretthatcher.org/document/104576 (accessed 26 July 2012).

30 Reefer Trades, *A Survey of Business Opportunities for APM*, April 1986, A.P. Moller – Maersk archives.

31 The development picked up speed after 1971 with the cooperation between Lauritzen and P&O, the forerunner of Lauritzen Reefers, similarly the formation of Maritime Fruit Carriers in cooperation with Salén. Both these were specialists at the time in refrigerated shipping.

32 A small number of units were not usable to Australia as they contained wooden material that had not been treated to Australian quarantine standards.

33 Rolls, p. 37.

34 Rolls, p. 37.

35 *Containerisation International Yearbook 1983*, p. 7.

36 *Containerisation International Yearbook 1984*, pp. 7–8.

Economist Intelligence Unit

37 *The New York Times*: http://topics.nytimes.com/top/reference/timestopics/organizations/k/khmer_rouge/index.html (accessed on 24th July 2012).

38 BBC: http://news.bbc.co.uk/onthisday/hi/dates/stories/april/30/newsid_2498000/2498441.stm (accessed on 25th July 2012).

39 BBC: http://www.bbc.co.uk/news/world-europe-17761153 (accessed on 25th July 2012).

40 Voice of America: http://www.voanews.com/content/a-13-2008-12-15-voa39–66618542/556463.html (accessed on 25th July 2012).

41 US Department of State: http://www.state.gov/www/global/arms/treaties/salt2–1.html (accessed on 25th July 2012).

42 Arms Control Association: http://www.armscontrol.org/factsheets/INFtreaty (accessed on 25th July 2012).

43 *Encyclopaedia Britannica*: http://www.britannica.com/EBchecked/topic/1499983/Soviet-invasion-of-Afghanistan (accessed on 25th July 2012).

44 Vanessa Sumo, The Federal Reserve Bank of Richmond, *Region Focus* (Summer 2006): http://www.richmondfed.org/publications/research/region_focus/2006/summer/pdf/federal_reserve.pdf (accessed on 25th July 2012).

45 Bank for International Settlements: http://www.bis.org/about/chronology/1970–1979.htm (accessed on 25th July 2012).

46 BBC: http://news.bbc.co.uk/nol/shared/spl/hi/pop_ups/quick_guides/05/asia_pac_china0s_economic_reform/html/2.stm (accessed on 25th July 2012).

47 BBC: http://news.bbc.co.uk/onthisday/hi/dates/stories/april/18/newsid_2525000/2525147.stm (accessed on 25th July 2012).

48 J. Hamilton, *Historical Oil Shocks* (San Diego: University of California, 2011): http://dss.ucsd.edu/~jhamilto/oil_history.pdf (accessed on 26th July 2012).

49 Bank for International Settlements: http://www.bis.org/about/chronology/1970–1979.htm (accessed on 26th July 2012).

50 United Nations: http://www.un.org/womenwatch/daw/beijing/mexico.html (accessed on 26th July 2012).

51 BBC: http://www.bbc.co.uk/sn/prehistoric_life/human/human_evolution/mother_of_man1.shtml (accessed on 26th July 2012).

52 BBC: http://news.bbc.co.uk/1/hi/world/europe/851027.stm (accessed on 26th July 2012).

53 BBC: http://news.bbc.co.uk/onthisday/hi/dates/stories/july/25/newsid_2499000/2499411.stm (accessed on 26th July 2012).

54 K. Pollson, 'Chronology of Personal Computers' (2012): http://pctimeline.info/comp1976.htm (accessed on 26th July 2012).

55 BBC: http://www.bbc.co.uk/news/business-17669078 (accessed on 26th July 2012).

56 B. Kundle, 'A Brief History of Word Processing (Through 1986)', Stanford University (1986): http://www.stanford.edu/~bkunde/fb-press/articles/wdprhist.html (accessed on 26th July 2012).

57 The Lemelson-MIT Program: http://web.mit.edu/invent/iow/jarvik.html (accessed on 26th July 2012).

58 BBC: http://www.bbc.co.uk/archive/tomorrowsworld/8018.shtml (accessed on 26th July 2012).

59 *The Telegraph*: http://www.telegraph.co.uk/comment/personal-view/8088232/ Why-I-will-mourn-the-death-of-the-Walkman.html (accessed on 26th July 2012).

60 International Committee of the Red Cross: http://www.icrc.org/ihl.nsf/full/470? opendocument (accessed on 26th July 2012).

61 United Nations: http://www.un.org/womenwatch/daw/cedaw/cedaw.htm (accessed on 26th July 2012).

62 *National Geographic*: http://greenliving.nationalgeographic.com/freon-really-affect-ozone-20345.html (accessed on 26th July 2012).

63 ADM: http://www.adm.com/en-US/company/history/Pages/1960–1979.aspx (accessed on 26th July 2012).

64 Renewable Fuels Association: http://www.ethanolrfa.org/pages/statistics (accessed on 26th July 2012).

65 Environmental History Timeline, Radford University: http://www.radford.edu/ wkovarik/envhist/9seventies.html (accessed on 26th July 2012).

66 The Nobel Prize: http://www.nobelprize.org/nobel_prizes/peace/laureates/1983/ walesa-bio.html (accessed on 26th July 2012).

67 BBC: http://www.bbc.co.uk/news/uk-17369334 (accessed on 26th July 2012).

68 Margaret Thatcher Foundation: http://www.margaretthatcher.org/document/ 104576 (accessed on 26th July 2012).

69 BBC: http://news.bbc.co.uk/onthisday/hi/dates/stories/october/6/newsid_2515000/ 2515841.stm (accessed on 26th July 2012).

70 BBC: http://www.bbc.co.uk/news/world-middle-east-12301713 (accessed on 26th July 2012).

71 *TIME*: http://www.time.com/time/magazine/article/0,9171,921207,00.html (accessed on 26th July 2012).

72 BBC: http://news.bbc.co.uk/onthisday/hi/dates/stories/march/23/newsid_2794000/ 2794525.stm (accessed on 27th July 2012).

73 BBC: http://news.bbc.co.uk/onthisday/hi/dates/stories/september/26/newsid_ 2538000/2538843.stm (accessed on 27th July 2012).

74 BBC: http://news.bbc.co.uk/onthisday/hi/dates/stories/october/31/newsid_2464000/ 2464423.stm (accessed on 27th July 2012).

75 Forbes: http://www.forbes.com/sites/peterferrara/2011/05/05/reaganomics-vs-obamanomics-facts-and-figures/ (accessed on 27th July 2012).

76 J. Powers, 'The history of private equity and venture capital', Corporate LiveWire (2012): http://www.corporatelivewire.com/top-story.html?id = the-history-of-private-equity-venture-capital (accessed on 27th July 2012).

77 Federal Deposit Insurance Corporation: http://www.fdic.gov/bank/historical/ history/191_210.pdf (accessed on 27th July 2012).

78 A. Blundell-Wignal, J. Fahrer, and A. Heath, '*Major influences on the Australian dollar exchange rate*', Reserve Bank of Australia (1993): http://www.rba.gov.au/ publications/confs/1993/blundell-wignall-fahrer-heath.pdf (accessed on 27th July 2012).

79 University of Bath: http://people.bath.ac.uk/liskmj/living-spring/sourcearchive/ fs2/fs2ed1.htm (accessed on 27th July 2012).

80 CNN: http://us.cnn.com/about/ (accessed on 28th July 2012).

81 *The Economist*: http://www.economist.com/node/9249262 (accessed on 28th July 2012).

82 *Science News*: http://www.sciencenews.org/view/feature/id/339020/title/ 90th_Anniversary_Issue_1980s (accessed on 28th July 2012).

83 Google Patents: http://www.google.com/patents/US4311434 (accessed on 28th July 2012).

84 International Organization for Standardization: http://www.iso.org/iso/home/ store/catalogue_ics/catalogue_detail_ics.htm?csnumber = 12647 (accessed on 28th July 2012).

85 IBM: http://www-03.ibm.com/ibm/history/exhibits/pc25/pc25_birth.html (accessed on 28th July 2012).

86 BBC: http://news.bbc.co.uk/1/hi/technology/8366703.stm (accessed on 28th July 2012).

87 PricewaterhouseCoopers: 'Cyber Security M&A: Decoding deals in the global Cyber Security industry' (2011): http://www.pwc.com/en_GX/gx/aerospace-defence/pdf/ cyber-security-mergers-acquisitions.pdf (accessed on 28th July 2012).

88 *TIME*: http://www.time.com/time/specials/packages/article/0,28804,2023689_ 2023708_2023656,00.html (accessed on 28th July 2012).

89 *The Guardian*: http://www.guardian.co.uk/science/2009/may/24/dna-fingerprinting-alec-jeffreys (accessed on 28th July 2012).

90 *The Paris Memorandum of Understanding on Port State Control*: http://www. parismou.org/Organization/About_us/2010.12.28/History.htm (accessed on 28th July 2012).

91 International Maritime Organization: http://www.imo.org/OurWork/ Environment/PollutionPrevention/OilPollution/Pages/Default.aspx (accessed on 28th July 2012).

92 NOAA General Counsel: http://www.gc.noaa.gov/gcil_los.html (accessed on 28th July 2012).

93 United Nations: http://www.un.org/en/aboutun/history/1981–1990.shtml (accessed on 28th July 2012).

94 European Green Party: http://europeangreens.eu/countries/belgium?page = 2 (accessed on 28th July 2012).

95 *Science News*: http://www.sciencenews.org/view/feature/id/339020/title/ 90th_Anniversary_Issue_1980s (accessed on 28th July 2012).

96 United Nations: http://www.un.org/documents/ga/res/37/a37r007.htm (accessed on 28th July 2012).

97 BBC: http://news.bbc.co.uk/onthisday/hi/dates/stories/december/3/newsid_ 2698000/2698709.stm (accessed on 28th July 2012).

Chapter 5

1 Nariman Behravesh, Chief Economist, *Global Insight*, quoted in the *Journal of Commerce, 50 Years of Containerisation*, April 2006, p. 12A. A.P. Moller – Maersk archives.

2 Paper dated 24 July 1984, p. 1, Box 122118, A.P. Moller – Maersk archives.

3 Kruse's statement was 'people always talk about strategies. There wasn't really any strategy, it was just opportunity. We were successful, we wanted to expand and of course make money expanding. It was just seizing opportunities and providing for a better business venture, but no great strategy.'

4 Interview with Jørgen Harling, 11 September 2012, A.P. Moller – Maersk archives.

5 A.P. Moller – Maersk archives.

6 The systems would be unique to Maersk Line, accessible from any online office and designed to ensure that Maersk Line stayed ahead in terms of systems capabilities.

7 Box 122118, A.P. Moller – Maersk archives.

8 Interview with Carsten Melchiors, 29 June 2012, A.P. Moller – Maersk archives.

9 Agreement No. 010099–034 dated 5 April 2002, Federal Maritime Commission, A.P. Moller – Maersk archives.

10 Agreement No. 010099–034, 5 April 2002, Federal Maritime Commission, A.P. Moller – Maersk archives.

11 Box 122052, A.P. Moller – Maersk archives.

12 Memo from Ib Kruse to Mærsk McKinney Møller, 3 June 1986, Box 122118, A.P. Moller – Maersk archives.

13 The PCG was to 'coordinate Maersk Line's global activities, recognising the overriding importance of ensuring total profitability; coordinate development of new ideas for rationalisation and additional activities and to foster initiatives'. It was also to 'assist the A. P. Moller Staff Department in coordinating training, development and management of staff resources and to bring Maersk Line's agencies and Copenhagen closer together'.

14 Box 122052, A.P. Moller – Mærsk archives.

15 Box 122052, A.P. Moller – Mærsk archives.

16 M. W. Hansen, M. Greve and H. Schaumburg-Müller, *Container Shipping & Economic Development*, Copenhagen Business School, 2007, p. 36.

17 Interview with Jørgen Harling, 11 September 2012, A.P. Moller – Maersk archives.

18 Production with two cranes was running at about 22 moves per crane-hour, or 44 moves per berth hour.

19 Correspondence with Crisanto Dominguez, Head of Health and Safety, APM Terminals, Algeciras, Spain, 16 November 2012.

20 Box 158854, A.P. Moller – Mærsk archives.

21 Similar steps were taken at the New York terminal, where the cranes were raised so that they could handle containers on the fifth tier on deck.

22 Box 122052, A.P. Moller – Maersk archives.

23 *Preamble to the General Agreement on Tariffs and Trade.* Internal A.P. Moller – Maersk analyses and Duke University School of Law Research Guide on GATT/ WTO.

24 *Containerisation International Yearbook 1986*, p. 6.

25 L. O. Blanco, *Shipping Conferences under EC Anti-Trust Law*, Hart Publishing, 2007, p. 36.

26 Interview with John Clancey, 16 August 2012, A.P. Moller – Maersk archives.

27 Interview with Ib Kruse, 29 August 2012, A.P. Moller – Maersk archives.

28 Box 158854, A.P. Moller – Maersk archives.

29 *Containerisation International Yearbook 1987*, p. 6.

30 Senator Line continued to operate as an outsider until March 1996, when it followed Taiwan's Yang Ming into the FEFC, the latter having joined in August 1995.

31 Jeffrey Sachs, Director of Columbia University's Earth Institute, Columbia Business School, 25 June 2012, A.P. Moller – Maersk archives.

32 Review of Maritime Transport, UNCTAD, 2011, p. 2.

33 Box 122063, A.P. Moller – Maersk archives.

34 Box 122061, A.P. Moller – Maersk archives.
35 Box 122061, A.P. Moller – Maersk archives.
36 *Containerisation International Yearbook 1986*, p. 5. The quote continues: 'The revolution, for that is what some are already calling the metamorphosis now taking place, is already producing a more efficient, cost-effective industry, eager to seek economies of scale through deployment of larger vessels at sea and double stack, high density trains on land.'
37 Offices in China were also needed to manage the challenges of providing effective transport services due to the relative lack of infrastructure at the time.
38 Minutes of Policy Coordination Group, November 1985, A.P. Moller – Maersk archives.
39 These included Singapore, Taiwan, Rotterdam and the UAE, as well as in Italy, the UK and in China.
40 F. Broeze, *The Globalisation of the Oceans: Containerisation from the 1950s to the Present*, International Maritime Economic History Association, 2002, p. 79.
41 Knud Erik Moller Nielsen, *Summary of Caribbean, Central and South America*, May 1986, Box 122062, A.P. Moller – Maersk archives.
42 Summary memo from F. R. Jacobs to M. M. Møller, 8 August 1986, Box 122062, A.P. Moller – Maersk archives.
43 M. Levinson, *The Box: How the Shipping Container Made the World Smaller and the World Economy Bigger*, Princeton University Press, 2006, p. 7.
44 M. F. Guillén, 'Is Globalisation Civilising, Destructive or Feeble?', *Annual Review of Sociology*, 2001, p. 27.
45 D. Held, A. McGrew, D. Goldblatt and J. Perraton, *Global Transformations*, Stanford University Press, 1999.
46 G. Gereffi, *The Organisation of Buyer-Driven Global Commodity Chains*, Greenwood Press, 1994.
47 J. Stiglitz, *Globalisation and Its Discontents*, Allen Lane, 2002.
48 Unemployment at the time was running at about 7 per cent in the USA, 11.5 per cent in Spain, 8 per cent in Belgium, over 7 per cent in Holland and about 5.7 per cent in the UK.
49 Guillén, 2001.
50 C. Y. Tung, quoted in '50 Years of Containerisation', *Journal of Commerce*, April 2006, p. 12A. A.P. Moller – Maersk archives.
51 Interview with Ken Park, 21 June 2012, A.P. Moller – Maersk archives.
52 Harvard Business School paper, 9 November 2005, A.P. Moller – Maersk archives.
53 HBS Alumni Bulletin, December 2011, p. 34, A.P. Moller – Maersk archives.
54 S. Tenold, M. J. Iversen and E. Lange, *Global Shipping in Small Nations*, Palgrave Macmillan, 2012, p. 1.

Chapter 6

1 Interview with Søren Skou, 21 August 2012, A.P. Moller – Maersk archives.
2 Live reefers, that is reefers carrying cargo that require their cooling system to be turned on, were mainly used outbound from Europe and the USA. There was not the same volume requirement on the return journey. Rather than re-position them empty to Europe or the USA, they might be positioned to Australia–New Zealand for usage outbound from that area.

3 *Containerisation International Yearbook 1987*, p. 5.

4 Box 122117, A.P. Moller – Maersk archives.

5 The dominant shipping company in Denmark, the East Asiatic Company, stood out for having established its own internal training scheme around the year 1900.

6 P. Boje, Ledere, *Ledelse og organisation 1870–1972: Dansk industri efter 1870*, Bind 5, Odense Universitetsforlag, 1997.

7 Originally established just after the Second World War as a three-year programme, the school had run daily classes in Copenhagen from 08.00 am to 10.00 am, with homework and sometimes evening classes.

8 Interview with Eric B. Williams, 30 May 2012, A.P. Moller – Maersk archives.

9 Interview with Jessica Lauren Cohen, 27 June 2012, Box 122117, A.P. Moller – Maersk archives.

10 A.P. Moller – Maersk archives.

11 Box 122120, A.P. Moller – Maersk archives.

12 Economist Intelligence Unit 1985–9, Technological Review, A.P. Moller – Maersk archives.

13 Interview with Duncan McGrath, 3 September 2012, A.P. Moller – Maersk archives.

14 Notes from Policy Coordination Group meeting, London, 3–4 September 1987, Box 122117, A.P. Moller – Maersk archives.

15 Interview with Martin Christopher, Emeritus Professor of Marketing and Logistics, Cranfield University, 26 November 2012, A.P. Moller – Maersk archives.

16 Interview with Duncan McGrath, 3 September 2012, A.P. Moller – Maersk archives.

17 In 1988, the carriers did have success with the decision by the Federal Maritime Commission to end the use of the 'crazy eddie' clauses in service contracts which had been a source of substantial rate instability.

18 O. Hornby, '*With Constant Care . . .' A. P. Møller: Shipowner 1876–1965*, Schultz, 1988, pp. 217–18.

19 The service from the Far East would continue on across the Atlantic from New York, the last US port, direct to Le Havre in northern France, Felixstowe in the UK, Rotterdam in Holland and Bremerhaven in Germany. From there it would cross back to Halifax in Canada, New York and then follow the existing rotation of the Panama service to Baltimore, Charleston, Long Beach, Oakland and out to Asia. In the United States, local feeder services would connect Halifax with Boston and Baltimore with Philadelphia. In Europe, feeders would serve Dublin in Ireland, Bilbao in Spain, Lisbon and Leixoes in Portugal, while other feeders would serve Grangemouth in Scotland and all the main Scandinavian ports in Denmark, Norway, Sweden and Finland.

20 The objective was to 'improve our service package and significantly exceed what was offered by competitors in the trade'.

21 Birger Jorgensen, memo to Mærsk Mc-Kinney Møller and Ib Kruse, 31 August 1987, Box 122076, A.P. Moller – Maersk archives.

22 Interview with Tim Harris, 23 August 2012, A.P. Moller – Maersk archives.

23 Interview with Carsten Melchiors, 29 June 2012, A.P. Moller – Maersk archives.

24 The Optima ships were built between 1978 and 1980 at Odense Steel Shipyard and were named *Emma, Eleo, Estelle, Emilie, Evelyn* and *Elisabeth Mærsk*.

25 While Showa Line was merged with Nippon Yusen Kaisha (NYK Line) in October 1998, Yamashita Shinnihon Line was ultimately merged with Mitsui-OSK Lines in 1999.

26 Box 122117, A.P. Moller – Maersk archives.
27 Box 122117, A.P. Moller – Maersk archives.
28 *Containerisation International Yearbook 1988*, p. 5.
29 Interview with Flemming Jacobs, 31 July 2012, A.P. Moller – Maersk archives.
30 Box 122120, A.P. Moller – Maersk archives.

Economist Intelligence Unit

31 BBC: http://news.bbc.co.uk/onthisday/hi/dates/stories/february/22/newsid_2519000/2519155.stm (accessed on 28th July 2012).
32 J. Young and J. Kent, *International relations since 1945* (Oxford: Oxford University Press, 2006) : http://fdslive.oup.com/www.oup.com/orc/resources/politics/intro/young_kent/01student/timeline/timeline.pdf (accessed on 29th July 2012).
33 J. Young and J. Kent, *International relations since 1945* (Oxford: Oxford University Press, 2006): http://fdslive.oup.com/www.oup.com/orc/resources/politics/intro/young_kent/01student/timeline/timeline.pdf (accessed on 29th July 2012).
34 J. Young and J. Kent, *International relations since 1945* (Oxford: Oxford University Press, 2006): http://fdslive.oup.com/www.oup.com/orc/resources/politics/intro/young_kent/01student/timeline/timeline.pdf (accessed on 29th July 2012).
35 J. Young and J. Kent, *International relations since 1945* (Oxford: Oxford University Press, 2006): http://fdslive.oup.com/www.oup.com/orc/resources/politics/intro/young_kent/01student/timeline/timeline.pdf (accessed on 29th July 2012).
36 BBC: http://news.bbc.co.uk/onthisday/hi/dates/stories/november/9/newsid_2515000/2515869.stm (accessed on 29th July 2012).
37 Bank for International Settlements: http://www.bis.org/about/chronology/1980–1989.htm (accessed on 29th July 2012).
38 J. Young and J. Kent, *International relations since 1945* (Oxford: Oxford University Press, 2006): http://fdslive.oup.com/www.oup.com/orc/resources/politics/intro/young_kent/01student/timeline/timeline.pdf (accessed on 29th July 2012).
39 *Financial Times*: http://www.ft.com/cms/s/0/5be5e788-c1ba-11df-9d90-00144feab49a.html#axzz21ZQ9ed55 (accessed on 29th July 2012).
40 *Financial Times*: http://www.ft.com/cms/s/0/198db6c4-a3f7-11e1-84b1-00144feabdc0.html#axzz21ZQ9ed55 (accessed on 29th July 2012).
41 The Cairns Group: http://cairnsgroup.org/Pages/default.aspx (accessed on 29th July 2012).
42 *The New York Times*: http://learning.blogs.nytimes.com/2011/10/19/oct-19–1987-stock-market-crashes-on-black-monday/ (accessed on 29th July 2012).
43 Council of Mortgage Lenders: http://www.cml.org.uk/cml/policy/issues/721 (accessed on 29th July 2012).
44 BBC: http://news.bbc.co.uk/1/hi/8433652.stm (accessed on 29th July 2012).
45 Bloomberg: http://www.bloomberg.com/markets/stocks/movers/nikkei-225/ (accessed on 12th March 2013).
46 APEC: http://www.apec.org/About-Us/About-APEC/History.aspx (accessed on 29th July 2012).
47 BBC: http://www.bbc.co.uk/religion/religions/christianity/beliefs/liberationtheology.shtml (accessed on 29th July 2012).
48 Free Software Foundation: http://www.fsf.org/about/leadership/ (accessed on 29th July 2012).

49 BBC: http://www.bbc.co.uk/news/world-africa-15202021 (accessed on 29th July 2012).

50 BBC: http://www.bbc.co.uk/news/world-africa-10725711 (accessed on 29th July 2012).

51 Fairtrade Foundation: http://www.fairtrade.org.uk/what_is_fairtrade/history.aspx (accessed on 29th July 2012).

52 World Trade Organization, *World Trade Report 2008* (Geneva), p.22: http://www.wto.org/english/res_e/booksp_e/anrep_e/world_trade_report08_e.pdf (accessed on 14th July 2012).

53 W3Schools: http://www.w3schools.com/browsers/browsers_os.asp (accessed on 29th July 2012).

54 The Singularity: http://singularity.com/charts/page75.html (accessed on 29th July 2012).

55 *Science News*: http://www.sciencenews.org/view/feature/id/339020/title/90th_Anniversary_Issue_1980s (accessed on 29th July 2012).

56 Manufacturing Management Research Center: http://merc.e.u-tokyo.ac.jp/mmrc/dp/pdf/MMRC269_2009.pdf (accessed on 29th July 2012).

57 The Lemelson-MIT Program: http://web.mit.edu/invent/iow/berners-lee.html (accessed on 29th July 2012).

58 Internet World Stats: http://www.internetworldstats.com/stats.htm (accessed on 29th July 2012).

59 US Department of Justice: http://www.justice.gov/criminal/cybercrime/docs/ccmanual.pdf (accessed on 29th July 2012).

60 United Nations Environment Programme: http://ozone.unep.org/new_site/en/index.php (accessed on 29th July 2012).

61 United Nations: http://www2.ohchr.org/english/law/crc.htm (accessed on 29th July 2012).

62 *Science News*: http://www.sciencenews.org/view/feature/id/339020/title/90th_Anniversary_Issue_1980s (accessed on 29th July 2012).

63 International Whaling Commission: http://iwcoffice.org/commission/iwcmain.htm (accessed on 30th July 2012).

64 Intergovernmental Panel on Climate Change: http://www.ipcc.ch/organization/organization_history.shtml#.UAvGRbR8Asc (accessed on 30th July 2012).

65 NEC: http://www.nec.com/en/global/environment/featured/space/06_esim_iv01.html (accessed on 29th July 2012).

66 *Science News*: http://www.sciencenews.org/view/feature/id/339020/title/90th_Anniversary_Issue_1980s (accessed on 30th July 2012).

Chapter 7

1 '50 Years of Containerisation' *Journal of Commerce*, April 2006, pp. 16A, 18A, A.P. Moller – Maersk archives.

2 Box 122120, A.P. Moller – Maersk archives.

3 Box 122139, A.P. Moller – Maersk archives.

4 Vagn Lehd Moller and Bjarne Kolbo Nielsen, letter to main offices, 29 August 1989, Box 122139, A.P. Moller – Maersk archives.

5 In the Trans Pacific, outsiders included Evergreen, Yang Ming, Hanjin, Hyundai, OOCL, COSCO and Senator Lines. In the Europe–Far East trades, Evergreen, Yang Ming, Hanjin, Cho Yang, COSCO, Senator and NorAsia/Sea-Land; in the Trans

Atlantic, Evergreen, OOCL, Senator, Polish Ocean Lines and Mediterranean Shipping Company (the first time this company features seriously on the competitive landscape.

6 Flemming Jacobs, *Confidential memo to Ib Kruse*, 22 February 1990, A.P. Moller – Maersk archives.

7 Memo, 20 August 1990, Box 122139, A.P. Moller – Maersk archives.

8 Line Department, Cost-Efficiency Report, August 1990, p. 3, A.P. Moller – Maersk archives.

9 The invasion and the later Operation Desert Storm made it difficult to deliver commercial goods to customers in Iraq and Kuwait. Working with Maersk Line's legal advisors and insurance company (in shipping, known as Protection & Indemnity Clubs (P&I)) letters were sent to each cargo owner outlining what Maersk Line planned to do under the UN sanctions. With patience and persistence, Maersk Line's organisations in the area ultimately resolved the issues, despite the somewhat challenging situation.

10 Flemming Jacobs, *Memo to Mærsk Mc-Kinney Møller*, 11 October 1990, A.P. Moller – Maersk archives.

11 *Containerisation International Yearbook 1991*, p. 5.

12 Maersk Line provided the training and spare part kits so that running repairs could be carried out en route, if needed.

13 The concept behind these coming supply chain services was that they could be used to strengthen the day-to-day working relationship with major customers by offering services that provided them with substantial added-value while differentiating Maersk Line from the competition. In many ways, Maersk was ahead of the game with its plans for Mercantile.

14 *Maersk Materials Management, Evaluation of Concept Report*, 9 February 1989, p. 1, A.P. Moller – Maersk archives.

15 Rune Svenson, President of Volvo Transport Corp., *SeaTrade Business Review*, November 1988, A.P. Moller – Maersk archives.

16 *Maersk Materials Management, Evaluation of Concept Report*, 9 February 1989, p. 25, A.P. Moller – Maersk archives.

17 Subject to finding a suitable legal structure to avoid any potential conflict of interest under the terms of the 1984 US Shipping Act, the recommendations were 'to fully develop Mercantile globally as the general contractor for the 3M concept; to develop a global logistics package fully supported by IT services and comprising consultancy on logistics services, information exchange via EDI; follow up with suppliers at origin; management of trucking, rail and inland transport arrangements; export licensing and permit management; Certificates of Origin management; warehousing at origin; consolidation; insurance; ocean transport; inward Customs clearances; inland transport management; warehousing, storage and inventory management at destination as well as just-in-time delivery. The package was to be tied together by one electronic invoice covering the entire transport chain.'

The Maersk Double Star Distribution Service was to consist of the existing consolidation and distribution services already offered by Mercantile, providing a 'push' process for goods flowing through the pipelines. Mercantile was to be strengthened with the addition of freight forwarding and airfreight services.

The third product was Maersk's Star Transportation Services providing door-to-door and port-to-port services as required by the customers. It was envisaged that some customers initially buying this service would gradually move up the chain to the Double or Triple Star services over time.

18 *Maersk Materials Management, Evaluation of Concept Report*, 9 February 1989, p. 16, A.P. Moller – Maersk archives.

19 Timothy J. Rhein, *President of American President Line*, to Containerisation and Intermodal Institute, Oakland, California, 10 June 1988, A.P. Moller – Maersk archives.

20 *Maersk Materials Management, Evaluation of Concept Report*, 9 February 1989, pp. 30–33, A.P. Moller – Maersk archives.

21 *Maersk Materials Management, Evaluation of Concept Report*, 9 February 1989, pp. 46–7, A.P. Moller – Maersk archives.

22 The team was initially housed in the old, restored Post Office across the street from the Maersk headquarters in Esplanaden.

23 Letter and attachments from Dave Easton, Vice President, Meldisco and Project Sponsor, 26 July 1990, A.P. Moller – Maersk archives.

24 O. Hornby, '*With Constant Care . . .' A. P. Møller: Shipowner 1876–1965*, Schultz, 1988, p. 56.

25 Two of the issues centred around getting the Log*IT system to operate effectively. Once the system was up and running with each Division, the next challenge was getting consistent, complete, timely and high-quality information from each origin for those who needed it at destination. This was essential if distribution and store planning was to operate effectively. With Divisions running on a variety of different purchase order management systems, each migration meant largely starting from scratch.

26 As the business relationship with the Divisions settled down, it became more important to work with each of them on their supply chains in a developmental manner. As each Division was different from the others, Michael Christensen developed a 'Black Book' with each of them that established forward-looking plans and aspirations, as well as details of timelines, resources and who would pay for what, so that there was a continuous improvement process built into the working relationship with each Division.

27 'A Review of the Melville/Mercantile Partnership in International Logistics 1991–1996', *Melville Corporation*, February 1996, A.P. Moller – Maersk archives.

28 Box 154089, A.P. Moller – Maersk archives.

29 Mercantile M*Power brochure, A.P. Moller – Maersk archives. A new technical visibility platform, M*Power, was under development. Designed to run on top of the existing and, at that time, probably world leading technical platforms of MODS and Log*IT, it would provide customers with easier access to their data. A new and modern Windows-based entry to information, M*Power was launched in mid-1996. Shortly afterwards, a further enhanced version based on an Information Library and powered by *Business Objects* added 'a new dimension to information services'.

30 Vagn Lehd Møller letter to Maersk Country Managers, 12 June 1996, A.P. Moller – Maersk archives.

31 Operating Agreement with P&O, 1 March 1991, A.P. Moller – Maersk archives.

32 Press release, 4 April 1991, A.P. Moller – Maersk archives.

33 This deployment would allow Maersk Line to increase its share of the trade and enhance the bottom line, giving an expected return on investment of about 21 per cent.

34 Vagn Lehd Møller, memo to Mærsk Mc-Kinney Møller, Jess Søderberg and Ib Kruse, 20 December 1991, A.P. Moller – Maersk archives.

35 'World Economic Outlook, a Survey by the Staff of the International Monetary Fund', quoted in *Containerisation International Yearbook 1992*, p. 5, A.P. Moller – Maersk archives.

36 *Containerisation International Yearbook 1992*, p. 5.

37 Box 122120, A.P. Moller – Maersk archives.

38 M. Levinson, *The Box: How the Shipping Container Made the World Smaller and the World Economy Bigger*, Princeton University Press, 2006, pp. 259–62.

39 Palle Weidlich, memo to Ib Kruse, copy to Vagn Lehd Møller, Niels Vallø Kristiansen, 10 October 1991, A.P. Moller – Maersk archives.

40 TBS provided a report on global trade and container growth prospects and projections through to 1997.

41 Vagn Lehd Møller, memo to Mærsk Mc-Kinney Møller, Jess Søderberg and Ib Kruse, 3 February 1992, A.P. Moller – Maersk archives.

42 Economist Intelligence Unit 1995–1999 A Selection of Important Developments.

43 Economist Intelligence Unit 1995–1999 A Selection of Important Developments.

44 *Containerisation International Yearbook 1990*, p. 5.

45 *Containerisation International Yearbook 1990*, p. 5.

46 *Containerisation International Yearbook 1990*, p. 6.

Economist Intelligence Unit

47 BBC: http://www.bbc.co.uk/news/world-middle-east-14546763 (accessed on 22nd July 2012).

48 *Los Angeles Times*: http://articles.latimes.com/1991–07–02/news/mn-1648_1_warsaw-pact (accessed on 21st July 2012).

49 *Encyclopaedia Britannica*: http://www.britannica.com/EBchecked/topic/652816/Boris-Yeltsin (accessed on 21st July 2012).

50 BBC: http://news.bbc.co.uk/1/hi/world/europe/4997380.stm (accessed on 21st July 2012).

51 *Los Angeles Times*: http://articles.latimes.com/1991–06–18/news/mn-929_1_population-registration-act (accessed on 21st July 2012).

52 BBC: http://news.bbc.co.uk/onthisday/hi/dates/stories/may/10/newsid_2661000/2661503.stm (accessed on 24th July 2012).

53 *Encyclopaedia Britannica*: http://www.britannica.com/EBchecked/topic/476968/Oslo-Accords (accessed on 24th July 2012).

54 BBC: http://www.bbc.co.uk/news/world-africa-14093238 (accessed on 24th July 2012).

55 World Trade Organization: http://www.wto.org/english/res_e/booksp_e/anrep_e/wtr08–2b_e.pdf (accessed on 24th July 2012).

56 *The Guardian*: http://www.guardian.co.uk/business/2008/sep/30/japan.japan (accessed on 24th July 2012).

57 World Trade Organization: https://www.wto.org/english/res_e/booksp_e/discussion_papers8_e.pdf (accessed on 30th July 2012).

58 BBC: http://news.bbc.co.uk/1/hi/world/americas/5195834.stm (accessed on 24th July 2012).

59 A. Panagariya, 'India's economic reforms: what has been accomplished? What remains to be done?', EDRC Policy Brief No. 2 (2001): http://www.columbia.edu/~ap2231/Policy%20Papers/OPB2.pdf (accessed on 24th July 2012).

60 *TIME*: http://www.time.com/time/nation/article/0,8599,1868997,00.html (accessed on 24th July 2012).

61 Free Trade Area of the Americas: http://www.ftaa-alca.org/View_e.asp (accessed on 24th July 2012).

62 Bloomberg: http://www.bloomberg.com/news/2012–10–29/romney-must-romance-brazil-to-boost-latin-american-trade.html (accessed on 29th October 2012).

63 World Trade Organization: https://www.wto.org/english/docs_e/legal_e/04-wto.pdf (accessed on 24th July 2012).

64 *China Daily*: http://www.chinadaily.com.cn/business/2008–09/08/content_7007412.htm (accessed on 24th July 2012).

65 S. Arita, S. La Croix and James Mak, 'How Big? The Impact of Approved Destination Status on Mainland Chinese Travel Abroad', Working Paper No. 2012–3, The Economic Research Organization at the University of Hawaii (June 2012): http://www.uhero.hawaii.edu/assets/WP_2012–3.pdf (accessed on 24th July 2012).

66 J. Rose and J. Ganz, 'The MP3: A History Of Innovation And Betrayal' (2011): http://www.npr.org/blogs/therecord/2011/03/23/134622940/the-mp3-a-history-of-innovation-and-betrayal (accessed on 24th July 2012).

67 International Telecommunication Union: http://www.itu.int/en/history/overview/Pages/dates.aspx (accessed on 24th July 2012).

68 National Aeronautics and Space Administration (NASA): http://imagine.gsfc.nasa.gov/docs/features/exhibit/tenyear/age.html (accessed on 24th July 2012).

69 UW Food Irradiation Education Group: http://uw-food-irradiation.engr.wisc.edu/Facts.html (accessed on 24th July 2012).

70 UW Food Irradiation Education Group: http://uw-food-irradiation.engr.wisc.edu/Facts.html (accessed on 24th July 2012).

71 International Telecommunication Union: http://www.itu.int/osg/spu/ip/chapter_two.html (accessed on 24th July 2012).

72 *The New York Times*: http://www.nytimes.com/1993/10/24/us/scientist-clones-human-embryos-and-creates-an-ethical-challenge.html?pagewanted = all&src = pm (accessed on 24th July 2012).

73 Carrier Corporation: http://www.container.carrier.com/Carrier + Brand + Sites/Carrier + Transicold + Container/Side + Bar + Links/Overview/ch.Timeline.printerfriendly?hidLocale = en (accessed on 24th July 2012).

74 Penguin Readers: http://www.penguinreaders.com/pdf/downloads/pr/teachers-notes/9781405880138.pdf (accessed on 24th July 2012).

75 NSW Department of Aboriginal Affairs: http://www.daa.nsw.gov.au/publications/Fact%20Sheets.pdf (accessed on 24th July 2012).

76 World Trade Organization: http://www.wto.org/english/thewto_e/whatis_e/tif_e/agrm7_e.htm (accessed on 24th July 2012).

77 BBC: http://news.bbc.co.uk/1/hi/business/393199.stm (accessed on 24th July 2012).

78 Canada's World: http://www.canadasworld.ca/timeline/19841993 (accessed on 24th July 2012).
79 Convention on Biological Diversity: http://www.cbd.int/convention/ (accessed on 25th July 2012).
80 CNN: http://edition.cnn.com/SPECIALS/1999/china.50/asian.superpower/three.gorges/ (accessed on 25th July 2012).
81 United Nations: http://www.un.org/geninfo/bp/enviro.html (accessed on 25th July 2012).
82 Groupe Eurotunnel: http://www.eurotunnelgroup.com/uk/the-channel-tunnel/history/ (accessed on 23rd July 2012).

Chapter 8

1 Hans Henrik Sørensen, note, 1 May 1992, A.P. Moller – Maersk archives.
2 Michael Fiorini, *Note of meeting 24 July 1992 with Ib Kruse and Karsten Stock Andresen of ØK*, 27 July 1992, A.P. Moller – Maersk archives.
3 ACL letter, dated 6 November 1992, A.P. Moller – Maersk archives.
4 *Containerisation International Yearbook 1993*, p. 11, A.P. Moller – Maersk archives.
5 Jess Søderberg, file note, 23 March 1993, A.P. Moller – Maersk archives.
6 S. Tenold, M. J. Iversen and E. Lange, *Global Shipping in Small Nations*, Palgrave Macmillan, 2012, p. 83.
7 www.australia-information.com (accessed 20 January 2013).
8 Internal analysis of Australia, A.P. Moller – Maersk archives.
9 http://en.wikipedia.org/wiki/New_Zealand (accessed 20 January 2013).
10 Internal analysis of New Zealand, A.P. Moller – Maersk archives.
11 MCC Transport presentation, October 2012, A.P. Moller – Maersk archives.
12 O. Hornby, *'With Constant Care . . .' A. P. Møller: Shipowner 1876–1965*, Schultz, 1988, p. 214.
13 By the end of 1993, Maersk Line was operating in more than 50 countries through more than 200 offices. In 1993 alone, 24 new offices were opened and Maersk Line entered 9 new countries: Australia, Brazil, the Gambia, Cambodia, Guinea, Ukraine, Jamaica, Ecuador and Venezuela.
14 Memo from the Andean Team to K. Erik Møller-Nielsen, 25 February 1991, A.P. Moller – Maersk archives.
15 Interview with Robbert Jan van Trooijen, 28 June 2012, A.P. Moller – Maersk archives.
16 Memo from the Andean Team to K. Erik Møller-Nielsen, 25 February 1991, A.P. Moller – Maersk archives.
17 Andean Service Mission, Budget file 1993, prepared October 1992, A.P. Moller – Maersk archives.
18 *Containerisation International Yearbook 1994*, p. 5, A.P. Moller – Maersk archives.
19 McKinsey & Company report, 'Where is the Value in Transportation', February 2012.
20 Examples of projects included: (a) coverage of Greece through agency representation with an own office opened in 1997; (b) coverage of Turkey from 1993 via an agent with Maersk Line Turkey opening in 2001; (c) coverage of Morocco in 1993 via a feeder from Algeciras; (d) coverage of the Eastern Mediterranean from 1994, as well as dedicated feeder services to and from Bilbao, Vigo, Lisbon and Leixos, later with Spanish flag ships owned by Maersk Spain covering the Canary Islands.

21 Maersk Line 1993–7 Budget file, EDP Budget – Data Processing, A.P. Moller – Maersk archives.

22 A different view of costs was summarised by Equipment Management. It showed that on average, a Maersk container carried 5.4 loads each year, being, per load, at sea full for 20 days, on land full for 21 days and on land empty for 23 days. The plan was to bring this usage up to an average of 6 loads per year.

23 Maersk Line 1993–7 Budget file, EDP Budget – Data Processing, A.P. Moller – Maersk archives.

24 J. D. Lewis, *Trusted Partners*, 1999, The Free Press.

25 Lewis, p. 7.

26 Lewis, p. 24.

27 Lewis, p. 46.

28 Lewis, p. 77.

29 Robert Woods of P&OCL, letter to Per Jørgensen of Maersk Line, 11 May 1994, A.P. Moller – Maersk archives.

30 Letter from Mærsk Mc-Kinney Møller and Jess Søderberg to executives and managers, 30 September 1994, A.P. Moller – Maersk archives.

31 Letter from Ib Kruse to the Country Managers, 22 December 1995, A.P. Moller – Maersk archives.

32 Maersk Line had a surplus of both dry and reefer equipment in South America. Implementing the service would enhance equipment use and turn-around. Minimal extra staff were needed to support the service.

33 Senior Committee on Future VSA Arrangements, memo 17 May 1995, A.P. Moller – Maersk archives.

34 Mærsk Mc-Kinney Møller, memo to Jess Søderberg, 15 May 1995, Box 152537, A.P. Moller – Maersk archives.

35 Interview with Peter Spiller, 26 July 2012, A.P. Moller – Maersk archives.

36 For example, terminal arrangements in North America, Algeciras and Japan; the integration of chassis fleets in North America.

37 E-mail from John Clancey and Ib Kruse to all main office managers, 16 September 1996, A.P. Moller – Maersk archives.

38 *Containerisation International Yearbook 1996*, p. 5, A.P. Moller – Maersk archives.

39 *Containerisation International Yearbook 1994*, p. 5, A.P. Moller – Maersk archives.

40 *American Shipper Magazine*, June 1995, p. 26, A.P. Moller – Maersk archives.

41 Interview with Duncan McGrath, *Cargill Incorporated*, 3 September 2012, A.P. Moller – Maersk archives.

42 *Containerisation International Yearbook 1995*, p. 5. A.P. Moller – Maersk archives.

43 *Containerisation International Yearbook 1995*, p. 5. A.P. Moller – Maersk archives.

44 Ib Kruse, *Presentation to the International Council of Containership Operators*, Langelinie, Copenhagen, 7 May 1996, on board *Knud Mærsk*, A.P. Moller – Maersk archives.

45 As part of the process, Maersk Net, the communications network that linked all offices, was upgraded, a new distributed computing environment was implemented based on Windows NT 3.51, and Office and Maersk Line's initial home page was released to the public.

46 Ib Kruse, *Letter to Maersk Line Country Management*, 16 December 1996, A.P. Moller – Maersk archives.

47 Ib Kruse, *Letter to Maersk Line Country Management*, 7 April 1997, A.P. Moller – Maersk archives.

48 Other enhancements included opening direct services from South Florida to Colombia and Venezuela, and separately to Guatemala and Honduras; adding the Bahamas as a hub-port; adding a Mauritius feeder between Durban, South Africa and Port Louis, Mauritius, later extended to La Réunion; and a fortnightly feeder serving Brest, Montoir, Dunkirk and Rouen catering to the African and Indian Ocean markets via Algeciras and others.

Chapter 9

1 Interview with John Clancey, 16 August 2012, A.P. Moller – Maersk archives.

2 *Containerisation International Yearbook 1997*, p. 6, A.P. Moller – Maersk archives.

3 Pilot projects were established in Algeciras, Miami and Kaohsiung, where both carriers had adjacent terminals. Meantime, terminals were owned or operated at Algeciras, Kaohsiung, Oakland, Long Beach, Miami, Charleston, Baltimore, New York, Yokohama and Kobe. Investments had been made in terminals at Yantian, Salalah and Laem Chabang.

4 Maersk Line Strategy 1997, *Box 152514*, A.P. Moller – Maersk archives.

5 Letter from Ib Kruse, with attachments summarising the carriers' talking paper and notes, 26 January 1998, Box 154081, A.P. Moller – Maersk archives.

6 The paper saw the EU approach as 'clearly mapped to increase free competition in the shipping sector and move it closer to other industries in that regard'.

7 Memo from Line Department to Ib Kruse, 25 June 1998, A.P. Moller – Maersk archives.

8 The ANERA and the TWRA were required to cease operations from the end of April that year.

9 The Mercantile objectives read: 'Mercantile will be the customers' competitive edge in logistics by offering the best quality products in the tradition of the A.P. Moller Group. It will provide cost effective services to customers in order to maximize the profitability of the A.P. Moller Group. It will respect the individual employee and offer a unique and motivating working environment.'

10 Box 154089, A.P. Moller – Maersk archives.

11 Interview with Professor Emeritus Martin Christopher, Cranfield University, 26 November 2012, A.P. Moller – Maersk archives.

12 The Mercantile Strategy had also moved forward and was now 'to develop into a total logistics provider and market leader, organised as a global business and ensuring financial independence from Maersk Line'.

13 Memo from Søren Skou to Knud Stubkjær, 4 January 1999, A.P. Moller – Maersk archives.

14 Memo from Thomas Eskesen, Lars Kastrup, Jakob Oehrstrem, John Reinhart and Thomas Woldbye, *to Knud Stubkjær, CEO, Maersk Line*, 28 October 1998, circulated to members of the BDC by his letter of 2 November 1998, A.P. Moller – Maersk archives.

15 Classical Japanese dance-drama.

16 Interview with Dick McGregor, *Copenhagen*, 29 June 2012, A.P. Moller – Maersk archives.

17 Letter from Ib Kruse to country managers, 15 July 1998, A.P. Moller – Maersk archives.

18 Memo from Knud Stubkjær to Ib Kruse, 10 August 1998, A.P. Moller – Maersk archives.

19 For example, the US to east coast South America service was reduced from seven to six ships and the California to west coast South America service from five to three.

20 Material provided by Dansk Supermarked.

21 Interview with Thomas Eskesen, 25 June 2012, A.P. Moller – Maersk archives.

22 Jørgen Engell, Søren Skou, memo, 27 November 1998, Box 154082, A.P. Moller – Maersk archives.

23 Interview with Knud Stubkjær, 19 September 2012, A.P. Moller – Maersk archives.

24 Michael Benson, 'What Makes a Brand Great – and Your Role in It', *Navigator*, January 2013, p. 4, A.P. Moller – Maersk archives.

25 Grant Daly, CEO, Safmarine, 'Milestones and Reflections', *Navigator*, January 2013, p. 3, A.P. Moller – Maersk archives.

26 Vagn Lehd Møller, Mattias Hellström, Søren Laungaard, Thomas Woldbye, *Draft of Maersk Line Acquisition/Expansion Strategy*, 19 March 1999, A.P. Moller – Maersk archives.

27 Interview with Ib Kruse, 29 August 2012, A.P. Moller – Maersk archives.

28 Interview with Dick Murphy, 24 July 2012, A.P. Moller – Maersk archives.

29 Interview with Dick McGregor, 29 June 2012, A.P. Moller – Maersk archives.

30 Interview with Nick Taro, 2 August 2012, A.P. Moller – Maersk archives.

31 Interview with Flemming Jacobs, 14 September 2012, A.P. Moller – Maersk archives.

32 One measure of the jump in numbers is the stock of available containers, which totalled 316,300 FFE for Maersk Line in 1998, climbed to 623,400 FFE in 1999 and was expected to hit 700,000 FFE in 2000.

33 Interview with Nick Taro, 2 August 2012, A.P. Moller – Maersk archives.

34 Richard McGregor, *Presentation to BDC*, 10 January 2000, A.P. Moller – Maersk archives.

35 D. M. Lambert, M. A. Emmelhainz and J. T. Gardner, 'So You Think You Want a Partner?', *Marketing Management*, 5, 2, 1996, A.P. Moller – Maersk archives.

36 Interview with Ib Kruse, 29 August 2012, A.P. Moller – Maersk archives.

37 Interview with John Clancey, 16 August 2012, A.P. Moller – Maersk archives.

38 Interview with Knud Stubkjær, 19 September 2012, A.P. Moller – Maersk archives.

Economist Intelligence Unit

39 BBC: http://news.bbc.co.uk/onthisday/hi/dates/stories/december/14/newsid_2559000/2559699.stm (accessed on 25th July 2012).

40 *The New York Times*: http://www.nytimes.com/1997/05/13/world/yeltsin-signs-peace-treaty-with-chechnya.html?pagewanted = all&src = pm (accessed on 25th July 2012).

41 *The New York Times*: http://www.nytimes.com/learning/general/onthisday/big/0630.html (accessed on 30th July 2012).

42 *The New York Times*: http://www.nytimes.com/1998/05/21/world/fall-suharto-overview-suharto-besieged-steps-down-after-32-year-rule-indonesia.html?pagewanted = all&src = pm (accessed on 30th July 2012).

43 BBC: http://news.bbc.co.uk/1/hi/events/indonesia/special_report/353229.stm (accessed on 30th July 2012).

44 BBC: http://news.bbc.co.uk/hi/english/static/northern_ireland/understanding/events/good_friday.stm (accessed on 30th July 2012).

45 BBC: http://www.bbc.co.uk/news/world-africa-17817673 (accessed on 30th July 2012).

46 BBC: http://news.bbc.co.uk/onthisday/hi/dates/stories/may/9/newsid_2519000/2519271.stm (accessed on 30th July 2012).

47 CNN: http://articles.cnn.com/1999-05-08/world/9905_08_kosovo.01_1_ambassador-vladislav-jovanovic-embassy-attack-nato-officials?_s = PM:WORLD (accessed on 30th July 2012).

48 P. Sheehan and J. Houghton, 'A primer on the knowledge economy', Centre for Strategic Economic Studies, Victoria University (2000): http://www.cfses.com/documents/knowledgeeconprimer.pdf (accessed on 30th July 2012).

49 D. Mihaljek and J. Hawkins, 'The banking industry in the emerging market economies: competition, consolidation and systemic stability – an overview', BIS Papers, no. 4 (2001): http://www.bis.org/publ/bppdf/bispap04a.pdf (accessed on 24th July 2012).

50 BBC: http://news.bbc.co.uk/onthisday/hi/dates/stories/december/2/newsid_2518000/2518423.stm (accessed on 30th July 2012).

51 International Monetary Fund: http://www.imf.org/external/pubs/ft/fandd/1998/06/lipsky.htm (accessed on 30th July 2012).

52 BBC: http://news.bbc.co.uk/1/hi/special_report/1998/08/98/russia_crisis/165646.stm (accessed on 31st July 2012).

53 International Telecommunication Union: http://www.itu.int/osg/spu/ip/chapter_two.html (accessed on 31st July 2012).

54 International Telecommunication Union: http://www.itu.int/ITU-D/ict/statistics/material/pdf/2011%20Statistical%20highlights_June_2012.pdf (accessed on 31st July 2012).

55 Canada's World: http://www.canadasworld.ca/timeline/19841993 (accessed on 31st July 2012).

56 TIME: http://www.time.com/time/business/article/0,8599,2004089,00.html (accessed on 31st July 2012).

57 INSEAD: http://www.insead.edu/facultyresearch/faculty/documents/Al-Jazeera-w.pdf (accessed on 31st July 2012).

58 Google: http://www.google.co.uk/about/company/ (accessed on 31st July 2012).

59 Jeffbullas.com: http://www.jeffbullas.com/2011/05/16/50-amazing-facts-and-figures-about-google/ (accessed on 31st July 2012).

60 USA Today: http://www.usatoday.com/life/2002–10–17-dvd-timeline_x.htm (accessed on 31st July 2012).

61 BBC: http://news.bbc.co.uk/onthisday/hi/dates/stories/february/22/newsid_4245000/4245877.stm (accessed on 31st July 2012).

62 Science News: http://www.sciencenews.org/view/feature/id/339020/title/90th_Anniversary_Issue_1990s (accessed on 31st July 2012).

63 BBC: http://www.bbc.co.uk/news/health-11518539 (accessed on 31st July 2012).

64 BBC: http://news.bbc.co.uk/1/hi/special_report/1997/schengen/13508.stm (accessed on 31st July 2012).

65 BBC: http://www.bbc.co.uk/news/world-europe-13194723 (accessed on 31st July 2012).

66 World Trade Organization: http://www.wto.org/english/tratop_e/sps_e/sps_e.htm (accessed on 31st July 2012).

67 United Nations: http://www.unog.ch/80256EE600585943/(httpPages)/ CA826818C8330D2BC1257180004B1B2E?OpenDocument (accessed on 31st July 2012).

68 International Criminal Court: http://www.icc-cpi.int/Menus/ICC/About + the + Court/ ICC + at + a + glance/Chronology + of + the + ICC.htm (accessed on 31st July 2012).

69 Australian Government Bureau of Meteorology: http://www.bom.gov.au/lam/ climate/levelthree/c20thc/drought5.htm (accessed on 31st July 2012).

70 *Science News*: http://www.sciencenews.org/view/feature/id/339020/title/90th_ Anniversary_Issue_1990s (accessed on 1st August 2012).

71 World Health Organization: http://www.euro.who.int/__data/assets/pdf_file/0003/ 97050/4.5.-Levels-of-lead-in-childrens-blood-EDITING_layouted.pdf (accessed on 1st August 2012).

72 United Nations: http://unfccc.int/kyoto_protocol/items/2830.php/ (accessed on 1st August 2012).

Chapter 10

1 Interview with Kim Fejfer, *APM Terminals*, 8 October 2012, A.P. Moller – Maersk archives.

2 *Containerisation International Yearbook 1997*, p. 5, A.P. Moller – Maersk archives.

3 *Containerisation International Yearbook 1998*, p. 7, A.P. Moller – Maersk archives.

4 *Containerisation International Yearbook 1999*, p. 5, A.P. Moller – Maersk archives.

5 The new paradigm was driven by a combination of pressures from shipper associations, US and EU moves to remove carriers' anti-trust immunity, an over-supply of container shipping capacity leading to tough contract negotiations with customers, and an ample supply of low-cost carriers as well as the growing influence of the freight forwarding industry.

6 Interview with Tim Harris, 23 August 2012, A.P. Moller – Maersk archives.

7 Presentation on the Global Logistics Study, 1 September 2000, A.P. Moller – Maersk archives.

8 A.P. Moller Finance Department, cited in 'The Integrated Logistics Management Report, February 2001'.

9 PricewaterhouseCoopers, cited in 'The Integrated Logistics Management Report, February 2001'.

10 Outsourced was defined as 'the activity where management remains in control of the product or service it is delivering to its customers, but does not control the resources which contribute to that end product or service'. This definition was taken from Andersen Consulting/Accenture.

11 KPMG Report, 'Outsourcing Logistics', cited in 'The Integrated Logistics Management Report, February 2001'.

12 *Containerisation International Yearbook 2000*, p. 5, A.P. Moller – Maersk archives.

13 Henning Morgen, *Memo on the start-up of APM Terminals*, 25 June 2010, A.P. Moller – Maersk archives.

14 *Containerisation International Yearbook 2001*, p. 5, A.P. Moller – Maersk archives.

15 Interview with Thomas Eskesen, 25 June 2012, A.P. Moller – Maersk archives.

16 *Containerisation International Yearbook 2001*, p. 7, A.P. Moller – Maersk archives.

17 *Containerisation International Yearbook 2002*, p. 5, A.P. Moller – Maersk archives.

18 *Containerisation International Yearbook 2002*, p. 5, A.P. Moller – Maersk archives.

19 *Containerisation International Yearbook 2003*, pp. 6–7, A.P. Moller – Maersk archives.

20 *Maersk-Sealand Budget*, 2002–6, p. 1, A.P. Moller – Maersk archives.

21 Interview with Knud Stubkjær, 19 September 2012, A.P. Moller – Maersk archives.

22 Interview with Claus Hemmingsen, 17 August 2012, A.P. Moller – Maersk archives.

23 Rates rose by about 12 per cent in the Trans Pacific and about 10 per cent in the Far East to Europe trades.

24 *Containerisation International Yearbook 2004*, p. 5, A.P. Moller – Maersk archives.

25 Interview with Søren K. Brandt, 28 August 2012, A.P. Moller – Maersk archives.

26 Interview with Søren K. Brandt, 28 August 2012, A.P. Moller – Maersk archives.

27 *Containerisation International Yearbook 1988*, p. 6, A.P. Moller – Maersk archives.

28 John Isbell, *former Vice President of Nike*, 19 December 2012, A.P. Moller – Maersk archives.

29 Interview with Frans Smit, *Nike*, 9 November 2012, A.P. Moller – Maersk archives.

30 Interview with Søren K. Brandt, 28 August 2012, A.P. Moller – Maersk archives.

31 Project StarLight Management Presentation, 19 August 2002, A.P. Moller – Maersk archives.

32 Interview with Søren K. Brandt, 28 August 2012, A.P. Moller – Maersk archives.

33 *Containerisation International Yearbook 2005*, p. 5, A.P. Moller – Maersk archives.

34 *Containerisation International Yearbook 2005*, pp. 6–7, A.P. Moller – Maersk archives.

35 *Containerisation International Yearbook 2005*, p. 5, A.P. Moller – Maersk archives.

Economist Intelligence Unit

36 BBC: http://news.bbc.co.uk/onthisday/hi/dates/stories/september/11/newsid_2514000/2514627.stm (accessed on 1st August 2012).

37 BBC: http://news.bbc.co.uk/onthisday/hi/dates/stories/september/12/newsid_2515000/2515239.stm (accessed on 1st August 2012).

38 Federation of American Scientists: http://www.fas.org/nuke/control/start1/index.html (accessed on 1st August 2012).

39 BBC: http://news.bbc.co.uk/1/hi/world/asia-pacific/3126241.stm (accessed on 1st August 2012).

40 BBC: http://news.bbc.co.uk/onthisday/hi/dates/stories/june/28/newsid_4517000/4517865.stm (accessed on 1st August 2012).

41 BBC: http://news.bbc.co.uk/1/hi/world/europe/country_profiles/3498746.stm (accessed on 1st August 2012).

42 *The New York Times*: http://www.nytimes.com/2008/12/21/business/worldbusiness/21iht-admin.4.18853088.html?pagewanted = all (accessed on 30th July 2012).

43 *The Boston Globe*: http://www.bostonglobe.com/news/nation/2012/06/14/fact-check-where-obama-romney-missed-mark/gss69SFPebBveEeZrgEaJL/story.html (accessed on 1st August 2012).

44 Food and Agriculture Organization: http://www.fao.org/docrep/005/y4252e/y4252e12.htm (accessed on 1st August 2012).

45 *The Wall Street Journal*: http://online.wsj.com/article/SB10001424052748703915204575104190814015302.html (accessed on 1st August 2012).

46 Google Finance: http://www.google.com/finance/historical?cid = 13756934&startdate = Mar%2010%2C%202010&enddate = Sep%2021%2C%202010&num = 30&ei = am9cUODCCcWCwAPrRg&start = 120 (accessed on 1st August 2012).

47 World Trade Organization: http://www.wto.org/english/tratop_e/dda_e/dda_e.htm (accessed on 1st August 2012).

48 World Trade Organization: http://www.wto.org/english/thewto_e/countries_e/china_e.htm (accessed on 1st August 2012).

49 World Bank: http://data.worldbank.org/indicator/TX.VAL.MRCH.CD.WT?page = 2 (accessed on 1st August 2012).

50 Bank for International Settlements: http://www.bis.org/about/chronology/2000–2009.htm http://www.bis.org/about/chronology/2000-2009.htm (accessed on 1st August 2012).

51 United Nations: http://www.un.org/millenniumgoals/ (accessed on 1st August 2012).

52 *TIME*: http://www.time.com/time/business/article/0,8599,1917002,00.html (accessed on 1st August 2012).

53 Wikipedia: https://en.wikipedia.org/wiki/Special:Statistics (accessed on 1st August 2012).

54 *Los Angeles Times*: http://articles.latimes.com/2003/feb/12/science/sci-universe12 (accessed on 31st July 2012).

55 Google: http://www.google.com/earth/explore/showcase/historical.html (accessed on 1st August 2012).

56 BBC: http://news.bbc.co.uk/onthisday/hi/dates/stories/january/25/newsid_4606000/4606576.stm (accessed on 1st August 2012).

57 *The Guardian*: http://www.guardian.co.uk/technology/2007/jul/25/media.newmedia (accessed on 1st August 2012).

58 Foresight for Development: http://www.foresightfordevelopment.org/sobi2/Resources/The-State-of-Science-and-Technology-in-Africa-2000–2004 (accessed on 1st August 2012).

59 US Department of Energy: http://www.ornl.gov/sci/techresources/Human_Genome/home.shtml (accessed on 1st August 2012).

60 *Wired*: http://www.wired.com/medtech/health/news/2003/04/58508 (accessed on 1st August 2012).

61 Council of Europe: http://conventions.coe.int/Treaty/en/Treaties/Html/185.htm (accessed on 1st August 2012).

62 United Nations: http://www.un.org/en/aboutun/history/2001–2010.shtml (accessed on 1st August 2012).

63 Australian Government Department of Infrastructure and Transport: http://www.infrastructure.gov.au/transport/security/maritime/isps/index.aspx (accessed on 1st August 2012).

64 United Nations: http://unfccc.int/files/cooperation_and_support/capacity_building/application/pdf/unepcdmintro.pdf (accessed on 1st August 2012).

65 European Commission: http://ec.europa.eu/environment/waste/weee/index_en. htm (accessed on 1st August 2012).

66 *New Scientist*: http://www.newscientist.com/article/dn9931-facts-and-figures-asian-tsunami-disaster.html (accessed on 1st August 2012).

Chapter 11

1 A. Donovan and J. Bonney, *The Box that Changed the World: 50 Years of Container Shipping – an Illustrated History*, Commonwealth Business Media, 2006, p. 194.

2 *Containerisation International Yearbook 2006*, p. 5, A.P. Moller – Maersk archives.

3 *Containerisation International Yearbook* 2007, p. 5, A.P. Moller – Maersk archives.

4 Interview with Claus Hemmingsen, 17 August 2012, A.P. Moller – Maersk archives.

5 CBC Minutes, 22 September 2004, Box 226033, A.P. Moller – Maersk archives.

6 Interview with Claus Hemmingsen, 17 August 2012, A.P. Moller – Maersk archives.

7 Interview with Tim Harris, 23 August 2012, A.P. Moller – Maersk archives.

8 Interview with Jeremy Nixon, 19 June 2012, A.P. Moller – Maersk archives.

9 Interview with Jeremy Nixon, 19 June 2012, A.P. Moller – Maersk archives.

10 Interview with Robbert Jan van Trooijen, 28 June 2012, A.P. Moller – Maersk archives.

11 Interview with Lucas Vos, 30 July 2012, A.P. Moller – Maersk archives.

12 Interview with Lucas Vos, 30 July 2012, A.P. Moller – Maersk archives.

13 Interview with Tim Smith, 20 June 2012, A.P. Moller – Maersk archives.

14 Interview with Jeremy Nixon, 19 June 2012, A.P. Moller – Maersk archives.

15 Interview with Eivind Kolding, 7 September 2012, A.P. Moller – Maersk archives.

16 Interview with Eivind Kolding, 7 September 2012, A.P. Moller – Maersk archives.

17 It is also noteworthy that no training could take place before the acquisition was approved by the authorities.

18 Interview with John M. Nielsen, 31 May 2012, A.P. Moller – Maersk archives.

19 Interview with Knud Stubkjær, 19 September 2012, A.P. Moller – Maersk archives.

20 *Containerisation International Yearbook 2008*, p. 6, A.P. Moller – Maersk archives.

21 Interview with Jørgen Harling, 11 September 2012, A.P. Moller – Maersk archives.

22 Area coordination memo, 24 August 2004, A.P. Moller – Maersk archives.

23 Six-page memo, 22 September 2005, A.P. Moller – Maersk archives.

24 E-mail from Vagn Lehd Møller to Knud Stubkjær, 24 August 2006, A.P. Moller – Maersk archives.

25 Interview with Knud Stubkjær, 19 September 2012, A.P. Moller – Maersk archives.

26 Interview with Eivind Kolding, 7 September 2012, A.P. Moller – Maersk archives.

27 Interview with Claus Hemmingsen, 17 August 2012, A.P. Moller – Maersk archives.

28 *Containerisation International Yearbook 2007*, p. 5, A.P. Moller – Maersk archives.

29 Interview with Captain Henrik Solmer, 11 October 2012, A.P. Moller – Maersk archives.

Chapter 12

1 UNCTAD, *Review of Maritime Transport, 2011*, p. 7, A.P. Moller – Maersk archives.

2 Interview with Flemming Steen, 13 July 2012, A.P. Moller – Maersk archives.

3 Interview with Eivind Kolding, 7 September 2012, A.P. Moller – Maersk archives.

4 Those who had earlier built up their country organisations to manage a broad portfolio of shipping and logistics activities, naturally saw their role substantially reduced and focused mainly on liner sales and customer service.

5 Interview with Hanne B. Sørensen, 16 August 2012, A.P. Moller – Maersk archives.

6 Interview with Hanne B. Sørensen, 16 August 2012, A.P. Moller – Maersk archives.

7 Interview with Flemming Steen, 13 July 2012, A.P. Moller – Maersk archives.

8 Interview with Morten Engelstoft, 21 August 2012, A.P. Moller – Maersk archives.

9 Interview with Morten Engelstoft, 21 August 2012, A.P. Moller – Maersk archives.

10 Interview with Lars Reno Jakobsen, 16 August 2012, A.P. Moller – Maersk archives.

11 Eivind Kolding, quoted by Philip Lee and John Churchill in 'We Will Change the Game', *Mærsk Post*, 2010, 2, pp. 14–15.

12 Maersk Line Budget file 2007–11, A.P. Moller – Maersk archives.

13 Interview with Eivind Kolding, 7 September 2012, A.P. Moller – Maersk archives.

14 First half results indicated just how serious the situation was: Maersk losses of $ 961 million, OOCL losses of $ 232 million, Hanjin Shipping with losses of $ 516 million, China Shipping Container Line with losses of $ 499 million, NOL/APL with losses of $ 391 million.

15 *Containerisation International Yearbook 2011*, p. 5, A.P. Moller – Maersk archives.

16 Interview with Eivind Kolding, 7 September 2012, A.P. Moller – Maersk archives.

17 *Containerisation International Yearbook 2011*, p. 5, A.P. Moller – Maersk archives.

18 Eivind Kolding, *Strategy launch video*, 2009, A.P. Moller – Maersk archives.

19 Interview with Eivind Kolding, 7 September 2012, A.P. Moller – Maersk archives.

20 *Containerisation International Yearbook 2012*, p. 5, A.P. Moller – Maersk archives.

21 Interview with Hanne B. Sørensen, 16 August 2012, A.P. Moller – Maersk archives.

22 Interview with Eric Williams, 30 May 2012, A.P. Moller – Maersk archives.

23 Interview with Tom Sproat, 26 July 2012, A.P. Moller – Maersk archives.

24 O. Hornby, '*With Constant Care . . .*' A. P. Møller: Shipowner 1876–1965, Schultz, 1988, p. 144.

25 Interview with Søren Skou, 21 August 2012, A.P. Moller – Maersk archives.

26 Interview with Søren Skou, 21 August 2012, A.P. Moller – Maersk archives.

27 Interview with Thomas Eskesen, 25 June 2012, A.P. Moller – Maersk archives.

28 Interview with Søren Skou, 21 August 2012, A.P. Moller – Maersk archives.

29 Interview with Tim Harris, 23 August 2012, A.P. Moller – Maersk archives.

Economist Intelligence Unit

30 PBS: www.pbs.org/newshour/bb/middle_east/july-dec05/iraq_12–12.html (accessed on 2nd August 2012).

31 BBC: http://news.bbc.co.uk/1/shared/spl/hi/europe/04/enlarging_europe/html/eu_expansion.stm (accessed on 2nd August 2012).

32 *The New York Times*: http://topics.nytimes.com/top/reference/timestopics/subjects/c/credit_crisis/bailout_plan/index.html (accessed on 2nd August 2012).

33 *The New York Times*: http://learning.blogs.nytimes.com/2011/11/04/nov-4–2008-barack-obama-elected-president/ (accessed on 2nd August 2012).

34 *Foreign Affairs*: http://www.foreignaffairs.com/articles/67693/lisa-anderson/demystifying-the-arab-spring (accessed on 2nd August 2012).

35 BBC: http://www.bbc.co.uk/news/world-middle-east-12813859 (accessed on 2nd August 2012).

36 BBC: http://www.bbc.co.uk/news/world-asia-19645305 (accessed on 2nd August 2012).

37 BBC: http://www.bbc.co.uk/news/world-europe-13597627 (accessed on 2nd August 2012).

38 United Nations Conference on Trade and Development: http://unctad.org/en/docs/rmt2011_en.pdf (accessed on 2nd August 2012).

39 A. Heerden, M. Prieto, M. Caspari, 'Rags or riches? Phasing out the multi-fibre arrangement', International Labour Organization, SEED working paper no.40 (2003): http://www.ilo.org/wcmsp5/groups/public/@ed_emp/@emp_ent/@ifp_seed/documents/publication/wcms_117697.pdf (accessed on 2nd August 2012).

40 BBC: http://news.bbc.co.uk/1/hi/business/4100249.stm (accessed on 2nd August 2012).

41 EU SME Centre: http://www.eusmecentre.org.cn/content/textiles-and-apparel-sector-report (accessed on 2nd August 2012).

42 International Monetary Fund: http://www.imf.org/external/np/exr/chron/chron.asp (accessed on 1st August 2012).

43 BBC: http://news.bbc.co.uk/1/hi/7521250.stm (accessed on 2nd August 2012).

44 BBC: http://www.bbc.co.uk/news/business-13856580 (accessed on 2nd August 2012).

45 The Guardian: http://www.guardian.co.uk/business/economics-blog/2012/aug/22/russia-entry-world-trade-organisation (accessed on 2nd August 2012).

46 World Health Organization: http://www.who.int/gho/hiv/epidemic_status/deaths_text/en/index.html (accessed on 2nd August 2012).

47 BBC: http://news.bbc.co.uk/1/hi/business/6034577.stm (accessed on 2nd August 2012).

48 Forbes: http://www.forbes.com/2009/06/12/novartis-swine-flu-markets-equity-pharmaceuticals.html (accessed on 2nd August 2012).

49 World Bank: http://web.worldbank.org/WBSITE/EXTERNAL/EXTABOUTUS/EXTARCHIVES/0,contentMDK:22540075~menuPK:8045142~pagePK:36726~piPK:437378~theSitePK:29506,00.html (accessed on 2nd August 2012).

50 United Nations: http://www.un.org/en/aboutun/history/2011–2020.shtml (accessed on 2nd August 2012).

51 United Nations: http://data.un.org/Data.aspx?q = population&d = PopDiv&f = variableID%3a12 (accessed on 2nd August 2012).

52 J. Tharamangalam, 'Occupy Wall Street: Poverty and Rising Social Inequality, Interrogating Democracy in America', Centre for Research on Globalization (13th December 2011): http://www.globalresearch.ca/occupy-wall-street-poverty-and-rising-social-inequality-interrogating-democracy-in-america/ (accessed on 2nd August 2012).

53 International Agency for Research on Cancer (World Health Organization): http://press.iarc.fr/pr213_E.pdf (accessed on 2nd August 2012).

54 BBC: http://www.bbc.co.uk/news/world-middle-east-18813543 (accessed on 2nd August 2012).

55 Apple: http://www.apple.com/pr/products/ipodhistory/ (accessed on 2nd August 2012).

56 BBC: http://news.bbc.co.uk/1/hi/sci/tech/8375486.stm (accessed on 2nd August 2012).

57 *The Independent*: http://www.independent.co.uk/news/science/peter-higgs-grandfather-behind-the-god-particle-is-nobel-contender-8191515.html (accessed on 2nd August 2012).

58 Dataversity: http://www.dataversity.net/the-growth-of-unstructured-data-what-are-we-going-to-do-with-all-those-zettabytes/ (accessed on 2nd August 2012).

59 BBC: http://www.bbc.co.uk/news/science-environment-18396655 (accessed on 2nd August 2012).

60 *Garnaut Climate Change Review*: http://www.garnautreview.org.au/pdf/Garnaut_Chapter8.pdf (accessed on 2nd August 2012).

61 *The Guardian*: http://www.guardian.co.uk/world/2012/mar/14/congo-thomas-lubanga-child-soldiers (accessed on 2nd August 2012).

62 Radford University: http://www.radford.edu/wkovarik/envhist/12oughties.html (accessed on 2nd August 2012).

63 *National Geographic*: http://news.nationalgeographic.com/news/2007/09/070917-northwest-passage.html (accessed on 2nd August 2012).

64 *Science News*: www.sciencenews.org/view/feature/id/339023/title/90th_Anniversary_Issue_Science_News_marks_a_milestone (accessed on 2nd August 2012).

Epilogue

1 P. F. Drucker, quoted in A. Donovan and J. Bonney, *The Box that Changed the World: 50 Years of Container Shipping – an Illustrated History*, Commonwealth Business Media, 2006, p. 209.

2 Mauro F. Guillén, 'Is Globalisation Civilising, Destructive or Feeble?', *Annual Review of Sociology*, 2001, pp. 247, 252.

3 S. Panitchpakdi, Secretary General, UNCTAD, Foreword to 2011 Report, p. xiii.

4 Institute for Public Policy, 'The Third Wave of Globalisation', *Research paper*, January 2012, p. 2.

5 Institute for Public Policy, p. 3.

6 The Hurun Global Rich List for 2013, issued 28 February 2013.

7 *UNCTAD Review of Maritime Transport 2012*, Section 1, Developments in International Seaborne Trade, p. 25.

8 United Nations 2013 *Human Development Report*, 'The Rise of the South: Human Progress in a Diverse World', press release, 14 March 2013.

9 Schumpeter column, 'The Best Since Sliced Bread', *Economist*, 19 January 2013.

10 Schumpeter column, 'The Case Against Globaloney', *Economist*, 23 April 2011, referencing P. Ghemawat, *World 3.0: Global Prosperity and How to Achieve It*, Harvard Business Review Press, 2011.

11 M. Shermer, 'Globaloney: Why the World is Not Flat – Yet', *Scientific American*, August 2011.

12 'Value-added Trade', *Economist*, 19 January 2013, p. 85.

13 Professor Shang-Jin Wei, Professor of Finance and Economics, and N. T. Wang Professor of Chinese Business and Economy, Graduate School of Business, Columbia University, 14 June 2012.

14 Pascal Lamy, '"Made in China" Tells Us Little About Global Trade', *Financial Times*, 25 January 2011, A.P. Moller – Maersk archives.

15 *UNCTAD Review of Maritime Transport 2012*, Section 1, Developments in International Seaborne Trade, p. 5.

16 World Economic Forum, 'Enabling Trade, Valuing Growth Opportunities', Foreword, p. 3.

17 World Economic Forum, p. 5.

18 World Economic Forum, p. 6.

19 *UNCTAD Review of Maritime Transport 2012*, Section 1, Developments in International Seaborne Trade, p. 112.

20 'The Gift That goes on Giving', *Economist*, 22 December 2012.

21 United Nations, 'World Economic Situation and Prospects 2012', Executive Summary, p. ix.

22 Interview with Thomas Riber Knudsen, 25 June 2012, A.P. Moller – Maersk archives.

23 S. Mallaby, 'Africa Hooked on Growth After 12 Years of Progress', *Financial Times*, 2 January 2013, A.P. Moller – Maersk archives.

24 N. Okonjo-Iweala, 'Emerging from the Frontier', *Economist*, A.P. Moller – Maersk archives.

25 'Unlocking the Potential of the Indian Banana Trade', developed by Maersk Line, AEHR and First Line, 2011, A.P. Moller – Maersk archives.

26 'Impact Assessment of Maersk in Brazil', Copenhagen Economics, 12 February 2013.

27 Interview with Thomas Riber Knudsen, 25 June 2012, A.P. Moller – Maersk archives.

28 *UNCTAD Review of Maritime Transport 2012*, Section 1, Developments in International Seaborne Trade, p. 25.

29 Source: Bank of America Merrill Lynch Global Research estimates from April 2012.

30 Internal Maersk Line booklet, '*The Reality*', February 2013, A.P. Moller – Maersk archives.

31 The paper included the estimate that 'the aggressive price wars led the shipping industry to destroy 10 times more value (approximately USD 40 billion) from 2008–11 than if everybody had just accepted the cost of sailing with lower utilization'.

32 Boston Consulting Group, '*Charting a New Course: Restoring Profitability to Container Shipping*', pp. 22–23, A.P. Moller – Maersk archives.

33 '50 Years of Containerisation', *Journal of Commerce*, p. 7a, A.P. Moller – Maersk archives.

Index